The Science and Technology of Counterterrorism

The Science and Technology of Counterterrorism

Measuring Physical and Electronic Security Risk

Carl S. Young

ELSEVIER

AMSTERDAM • BOSTON • HEIDELBERG • LONDON
NEW YORK • OXFORD • PARIS • SAN DIEGO
SAN FRANCISCO • SINGAPORE • SYDNEY • TOKYO

Butterworth-Heinemann is an imprint of Elsevier

Acquiring Editor: Pamela Chester
Editorial Project Manager: Marisa LaFleur
Project Manager: Punithavathy Govindaradjane
Designer: Russell Purdy

Butterworth-Heinemann is an imprint of Elsevier
225 Wyman Street, Waltham, MA 02451, USA
The Boulevard, Langford Lane, Kidlington, Oxford, OX5 1 GB, UK

Library of Congress Cataloging-in-Publication Data
Application submitted

British Library Cataloguing-in-Publication Data
A catalogue record for this book is available from the British Library

ISBN: 978-0-12-420056-2

Printed and bound in the United States of America
14   15   16   17   18   10   9   8   7   6   5   4   3   2   1

For information on all Butterworth–Heinemann publications
visit our website at *http://store.elsevier.com*

Dedication

**To my nieces and nephews, Claire Melin, Julia Melin,
Harry Uniman, and Max Uniman**

Contents

Acknowledgments

With respect to acknowledgements, I am most indebted to my parents, Dr. Irving Young and Dr. Geraldine Young. In addition to their continued love and support, they encouraged me to take the "road not taken" in the words of Robert Frost. In that vein, I am thankful that I chose not to follow in their footsteps, and became a physicist rather than a physician.

Other individuals have played a disproportionate role in the creation of this book, and they are noted below.

The first such individual is Mr. Jean Gobin. He contributed significantly to the material on electronic security risk in Chapter 8 and the section on virtualization in Chapter 9. Jean is one of the most talented and knowledgable electronic security professionals in the business. I am indebted to him for his contributions to this book as well as for his efforts in support of the Security Science group at Stroz Friedberg.

My longtime colleague, friend, and mentor, Dr. David Chang, deserves mention. Dave performed the heavy lifting on the probability of protection method applied to explosive threats, the results on window protection from ballistic and explosive loading and the calculation of the passive RFID field magnitudes specified in Appendix G. I have had the privilege of learning from Dave for over 25 years as well as bearing witness to his humility that belies his exceptional scientific talent.

Jim King was a colleague when we both worked for our respective governments. Jim emerged from fighting the forces of evil for Her Majesty to face the more daunting task of being my boss at Goldman Sachs. In his capacity as Global Head of Physical Security, he encouraged me, and others, to think expansively about security. Many of the ideas explored in this book originated while working for Jim. I hope he finds this book "helpful."

Roger Pike, President of RPA Ltd. in the UK, is another key security figure that directly and indirectly contributed to this book. Roger has an encyclopedic knowledge of physical security technologies, and also possesses a remarkable problem-solving capability. In my view he has no equal as a physical security expert on either side of the Atlantic.

Chris Hogan and I met relatively late in the evolution of this book, but he nonetheless had a significant impact. He and I spent months together in Pittsburgh, Pennsylvania and Portage, Indiana (of all places). During this time I had the privilege of learning from a truly iconic security practitioner. Moreover, he gave me encouragement and inspiration to complete this journey, and I am indebted to him for his knowledge, wisdom, and friendship.

I am most appreciative of the support provided by various individuals at Stroz Friedberg, LLC. Specifically, Ed Stroz, who befriended me when I arrived from Washington in 2000. We were both escapees from government service, and he made me feel at home in my newly adopted city. I recall our many dinners at Gus' Place (now extinct) in the West Village with fondness. In 2011 he gave me the opportunity to start a security consulting practice at his company, possibly because he became bored with hearing me complain about security consultants. I am grateful for that opportunity as well as his continued friendship and support in writing this book. I would also like to acknowledge Bob Lynch, Chief Financial Officer. Our brainstorming sessions over lunch at Walker's in TriBeCa have been an important source of nutrition, mentally and otherwise.

If this book is successful, it will largely be due to the efforts of the team at Elsevier. They toiled long and hard behind the scenes, and managed to overcome the many hurdles I consistently if unintentionally placed in their way. Specifically, I am most grateful to Pam Chester (acquiring editor), Marisa LaFleur (editorial project manager), Punithavathy Govindaradjane (project manager), and Russell Purdy (designer).

I happened to have the good fortune to have worked with the Cyber Security team at United States Steel while writing this book. This team of bona fide security-risk professionals includes Andrew Blasko, John Eshenbaugh, Tom Lentz, Caryn Mckenna, Stephanie Sjoberg, and Nicole Trimbey. I was inspired by their dedication and unwavering enthusiasm as exemplified by their signature greeting, "Carl! Good to see you!!"

The Security Science team at Stroz Friedberg is a remarkable collection of technical talent. I have never worked with a more knowledgeable group of security professionals and I am indebted to them for all they have taught me. Contributions from specific individuals are interspersed, and so acknowledged, throughout this book. Team members as of this writing include Chris Briscoe, Chantnu Chandel, Dave Dalva, Steve Doty, Kendra Garwin, Jean Gobin, Nitai Mandhyan, Steve Ruzila, and Dominic Spinosa.

Finally, readers of this book will definitely note my bias in applying statistics to all types of phenomena. But the laws of probability alone cannot fully explain how one family suddenly appeared and altered my perspective on risk and reward. So I must acknowledge their contribution to this book without adequate explanation, but with profound appreciation nonetheless. Family members in order of seniority include Josefina Quinn, Mariana Ramirez, Michael Kowalski, and Aidan Quinn.

There are many others I have not mentioned because of space limitations or I have acknowledged previously. I am fortunate to have many friends and acquaintances to whom I am personally and professionally indebted. I sincerely hope they are not offended by not being mentioned by name.

About the Author

Carl S. Young has specialized in applying science and quantitative methods to problems in security risk management. He was a Supervisory Special Agent and Senior Executive in the FBI as well as the Global Head of physical security technology at Goldman Sachs & Co. in New York, and Goldman Sachs International in London. He is currently the head of the Security Science consulting practice and Chief Security Officer at Stroz Friedberg, LLC in New York City. He is also an adjunct professor in the Protection Management Department of the John Jay College of Criminal Justice, City University of New York (CUNY).

Mr. Young was a consultant to the JASON Defense Advisory Group, and was selected by the Director of Central Intelligence to advise the intelligence community on technology as part of a blue ribbon panel. In 1997 he was awarded the James R. Killian Medal by the White House for individual contributions to national security. He is the author of *Metrics and Methods for Security Risk Management* (Syngress, 2010) as well as numerous technical papers related to security risk management. Mr. Young received undergraduate and graduate degrees in mathematics and physics respectively from the Massachusetts Institute of Technology (MIT), Cambridge, MA.

Preface

This is my second book on security risk management. In *Metrics and Methods for Security Risk Management*, I examined the individual components of risk for a variety of physical security threats. I also discussed the importance of identifying the risk factors that affect those components of risk. This book expands on those themes, and there is admittedly some duplication in specific areas.

However, I had different objectives in writing this book, and therefore this is a very different work. In both books I provide a framework for security risk assessments. This is fundamental to addressing counterterrorism issues from first principles and to developing truly strategic solutions.

But in this book I hope to create a comprehensive reference that is useful to practicing security professionals. To that end, I specify the theory that underpins fundamental security controls, and importantly, how theory affects implementation. The focus is clearly on technology controls related to counterterrorism, but I include other methods that apply to more general problems in security.

The main objective of this book is to teach the reader how to think *strategically* about security risk management by understanding fundamental security principles and methods. I also provide supporting technical details to enable the application of those principles to realistic terrorism scenarios. Anyone can memorize a list of widgets and technical specifications. When security technologies are viewed as controls that affect the overall security risk profile, the development of a risk-based strategy is possible.

To that end, the risk assessment framework specified in Chapter 1 is a recurring theme throughout this book. This is because it provides the rationale for every counterterrorism control discussed thereafter and is essential to developing a risk-based mitigation strategy. Although it is a relatively simple framework, examples are always helpful. I therefore provide numerous examples gleaned from actual security scenarios. Such examples also illustrate the practical limits on controls that are often imposed by Mother Nature.

In some cases these examples may seem a bit esoteric. I might indeed agree, but sometimes it is valuable to stretch the limits of the imagination in thinking about security. Our field can be constrained by templated thinking and the reflexive use of checklists. There is a benefit to thinking about security in nontraditional ways.

Chapters 2 and 3 discuss tools that could be used to "measure" security and counterterrorism risk. The word measure is in quotation marks because the results are typically estimates; exact measurements of security risk are frequently elusive. The importance of uncertainty in terrorism is also explained, and this includes a discussion on random variables. Ironically, the assumption that a risk factor is a normally distributed random variable introduces a degree of certainty to the inherently uncertain world of counterterrorism.

It is important to know how security technologies work mainly because it is relevant to evaluating their effectiveness in addressing risk. Understanding threats on a scientific level is also important, in part because it is the science that often dictates the magnitude of the vulnerability component of risk. Moreover, scientific and risk-based explanations of security threats and mitigation technologies are typically absent from traditional security references or are presented in nonsecurity-related contexts. When such concepts are not coupled to security issues they can seem too abstract to be useful.

In that vein, simple physical models are presented in Chapter 4 along with their application to broad classes of security problems. These models include point sources of radiation, exponentially increasing and decreasing processes, harmonic motion, and Gaussian plumes. In my experience these are most useful in performing "back of the envelope" calculations to yield order of magnitude estimates of security risk. Such estimates also provide a valuable reality check on intuition.

Chapter 5 provides a unique method of examining risk. Specifically, the risk factors of various threats are assumed to be normally distributed random variables. What evolves from this assumption is a means of determining the likelihood of the effectiveness of security controls. This is fundamentally different than calculating the likelihood of a future terrorist incident, a typically fruitless endeavor.

Chapter 6 is devoted exclusively to analyzing the risk associated with conventional explosive threats. Understanding how such threats scale, i.e., change, with distance and payload is central to estimating vulnerability. As always, specifying the risk factors for a given threat or attack vector is essential to developing an effective risk mitigation strategy.

Chapter 7 discusses "nontraditional" terrorism threats. These include radiological, chemical, biological, and electromagnetic pulse weapons. The models discussed in Chapter 4 are used to develop a realistic if coarse estimate of the vulnerability to these threats and the effectiveness of controls.

Another key objective of this book is to provide a deeper understanding of electronic terrorism risk. The distinction between electronic terrorists and other "cyber" criminals may be mostly semantic. However, in Chapter 8 the focus is on electronic threats that might have particular appeal to a terrorist, based on the potential damage inflicted and/or headlines achieved through such an attack. Detailed analyses of relevant controls and how they address common modes of attack follow discussions of the threats themselves. With respect to controls, emphasis is placed on monitoring inter-zone network traffic in the spirit of "measuring" risk in this context.

Importantly, in Chapter 9 there is a detailed discussion on the increasing convergence of physical and electronic security risk. In that discussion, specific physical security system components with potential electronic vulnerabilities are identified in addition to showing how physical vulnerabilities facilitate electronic attacks. This convergence is often mentioned in security literature but the details are sometimes missing. Absent information showing where and how this convergence occurs, such treatments do not convey a full appreciation of the risks.

Providing the proper balance between theory and practice is important in a book that strives to be useful for both practitioners and academics. Chapters 10, 11, and 12 cover the fundamental controls of physical security. The treatment is risk-based with explanations grounded in science and augmented by quantitative analyses. Physical access control systems, sensors, and CCTV are discussed in detail as well as their application to various counterterrorism scenarios. A statistical treatment of security device/sensor performance is also presented, an analysis that is in keeping with a more quantitative treatment of risk.

The theoretical foundations of threats and technologies are central to understanding risk, but as noted above, a key objective is to provide a useful reference for security practitioners. Therefore, I attempt to identify "rules of thumb" and simple performance metrics associated with security technologies. These are approximations that are useful in quickly assessing risk and/or in performing back-of-the-envelope calculations of system performance. The pixel density for CCTV systems immediately comes to mind. Numerous tables with security technology specifications are included that are useful in examining risk, and which are particularly handy when compiled in a single reference.

Although some readers might be put off by the occasional mathematical excursions, I believe the game is worth the chase. These may also save the day the next time you are asked for a more rigorous justification of a security-related expenditure. Hopefully you will agree, and thereafter view security risk management in a more analytic light.

Problems are provided at the conclusion of each chapter. These are intended to test the student's grasp of the fundamental concepts. Many of these problems derive from real-life scenarios and I often attempt to put the reader in the shoes of security decision-makers. Despite my occasional attempt at humor, it is important to keep in mind that decisions made by security professionals can have significant consequences. All problems are tightly coupled to the concepts imparted in the text. In my view this is essential in order to satisfy the book's objectives.

Finally, I must comment on terrorism itself. Terrorism has become useful to politicians, and is sometimes invoked to further nonsecurity-related agendas. Those in power get to determine who is a terrorist and who is a legitimate defender of the realm. Dictators are fond of labeling opponents who favor democracy as terrorists.

Security professionals are obliged to demonstrate more integrity and intellectual rigor than politicians, which fortunately is not difficult. There is a science to measuring security risk, and that is what this book is all about.

"The most important questions of life are indeed, for the most part, really only problems of probability."

Pierre-Simon Laplace
(Théorie Analytique des Probabilités: 1812)

Modeling Terrorism Risk

CHAPTER 1

Terrorism Threats, Risk, and Risk Assessments

1.1 INTRODUCTION: DECISIONS AND RISK

Risk management has an image problem. There seems to be a never-ending stream of headlines about some corporate misstep resulting in billions of dollars in losses that is blamed on poor risk management. We typically only hear about the significant transgressions since big losses and major tragedies make news. The fact is that every financial transaction with a buyer and a seller has a winner and a loser. Therefore, gains and losses are happening all the time. Risk management is presumably at work with little notice until an issue becomes public.

Significant losses often point to a disregard for existing risk management processes rather than flaws in the process itself. So it would seem that risk management is not fundamentally flawed. Rather, it is often selectively applied or intentionally disregarded.

It is also important to appreciate that the tolerance for risk is not constant across professions, and this contributes to an imbalance in expectations on performance. In some fields of endeavor, the tolerance for risk is thankfully quite low. Few people would willingly fly on an airline whose risk management efforts resulted in a 70 percent success rate. Similar statistical expectations exist for other professionals such as surgeons, electricians, riggers, and plumbers. Most people would not be very happy if they had a 70 percent chance of a functional toilet following a visit by the plumber.

On the other hand, the manager of a major league baseball team would be handsomely rewarded for a 70 percent winning percentage. The services of a major league hitter with a mere 30 percent success rate would be even more valued, and no doubt rewarded in kind. Maybe the real lesson here is to carefully choose your profession . . . and your plumber.

There is a tacit assumption that winning at the professional level in baseball is inherently more difficult than plumbing. Note this says nothing about the relative importance of a plumber versus a baseball manager. This likely depends on the status of one's bathroom at the time the question is posed.

3

Society's tolerance or intolerance for varying levels of risk management is based on expectations informed by statistical norms. These expectations will change as these statistics evolve and a new mean and standard deviation for performance emerge over time. Usually this is a slow process.

A precipitous change in performance statistics for a large population is a strong indicator that some external influence is at work. For example, during the baseball steroid era (approximately from 1998 to 2005), the home run production from hitters increased dramatically across the major leagues. As if by magic, hitting 40 home runs in a season became a regular occurrence. Just as suddenly, hitters' home run statistics and fan expectations reverted to the previous mean, probably as a consequence of stringent testing for performance-enhancing drugs.

Statistical outliers in sports do occur, and they take their rightful place at the extreme tails of a normal distribution. For example, Bob Beamon shattered the world long jump record at the 1968 Olympics in Mexico City. In a single attempt he beat the existing record by 21.75 inches. Prior to this effort, the average improvement of the world record was 2.5 inches/jump. So Beamon's singular effort in Mexico City was nearly nine times the average incremental improvement. However, this type of rare event is not the same as a wholesale shift in the performance of a large population over a short time period.

Risk management is also more easily measured in some professions than others. Fortunately or not, this ease of measurement enhances the intensity of the public spotlight. For example, if planes crash, large numbers of people die in surgery at a hospital, or the Yankees lose to the Red Sox and vice versa (the latter is a more likely outcome), a number of people will be upset. Performance statistics in certain industries are intensely reviewed, and outcomes are constantly compared among peer organizations.

Decisions based on risk management are central to our personal and professional lives. In fact, each and every decision we make *is* a form of risk management. This is because every decision, no matter how trivial, boils down to a choice between outcomes with varying effects on our lives. Therefore, each outcome carries risk in the broadest sense of the word. This process applies to any issue, whether it is deciding between green beans and carrots for dinner, swinging at a pitch or not, selecting Harvard or Yale for college, or choosing between Betty and Barbara as a spouse.

The pros and cons of Betty versus Barbara notwithstanding, most decisions that require our attention are not very difficult. This probably has more to do with the types of decisions we face than our native decision-making ability. It is a good bet that nearly all readers of this book live in a stable environment and do not lack the necessities of life. Therefore, we are spared the burden of making choices with life-and-death consequences.

It was not so long ago that life-and-death decisions were an everyday event for most humans on the planet. In some parts of the world this is likely still the case. One crude performance metric for the success of a nation might be the average rate of life-and-death decisions faced by its citizens.

This facility for decision-making may be an evolutionary artifact of *Homo sapiens* and therefore indicative of our evolved thought process. Whatever the explanation, the fact is that risk is built into all our decisions. Whether decision-making is an innate human characteristic is a topic best suited for scientists who study such things.

But it does not require a Ph.D. in zoology to appreciate that animals do not make decisions in the same way that humans do, if at all. Animals rely on instinct whereas humans leverage experience and are clearly influenced by factors like emotion and peer pressure. That said, the reader is referred to a fascinating article describing vervet monkeys who gave up their dislike of colored corn when they changed locations and observed other monkeys eating it.[1]

Consider the daily struggles of your average jungle carnivore. Such animals are focused on survival, which in the near- and long-term translates to eating and procreating, respectively. They do not have the luxury of succumbing to trivial distractions from the Darwinian competition for survival that occurs up and down the food chain every day.

The long-term prospects for a lioness would be dire if she was racked with indecision before each day's hunt on the savanna. Such indulgences would adversely affect her as well as the entire pride. The lioness is programmed for survival, and food obtained through killing or scavenging is essential to her and her pride's survival.

The challenge for the lioness is particularly daunting, especially since she does not have a credit card at her disposal. Her pre-dining efforts entail searching, locating, stalking, chasing, catching, and killing her prey. Contrast this with the trivial effort required to order my quotidian dose of Asian takeout. Fortunately, evolution has served the lioness well, although the statistics show that success at hunting is not at all guaranteed.[2]

The daily quest for food by humans is likely not too difficult for those individuals reading this book. This is clearly the case because if you have paid for this book then acquiring food was a lesser priority. If you received this book as a gift then I assume your kindly benefactor would have chosen to buy you a meal rather than a book notwithstanding this particular book's intrinsic value. In fact, in New York City one merely has to pick up the phone, mumble a 10-digit number plus an expiration date, and food will magically appear at your doorstep. Death through overindulgence is a more likely outcome for the more fortunate members of our species.

In contrast to most of our mammalian counterparts, humans have the simultaneous luxury and curse of distractions resulting from an avalanche of trivial exercises in risk management known as decisions. Most of these are resolved with relative ease despite the consequences of a bad choice.

Consider the decisions required during a routine trip to the grocery store. Do I hop in the car or take public transportation? If I do take the car, should I exceed the speed limit or obey the law? Should I run the yellow light or sit through another frustrating cycle of signal changes? How about knocking down a cold beer (or two) versus drinking Diet Coke before departing? Should I snag a few uninspiring Brussels sprouts or indulge in a bag of artery-hardening potato chips? It is no wonder that ordering takeout seems so liberating.

In any decision, choosing one option over another has consequences. Absent risk, all choices would essentially be equivalent, and you would end up staring at the grocery shelf in perpetuity. This actually happens to me when I am in the vegetable section since all possible outcomes seem equally bad. I attribute this to a personal failure in risk management rather than a penchant for unhealthy food.

Humans often make the wrong decision on relatively significant issues. The silver lining is that these decisions appear to be having a limited impact on the survival of our species, although the final chapter has not been written on the effects of our current cycle of climate change.

More impactful decisions such as which person to marry might make the point more convincingly. Although humans may be innate decision makers, we clearly have not perfected the process. As noted above, it is possible that modern decisions have limited biological consequences, hence there is no evolutionary pressure to improve. Nature may therefore be agnostic to our decision-making efforts, flawed or otherwise, which means we have the potential to continue this way in perpetuity.

1.2   THREATS AND THE COMPONENTS OF RISK

Questions regarding the risk of marriage and successful lion hunting are no doubt fascinating, but exploring the risk associated with the threat of terrorism should be our main focus.

Understanding the threats posed by terrorists is fundamental to developing an effective security risk-mitigation strategy. In fact, identifying the spectrum of what I choose to call the set of "distinct and impactful threats" should be the starting point for a rigorous assessment of security risk. Let's explore what we mean by distinct and impactful threats.

Later in this section we will spell out and examine the three components of risk in more detail. However, one of those components requires mention up front: impact. The impact component of risk specifies how important or meaningful that threat is to the affected entities. After all, not all threats will be of consequence, so identifying what is and is not impactful represents an essential filter in determining "risk relevance." In addition, the impact component of risk is important in determining if it is worth expending resources on addressing the risk associated with that threat.

It should not be too difficult to understand whether a specific threat is impactful. For example, a boat owner in Miami should probably not be too concerned about blizzards in Canada.

The notion of distinctness can be trickier to understand, but it is key to identifying risk mitigation. Threats that are commonly lumped together as terrorism, can actually be quite dissimilar, and different mitigation measures might be required to reflect those differences. There needs to be a test for distinctness, and fortunately there is one, which will also be discussed later in this chapter.

Specific attack vectors must also be identified as part of the exercise in identifying threats. An attack vector is a fancy name for a specific mode of implementing a threat. Vehicle-borne explosives, the use of firearms with the purpose of terrorizing the population, and the dispersal of biological agents are examples of attack vectors that are subsumed under the more general heading of "terrorism."

A security strategy is not very strategic if the threats of concern are not appreciated and/or their relative impact is not understood. A brief digression regarding the distinction between threats and risk is warranted at this point.

A threat can be defined as anything that causes harm or loss, intentional or not. We will accept it as a fact that the outcome of a threat is to make one worse off than before the threat occurred. Of course, the notion of "worse" is subjective. The same threat will not affect all individuals in the same way. In fact, some things in everyday life are viewed as a scourge by some and embraced by others.

Religion and television immediately come to mind. Religion is too controversial, so I will sidestep that issue. Although some might argue that television expands our collective consciousness, it might not be so beneficial for the more impressionable members of society, as Figure 1.1 suggests. It appears from this data that the number of hours spent watching television and grade point average is moderately anticorrelated.

Yet aspiring to a rigorous approach in assessing security risk imposes certain demands. At a minimum, one should be precise about terminology. People

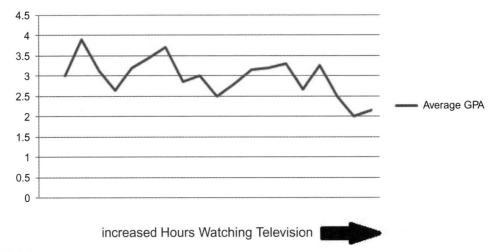

FIGURE 1.1

Televison risk. *(Information from: "The 'Evils' of Television: The Amount of Television Viewing and School Performance Levels." Indiana University South Bend.* https://www.iusb.edu/ugr-journal/static/2002/hershberger.php.*)*

often conflate the terms "threat" and "risk," which can cause confusion regarding the precise focus of a strategy. Even experts get this wrong.

In addition, the verb "threaten" is sometimes confused with the noun, "threat." To threaten actually implies the existence of an underlying threat (e.g., physical assault, firing from a job, withholding support such as food or money, etc.), so the act of threatening is merely an explicit announcement of an impending threat. But this begs the important question, "What is risk?" Simply put, if a threat causes harm and generally makes one worse off, the risk associated with a threat defines the essential properties of that threat. These are admittedly abstract concepts that need more concrete descriptions in order to be fully appreciated.

A threat is analogous to a force in physics. A force requires certain features in order to have an effect. For example, the force of gravity requires at least two objects with mass in order for the familiar pull to occur. In the same way, a threat requires risk in order to have an effect. In other words, a threat is not *threatening* without risk, just as gravity is not *gravitational* (i.e., an attracting influence) without objects that have mass.

In Section 1.1 it was noted how each decision was an exercise in risk management since all decisions carried risk. It turns out that security-related decisions are no different than any other types of decision in terms of the underlying assessment process. The problem with decisions on security is that security solutions sometimes become decoupled from the drivers of those solutions, i.e., threats. In fact, decisions on security risk mitigation can sometimes seem whimsical as a result of a reflexive deployment of a standard set of equipment. This can happen when the risk associated with a threat is not carefully evaluated and understood.

Moreover, in the absence of security incident statistics or a proper laboratory to conduct controlled experiments, the effectiveness of counterterrorism controls cannot be rigorously tested. Inevitably, solutions are implemented without really understanding their effect on the security risk profile.

What is missing? At the highest level, a process is required to assess security risk and then determine the appropriate controls required to manage that risk. What are the benefits of such a process? Most importantly, it provides an explicit connection between security threats and risk mitigation. Of course this presumes one has a genuine understanding of the relevant threats and associated risk. This can be a nontrivial exercise, and learning how to do this is a key objective of this book.

Before we can examine the risk assessment process in detail, we must describe risk with precision. It has been previously stated without accompanying detail that risk has three components. Understanding these components is critical to developing an effective security strategy. These components are as follows:

- Threat impact (i.e., importance)
- Threat likelihood (i.e., potential for occurrence)
- Threat vulnerability (i.e., the consequences or the exposure to loss if the threat does occur)

Each of these three components of risk must exist for a threat to be threatening. If the magnitude of a single component is zero then the threat is merely an abstraction. We can express the relationship between threats and risk in compact form in what I dramatically call the Fundamental Expression of Risk.

$$\text{RISK}(\text{threat}) = \text{Impact} \times \text{Likelihood} \times \text{Vulnerability}$$

The proper way to read this expression is as follows: "The risk associated with a given threat is equal to the product of that threat's impact times the threat likelihood times the vulnerability to that threat."

One should not be too literal in the mathematical interpretation of this expression. Each component of risk is not necessarily equally weighted, contrary to how it is written. In fact, assessing the relative magnitude of each component of risk for a given threat is the first step in conducting a proper security risk assessment.

1.3 RISK ASSESSMENTS

There are typically many issues to address when defending an organization against the spectrum of distinct and impactful threats. If unlimited resources are available, one can avoid the mental effort inherent in a risk-based approach. One can also ignore this book. Fortunately I am relatively safe in assuming that infinite budgets are not generally available. So, how should one apportion resources in accordance with a finite security budget and thereby address the set of distinct and impactful threats?

Those constrained by budgets need to be judicious in applying risk mitigation. Specifically, they require a *strategy* that prioritizes the set of distinct and impactful threats and suggest risk-mitigation measures that are proportionate to those threats. A security strategy is actually a prioritized set of risk-mitigation measures. Identifying such a strategy is often easier said than done, and it can be a daunting task for complex organizations with numerous business units, a global footprint, etc.

Developing a *bona fide* security strategy requires a proper risk assessment using a rigorous methodology. However, one warning from the outset is that it is easy to get hung up on details in the process. The breadth and scope of assessing a large organization can seem overwhelming, so latching on to the most visible, low-hanging fruit is tempting. Although details are important, an initial focus on minutiae can obfuscate systemic issues. In general, when tackling a complex problem it is advantageous to identify general areas first and then drill down on the details rather than vice versa.

We actually specified the first step in a proper security risk assessment process in the previous section. Namely, identify all the distinct and impactful threats and threat attack vectors. In other words, an evaluation of the impact component of risk for each distinct threat or threat attack vector represents the initial phase of a security risk assessment.

This seems straightforward, but it can actually be a nontrivial exercise. Identifying the precise threats and attack vectors of concern requires insight into the various modes of attack as well as an understanding of how an organization conducts business to determine which threats are indeed impactful.

The next step is to assess the relative magnitude of the remaining components of risk associated with each of the identified threats and attack vectors. Importantly, it is essential to specify which component of risk is driving the mitigation strategy. For example, consider a counterterrorism strategy designed to protect the lobby of a building. The security director has wisely decided to install turnstiles to minimize the risk of terrorism and the possibility of other threats by reducing the vulnerability to unauthorized physical access via piggybacking. However, the individual who passes through a turnstile may be using someone else's ID to gain unauthorized physical access. If the likelihood of this is deemed to be low, should some form of authentication be employed as an added control such as a biometric or a security officer checking ID photographs? The answers to this and similar security questions are not always clear since such moves involve a cost.

I once asked my class at John Jay College to estimate the rate at which individuals were bypassing the turnstiles in the lobby of our classroom building. I asked the question to see whether they would recommend adding authentication as a security control, and if so, how would they justify their decision. Their estimates of risk varied wildly since they were relying on impressions based on informal observations and anecdote. My point was less about arriving at the correct answer (note: there is often no correct or incorrect answer to risk-type problems; there are only substantiated or unsubstantiated explanations about risk) than to illustrate the importance of making decisions based on a rigorous assessment of risk.

It is possible that the cost of implementing authentication does not make sense in view of limited vulnerability and/or a smallish likelihood component of risk. However, such a decision should be based on an actual evaluation of the components of risk. In my experience such an evaluation is often lacking.

Returning to the assessment process, it is imperative that each distinct and impactful attack vector be identified when assessing terrorism risk, otherwise the risk-mitigation strategy might address irrelevant vulnerabilities or miss them altogether. Fortunately there is a way to test for distinctness, and this conveniently leads to the next step in the security risk assessment process as discussed in Section 1.6. Figure 1.2 illustrates the balance required in assessing the likelihood and vulnerability components of risk.

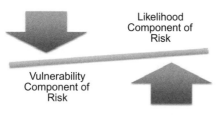

Likelihood
Component of
Risk

Vulnerability
Component of
Risk

FIGURE 1.2
Assessing the components of risk.

1.4 SECURITY RISK TRADE-OFFS

Operational decisions with security implications often require trade-offs that are driven by an organization's business model. A good example of this occurs at museums. I sometimes visit the Metropolitan Museum of Art in New York City, which is just across the park from my home. The "Met" is an iconic institution that possesses countless art treasures. I am personally fond of the baseball card collection, much to the frustration of my more cultured friends.

One day I found myself hanging around the museum lobby deciding which collection to visit. After watching the security staff in action, it dawned on me that the museum does not authenticate the identity of visitors prior to allowing physical access to the exhibits. How is that possible in light of the priceless collections, of art and the close proximity of millions of visitors to those items?

The Met does inspect bags upon entry, but I believe this is primarily intended as a counterterrorism measure. In all candor, inspection of bags alone does not make a lot of sense unless art-loving terrorists are preternaturally averse to hand-carrying their weapons. Absent evidence to the contrary, this likely qualifies as "security theatre," a concept explored in Section 2.5. However, a brief digression on this point is warranted.

Goldman Sachs implemented X-ray inspections of bags carried into their New York City buildings immediately after 9/11. In a scenario reminiscent of the Met, individuals were not personally inspected for weapons. Therefore, any terrorist who hand-carried a firearm or a bomb was relatively immune to detection.

Setting aside the potential for someone attacking Goldman Sachs in this way, it was clear to even the casual observer that inspecting bags alone was ineffective. This was certainly apparent to my nonsecurity-trained friends, who reminded me of the flawed logic at every opportunity. Adding insult to injury, the X-ray inspectors themselves were often observed to be inattentive.

The X-ray procedure was not just a waste of time and money. It actually had a more damaging effect: it caused employees to lose faith in the physical security program. This experience provided a valuable lesson about the collateral effects of security theatre. Goldman Sachs employees are generally quite intelligent, so when subjected to a nonrisk-based and inconvenient procedure the result was collective cynicism and distrust.

Returning to the Metropolitan Museum of Art's security strategy, it too focuses on confirming that one is authorized to enter the facility. However, this translates to ensuring the entrance fee is paid. So 25 bucks allows any person to get within inches of many extremely expensive assets. Is this a prudent security strategy?

A museum's security professionals probably recognize that this strategy is not ideal, but they also realize it is driven by necessity. The museum assumes that the risk associated with theft, sabotage, etc., is roughly the same from person-to-person. Absent evidence to the contrary, the assumption is that the security risks posed by "Carl Young" are the same as anyone else relative to the threats just noted. This is a necessary assumption since accommodating visitors is the whole point of a museum. If you overly inhibit visitors, the entire museum could come to a grinding halt. This highlights the importance of understanding an organization's business model before prescribing security measures.

What other controls might help manage the risk in this context? Adding a control such as background checks on each of the nearly 6 million annual visitors might reduce risk, but this is not a realistic option. Other standard physical security controls such as authentication of identity and confirmation of authorized physical access are also not compatible with the museum's business model. As noted above, it does not matter if "Carl Young" is a mass murderer in this context. All visitors are assumed to pose an equivalent risk to the museum with respect to the physical threats of concern.

What controls *do* the museum use to address the risk factor of close physical proximity to high-value items? The answer is they saturate the environment with security officers and antitheft technology. This is an expensive strategy.

Museum security directors, like all security professionals, must develop a security strategy that comports with their organization's culture and business model. This same strategy would certainly not be viable in most commercial facilities since the cost of implementation would be prohibitive. Also, lots of security officers might spook the employees and visitors. I suspect most firms' cultures would not tolerate such a posture. On the other hand, everyone expects a massive security presence at museums, and the associated costs are presumably built into the ticket price and anticipated donations.

A more extreme example of the vulnerability-likelihood tradeoff is the threat of a nuclear attack. It is almost guaranteed that every commercial facility in New York City and every other U.S. city is quite vulnerable to this threat. Assuming a security director gave it any thought, he or she most likely estimated the potential for an incident occurrence to be extremely low. In other words, the security director is probably comfortable trading extreme vulnerability for infinitesimal likelihood with respect to this threat.

An important consideration in a real-world risk assessment is the cost of addressing the vulnerability in light of the potential for incident occurrence. This will be discussed in more detail in Chapter 2. I doubt that a recommendation to construct a building deep underground or to renovate the office space with the latest in lead-lined decor is an option that would be warmly received by most organizations.

However, the strategy for nuclear defense might change if an extremely cheap and easily implemented means of addressing this threat were available despite the extremely low potential for occurrence. Such is the essence of security risk decisions.

Although the proper approach to addressing nuclear threats may seem trivial in light of the obvious likelihood-vulnerability imbalance, this is atypical of many security decisions. In general, such trade-offs can be difficult and require rigorous analyses informed by judgment and experience to arrive at a thoughtful and defensible position.

1.5   SECURITY RISK IN CONTEXT

The individual components of terrorism risk do not exist in a vacuum. It is impossible to accurately assess risk without appreciating the context of a particular threat. Events or circumstances that might appear to enhance the potential for a threat or attack vector in one context may be completely benign or irrelevant in another.

Frequent references to the New York City subway system are made in this book. There is a good reason for this. Many New Yorkers such as myself spend some part of each day on a train with little else to do than observe the sociology experiment unfolding before their eyes. Interesting lessons on human behavior can be learned when large numbers of people are forced to interact in close proximity to one another.

It is always slightly amusing to hear the canned subway announcement warning passengers to "immediately report any suspicious activity to the police." One invariably looks around at the spectacle and wonders how a tourist from Europe, Japan, Kansas, etc. decides whom or what to report first!

Of course the word "suspicious" has a very specific meaning in this context. In the language of risk, the city is actually asking passengers to identify a risk factor for terrorism: "suspicious" behavior. However, the point is that suspicious behavior is highly contextual and open to broad interpretation. For example, New Yorkers are inured to events that might freak out your average Kansan and vice versa. A large quantity of ammonium nitrate fertilizer would hopefully raise a few eyebrows in Columbus Circle but might be considered standard operating procedure on a farm in Kansas.

Human behavior will likely be quite different from venue-to-venue depending on local customs and cultures. People who are socially aware often try to adapt to the local norm, possibly because of a characteristically human desire to "fit in." Individuals who do not fit in are considered at odds with their peers and they risk alienation from the group at large.

Why is this important to terrorism? Terrorists who do not want to get caught *before* they commit an act of terrorism would likely aspire to blend in to their surroundings. They would seek to exhibit "average" behavior relative to those around them. In other words, they would not want to call attention to themselves, although this is probably not due to a concern over a diminished social status. Unusual or suspicious behavior must be defined in context in order to be meaningful and/or relevant to a counterterrorism strategy.

However, certain features of terrorism will be relevant irrespective of the setting, and these need to be monitored and detected. All terrorists require a method of implementing their terror. An effective terrorism risk management strategy will consist of an exhaustive examination of likely attack vectors and their respective components of risk followed by a rigorous examination of the so-called risk factors.

1.6 RISK FACTORS

Once the magnitude of each component of risk for each distinct and impactful threat is determined, the next step is to identify the risk factors associated with each threat. A risk factor is anything that enhances one or more components of risk. The world of medicine offers ample illustrations of this important concept.

The problems in medicine and security are often strikingly similar from a risk management perspective. However, the examples in medicine have one important advantage over those in security. Medical professionals are able to leverage statistically significant data on threats (i.e., diseases) and the effect of mitigation (therapies) in making decisions. Because of an abundance of incidents, the insights gleaned from controlled experiments, and the consistency of the human body from individual-to-individual, significant data is available to make accurate predictions about the likelihood of future incidents as well as the effectiveness of remediation.

The role of the security professional is similar to the physician. The physician prescribes medicine that is the functional equivalent of risk mitigation in the world of security. Medical histories coupled with a physical examination are analogous to security risk assessments. However, the security professional often has a more difficult time substantiating the effectiveness of mitigation because there is little data to support claims of success or failure. Establishing cause and effect are statistical luxuries in counterterrorism. For example, suppose you are the security director of a large international corporation and you are asked whether the newly installed closed circuit television (CCTV) and physical access control systems have been effective in thwarting terrorism? You might respond by saying you have not had an incident since these systems were installed. But the whole truth is that there were also no incidents *before* such systems were installed. So was the risk mitigation effective or was there merely extreme disinterest by terrorists? Chapter 5 examines ways of dealing with the mixed blessing of small numbers of terrorism incidents.

A pet peeve of mine occurs when a consumer of a security strategy demands a specific risk-mitigation method. Imagine visiting the cardiologist and demanding an EKG or echocardiogram? The appropriate procedure is to state your symptoms and let the good doctor decide what is required in the way of tests, medicines, etc. Of course you must trust that your doctor knows how to evaluate risk. Although it might seem slightly presumptuous, let's review how a physician should diagnose diseases.

Suppose you wake up one day and feel absolutely awful. It is not even Monday, so the prospect of an agonizing week at work cannot account for your abject misery. You have a fever, headache, and notice that a rash has mysteriously appeared on your body. Coincidentally, you have just returned from a tropical vacation. You pick up the phone and attempt to make an appointment with a physician.

Let's suspend reality and assume that the doctor agrees to see you that day. In fact, this particular physician is not only compassionate but is also astute. After learning of your symptoms, she notices your sporty suntan and asks if you have recently traveled overseas. Upon hearing your answer and taking note of your symptoms, she suspects you may have contracted a tropical illness.

She fires up her browser to query her trusty colleague, "Dr. Internet." After clicking on *www.google.com*, she types in your symptoms. It seems that both physicians and their anxious patients do the same thing these days. This physician knows that traveling to a tropical climate is a risk factor for certain diseases. The next step is to attempt to match the patient's symptoms with those of a particular illness.

In a fraction of a second, the search engine, whose designers never attended a day of medical school, renders a website that describes a disease with symptoms of a fever, headache, and a rash. This adds weight to the doctor's hunch that you are indeed suffering from a tropical disease. In fact, she suspects that you have contracted dengue fever based on the so-called "dengue triad" of symptoms. Blood tests are required to confirm the diagnosis, but she is now more confident in commencing with a regimen of drugs in anticipation of the laboratory results.

She now researches remedies that are hopefully covered by your insurance plan. Unfortunately, the financial implications of illness also carry risk in some countries.

Identifying the distinct and impactful threats represents the first step in a security risk assessment, but determining the risk factors associated with each of these threats is what drives mitigation. The reason is obvious from the definition since a risk factor is defined as a feature that enhances one or more components of risk. Let's examine a few threats and associated risk factors.

One of my personal "favorites" is the threat of death due to lung cancer. In this case, smoking has been conclusively shown to be a risk factor. Just to clarify, I am not a fan of lung cancer, but it is illustrative because the causal relationship between the disease and an environmental influence is so compelling. Figure 1.3 tells the story.

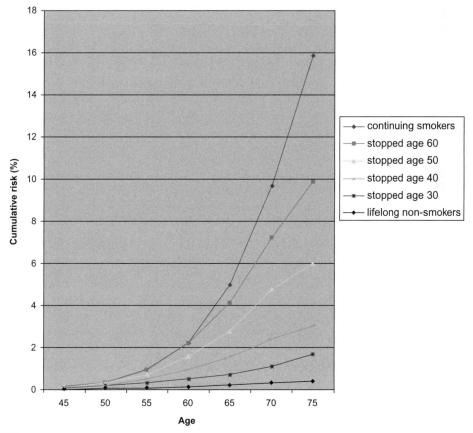

FIGURE 1.3

Effects of stopping smoking at various ages on the cumulative risk (%) of death from lung cancer by age 75, calculated by combining results from the 1990 study with mortality rates for men in the UK in 1990. *(From Peto, R. et al. (200). "Smoking, Smoking Cessation, and Lung Cancer in the UK Since 1950: Combination of National Statistics with Two Case-Control Studies." National Center for Biotechnology Information.* http://www.ncbi.nlm.nih.gov/pmc/articles/PMC27446/.)

The data establishes a definitive relationship between the number of years of smoking cigarettes and the likelihood of dying from lung cancer. In this study, comparisons were made among groups of people who persisted in the same behavior for varying lengths of time, and the length of time smoking represented the only significant variation in their behavior. It therefore directly addressed the question of whether the mortality from lung cancer as a result of cigarette smoking increases with additional years of smoking.

At the risk of seeming pedantic, one should be precise about which component of risk is being affected by cigarette smoking or any risk factor. The phrase "increases the risk of . . ." is imprecise since it does not specify the affected component of risk. Sometimes multiple components are affected by a single risk factor, but in unequal amounts.

In the case of the threat of lung cancer, it is indeed both the likelihood and vulnerability components of risk that are affected by the smoking risk factor. There is a direct relationship between the number of cigarettes smoked and the probability of dying from lung cancer. The availability of statistically significant data on lung cancer incidents facilitates a more quantitative statement about the likelihood component of risk. In general, if there is a positive correlation (see the discussion on correlation later in this section) between the occurrence of a risk factor and a threat, then that risk factor affects the likelihood component of risk.

However, increased exposure to tobacco also increases one's vulnerability to carcinogens. Recall the general threat is lung cancer, which can occur as a result of other risk factors including genetics. In this case we are examining the specific risk factor of cigarette smoking, and increasing the level of tobacco exposure increases the vulnerability to lung cancer.

In a similar vein, consider the theft of valuables and the risk factor of unauthorized physical access to a facility. This risk factor affects the vulnerability component of risk since physical proximity facilitates various modes of attack that otherwise are not feasible. It also increases the potential for this threat. If the rate of unauthorized physical access to a facility increases, the potential for theft increases. However, unless there were multiple instances of thefts, one could not make a more quantitative statement on the likelihood component of risk.

This makes intuitive sense, but can one make a more precise statement on the correlation between the likelihood of theft and the unauthorized physical access risk factor? Later in this chapter we will discuss the concept of a correlation coefficient. This specifies the magnitude of the linear relationship between two variables. For example, the extremely rigorous security professional might want to calculate the correlation coefficient between the number of thefts and the number of unauthorized physical access incidents.

What about the threat of vehicle-borne explosives? This is a good illustration of the distinction between "likelihood" and "potential." Here a risk factor is also physical proximity, and it affects the vulnerability component of risk. The closer the vehicle is to the target, the greater the exposure to physical damage or loss.

However, the potential for a vehicle-borne explosive incident is affected by current political, economic, and/or religious risk factors. The potential expresses the general conditions or climate for an attack. Importantly, it is a qualitative and quite useful statement on the risk associated with the general state of play relative to this threat.

In contrast, assessing the likelihood of a single explosive incident is inherently statistical. So a risk factor for the likelihood of an incident would be the number of instances of unauthorized vehicles in proximity to a facility. Why?

In the statistical view of the likelihood component of risk, each vehicle has a well-defined and equal probability of exploding. Let's assume the probability of any single vehicle exploding is given by $p(x)$. If there are n vehicles, the likelihood of any one of these vehicles exploding and thereby affecting a given facility is equal to $1 - [p(x)]^n$.

Therefore, in this view of risk, the greater the number of vehicles, the higher the likelihood of an explosive incident all things being equal.

However, there could be a large number of such events in a given time frame yet the potential for an attack as determined by a qualitative assessment of relevant risk factors might be low. How should one proceed to identify a strategy to address this threat?

A prudent counterterrorism strategy might not completely discount the statistical view of risk, and therefore seek to address the relevant risk factors (i.e., limit the number of unauthorized vehicles in physical proximity to a facility), assuming the cost of risk remediation was within acceptable limits.

The lesson here is that one must be linguistically precise in characterizing the components of risk and relevant risk factors. Clearly, the risk factors might vary depending on the view of risk at the component level so the defensive strategy would also change. As always, there is no escaping the need for rigor, precision and judgment in assessing risk.

That said, an actual incident might never happen since someone must be predisposed to actually commit such a heinous crime. Again, a more precise statement on the likelihood component of risk is not possible without actual incidents or events related to threat risk factors.

Returning to medical analogies and risk, smoking as a risk factor for lung cancer is old news. What about cause-and-effect relationships for other diseases?

Diabetes mellitus is a condition where the body has excessive sugar in the blood. This is caused by the cells' inability to process insulin or an insufficient amount of insulin in the bloodstream. Obesity is a scientifically confirmed risk factor for certain types of diabetes.

It should not require a huge stretch of the imagination to speculate that a predilection for fast food might be a risk factor for diabetes given the connection between fast food and obesity. This is the gist of Figure 1.4, which indicates trends in the rate of diabetes and the proliferation of McDonald's restaurants.

However, this data does not prove a cause-and-effect relationship between eating fast food and the rate of diabetes in the same way as the data for smoking and lung cancer did. It merely shows potentially related trends, or to put this into statistical jargon, it shows a correlation. Therefore, one cannot say for sure that eating at McDonald's is a risk factor for diabetes. There are too many other factors that might influence the prevalence of diabetes for McDonald's to claim exclusive bragging rights. Confirming the hypothesis that eating at McDonald's causes diabetes would require a direct test for it. Nevertheless, these results are interesting and might inspire further investigation by health officials. Imagine requiring a prescription for a Big Mac.

Whatever else, it is critical that reliable data is used to assess risk issues rather than relying on intuition. For example, the results of four independent studies shown in Figure 1.5 confirm a decrease in the frequency of sex with age among married couples. The overwhelming consensus on this point might lead one to believe that a downward trend in the lack of amorous interaction between married couples contributes to the rate of divorce.

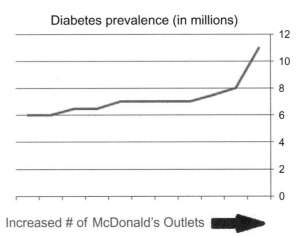

FIGURE 1.4

Correlation of diabetes with fast food. *(Information from Nicholas, W. Webinquiry.org. "The Fast Food Freeway to Diabetes". http://webinquiry.org/examples/diabetes/.)*

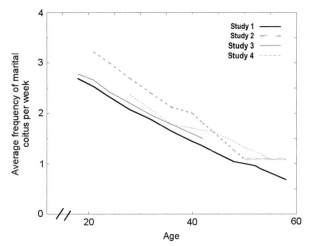

FIGURE 1.5

Frequency of marital sex. *(Data from Divorceinfo.* http://www.divorceinfo.com/statistics.htm.*)*

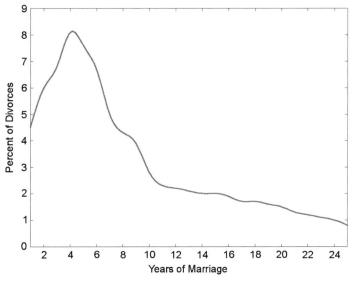

FIGURE 1.6

Correlation or anticorrelation? Lack of sex and divorce. *(Data from Divorceinfo.* http://www
.divorceinfo.com/statistics.htm.*)*

However, Figure 1.6 shows a steep decline in the divorce rate for marriages last-ing more than 5 years. Presumably those couples that are married 5 years or more are having decreasing sexual activity based on the data in Figure 1.5. That would seem to counter the supposition that sex, or a lack thereof, plays a signifi-cant or exclusive role in couples splitting up. In other words, maybe a lack of sex is not a risk factor for divorce, at least over the long term. Again, the only way to determine if there is a causal relationship is to directly test for the hypothesis.

In my experience, humans are notoriously bad at reasoning about cause and effect. They often draw conclusions based on personal accounts or events that are closely linked in time. They typically do not account for other factors that could be at work since proper experimental controls are lacking. Everyone has heard comments like, "My Uncle Seymour smoked 3 packs a day for 50 years and he never developed lung cancer!"

In fact, medical experts do not claim that everyone who smokes is destined to develop lung cancer. If they did, Uncle Seymour's experience would offer an instructive counterexample. The medical experts who opine on smoking are making a statement about risk, which is inherently statistical in this case. Uncle Seymour is merely a solitary example among many other examples, each with a different and likely more somber outcome.

What blinds people to reality is that their personal experience represents a single data point that may lie at the tail end of a broad distribution. The bigger picture often tells a very different story depending on the breadth of that distribution.

Sometimes it is easy to predict a correlation between two variables, but other times less so. For example, it does not require a big stretch of the imagination to think there would be a high correlation between proficiency at basketball and height as measured by the number of points scored by each player. What about measuring other possible relationships, and especially those relevant to security risk?

One method used to determine a linear relationship between two variables is the Pearson product-moment correlation coefficient or Pearson correlation coefficient. This coefficient is often denoted by "r." A Pearson correlation coefficient attempts to draw a line of best fit through the data of two variables. It indicates how far these data points are from this line of best fit. In other words, it indicates how well the data points fit this model for the best fit.

The Pearson correlation coefficient can take a range of values from +1 to −1. A value of 0 indicates that there is no linear relationship between the two variables. A value greater than 0 indicates a positive linear relationship. That is, as the value of one variable increases, so does the value of the other variable. A value less than 0 indicates a negative association. In other words, as the value of one variable increases, the value of the other variable decreases.

The formula for the Pearson correlation coefficient is the following:

$$r = \frac{\sum XY - \dfrac{\sum X \sum Y}{N}}{\sqrt{\left(\sum X^2 - \dfrac{\left(\sum X\right)^2}{N}\right)\left(\sum Y^2 - \dfrac{\left(\sum Y\right)^2}{N}\right)}}$$

N is the total number of samples, X represents all the x values, and Y corresponds to all the y values; "r" can be used to determine a correlation between the occurrence of a threat or threat attack vector and a risk factor for that threat. Suppose it is hypothesized that there is a correlation between the number of terrorist events and the day of the month. In other words, the hypothesis is that the number of terrorist incidents increases linearly with increasing days of the month. Moreover, a strategy is suggested that involves deploying more counterterrorist controls toward the end of the month to effectively deploy resources. A rigorous analysis of this hypothesis is required to determine if this strategy will indeed be effective.

The Pearson correlation coefficient can be used to test this hypothesis using phony data. We will also make use of an online calculator, such as the following, to perform the calculation, thereby saving a lot of time: *http://www .socscistatistics.com/tests/pearson/Default2.aspx*.

The first step is to create a table (Table 1.1) of the scores for each variable and the product of the two scores. The first column represents the days of the month

Table 1.1 Pearson Correlation Coefficient Example

X (Day of the Month)	Y (Number of Terrorist Incidents)	X^2	Y^2	XY
1	2	1	4	2
2	1	4	1	2
3	3	9	9	9
4	1	16	1	4
5	4	25	16	20
6	2	36	4	12
7	3	49	9	21
8	2	64	4	16
9	2	81	4	18
10	2	100	4	20
11	5	121	25	55
12	1	144	1	12
13	2	169	4	26
14	3	196	9	42
15	3	225	9	45
16	1	256	1	16
17	1	289	1	17
18	2	324	4	36
19	3	361	9	57
20	3	400	9	60
210	46	2870	128	490

up to day 20 and the second column indicates a contrived number of terrorist incidents that occurred on the corresponding day of the month.

Plugging the values shown in the table into the formula for "r" we get the following:

$$r = \left(490 - \left(210 \times (46/20)\right)\right) / \sqrt{\left(\left(2870 - (210)^2/20\right)\right)\left(128 - \left(46^2/20\right)\right)}$$

Cranking through this expression yields a correlation coefficient of $r = 0.058$.

Recall that the correlation coefficient ranges from -1 to 1, where -1 is perfect anticorrelation (e.g., the number of terrorist incidents *decreases* linearly as the days of the month progress), 0 corresponds to no correlation, and 1 indicates perfect positive linear correlation.

A 0.058 coefficient implies that there is only a very slight correlation between the day of the month and the number of terrorism incidents. The magnitude of this correlation should counter any anecdotal evidence to support the supposition and hopefully undermine attempts at implementing a strategy based on this hypothesis.

Let's investigate another terrorism-related example that highlights the relevance of risk factors. Suppose you are the security director of a large international corporation and you are put in charge of identifying a site for your company's new global headquarters. This company is a high-profile firm and would likely make the hit list of any moderately informed anti-Western terrorist group.

As noted previously, a common terrorist attack vector is the use of vehicle-borne explosives. This is certainly not the only attack vector at their disposal, but it is a popular terrorist technique. The risk factors for vulnerability to vehicle-borne explosives include physical proximity to vehicles and proximity to "iconic" structures that are themselves targets.

Now suppose you have studied the problem carefully, and you have even consulted a physical security expert. Thankfully, your security consultant is a physicist by training and therefore is capable of making quantitative estimates of risk.

The security consultant advises that the vulnerability to explosive forces decreases nonlinearly with distance from the explosive source. In other words, the helpful effect of distance is disproportionately enhanced with increasing distance. The converse is, of course, true as well. The negative effects of close proximity are disproportionately amplified with decreasing distance between the explosive source and the target. The physics of explosive detonations makes a compelling argument in favor of getting as far away as possible from potential terrorist targets.

The risk-based mitigation strategy calls for selecting a site that is as far away as possible from iconic structures, a risk factor affecting the vulnerability component of risk for the vehicle-borne explosive attack vector. You have justified this approach based on a rigorous analysis of the components of risk. This analysis included a *qualitative* estimate of the increase in the potential for a vehicle-borne explosive attack (i.e., risk factor number 1) and a *quantitative* estimate of the increased vulnerability to vehicle-borne explosive threats as a function of decreasing distance between a vehicle and your facility (i.e., risk factor number 2).

Unfortunately, this strategy antagonizes the company CEO. It turns out that the firm is being offered significant financial incentives to build a facility across the street from a very iconic facility.

However, the news gets even worse for the CEO. The security budget calls for the installation of bollards with a high-energy rating. In other words, they are expensive. You have selected the Delta Scientific bollard model DSC720 with a K12 government rating (i.e., zero penetration of the barrier by a 15,000-lb vehicle moving at 50 mph).

The consultant did her homework and calculated the maximum kinetic energy of an accelerating vehicle upon impact in order to determine the appropriate bollard rating. She even plotted her results and created nice charts to assist in presenting a reasoned argument.

The plan calls for the bollards to be placed circumferentially around the headquarters facility and as far as possible from the façade, consistent with addressing risk factor number 2. Of course this increases the total number of bollards in direct proportion to the circle's radius.

Unfortunately, the CEO becomes apoplectic upon hearing the plan. Protecting the headquarters building from vehicle-borne explosives increases the security budget by a whopping 25 percent! Consequently, the bollards get scrapped and are replaced by a highly decorative fence.

As noted several times previously, identifying the complete set of distinct and impactful threats is step 1 in performing a security risk analysis. The good news is that identifying impactful (i.e., important) threats to an organization is usually not too difficult. However, and as noted previously, the notion of distinctness is a subtler concept. How can one determine if two threats or threat attack vectors are in fact distinct and therefore require different forms of risk mitigation?

There is a simple test for distinctness. That test is whether there are differences in the risk factors associated with each threat or threat attack vector. If the risk factors for two threats are identical then the threats are functionally indistinguishable in terms of required risk mitigation.

Consider another terrorist threat with various attack vectors, namely, an attack committed by an individual with a semiautomatic rifle. One vector might be a "random" maniac who goes berserk. A very different vector is an anti-Western religious fanatic. In each case the same weapon is being used to kill people in exactly the same manner. In fact, both cases can be considered acts of terrorism.

Although the *modus operandi* is identical in each case, key risk factors vary considerably and therefore would profoundly affect the risk-mitigation strategy. The potential for the maniac gunman scenario might be considered to be quite low. On the other hand, the anti-Western religious fanatic might be inspired by the iconic status of your company, and this would increase the potential for an attack.

Installing a metal detector along with a 24/7 staff to screen visitors at your building entrance might not be worth the cost to address the maniac gunman attack vector since the potential for occurrence is assessed to be quite low. However, such a cost might indeed be justified in addressing the threat of anti-Western fanatics based on the increased potential for attack against your iconic facility. Understanding the drivers of risk (i.e., risk factors) is a prerequisite for a meaningful cost-benefit analysis.

1.7 COUNTERTERRORISM CONTROLS

We now know that an effective security risk-mitigation strategy addresses all the risk factors associated with each distinct and impactful threat. Precise thinking is required to identify the complete set of risk factors associated with a given threat or threat attack vector. Successfully identifying these factors translates to a complete understanding of the risk relative to identified threats.

The logic is unassailable: If terrorist threats are characterized by three components of risk, and risk factors are those features that enhance one or more of these components, an effective counterterrorist strategy by definition must address each risk factor.

In another example, if the threat of concern is a radiological dispersion device (RDD), a.k.a. "dirty bomb," two risk factors affecting vulnerability are proximity to the explosion and exposure to the dispersed radioactive material. A control for risk mitigation might be radiological shielding, since it is designed to reduce the vulnerability component of risk.

Fortunately the laws of physics can be used to determine the relative effectiveness of various shielding materials. Specifically, these laws can be used to determine if a shield sufficiently reduces the vulnerability to absorbed radiation.

Controls are high-level forms of risk mitigation. A method is a means of implementing a given control. CCTV is a method used to implement the control of visual monitoring, but it is not the only method. One could also deploy a security officer to implement this control.

So why not do just that? After all, a security officer can immediately report problems and respond to incidents. The answer is, of course, money. A security officer has recurring costs such as a salary, vacations, health insurance, etc., and will likely cost tens of thousands of dollars per year. In contrast, a high quality CCTV camera costs between $1000 and $2000, and the expense can be amortized over time.

It is true that a security officer does not continuously record what he or she observes. But if the objective is to deter threats, a security officer is arguably more effective than a camera. Unfortunately, and as I noted above, they are considerably more expensive.

Since security officers do not just stare at their surroundings, a more precise term for this form of control is "active visual monitoring." In contrast, CCTV systems are inanimate devices that merely provide visual access and record activity. They more accurately perform "passive visual monitoring." The individual component and system-level specifications for CCTV systems determine their performance. These specifications might seem overly technical, but they are extremely relevant to an effective counterterrorism strategy. CCTV specifications will be discussed in detail in Chapter 11, and specifications for other key counterterrorism controls are provided in Chapters 10 and 12.

If passive or active visual monitoring is deemed to be a required control based on the results of a risk assessment as described herein, one must then determine a means of implementing that control. Visual monitoring is only one control among a spectrum of controls that might be relevant to a comprehensive counterterrorism strategy.

An effective counterterrorism strategy mandates *at least one control for each risk factor*. Again the logic is clear: if risk factors enhance one or more components of risk, then a control is required to address each identified risk factor. If a risk factor has not been addressed, this implies that there could be a gaping hole in the counterterrorism strategy. The choice of a specific control will be a matter of judgment that is informed by experience and analysis.

A control characterizes *what* activity must be done to address a risk factor, but it does not specify *how* to address it. Although controls are essential to developing an effective counterterrorism strategy, one would be hard pressed to protect anything by merely specifying a set of controls. More detail is required to make the strategy actionable.

1.8   COUNTERTERRORISM METHODS

What is missing from this security risk assessment framework is a means of implementing each control. Resisting even the slightest creative urge, these modes of implementation are referred to as "methods." We have already encountered several methods, the most prominent being CCTV, a method used to implement visual monitoring.

It is true that many security professionals prescribe methods without examining the risk factors. They get away with it because their "strategy" often goes unchallenged, either by their management or by the terrorists. In my experience, security professionals are rarely asked to provide rigorous justifications for security expenditures. If they are queried on how they arrived at a specific solution, it is often intuition or an anecdote that is used for justification.

If a method is required to implement a control, and a control is required for each risk factor, then every counterterrorism strategy must also specify at least one method per risk factor. This is true unless one method addresses more than one risk factor. Again, there is flexibility in deciding on the number and types of methods. After analyzing the risk according to the process defined herein, that particular decision is ultimately based on judgment.

But judgment should be informed by experience that is supported by analysis. For example, both judgment and experience should be invoked to determine whether visual monitoring is in fact required to address a particular terrorism risk factor. Moreover, experience might suggest that CCTV is the appropriate method to implement visual monitoring. Furthermore, the ability to identify a specific individual from the image on the monitor may be determined to be an operational requirement, a concept discussed in the next section. So judgment plays a major role in developing a counterterrorism strategy and, specifically, in determining appropriate security controls and methods as well as in defining their operational requirements.

Continuing with CCTV, the set of operational requirements for this method will always include system resolution. CCTV system resolution is directly related to technical parameters like lens focal length, the distance from lens to object, etc. Once the operational requirements have been defined, determining the precise technical performance specifications is where experience and intuition must take a back seat to science and engineering.

1.9   OPERATIONAL REQUIREMENTS

Specifying the operational requirements for each method used in a counterterrorism strategy is another key step in the risk assessment process. Technical specifications that affect the performance of each method should be linked to an operational requirement. In other words, you need to specify what you want the method to do and how well you want it to perform.

Consider the insider threat, where an individual who is authorized to have physical access to the premises is the adversary. CCTV is being deployed as a method to implement the visual monitoring of sensitive areas. But suppose the optical resolution of the system merely provides for situational awareness. In other words, one can only determine what is generally happening in the field-of-view based on the image on the monitor, and the operator is unable to recognize the identity of a particular individual. Better resolution is required to confirm the identity of someone suspected of being up to no good.

The need to delineate operational requirements might seem obvious since purchasing security equipment is substantively no different than any other purchase. For example, when buying a car one has requirements like passenger capacity, fuel efficiency, etc. Consider the automobile requirements of a suburban parent versus a 20-something hot shot. Although the operational requirements for terrorism risk mitigation are likely quite different from buying a car, the decision process is the same.

If more incentives for this line of reasoning are required, specifying operational requirements also provides a path to meaningful risk metrics. Before seeing why this is so, we first must discuss performance specifications as they relate to operational requirements.

1.10 PERFORMANCE SPECIFICATIONS

Operational requirements are critical to a security risk management strategy because they specify *what* must be done to mitigate risk. However, knowing what a method must do does not say anything about its effectiveness. Invoking the automobile analogy once again, performance specifications will dictate the passenger capacity for the suburban couple and the horsepower of the turbocharged engine for the 20-something hot shot.

A slightly more relevant example that will be explored in great detail in Chapter 11 is as follows. If the operational requirement calls for identification-level resolution for a CCTV megapixel camera, then a 40 pixels/ft pixel density across the horizontal field-of-view is the minimum technical specification required to satisfy that requirement.

What is the consequence of not meeting a performance specification? If the CCTV camera does not perform to this level, it would potentially fall short in addressing a risk factor for an impactful threat. An unaddressed risk factor implies a component of risk is not being successfully managed.

It is worth mentioning that performance specifications are not restricted to technical devices. For example, if active monitoring is a required control for a facility, one might want to specify how many security officers are required to adequately protect that facility. The minimum number of required officers might be driven by the maximum allowable response time to a terrorist attack or any security incident, for that matter. So establishing a specification for the minimum number of security officers is relevant to addressing the vulnerability component of risk for general terrorist attack vectors. This particular issue will be explored in more detail in Chapter 5.

1.11   SECURITY RISK ASSESSMENT FRAMEWORKS, SECURITY STANDARDS, AND SECURITY RISK METRICS

The process noted in the previous sections leads directly to a convenient framework to assess the risk of terrorism. As noted previously, one does not often have the "luxury" of robust terrorism statistics in contrast with medical threats (i.e., diseases). Therefore, our only hope in identifying meaningful risk metrics is to establish a *risk-based* security standard and to measure the existing mitigation against that standard.

Table 1.2 is a risk assessment framework based on the methodology provided in this chapter. A simplified example is worked to illustrate its applicability to the vehicle-borne explosive attack vector.

This framework can be used to establish a security standard that specifies the appropriate controls to manage risk. It makes sense to tie the assessment framework to the standard since the point of the standard is to define the thresholds of risk. Moreover, a risk-based security standard leads immediately to a meaningful risk metric: compliance with the standard. If there is compliance, the risk is by definition being managed effectively. If not, there is so-called residual risk that must be addressed.

This may seem a bit circular, but it is a rigorous approach assuming you have done your homework in defining the precise threat, evaluating the components of risk for that threat, and identifying the risk factors that enhance each component of risk. This is precisely what is meant by a risk-based approach.

It is also important to note that standards so derived must comport with an organization's tolerance for risk, culture, and business requirements. Unless the corporate culture is completely dysfunctional and is actually contributing to the organization's decline, it would be counterproductive to impose security solutions that undermine the very thing that has made the organization successful. In other words, the security risk may decrease as a result of implementing a security standard, but the business risks might increase as a result if the standard does not align with the culture.

Table 1.2 Applying the Security Risk Assessment Framework to a Worked Example

Terrorism Attack Vector	Magnitude of Each Component of Risk	Risk Factors	Controls to Address Each Risk Factor (at least one control per risk factor)	Methods to Implement Each Control (at least one method per control) Plus Cost	Operational Requirements for Each Method	Performance Specifications to Satisfy the Operational Requirement	Meets the Standard (Y/N)?
Vehicle-borne explosive	Likelihood = low vulnerability before risk mitigation = high impact = high	Proximity of unauthorized vehicles to building façade	Barriers	Fixed and retractable bollards cost = $250,000 (installed) and included in security budget	Must withstand impact of a 15,000-lb vehicle traveling at 50 mph	K-12 rating; surrounds building perimeter; enforce vehicle distance of 20 feet	Yes

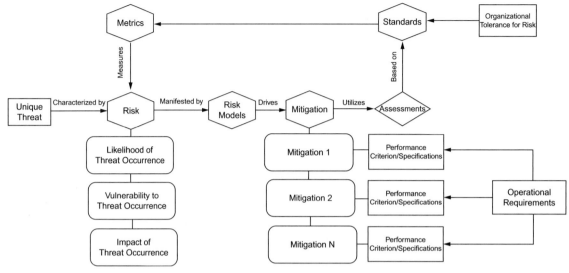

FIGURE 1.7
The security risk management process.

Finally, the security risk management process described in this chapter is summarized in Figure 1.7.

SUMMARY

Assessing the risk associated with terrorism, and security threats more generally, is a well-defined process. It begins with understanding the distinct and impactful threats to an organization as well as the magnitude of the components of risk associated with each of those threats.

The components of risk are by definition the likelihood or potential for threat occurrence, the vulnerability to loss or damage that would be experienced should a threat occur, and the threat's impact or importance to an organization. If any one of the components of risk is zero, then the threat does not exist in any real sense. The Fundamental Expression of Risk is written as follows:

$$RISK(threat) = Likelihood \times Vulnerability \times Impact$$

The risk factors for a threat are features that enhance one or more components of risk. Therefore, identifying the risk factors for a threat or threat attack vector is critical to the risk assessment process since the principal objective of security is to reduce the risk associated with threats of concern.

Once these risk factors are identified, security controls and methods can be applied that address each risk factor in order to develop an effective security risk management strategy.

A security standard can be developed that is based on the process noted herein, and compliance with that standard leads to meaningful security risk metrics in the absence of a statistically significant number of terrorism incidents.

REFERENCES

[1] The New York Times Co. http://www.nytimes.com/2013/04/26/science/science-study-shows-monkeys-pick-up-social-cues.html?_r=0&adxnnl=1&adxnnlx=1387481350-5r3wtMdgK flogXooUN1+Lw.

[2] Stander PE, Albon SD. Hunting success of lions in a semi-arid environment. In: Zoological Symposium; 1993. No. 65, http://www.desertlion.info/reports/lion_huntsuccess.pdf.

Problems

1. Describe a "threat" that you have personally witnessed or encountered. Analyze the magnitude of the three components of risk for that threat.
2. You are the security director of an international firm headquartered in the United States. Describe an impactful security threat to your firm. Analyze the likelihood and vulnerability components of risk for this threat.
3. In 2000 you invested $100,000 of your hard-earned money in the following three financial instruments in the hopes of buying your dream penthouse on Fifth Avenue:
   - Equities (diamond)
   - New York City bonds (square)
   - Wheat futures (triangle)

Figure 1.8 depicts these instruments' performance from 2000 to 2009 (horizontal axis). The vertical axis is specified in units of $1000 U.S.

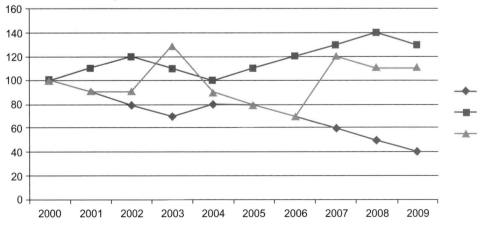

Refer to the individual curves and answer the following:
- **a.** How much money would you have in each financial instrument if you cashed out in 2009?
- **b.** What can you say about the historical risk associated with each instrument?
- **c.** What if anything does this say about what will happen in 2010 and beyond based on this data?

4. Indicate the risk factors for the following threats. Recall that the risk factors are those attributes, conditions, or features that enhance the magnitude of the individual components of risk. You are being asked to identify features that make the threat more likely to occur and/or increase its vulnerability/severity if it did occur:
   - **a.** Heart attacks.
   - **b.** Direct attack/damage to a facility using vehicle-borne explosives.
   - **c.** Collateral damage to a facility using vehicle-borne explosives directed against another facility.
   - **d.** Theft from an office.
   - **e.** Losing money in real estate.

5. Figure 1.9 below shows the aftermath of an explosion caused by an accumulation of dust. Although this is not a terror-related scenario, the result is quite similar to what one would expect with an explosive device. Figure 1.9 is used with permission from *http://www.csb.gov/csb-releases-new-safety-video-combustible-dust-an-insidious-hazard-features-three-new-animations-of-major-dust-accidents-shows-need-for-comprehensive-standard-and-improved-safety-practices/.*

A cartoon that explains what happened at a high level is shown directly below in Figure 1.10:

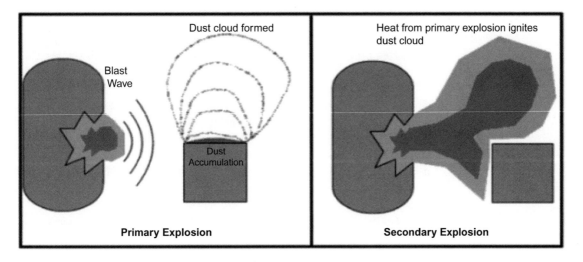

a. Analyze the risk associated with this threat, beginning with a precise statement of the threat and concluding with the hypothetical performance specifications for proposed risk mitigation.

b. Compare this to a risk analysis of a terror-related explosion.

In both cases, ensure you characterize the scenario in terms of the precise language of risk as conveyed in this chapter.

6. Choose a threat and analyze the risk associated with that threat using the chart in Figure 1.7.

7. You are the newly appointed director of security at a large financial institution. You are required to conduct a risk assessment of your headquarters building. However, the security department has a limited budget and there are a number of outstanding issues that were left unaddressed by your predecessor. How would you prioritize the required risk mitigation to address the spectrum of threats faced by your institution (Hint: what is the basis for a risk-based approach?).

8. You notice variations in your mood when you eat. You decide to do an experiment to figure out why this is happening. Interestingly, you informally notice that your mood seems to improve based on the number of hamburgers you consume. How would you test this hypothesis? How would you test the hypothesis that hamburgers *cause* mood changes?

9. Characterize the risk associated with the threat of divorce using the risk framework discussed in this chapter. What controls would you invoke to help manage the risk?

10. You are the police chief of a major U.S. city. Federal intelligence sources indicate a high potential for an attack by a suicide bomber via vehicle- or backpack-borne explosives (anti-Westerners again).

   a. What are the risk factors for this threat attack vector?

   b. What mitigation measures might be effective?

   c. You are being pressured by public sentiment to saturate high-risk venues with uniformed police officers. Would this be an effective mitigation method (i.e., would it address one or more risk factors)? Why or why not?

   d. How would you best communicate your risk-mitigation strategy to the public if this differed from their irrational demands?

11. You are a physician attending to a patient who is believed to have heart failure (a specific condition, not just a low-performing heart).

   a. Describe the process you would use to confirm or rule out this diagnosis (Hint: research the symptoms of heart failure).

   b. What would you guess are some of the risk factors for heart failure?

12. You are about to take a trip for your upcoming vacation and decide you want to do a rigorous analysis of the risk associated with various modes of travel.

   a. What information would you use for this risk analysis?

   b. How would you assess the relative risk of the threat of dying due to travel by air, auto, or train?

   c. Identify risk factors that would increase the likelihood and/or vulnerability component of risk.

13. Conduct a rigorous risk assessment in preparation for crossing a busy street using the process specified in Figure 1.7.

14. You are the director of security at a large university in the United States. Based on recent incidents, you are concerned about the threat of gun-related violence on campus. Specifically, you are concerned about the threat of an "active shooter" using automatic weapons.

   a. Characterize the components of risk for this threat.

   b. Describe the potential for threat occurrence versus the likelihood of a specific individual causing harm with an automatic weapon. Be as qualitative or quantitative as you like in your characterization of each view of risk.

   c. Would you say that easy access to automatic weapons in your state/jurisdiction is a risk factor for the potential for threat occurrence in this case? Why or why not?

   d. What are some risk factors for the potential and/or likelihood component of risk relative to this threat?

CHAPTER 2

Organizing and Assessing Terrorism Risk

2.1 A TAXONOMY OF TERRORISM THREATS

Whenever a complex problem presents itself, it is useful to organize that problem into large categories or "food groups," where the items in each food group possess common attributes. This often simplifies the problem and actually facilitates the identification of solutions.

An illustrative if extreme example is the problem of classifying the universe of insects. A naïve approach to this problem might be to examine each and every insect on the planet and label each one individually with descriptors. In case you are massively bored in your current job, the eminent entomologist E.O. Wilson estimates there are 10^{18} (i.e., a quintillion) insects on earth at any given time. Clearly loneliness is not an insect's problem.

A more systematic and efficient way to characterize such a prolific group might be to organize a statistically significant sampling of insects into groups and subgroups according to common attributes. One can then form a hierarchical structure based on these attributes. If future insects do not fit neatly in to a particular category, then a new category could be established. Over time, the rate of establishing new categories would diminish as the structure becomes more complete.

In fact, biologists have created such a hierarchal structure that extends to all living things. This structure is referred to as a *taxonomy*. The biologists' organization extends from the general to the specific as follows: kingdom, phylum, class, order, family, genus, and species.

Insects, or more accurately the class *Insecta*, exist within the *Animalia* kingdom and *Arthropoda* phylum. Organizing the world of insects into species is itself a daunting task. Estimates of the total number of species range from 30 million to the generally accepted figure of 2 million. To date about 925,000 species have been identified, so there are plenty of opportunities to make one's mark as an insect professional.

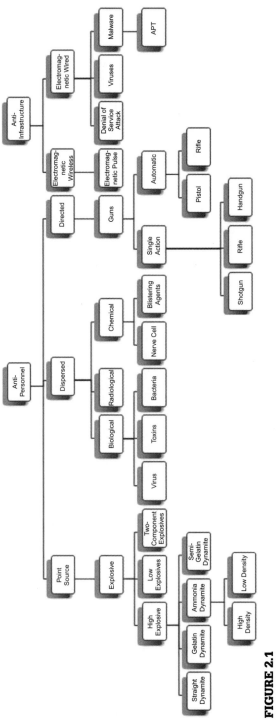

FIGURE 2.1

A terrorism threat taxonomy.

Thankfully, terrorism is not nearly so complicated. But in a similar vein, terrorism risk is better understood if the threats are organized according to a defined structure. Figure 2.1 describes one possible terrorism threat taxonomy, although this structure is not an exhaustive delineation of possible attack vectors.

The top of the taxonomy food chain divides neatly between the threats directed at personnel and those targeting infrastructure. The antipersonnel attack vectors are further divided according to the way they originate: distributed, point source, and directed.

Infrastructure-oriented vectors are exclusively electromagnetic. These divide again between wired and wireless modes. Of course these are very different vectors and, on the surface, would not appear to be related. But both are electromagnetic in nature, and that is what links them in the taxonomy. In a loose analogy, birds and dinosaurs are related as evidenced by similar anatomic features. I dare say that a casual observer of birds and dinosaurs would be hard pressed to recognize any relationship between these animals.

As one descends into lower elements of the food chain, the taxonomy is organized according to various modes of threat implementation or payload delivery followed by specific weapon types. These roughly align with the simple models that will be presented in Chapter 4.

Why bother developing a terrorism threat taxonomy? Security risk management is a descriptive science. It is similar to other descriptive sciences in that the identification and classification of objects being studied yields insights into common themes. In the case of terrorism, the objects being classified are threats and threat attack vectors. Fortunately, terrorism attack vectors are not particularly complex, but thinking about problems in this way is helpful in developing risk-mitigation strategies.

Specifically, organizing terrorism threats according to their mode of payload delivery is useful in identifying common mitigation methods. For example, certain dispersal-type attack vectors might seem quite dissimilar at first glance, e.g., radiological dispersion devices and biological weapons. However, when grouped in this way, the use of particulate filters as a risk-mitigation measure might be more readily identified.

2.2   COUNTERTERRORISM STANDARDS AND RISK METRICS

As noted in Chapter 1, the effectiveness of terrorism risk-mitigation measures is sometimes not easy to demonstrate. A direct measurement of cause and effect is not always possible because of a dearth of terrorist incidents. This, of course, is a good thing, but it is suboptimal from a strictly statistical perspective. For example, how might one show the benefit of an expensive set of bollards that was installed 5 years ago? Since there had not been a single terrorism incident before installation, and none after, it is impossible to draw a meaningful conclusion on cause and effect. But that does not necessarily imply that mitigation is not needed, i.e., that there is no risk.

What can be done to demonstrate sufficient "bang for the buck" for security mitigation in the absence of a statistically significant number of threat incidents? This is an ongoing conundrum in counterterrorism, and it is more generally an issue in security. Fortunately meaningful metrics can be generated, but it requires the adoption of risk-based methods.

There are at least three possible food groups of security risk metrics:

1. The number and type of mitigation measures that deviate from risk-based security standards.
2. The number of incidents associated with a risk factor for identified threats.
3. The effect of mitigation on the number of incidents related to risk factors.

Let's examine the aforementioned in sequence.

With respect to number 1, risk-based security standards are essential to developing a counterterrorism strategy. If an organization operates according to risk-based security standards, then compliance with those standards implies that the risk associated with the threats of concern is effectively being managed. Consequently, the development of such standards yields ready-made security risk metrics since one can now "measure" deviations from the standard. By definition, conditions that are below the standard imply there is residual security risk.

The second food group of security risk metrics is the measurement of one or more risk factors for a threat or attack vector. Statistical measurements of risk factors are what I choose to call *indirect* measurements of risk. Indirect measurements of risk are especially useful in the absence of actual security incidents. An example might be to measure the number of instances of unauthorized physical access to a facility or controlled space. Instances of unauthorized physical access do not imply that a terrorist or security incident will occur, but it signifies an enhanced vulnerability to the threat and/or an increased likelihood occurrence. This is what makes it a risk factor.

Moreover, measuring risk factor-related incidents provides a path to more quantitative statements on likelihood. However, this is only possible if and only if one can assign a probability that a risk factor incident will result in an actual terrorism incident. This is precisely the criterion that allows one to speak of the likelihood of a terrorist incident occurrence rather than the potential, and thereby adopt a statistical view of risk (Note: technically speaking we are modeling the spectrum of risk outcomes as a binomial distribution.

This process is equivalent to the distribution associated with flipping a coin). Recognize that in general identifying such a probability in terrorism scenarios is extremely difficult if not impossible, which is why the potential is usually a more apt term.

However, if this is indeed possible, it is important to note that even if the assigned probability of a terrorism incident occurrence is infinitesimally small, the occurrence of many risk factor incidents will lead to a large probability of an actual terrorism incident. Why? If $p(x)$ is the individual probability that a terrorism incident occurs as a result of a risk factor incident, and n is the number of risk factor incidents, then the likelihood of a terrorism incident is given by $1 - p(x)^n$ which approaches unity for large n. This means that the likelihood of a terrorist incident is a near certainty for large numbers of risk factor incidents. Again, it is important to emphasize that segueing from a qualitative (i.e., the potential) to a quantitative model (i.e., the likelihood) of risk is predicated on being able to identify the probability that a terrorist incident will occur as a result of any given risk factor incident.

The third security risk metric food group is the effect of mitigation on the number of actual incidents or incidents associated with a risk factor for a given threat. For example, one might show a reversal in the upward trend of unauthorized physical access following the implementation of enhanced authentication at the entrance to a facility. This is just one illustration of why identifying the risk factors associated with each distinct and impactful threat is so important to a meaningful assessment of security risk in the absence of statistics on actual threat incidents.

Recall Figure 1.3 showed the results of a study confirming an increased risk of death from lung cancer resulting from a greater number of years of cigarette smoking. In that case there was no ambiguity with respect to cause and effect. It was clear that the longer you smoked, the greater the chances of dying from lung cancer. These results were the product of a rigorous study involving large populations—a statistician's dream. This is a luxury that does not often present itself to security professionals.

Some metrics do not add much insight despite a plethora of data. Consider the airline safety statistic of passenger deaths per 100 million air miles. The difference between the top carriers is so small that it is difficult to draw a meaningful distinction. This is also a testament to the general safety of regulated air travel. Also, such statistics can be misleading for other reasons. To quote from *Slate.com*:[1]

> Even if historic accidents were a useful predictor of present safety, it is not clear how to denominate the metric. Some rankers consider crashes per passenger mile, but 70 percent of airline accidents occur during takeoff and landing, which constitute just 6 percent of flying time. This

makes commuter airlines, which takeoff and land more often, seem extra risky. You might count the number of deaths per flight instead, but that, too, would be misleading, since it discounts the dangers of accidents that happen in mid-flight.

It should be noted that there is nothing special about terrorism in terms of assessing risk or in the development of risk-based standards. In general, if a performance specification is required in order for a security system to satisfy an operational requirement, then a gap between the existing and required specifications is an indicator of risk. Absent a standard, there is more of an emphasis on intuition (or luck), which is not particularly reliable. This is equally true for terrorism as any other security threat.

For example, suppose visual monitoring is a required control to address the risk factor of unauthorized physical access to a facility. Furthermore, let's assume CCTV is selected as the method to implement that control. What are the operational requirements for the CCTV system in this case?

Is it sufficient to be able to see that the CCTV image shows a smallish human male or does one need to be able to recognize that the strikingly handsome individual on the monitor is Carl Young? The technical specifications that are required to satisfy each of these operational requirements could be quite different.

Of course, the underlying assumption is that the operational requirement and associated performance specification have been determined using a risk-based analysis. This is a critical assumption. If it is not true, then any purported security risk metric might seem impressive, but it might have little to do with effective risk management.

Not adopting a risk-based approach could certainly result in inadequate risk mitigation, but it might also lead to overkill. For example, it might be quite cost *ineffective* to saturate a building with CCTV cameras that perform significantly above the level required to satisfy the specified operational requirements. This would be especially true if there are hundreds or thousands of cameras on-site.

This situation is reminiscent of issues faced in designing the security strategy for the Goldman Sachs headquarters building in New York City. The legacy access control system in the former headquarters registered a staggering number of false positives at specific locations. Not surprisingly, the statistics showed a high correlation between the number of false positives and doors used frequently during business hours. Any reasonably intelligent person would expect a large number of "door held open" alarms on a busy trading floor during regular business hours.

One suggested remedy for the new facility was to focus a camera on every card reader in the building. The protocol would call for resolving alarms by viewing the scene from the control room. This would obviate the need to confirm the exact nature of the problem using a security officer. This strategy would certainly work, but is it a cost-effective use of resources?

In a multistory commercial building, the one card reader-one camera algorithm could have huge technical and financial implications. In addition to the cost of the cameras, system bandwidth and storage issues grow exponentially with the number of cameras. It is much more practical to limit the number of false positives using a risk-based approach.

The potential for impactful crimes occurring on a working floor during business hours is not a significant security risk issue assuming there are adequate security controls at the building perimeter. In addition, it is a fact of life that people will hold the door open for each other during business hours, thereby causing the "door held open" alarm to activate so frequently that it becomes irrelevant. These alarms are therefore likely to be ignored, which was precisely what occurred in this instance.

Therefore, the simplest and most cost-effective solution is to not detect "door forced" or "door held open" events during manifestly low-risk periods. Of course there is the infinitesimal likelihood that a "door forced" or "door held open" alarm represents a legitimate alarm during these times. However, there is also a security risk in a huge number of false-positive readings as well as a business risk associated with expensive security solutions.

There is always some residual risk associated with any threat. However, one of the components of risk might be deemed so insignificant that the prudent strategy is to address other threats with one's limited security budget. As noted previously, prioritization of risk mitigation is the essence of a security strategy.

The creation of security standards facilitates a strategy as well as risk metrics. A standard establishes a factual basis for assessing risk; it represents ground truth. Often this is the *only* basis for rigorously assessing risk.

Despite their name, security standards do not have to be rigid. The assessment framework provided in Chapter 1 that was used to establish a standard allowed for flexibility in choosing the number and type of risk-mitigation measures. But in every case, an effective security standard must address all the risk factors for a given threat.

If there are no security incidents then one might be tempted to assume there is no risk associated with a threat or threat attack vector. That assumption could be a crucial error. For example, the potential for a terrorist attack may be huge, yet miraculously no attack has taken place. Is that due to terrorist apathy? Is it a result of impenetrable security defenses? Or is it just plain luck?

Sometimes the response to the lack of threat incidents is to artificially assign quantitative values to inherently subjective security features. Unfortunately this merely gives the illusion of quantifiable results and precision. Surveys are often used for such purposes, and these are symptomatic of the flawed notion that artificially assigned precision is equivalent to accuracy, as Figure 2.2 poignantly illustrates. This point will be explored more rigorously in Chapter 12 when discussing security sensors.

In truth, identifying meaningful counterterrorism risk metrics is difficult and sometimes even impossible without security standards. To reiterate, the reason it is so difficult is because of the lack of incident statistics that might provide a cause-and-effect relationship between threats and mitigation. However, meaningful metrics are still possible, and three general types were provided in this section.

To complicate matters, terrorism activity is a function of a political, economic, and social landscape that changes with time. Of course, a lack of incidents is a mixed blessing, and a longing for statistical rigor should not be interpreted as a desire for increased terrorism!

In summary, the ephemeral conditions that spawn terrorism affect the potential for incident occurrence in nonquantifiable ways. However, incidents

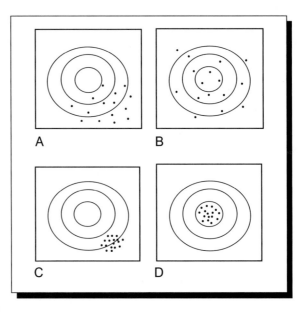

FIGURE 2.2

Precision versus accuracy. *(From EPA. "National Beach Guidance and Required Performance Criteria—Appendix 4B1: Data Quality and Sampling Design Considerations." http://water.epa.gov/grants_funding/beachgrants/app4b1.cfm.)*

relating to terrorism risk factors can provide meaningful security risk metrics. The physical principles that determine how well security technologies operate under various conditions can lead to quantitative estimates of the vulnerability component of risk. These two approaches offer the best opportunities for overcoming inherent statistical constraints.

2.3   THE COST OF RISK MITIGATION

In Chapter 1, the Fundamental Expression of Risk was introduced. This quasi-mathematical representation specified risk in terms of three components: impact, likelihood, and vulnerability. From a strictly theoretical perspective it completely characterizes the security risk associated with a terrorist threat and, more specifically, the risk associated with terrorist threats or specific terrorism attack vectors.

However, since we hope to address terrorism in the real world, there is a shadow issue that must be included when assessing security risk. Although this component is not an inherent element of risk per se, it is essential to conducting meaningful (read: practical) terrorism risk analyses.

Namely, the "cost" of risk mitigation must be considered when assessing terrorism risk and mitigation in the real world. Quotation marks are included around the word cost because this should not be thought of in strict financial terms, although money could indeed be a decision driver. Strictly speaking, cost is not a component of risk since it relates to mitigation and not to the threat itself. However, it would be naïve to think that cost does not play a major role in decisions about risk.

Terrorism strategies are governed by the realities imposed by constraints such as budgets, political capital, etc. This is not a negative commentary on life but reflects the fact that security cannot be divorced from practical considerations. In other words, although security decisions are based on an evaluation of the components of risk, these components do not tell the entire story when a decision on implementation is required. As noted in Chapter 1, such decisions do turn on the relative magnitude of the likelihood and vulnerability components of risk, assuming the threat is deemed impactful in the first place. But this magnitude must be weighed against the financial and/or operational burdens imposed by the proposed solution.

Recall the example noted in Chapter 1 regarding the addition of authentication at the turnstiles in the lobby of a building. Turnstiles are used to address the risk factor of unauthorized physical access by reducing the vulnerability to piggybacking. Of course if someone steals a valid ID and presents it at an unsuspecting turnstile, the device will respond exactly as it is programmed to do. One should not blame the turnstile!

What is lacking is a means of validating the identity of the cardholder. This typically requires the use of a security officer or biometric device deployed on the insecure side of the turnstile. To be precise, unauthorized physical access could be accomplished by stealing a valid ID. Turnstiles do nothing to mitigate the vulnerability to this attack vector. The use of authentication of identity in this context complements the confirmation of authorized access as a control.

However, there is always a cost associated with security risk mitigation. That cost may be financial or operational. If the cost of risk mitigation is minimal, the decision on implementation is likely to be easier. But suppose the cost of mitigating the risk of a given threat represents a significant fraction of the security budget? To complicate matters, what if there were a number of threats to be addressed and each required mitigation with attendant costs? This is the *raison d'etre* of a security risk management strategy.

2.4   MEDICAL ANALOGIES

Medical science has become quite proficient at measuring risk factors for disease. In fact, the ability to measure risk factors in medicine might be too good. Specifically, the ability of medical scientists to measure things has sometimes outpaced their ability to correlate those measurements with risk relative to the "cost" of risk mitigation. Consider the controversy over the prostate specific antigen (PSA) test for prostate cancer.[2]

In this case, the presence of an antigen in the bloodstream has been shown to be associated with the presence of a prostate malignancy. The problem is not in the measurement of the antigen, it is the significance of that measurement with respect to patient mortality *relative to the cost* of risk mitigation.

Figure 2.3 certainly shows a decrease in the rate of mortality in the United States from prostate cancer. The question is whether this decline can be directly attributed to the use of the PSA test.

An 11-year European study of 182,160 men 50 to 74 years old found that PSA screening significantly reduced the mortality from prostate cancer.[3]

However, a 20-year Swedish study of 9000 men showed no effect of periodic PSA screening on death from prostate cancer. Furthermore, in a study reported in the *Journal of the National Cancer Institute*, researchers found no difference in the effect of prostate cancer screening. Those researchers explained the decline in prostate cancer as follows:[4] "Improvements in prostate cancer treatment are probably at least in part responsible for declining prostate cancer mortality rates. Even if life is only prolonged by therapy,

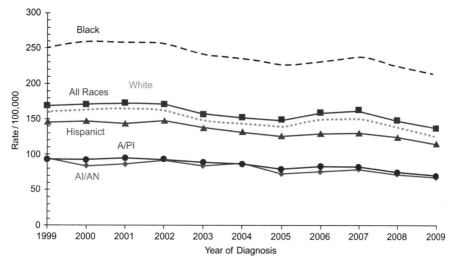

FIGURE 2.3

Rate of mortality from prostate cancer. *(From CDC. "Prostate Cancer Rates by Race and Ethnicity." http://www.cdc.gov/cancer/prostate/statistics/race.htm.)*

the opportunities for competing causes of death increase, especially among older men."

In addition, the researchers highlight that 455 (10.7 percent) of the 4250 prostate cancer case patients diagnosed in the intervention group died of other causes, while 377 (9.9 percent) of the 3815 men diagnosed with prostate cancer in the control group also died of other causes.

"Thus, a higher percentage of deaths from other causes rather than a deficit occurred among the prostate cancer patients diagnosed in the intervention arm, an indication of the over-diagnosis associated with PSA detection."

Clearly there is some controversy within the medical community regarding the benefits of the PSA test. But we need to be specific. It is not that PSA tests are ineffective in detecting prostate cancer. The controversy exists because the current treatments for prostate cancer have life-changing side effects (e.g., impotence, incontinence), and so experts are challenging these clinical costs relative to the benefit of the test in terms of decreased mortality.

In other words, the clinical cost of the procedure is high relative to the likelihood of succumbing to the disease.

If the detection of prostate cancer via PSA screening resulted in a high percentage of lifesaving interventions or the mitigation efforts were trivial, then the cost of the procedure would presumably be worth it.

So this debate is really about the cost versus benefit associated with risk mitigation. If a successful treatment for prostate cancer involved taking an innocuous little pill there would be no fuss.

A similar debate is inherent to security decisions. Each one entails weighing the relative magnitude of the components of risk for a given threat and the associated cost of risk mitigation. In this case cost could be the financial or operational burden associated with purchasing and maintaining a security system. There is no formula for this, and judgment plays a significant role in a series of decisions that ultimately form the basis for a comprehensive risk management strategy.

2.5   SIMPLE RISK ASSESSMENTS

It is instructive to use a simple chart to focus on the magnitude of the risk components for a given threat. These charts characterize the components of risk for impactful threats in terms of "high," "medium," and "low" ratings. Consider the results of the risk analysis for an unspecified impactful threat in Table 2.1. In the abstract this is a dream scenario for a security professional. The components of risk are categorized as high, but the cost of mitigation is low. Therefore, the decision to implement a solution for a high likelihood/ potential threat to which one is highly vulnerable *and* where the cost of mitigation is low should be relatively easy.

One might argue that absent exigent circumstances, if any of the components of risk are assessed as high, and the cost of remediation is low, such a scenario calls for implementing appropriate risk mitigation. To borrow a phrase from the modern vernacular, this might be considered a no-brainer decision.

Now let's consider another threat scenario. This time we will be specific and assume the table captures the high-level results of an assessment of the risk associated with the threat from nuclear weapons. This is a scenario we contemplated previously. Some might summarize the results of this high-level risk analysis as shown in Table 2.2.

Ensuring that an entire campus or even a particular facility is shielded from the effects of a nuclear blast would be very costly. Imagine the cost of lining the entire facility in lead or building the facility underground.

Table 2.1 High-Level Risk Assessment and a No-Brainer Decision

	High	Medium	Low
Likelihood/potential	Yes		
Vulnerability	Yes		
Mitigation cost			Yes

Table 2.2 High-Level Risk Assessment; The Threat of a Nuclear Attack

	High	Medium	Low
Likelihood/potential			Yes
Vulnerability	Yes		
Mitigation cost	Yes		

Security directors around the world seem to have figured this out, since almost every commercial facility is likely to have near-infinite vulnerability to this threat.

To put it more precisely, the high cost of risk mitigation in light of a very low potential for threat occurrence suggests a strategy of inaction. On the other hand, if shielding buildings and people required tinfoil rather than lead, the tipping point for this decision might change.

Unfortunately life is often even more complicated for the modern security professional. In Table 2.3, we show assessment results that will likely result in a difficult decision.

The cost of risk mitigation is high, which automatically raises the stakes with respect to a decision. One component of risk, the potential for occurrence, is high, possibly because there have been numerous incidents associated with a risk factor. The decision to add a control hinges on the outcome of this cost-benefit analysis. Does the high potential for occurrence offset the assessed vulnerability in view of the cost? This is the essence of a rigorous security risk assessment.

This juxtaposition of risk-relevant issues is inherent to all security risk decisions. Moreover, the decision to deploy risk mitigation is a function of competing priorities. To be clear, there is no formula or prescription for determining the appropriate risk-mitigation strategy. There is often a viable middle ground of options. Security strategies that result from this type of thinking represent a synthesis of experience and rigorous analysis that informs judgment.

Table 2.3 High-Level Risk Assessment and a Difficult Decision

	High	Medium	Low
Likelihood/potential	Yes		
Vulnerability		Yes	
Mitigation cost	Yes		

Recognize too that each decision on risk mitigation must be evaluated against similar risk decisions regarding other threats relative to available resources. This is the essence of a strategy; choices are required based on the relative magnitude of risk, modulated by the constraints imposed by cost, broadly defined. The ultimate point of a risk assessment is to establish priorities.

To summarize, the questions to ask when evaluating a threat or threat attack vector are as follows:

1. What is the potential for an attack to occur?
2. What is the magnitude of vulnerability should an attack occur? In other words, what is the exposure to damage/loss if an attack takes place?
3. If the vulnerability or potential is significant, what are the financial and/or operational costs of addressing the risk?
4. Can you justify the cost of remediation if the potential for occurrence is low but the vulnerability is high and vice versa?

2.6   SECURITY THEATRE

Sometimes implementing risk mitigation does nothing to affect the security risk profile. In some cases it can actually *increase* one or more components of risk. Most often this results from a lack of rigor in the assessment process. Other times the mitigation derives from a hidden agenda. The security expert Bruce Schneier has coined the phrase "security theatre" to describe measures that merely *appear* to address a security problem.

A possible example of security theatre occurs with some frequency in two cities that legitimately boast of having the best counterterrorism capabilities in the world: New York City and London. The New York Police Department (NYPD) and the London Metropolitan Police (aka "The Met" or "Scotland Yard") are exceptional police forces that do an effective job in countering terrorism in the face of difficult odds.

I happened to live in each of these cities during high-profile terrorist incidents and was in relatively close physical proximity each time. Fortunately I was only minimally inconvenienced in both instances. The first was in New York on September 11, 2001 and the second was in London on July 7, 2005.

In my experience the British have historically been quite strategic in their approach to counterterrorism. I attribute this to four factors: their extensive experience with the Irish Republican Army (IRA), a seriousness of purpose in addressing proximal and truly existential threats (recall the Battle of Britain), limited resources that drive the need for efficiency and effectiveness, and most importantly, the imposition of real accountability for government officials.

However, terrorist warnings in both the United States and Britain sometimes trigger reflexive if less than effective responses. For example, the flooding of an area with uniformed officers in a massive show of force in response to a terrorism alert might not address the risk factors for some of the more likely attack vectors.

I recall one such scenario when I was commuting to work from my apartment in Manhattan. A particular area was saturated with police officers and military personnel. They were brandishing a slew of weapons that would have been the envy of every Second Amendment enthusiast in the country. Presumably there had been some form of terrorism alert that triggered this response, with the intent of causing massive intimidation. The question is whether the correct people were being intimidated.

Arguably one of the intended effects of this show of force is to also reassure the public that the government is hard at work protecting them from harm. My view of the situation is not so sanguine.

Let's assume a suicide bomber is the attack vector. Such an individual is focused on killing or maiming as many people as possible. What could the presence of uniformed police officers realistically do to prevent an attack? How would the vulnerability of the public be reduced by the presence of 100 uniformed police officers? How about 1000 uniformed police officers?

The flaw in this strategy is that the concentration of so many *visible* security personnel represents a hugely attractive terrorist target. This is clearly not the intended effect. A determined bomber merely has to walk to a spot of his or her choosing, flick a switch, and hit the carnage jackpot. I am skeptical that anyone could successfully intervene before catastrophic damage ensues. This is what makes suicide attacks so confounding, and it highlights the difficulty of counterterrorism more generally.

The saturation of an area by uniformed police officers does little to reduce the vulnerability component of risk unless the circumstances of the attack are highly controlled and/or the terrorist is extraordinarily incompetent. This is sometimes the case, but it is not a reliable defensive strategy. Worse, law enforcement may have unwittingly *increased* the potential for an attack.

In fairness, the general population is comforted by a massive police presence, notwithstanding the fact that this may be completely opposite to how they should feel. The perception of security is admittedly a factor in security decisions, despite the potential irrelevance in addressing the risk factors. Moreover, if an incident did occur and the police were not present, there would be no end to the second-guessing and political fallout. Addressing counterterrorism in cities that are prime targets is extremely difficult, and the work of the NYPD and the London Metropolitan Police is commendable.

There is no clear fix to this predicament except for emphasizing the need for better intelligence and the implementation of clear-headed, risk-based approaches. Each case is different, and it is true that information may have been available that somehow justified this response by police. However, the presence of uniformed police could be a risk factor for terrorism activity. Therefore, a more discreet police presence might decrease the potential for an attack and possibly even enhance opportunities for preemptive intervention.

SUMMARY

Measuring terrorism risk and the effectiveness of risk mitigation is difficult because of a lack of terrorism incidents. Therefore, drawing accurate conclusions about cause and effect for risk mitigation is also difficult.

In the absence of a statistically significant number of incidents, there are at least three food groups of meaningful security risk metrics:

1. The number and type of mitigation measures that deviate from risk-based security standards.
2. The number of incidents associated with a risk factor for identified threats.
3. The effect of mitigation on the number of risk factor-related incidents or actual incidents.

Developing risk-based standards and identifying the risk factors of terrorism threats and attack vectors is essential to creating meaningful counterterrorism risk metrics. However, the cost of risk mitigation must be factored into a risk management strategy and weighed against the magnitude of the three components of risk. Such costs are not necessarily financial since operational costs can be equally burdensome and can also erode the population's confidence in the overall security posture.

Simple risk frameworks can be developed to assist in these decisions where the components of risk are evaluated according to "low-," "medium-," and "high-" risk designations. Decisions on mitigation versus cost can in some cases be easier when the magnitude of the components of risk is explicitly evaluated and listed relative to each other.

Moreover, a standard set of questions can be evoked to assist in evaluating a threat or threat attack vector. These are as follows:

1. What is the potential for an attack to occur?
2. What is the magnitude of vulnerability should an attack occur? In other words, what is the exposure to damage/loss if an attack happens?
3. If the vulnerability or likelihood is significant, what is the cost of addressing the vulnerability (i.e., remediation or risk mitigation)?

4. Can one justify the cost of remediation if the potential for incident occurrence is low but the vulnerability is high and vice versa?

Finally, it is important to assess terrorism threats analytically using a legitimate risk-based approach. This will help ensure that the prescribed mitigation actually addresses the risk factors associated with that distinct and impactful threat. This will avoid security theatre, i.e., addressing the wrong threat or merely appearing to address a threat of concern.

REFERENCES

[1] Palmer B. Is Qantas the World's safest airline? 2011. http://www.slate.com/articles/news_and_politics/explainer/2011/11/airline_safety_does_qantas_airlines_crash_free_record_make_it_th.html.

[2] Parker-Pope T. New data on harms of prostate cancer screening. New York Times 2012;. http://well.blogs.nytimes.com/2012/05/21/new-data-on-harms-of-prostate-cancer-testing/.

[3] Nat Rev Clin Oncol 2012;9:249.

[4] Medical News Today. PSA screening does not help mortality, http://www.medicalnewstoday.com/articles/240140.php.

Problems

1. List some risk factors for the vulnerability component of risk associated with the following threats:

   a. Terrorism by anti-Western elements using vehicle-borne explosives.

   b. Theft from desks in office spaces (distinguish between the threat during work hours and after work hours).

   c. Breaking and entering into a facility.

2. Discuss the relative effectiveness of the following methods in addressing the risk factors for theft from a facility:

   a. Control = visual monitoring

   Method = security officers versus CCTV

   b. Control = authorization

   Method = security officers versus card reader/turnstiles

   c. Control = authentication

   Method = security officers/photo ID recognition versus biometric-activated physical access

3. Use the risk assessment template specified below to analyze the threat and associated risk for the following scenarios:

   Scenario 1: The attack vector is the use of vehicle-borne explosives. Vehicles are in relatively close proximity to the company headquarters building entrance.

   Scenario 2: The attack vector is the kidnapping of senior executives from their cars and homes.

   Scenario 3: The attack vector is a disruption of the supply chain of an international company by armed gangs. Physical harm to the employees and the theft of the material in transit are both concerns.

> Distinct/impactful threat
> Likelihood component of risk (H/M/L)
> Vulnerability component of risk (H/M/L)
> Impact component of risk (H/M/L)
> Risk factor that increases one or more components of risk
> Control to address risk factor
> Specific method to implement control
> Operational requirement of the method
> Technical specification to ensure the method meets the operational requirement (per the standard)
> Cost of meeting this operational requirement (H/M/L)

4. Analyze ONE distinct threat and the associated risk for the following venues:
   a. Yankee Stadium (Bronx, NY)
   b. St. Patrick's Cathedral (NY, NY)
   c. The White House (Washington, D.C.)
   d. The Metropolitan Museum of Art (5th Ave., NY)
   e. Tiffany's flagship store (NY, NY)
   f. Your residence
   g. The Eiffel Tower (Paris, France)
   h. Buckingham Palace (London, UK)
   i. The Plaza Hotel (NY, NY)

5. You are the security director of a major international corporation. Your corporate headquarters is experiencing problems with clients and staff being robbed and/or accosted near your facility. Design a security strategy to be presented to the CEO that addresses this threat, noting it is important to maintain good relations with the local community.

6. You are the security director of a university. Create a high-level risk assessment and mitigation strategy for the lobby of the administration building. Specify the conditions that affect the risk factors and design the risk-mitigation strategy accordingly.

7. Match the following threats with the appropriate controls and explain why they apply in each case (i.e., how does it address one or more risk factors). Note that more than one control might apply to a single threat.

Threat	Risk Mitigation/Controls
1. Terrorism directed against a facility using vehicle-borne explosives	A. Physical restriction
2. Collateral damage to a facility due to vehicle-borne explosives	B. Authorization of physical access privilege
3. Theft via breaking and entering	C. Authentication of identity
4. Document theft from office areas	D. Visual monitoring
5. Information theft via radio frequency signal interception	E. Incident monitoring
6. Fire	F. Incident alerting

8. You are the newly appointed security director of an international manufacturing company headquartered in the United States. The previous security director mandated that visitors supply their social security account number (SSAN) when seeking entry to a company facility. Explain the security benefits of this control (if any) relative to the risk of storing records of personally identifying information (PII) for visitors in company databases. What risk factor does this procedure address, if any?

9. Explain the risk to society associated with the following threats and the "cost" of the identified control:
   a. Car accidents and seat belts
   b. Car accidents and speed limits
   c. Drowning and life guards
   d. Drowning and life preservers
   e. Death by firearms and gun locks
   f. Death by firearms and gun control legislation
   g. Diseases and government-funded medical programs

10. Life insurance can be viewed as a control to mitigate the risk of financial loss due to premature death (from various threat vectors). Explain how you would determine the amount of life insurance to purchase so that the "cost" of this control is proportionate to the risk.

11. You were recently appointed to be the security director for a large, multinational corporation. Your predecessor hired an expensive security consultant to conduct security risk assessments. The consultant used a security survey that required staff to qualitatively estimate risk and used the results to quantify risk. Discuss the pros and cons of this approach. Suggest an alternative methodology and indicate why it could be preferable.

12. You are the commander of an army that is about to attack the enemy. You have two distinct options: a beachhead assault that precedes a ground campaign or a sustained bombing effort. Provide a risk-based analysis of the pros and cons of each option.

13. During the Cold War, the United States' and the Soviet Union's nuclear policies were governed by a principle known as "mutually assured destruction." The point was to eliminate any perceived advantage of striking first because of the certainty that the defender would destroy the attacker as a result. Provide a (brief) risk-based analysis of this policy.

14. Choose three impactful threats and develop a simple risk assessment model as noted immediately below. Justify your assessment rankings for the two components of risk that are listed.

	High	Medium	Low
Likelihood/potential			
Vulnerability			
Mitigation cost			

15. You are the security director of a defense contractor that works on classified government programs. The viability of the company and the security of the United States in part depend on appropriate levels of security at your facility. There have been intelligence reports that the principal research facility has been under surveillance by known terrorist sympathizers. There is unobstructed line-of-sight between a house across the street and your research facility. The occupants of the house cannot be confirmed since it historically has been home to transients. The distance from the laboratory to the house is about 100 ft.

   a. Discuss the vulnerability component of risk with respect to information loss through the visual compromise of information. You can be as qualitative or quantitative as you like in your analysis, but you must base your argument on physical reality to bolster your claims of risk.

   b. Provide recommendations on risk mitigation.

   c. Do you think this is a priority security issue relative to others that are under your span of control as security director? Why or why not?

16. You are a high-priced security consultant who has been tasked with conducting a risk assessment of a campus with a number of facilities. You carefully calculate the vulnerability to explosive threats for a specific facility using the information gleaned from this book. Unfortunately, the likelihood component of risk relative to explosive threats is much higher at another facility on campus. Discuss the crux of the problem in terms of precision versus accuracy.

CHAPTER 3

Uncertainty and Terrorism

3.1 INTRODUCTION

Uncertainty is an inherent feature of terrorism that is exploited by its practitioners to great effect. Although uncertainty is linked to the notion of "randomness," a term with a mathematical definition, the two terms are not equivalent. Acts of terrorism are not generally predictable, but neither are they random in the strict sense of the word.

Predicting the exact time and location of a future act of terrorism is mostly a fruitless exercise. The problem of predicting terrorism is exacerbated by a lack of historical terrorism incidents and a highly dynamic risk profile. However, this does not mean that we are helpless in estimating the risk associated with specific attack vectors. For example, risk factors can yield clues about the effectiveness of risk mitigation should an attack occur. Moreover, if these risk factors are modeled as normally distributed random variables, the uncertainty associated with such distributions can be exploited to yield a statistical model of vulnerability. Therefore, the uncertainty of terrorism can be harnessed to make specific predictions about the vulnerability to future attacks. This chapter provides an introduction to these concepts applied to terrorism, and Chapter 5 provides more details.

3.2 UNCERTAINTY, ENTROPY, AND RANDOMNESS

The term "random" has become a fixture in the American vernacular. It is commonly used to describe what appear to be unpredictable events or behaviors. The truth is that humans act in highly nonrandom if irrational ways. In fact, the entire field of psychology is predicated on the predictability of human behavior.

Unpredictability and uncertainty are closely related concepts. The level of uncertainty associated with a future condition determines how predictable it is. The concept of entropy exemplifies this relationship. There is a strict technical definition of entropy, but qualitatively it is the number of possible states of a system.

57

Password complexity is often described in terms of entropy, which represents a means of quantifying the magnitude of uncertainty. The object of a password is to facilitate the confidentiality of information by defying an attacker's ability to guess its identity and thereby access the information protected by that password. Resilience to guessing is achieved by maximizing the possible number of available passwords, which is another way of saying that the uncertainty associated with the identity of a given password is a maximum. Entropy is therefore a measure of the resilience of a password relative to guessing, otherwise known as a brute force attack. A password or password type with greater entropy means it is more difficult to guess any single password since there are more possibilities to consider.

The entropy of a password is defined as $H = L\log_2 N$. L is the length of the password and N is the size of the alphabet, and it is usually measured in bits. Therefore, the entropy measures the number of bits it would take to represent every password of length L using an alphabet with N different symbols. For example, a password of seven lowercase characters (such as: *freedom*, csyoung, etc.) has an entropy of $H = 7\log_2 26 \approx 32.9$ bits. A password of 10 alphanumeric characters (such as *P4ssw0Rd97*, *K5lb42eQa2*) has an entropy of $H = 10\log_2 62 \approx 59.54$ bits. Table 3.1 specifies the entropy associated with various classes of characters.

The aforementioned describes the concept of entropy applied to passwords. But in general, the magnitude of uncertainty represents the hurdle to predicting a single outcome for any process. In our case, the set of outcomes is the breadth of possible terrorist incidents.

Terrorists exploit uncertainty to spread fear and to manipulate the emotions of individuals directly and indirectly affected by their actions. In fact, a defining feature of terrorism is the inherent uncertainty associated with where, when, and how a terrorist incident will occur. We immediately see that there is a very large set of possible outcomes since terrorists do not advertise their intentions in advance. In that vein, the uncertainty associated with terrorist outcomes (i.e., incidents) cannot be quantified in the same way as passwords. Therefore, the uncertainty of terrorism incidents resists being characterized in terms of entropy or any other convenient metric.

Table 3.1 Entropy of Character Classes

Character Class	Available Characters (n)	Entropy Per Character (bits)
Digits	10 (0 to 9)	3.32
Lowercase letters	26 (a to z)	4.7
Case-sensitive letters and digits	62 (A to Z, a to z, 0 to 9)	5.95
Standard keyboard characters	94	6.55

Information from Red Kestrel. "Random Password Strength." http://redkestrel.co.uk/articles/random-password-strength/.

Strictly speaking, uncertainty is related to the notion of randomness through the concept of a random variable. Let's assume the outcome of a measurement process is a random variable. Therefore, each measurement can assume a continuous range of values. If enough measurements are taken, and the value of each measurement is recorded, the resulting curve depicting the probability of the set of outcomes will be characterized by a distribution of a specific shape.

Although it is not possible to know the value of a single measurement of a random variable with certainty in advance (hence the word "random"), the shape of the curve allows one to opine on the *likelihood* that a future measurement will assume a specific value. One can also speculate with quantifiable limits on the certainty that a specific outcome will deviate from the average value. We will discuss such curves in the next section of this chapter.

Although uncertainty is an inherent feature of terrorism, and uncertainty is also an inherent feature of the probability distribution of a random variable, terrorism is not a random process. The reason for this is that it is affected by external factors, and these factors are well known. To be precise, terrorism incidents are not random variables. One can speculate on the relative likelihood that a terrorist incident will occur in one venue versus another during a given time period, but recognize that this is an inherently qualitative view of likelihood.

In fact, one outcome is that a terrorist incident may never happen at all. If terrorism is like a game of dice, imagine that those dice are loaded and also might never even be thrown! This is why the term "potential" is preferred over likelihood in this context. Likelihood has quantitative implications based on its use in connection with processes associated with random variables. Terrorists have reasons for their malevolent behavior, and these reasons provide a basis for expecting certain outcomes relative to others. In the language of probability, motivation and opportunity introduce a bias into the terrorism risk assessment process.

However, risk factors that affect the vulnerability component of terrorism risk can, in some cases, be specifically assumed to be a random variable. In theory, a risk factor can assume any prescribed value within scenario-specific limits. Certain physical constraints dictated by the terrorism methods themselves limit the range of risk factor values and consequently the magnitude of the vulnerability component of risk.

The fact that a terrorism risk factor can be assumed to be a random variable has implications to the modeling of terrorism risk. This is a topic that will be explored in Chapter 5, but first we must introduce the important concept of a normal distribution.

3.3   THE NORMAL DISTRIBUTION

Examples are often the best way to convey concepts. With respect to the concept of a random variable, consider my daily trek to the office each morning. Apologies to the non-New Yorkers who might have difficulty relating to the diurnal subterranean experience that is part of life in my home town.

For some reason I compulsively record the duration of my daily commute each day. This trek entails a walk to the subway followed by a ride on one or two subway lines. There is some variability in the subway I catch, and this contributes to fluctuations in the recorded travel times.

If I catch the "C" (local) train at 72nd Street, it is a straight shot to my office building. If, on the other hand, a "B" (express) train arrives first, I must switch at W. 4th Street and catch the "A" (also an express) for one stop or grab the "C" or "E" and take it two stops, eventually alighting at Canal Street. Since the "B" is an express train, it arrives at W. 4th Street more quickly than the "C," a local train. However, if I take the "B," I must switch trains at W. 4th, which introduces a delay that partially offsets the benefits of an express train.

There are a number of factors that contribute to variations in the total transit time: the particular subway line I choose, which impacts the walk to the initial stop. The volume of passengers on a train as well as the number of trains also contribute to variations in arrival time, since both of these peak during the morning and evening rush hours. The variability in any one of these parameters can be quite small, but their cumulative effect results in variations in the total transit time.

It turns out that my average door-to-door transit time is 25 min. This is not excessive by New York City standards. How much variability is there in this average value? As an aside that has important implications to the magnitude of uncertainty, I have made this trip hundreds of times so there is a statistically significant sample space of measurements.

It turns out that 68.2 percent of the trips were within 1 min of the average time of 25 min. In other words, approximately 68 percent of the recorded times were between 24 and 26 min; 95.4 percent of my trips were within 2 min of the average (i.e., 25 min ± 2 min); and 99.6 percent of the recorded times were within 3 min of the average.

When I plotted the time-per-trip against the number of trips of a specific duration divided by the total number of trips (i.e., the probability of the duration per trip), the resulting distribution of recorded times looked something like Figure 3.1.

The average or mean value of trip (μ) is 25 min. The spread about the mean or the dispersion, corresponding to one standard deviation (σ), is ±1 min (i.e., −1σ corresponds to 24 min and +1σ corresponds to 26 min). Two standard

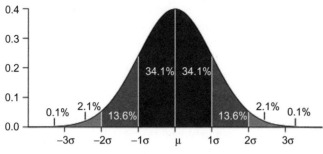

FIGURE 3.1

The Normal distribution. *(From The National Weather Service. "July 2009 One of the Hottest On Record."* http://www.srh.noaa.gov/bro/?n=2009event_hottestjuly.*)*

deviations or ±2σ accounts for 95.4 percent of the trips. Three standard deviations or ±3σ corresponds to 99.6 percent of the trips.

What can we conclude from this, and more importantly, what does this have to do with counterterrorism?

The first observation is that there is remarkably little variability in the average transit time. The New York City Transit System is both efficient and effective, as most New Yorkers would agree most of the time. My guess is there would be more variability if the distance traveled was longer and/or it occurred during rush hour.

Since hundreds of data points were recorded and travel time is a random variable, the Law of Large Numbers (LLN) dictates that the shape of the distribution will be a normal distribution. This is also known as a Gaussian distribution, named after the German physicist-mathematician Karl Friedrich Gauss. Such distributions have well-defined characteristics.

Specifically, a standard deviation about the mean of a normal distribution corresponds to a specific fraction of the total population of data points. A normal distribution immediately conveys the fraction of the measurements or incidents that differs from the mean and by how much that fraction differs.

The probability density function for a normally distributed random variable x, with a mean of 0 and a standard deviation of unity, is given by the following expression:

$$f(x) = 1 / \sqrt{2\pi}\left(e^{-x^2}\right)$$

To reiterate an important point, it is impossible to predict the value of a single value of a normally distributed random variable a priori. Hence the association with the use of the word "random." However, a probability distribution of random variable values allows one to estimate the likelihood that a specific value selected from the distribution is within a certain distance from the mean. Therefore, for every normally distributed set of values, ±1 standard deviation from the mean corresponds to 68.3 percent of the total population, 2 standard deviations equates to 95.5 percent of the total population, and 3 standard deviations is equivalent to 99.7 percent. Figure 3.2 is quite similar to Figure 3.1 and again illustrates this point nicely.

So if I attempted to predict the time of transit for my next trip to the office based on historical data, the likelihood that it will be greater than 24 min and less than 26 min is approximately 68 percent. Continuing in this way, there is roughly a 95 percent likelihood that the transit time would fall between 23 and 27 min, and over a 99 percent likelihood that a specific trip will require between 22 and 28 min.

Normal distributions are important because many processes in the real world are functions of random variables and the distribution of outcomes are normally distributed. I cannot say for certain why my subway transit time is a random variable. But it is likely that there are several independent features of each trip that vary from day-to-day in unpredictable ways. When these features are combined there is a collective uncertainty in the outcome, and the effect is a normal distribution for a sufficient number of trips.

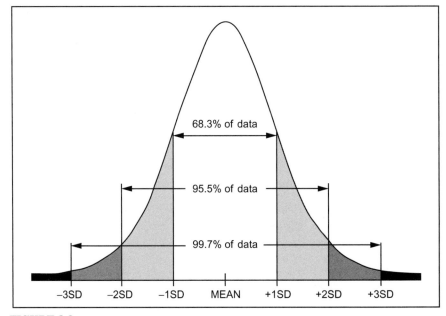

FIGURE 3.2

Normal distributions and standard deviations. *(From Centers for Disease Control and Prevention. "Lesson 2: Summarizing Data."* http://www.cdc.gov/osels/scientific_edu/ss1978/Lesson2/Section7.html.*)*

This begs the question of what constitutes a sufficient number of trips to achieve some desired level of statistical accuracy. This is a fancy way of asking how many data points are required to yield a particular spread about the mean. More relevantly, what can we say about the components of risk for terrorism by exploiting its inherent uncertainty?

The following section attempts to address these issues more quantitatively.

3.4 UNCERTAINTY APPLIED TO TERRORISM

We are now in a position to discuss terrorism risk and the role of uncertainty. As discussed in the last section, terrorism incidents do not occur randomly. Stated more precisely, terrorism incidents are not random variables. There is an underlying reason for such acts, and there is a bias in the process driven by a desire to commit the maximum damage further, political or religious causes, the availability of weapons, etc. Senselessness should not be confused with randomness.

If terrorism incidents were truly random we might conclude that the potential for an attack by anti-Western groups was roughly the same in Omaha, Nebraska, as Washington, D.C., or New York, New York. We know that is not the case, although we unfortunately cannot quantify the difference. Because there is an inherent bias in terrorists' behavior, we apply mitigation based on what we know about their intentions and modus operandi. These intentions and modes of implementation drive the risk factors for terrorist threats. Furthermore, the inherent bias allows for qualitative estimates of the potential for an attack against a specific target.

No one without insider knowledge can predict the next terrorist incident. That is, no one can say precisely *when* and/or *where* an attack will occur or what the losses will be as a result. However, we can make estimates about the vulnerability to attack by assuming the risk factors that affect vulnerability are normally distributed random variables.

Furthermore, uncertainty in the mean of a normally distributed random variable allows one to make statements about the likelihood of *invulnerability* or, conversely, the probability of protection provided by mitigation measures. Ironically, there is certainty in the inherent uncertainty associated with normally distributed random variables, and this turns out to be useful in estimating security risk.

As noted in Chapter 1, terrorists are intent on making headlines by killing or injuring as many people as possible. To optimize their killing strategy, they often use explosives, which are indiscriminate in their effect. People typically use the word terrorism to describe violent acts against innocent bystanders in furtherance of a political or religious cause. It is true that many individuals who commit terrorism do so in furtherance of a cause, yet this is a selective use of the term.

Is affiliation with a terrorist group an important characteristic with respect to a counterterrorism strategy? Although I believe acts of violence committed by individuals so affiliated or not qualify as acts of terror, affiliation with a group is indeed significant from a counterterrorism perspective. This is not because one type of terrorism is inherently worse than another. It is because an individual's affiliation with a particular group is a risk factor for specific terrorism threats, which in turn affects the choice of controls required to address those factors.

For example, individuals who commit mass murder in the United States appear to prefer high-capacity firearms in furtherance of their objective. It is unclear if government experts categorize this as a form of terrorism, but the surviving victims will most assuredly achieve consensus on that point. In contrast, "traditional" terrorists, both domestic and international, often use conventional explosives to further their respective causes. This knowledge is essential in developing a defensive posture since an effective risk-mitigation strategy addresses those terrorism attack vectors with the greatest potential for occurrence and in consideration of the mode of attack.

There has been much speculation about terrorists getting their hands on biological, chemical, and/or radiological weapons to further their respective agendas. We will analyze the effects of such weapons in Chapter 5 as well as the vulnerability component of risk for various scenarios. It is understandable that these would appeal to a terrorist based on the overarching desire to spread fear and panic.

The challenge for security professionals is to ignore subjective feelings and, where possible, to quantify the vulnerability component of risk. This will lead to a proportionate defensive strategy. Much of this book is about developing such strategies.

Specific parameters derived from physical laws are directly relevant to estimating the vulnerability to terrorist threats. For example, the overpressure and impulse directly relate to the damage caused by conventional explosives. The magnitude of both the overpressure and impulse is a function of distance from the explosive source to the target as well as the quantity of the explosive payload. Therefore, distance from the explosion and the explosive payload are risk factors for the conventional explosive attack vector since these directly affect the vulnerability component of risk.

The overpressure and impulse can be described by equations that are functions of the distance from an explosive source and the quantity of explosives used in an attack. These equations will be discussed in Chapter 6 and facilitate estimates of the vulnerability to damage as a result of a blast.

But vulnerability is only one of three components of risk. As noted in Chapter 1, we must also estimate the potential for incident occurrence in developing a counterterrorism strategy assuming one has already determined the threat is impactful.

Consider the problem that is one of the major themes of this book. Namely the fact that the number of terrorism incidents is typically quite low. This is of course a good thing from a security and safety perspective, but it is a statistical nightmare if accurate predictions of future losses are required.

One cannot make credible statements about the likelihood of a future terrorist incident in a specific locale or country based on one or two incidents. In addition, aggregating data from other countries is often irrelevant since the respective conditions that affect terrorism can vary significantly. Issues that affect the potential for terrorism are constantly changing due to political, economic, and social instabilities as well as the availability of weapons, the quality of defensive measures, etc.

Can risk-relevant information be derived from historical data on terrorist incidents? At least one paper posits that the losses due to terrorism incidents obey a so-called scale-free (i.e., power law) distribution.[1] In other words, the paper plots the number of incidents versus the magnitude of casualties. The results suggest that there are a few incidents with many casualties and many incidents with a lesser number of casualties. Figure 3.3 shows various power-law distributions for terrorism attacks in terms of injuries, death, and their aggregation as calculated in the reference.

For the interested reader, scale-free or power-law scaling has also been shown to characterize the distribution of nodes in a social network (e.g., email relationships).

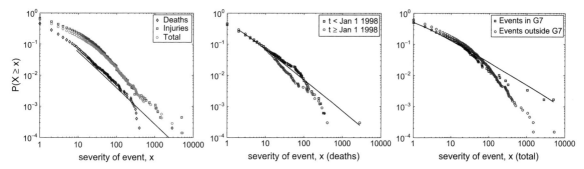

FIGURE 3.3

Power-law distributions for terrorism incidents. *(Used with permission from Clauset, A. and M. Young. 2005. "Scale Invariance in Global Terrorism." http://www.cs.unm.edu/~moore/tr/05-05/terrorism.pdf.)*

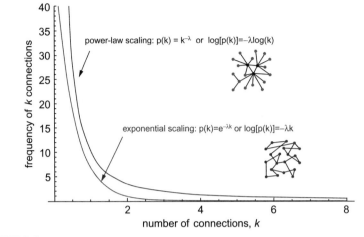

FIGURE 3.4

A scale-free or power-law scaling distribution. *(National Institutes of Health.* http://openi.nlm.nih.gov/detailedresult.php?img=1796610_1471-2148-7-S1-S16-1&req=4.*)*

If each individual point represents a network node, the distribution of nodes as a function of their connectivity to other nodes is such that there are a few nodes with many connections and many nodes with few connections. The distribution of nodes obeys an inverse power law, i.e., $p(k) = k^{-n}$. Figure 3.4 illustrates a scale-free network, plotting the number of connections for each node versus their frequency of occurrence.

This network structure facilitates communication, but also aids in the propagation of computer viruses for the same reason. In fact, the power-law representation of network connectivity may have application to electronic terrorism. For example, solutions have been obtained for an equation that characterizes computer virus infections and growth in scale-free networks.[2] In addition, a threshold condition was found for the persistence of computer infections, where the effect of connectivity-dependent growth and recovery rates was calculated.

Furthermore, it was theoretically shown to be possible to reduce the deleterious effects of computer viruses by preferentially discouraging growth and enhancing recovery in high-connectivity network nodes. Significantly, a security metric emerged from this analysis such that a sampling of the network environment in real time would facilitate the quantification of risk relative to email-borne threats.

If losses due to terrorism incidents do indeed follow a power-law distribution, we could possibly use this information to develop a risk-mitigation strategy since we know the expectation value or the probability of an incident loss, $p(k)$, multiplied by the cost of risk mitigation for each incident. Of course "losses" in this case include the loss of human life.

Unfortunately, the characterization of power laws is complicated by the large fluctuations that occur in the tail of the distribution. This is the part of the distribution representing large but infrequent events. Complications also arise due to the difficulty in identifying the range over which power-law behavior holds true.

Suppose that the number of terrorism incidents as a function of time is a normally distributed random variable. In other words, let's assume terrorism incidents occur in the same way that counts occur in a radiation detector. How many incidents are required to achieve a specific level of statistical accuracy?

Increasing the number of terrorism incidents would enhance statistical accuracy with the obvious downside of increasing damage to property and loss of human life. Enhancing the number of terrorism incidents just to achieve greater statistical precision seems like a profoundly bad idea. Although this point is likely to be completely obvious, it is worth a little math to demonstrate just how foolhardy it is. We will do this by showing how many incidents would be required to yield various levels of statistical precision.

Suppose we require the precision of our statistical measurement to be within 10 percent of the total number of incidents, N. This requirement in fact sets the minimum number of incidents required to achieve the prescribed level of precision. What is that minimum number in this case?

By assuming that the number of terrorism incidents is a normally distributed random variable, this implies that the standard deviation of a distribution of incidents is proportional to the square root of N, the total number of incidents. So the standard deviation $\sigma = \sqrt{N}$. But we also require that the standard deviation be within 10 percent of the total number of incidents. Therefore, $\sigma = (1/10)N$.

We can equate these expressions, so $\sqrt{N} = (1/10)N$. Performing some algebra and solving for N we see that the number of incidents N must be at least 100 to ensure that the dispersion about the mean is within 10 percent of N.

What if this is not good enough? Suppose we require 1 percent precision? In other words, $\sqrt{N} = (1/100)N$. In this case, $N = 10,000$. This implies that a rather large sample space of terrorist incidents is required to achieve the requisite precision. In fact the required precision scales with the square of the number of incidents. This exposes an inherent limitation of making predictions using a small number of incidents. Figure 3.5 plots precision versus the number of incidents required to achieve a specific level of precision for a normally distributed random variable.

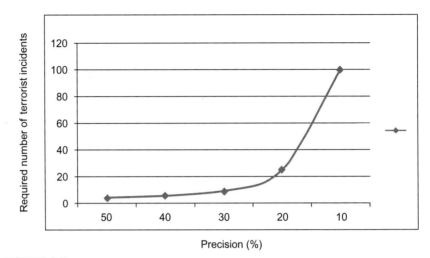

FIGURE 3.5

The number of terrorism incidents required to achieve a specified precision for a normally distributed random variable.

Clearly requiring a large number of terrorist incidents to assess the likelihood of loss in a future incident is less than ideal. In addition, we have made a strong claim that the occurrence of terrorism incidents is not a random variable. We must therefore look for other ways to assess terrorism risk in a rigorous and meaningful manner.

Finally, it is interesting to note that uncertainty is exploited in other contexts for fun and profit; uncertainty is big business. Insurance companies and Wall Street banks create sophisticated models of uncertainty and thereby establish confidence intervals to determine the likelihood of gains and losses. We will investigate confidence intervals in more detail in connection with the standard error in Chapter 12 as it relates to sensor performance.

Monte Carlo simulation is one technique used to model the behavior of financial instruments and others. Key parameters in the model are assumed to have a probability distribution with a prescribed uncertainty. Importantly, these models are used to limit the downside exposure to extreme financial events, although the financial wizards sometimes get it massively wrong, as the world witnessed in 2008. The probability of protection method in Chapter 5 is essentially a Monte Carlo-type analysis.

Casinos also capitalize on the properties of randomness to make big profits. However, although the outcomes of card games, dice, etc. are indeed random variables, a casino is not a level playing field. They adjust the rules of the games to ensure the house wins a greater proportion of the outcomes.

Although it is quite possible to beat the house over the course of a few encounters, the long-term prospects are grim. Short-term winnings by customers are actually good for the casinos as they inspire people to behave irrationally, i.e., make more frequent and larger bets. Individuals who attempt to move the odds in the other direction are banned from returning or worse.[3]

Casinos also capitalize on an immutable characteristic of human nature: greed. This ensures that there is a never-ending supply of people willing to forfeit their paychecks, annuities, and life savings in return for the illusory prospect of easy money.

SUMMARY

Uncertainty is a fundamental feature of terrorism. There is inherent uncertainty in the likelihood of a future terrorist incident. However, there is a quantifiable level of uncertainty in physical parameters that affect the vulnerability to loss or damage if one assumes that risk factors are normally distributed random variables.

A random variable is one where the spectrum of future outcomes/incidents for a given process is known but cannot be predicted a priori. The probability distribution of a normally distributed random variable is characterized by a mean and standard deviation that completely describe the likelihood of a specific outcome.

The inherent uncertainty of certain terrorism risk factors can be used to model these risk factors as normally distributed random variables for various terrorism attack vectors. Moreover, the uncertainty associated with normal distributions can be harnessed to assess the likelihood that terrorism mitigation measures are effective. This is the basis for the probability of protection method in Chapter 5.

For a normally distributed random variable, greater statistical precision requires a greater number of incidents. Specifically, statistical precision scales with the square of the number of incidents. In general, terrorism "suffers" from a small number of incidents, and this limits the ability to assess the effectiveness of risk mitigation as well as to predict the likelihood of a future incident.

Losses due to terrorism have been shown to follow a power-law distribution. In theory one could use this result to calculate the expectation value (i.e., probability of loss due to a terrorist incident times the magnitude of loss and resulting cost of mitigation) and thereby establish a risk-based mitigation strategy. Unfortunately, power-law distributions defy accurate modeling of their dispersion (i.e., deviation from the mean) due to large fluctuations in the tail, i.e., those incidents characterized by big losses and low frequency of occurrence.

REFERENCES

[1] Clauset A, Young M. Scale invariance in global terrorism. 2005. http://www.cs.unm.edu/~moore/tr/05-05/terrorism.pdf.

[2] Chang D, Young C. Infection dynamics on the internet. Comput Secur 2005;24(4):280–6.

[3] Mezrich B. Bringing down the house. New York: Free Press; 2003.

Problems

1. Estimate the potential for the following incidents and explain your reasoning:
   a. A terrorist attack in Washington, D.C., by anti-Western elements.
   b. A terrorist attack in Boise, Idaho, by anti-Western elements.
   c. A fire in your house or apartment.
   d. A theft from your car when it is parked near where you live.
   e. An electronic attack of your online account.
2. Can you quantify the likelihood of any of the incidents in problem number 1?
3. How is the likelihood or potential for the incidents in problem number 1 different from how you would calculate the odds of a particular outcome in a game of dice?
4. Indicate the potential for a terrorist incident due to anti-Western elements in TWO of the following venues and indicate at least one risk factor:
   a. Sioux Falls, Iowa
   b. The Washington Monument
   c. Times Square, New York
   d. The London Tube
   e. The Statue of Liberty
   f. The Hoover Dam
   g. The Golden Gate Bridge
   h. ABC News Headquarters
5. You are the police chief of a major city in the United States. Federal intelligence sources indicate a high potential for an attack by a suicide bomber via vehicle- or backpack-borne explosives (anti-Westerners again) against a local sports complex.
   a. What are the risk factors associated with this threat?
   b. What mitigation measures might be effective?
6. You are the security director of a major U.S. corporation. There have been a large number of thefts at your headquarters facility. Senior management is concerned, and they are putting pressure on you to do something about it. However, you are a skilled risk manager, and therefore you carefully analyze the situation before acting impulsively. You plot the number of thefts against the value of items stolen and observe that the values are normally distributed. The mean of the distribution is $1000 and 1 standard deviation from the mean equals $100.
   a. What is the range of values that encompasses 68 percent of all thefts (i.e., ±1 standard deviation from the mean)?
   b. 95 percent (i.e., ±2 standard deviations from the mean)?

    c. 99 percent (i.e., ±3 standard deviations from the mean)?

    d. How might you use this information to develop a cost-effective risk-mitigation strategy?

7. Normal distributions. The set of graphs (see below) are normal distributions with varying spreads about the same mean (i.e., varying dispersion). Do not worry about the units on the axes of the graph since only relative differences between the curves are of interest here.

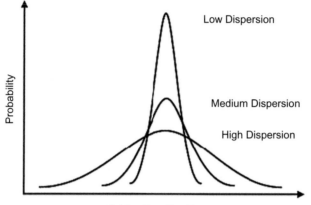

Cost or Duration Range

(From U. S. Department of Transportation. "Risk Analysis." http://international.fhwa.dot.gov/riskassess/risk_hcm06_04.cfm.)

    a. Which distribution depicts the widest variation in cost?

    b. Which curve depicts a cost with the highest probability of occurrence?

    c. Describe the *relative* certainty with respect to the mean cost for each distribution. In other words, if you picked a cost at random from each distribution, describe the relative likelihood you would be close to the mean value in each case. How would you quantitatively describe this certainty?

8. Describe a security threat where the outcomes or results of incidents might be a normally distributed random variable. Explain why.

9. You are the security director of a large international corporation headquartered in New York City. You are increasingly concerned about your company being targeted by international terrorists. You have developed a strategy to manage the risk, but you have been informed that the security budget for next year is 25 percent less than the current year. Unfortunately, your revised security strategy requires an increase of 25 percent! Provide a risk-based justification for an increase in the security budget (Hint: make arguments based on increasing threats and associated risk components, risk factors, required controls/methods and costs).

10. You are the security director of a department store in a U.S. city. Shoplifting is a big concern, and you are considering implementing measures to mitigate this risk.

    a. Would you expect the value of stolen items to be a normally distributed random variable? Why or why not?

b. Specify two security measures that might be effective. Would either of these measures also be effective against any form of terrorist threat? Why or why not?

c. How would you determine that the security measures you have implemented are effective relative to the threat of shoplifting?

d. Construct a hypothetical graph illustrating the number of thefts as a function of time, and indicate the effect of implementing security measures on shoplifting (Hint: hopefully the rate decreases as a result).

11. You are the security director of a major U.S. corporation. There have been a large number of thefts at your headquarters facility. Senior management is concerned, and they are putting pressure on you to do something about it immediately. However, you are a skilled risk manager, and therefore you carefully analyze the situation before acting impulsively. You plot the number of thefts against the approximate dollar value of each theft and you observe that the dollar amount-per-theft is normally distributed. The mean of the distribution of dollar amount-per-theft is $1000 and 1 standard deviation from the mean equals $\pm$ $100.

a. Use the figure below to label the range of values of the dollar amount-per-theft that includes 68 percent of all thefts (i.e., 1 standard deviation from the mean).

b. 95 percent (i.e., 2 standard deviations from the mean).

c. 99.7 percent (i.e., 3 standard deviations from the mean).

d. Could you use this information to inform your risk-mitigation strategy? If so, how? If not, explain why not?

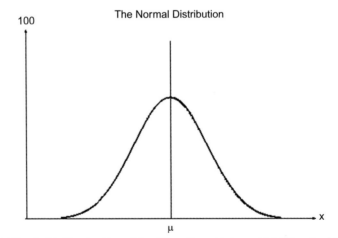

(From NIST. "What Do We Mean by 'Normal' Data?" http://www.itl.nist.gov/div898/handbook/pmc/section5/pmc51.htm.*)*

12. Extra Credit! The London Tube has five zones, and the price of a ride depends on how many zones you cross during each ride. You must swipe in and swipe out with your Oyster Card, so we can use the Poisson process to estimate the likelihood of traveling specific distances.

Let's say the probability of traveling a certain number of Tube stops, k, is given by a Poisson process:

$$p(K) = \lambda^k e^{-\lambda} / K!$$

$\lambda = 5 =$ the average number of Tube stops traveled/ride, and $k! = k \times (k-1) \times (k-2)....$ Assume one crosses a zone every 10 stops (Note: the Circle Line destroys this model since it continuously repeats itself in a loop).

Furthermore, every zone crossed costs £2. Calculate the probability that a person on the Tube who starts in zone 1 will cross zones 2, 3, 4, and 5 as well as the expected cost of each ride. The expected cost is the probability of the ride times the cost.

CHAPTER 4

Physical Models of Terrorism

4.1 INTRODUCTION

Certain physical models are broadly applicable to risk problems in terrorism. It is useful to recognize these models and understand how they can be applied to estimate the vulnerability component of risk for various threats or threat attack vectors.

Emphasis should be placed on the word "estimate." The utility of these models is embodied in their simplicity. This simplicity also places limits on their accuracy. Exact solutions to problems in physical security risk can be elusive. The good news is that exact solutions are often unnecessary since the effectiveness of risk-mitigation measures are not dependent on precision.

In fact, the proverbial back-of-the-envelope calculation can yield a perfectly adequate ballpark view of risk. Such approximations are useful in determining the vulnerability to a specific threat or threat vector. Moreover, they can be invaluable in estimating the effectiveness of proposed mitigation measures.

4.2 POINT SOURCES OF RADIATION

A point source of radiating energy is a process where two conditions can apply: (1) the physical dimensions of the radiating source are smaller than the wavelength of the radiated energy or (2) the distance from the radiating object to the point at which the energy is measured is much greater than the physical dimensions of the object.

The intensity of a radiating source of energy or the dispersal of some nasty substance is often relevant to assessing the vulnerability to terrorism. This is because it is the concentration of a substance or the power of an energy source over a given area that affects intervening objects. The effect of radiating energy on people and detectors is often determined by the intensity of that energy.

The human eye and ear are excellent examples of sensors that respond to energy intensity. It is the intensity of electromagnetic and mechanical energy, respectively, that trigger a sensory response in these two organs. In other words, the intensity of energy impinging on our eyes and ears is what allows us to see visible light and hear audible sounds.

You may recall from your days in geometry class that the surface area of a sphere is equal to $4\pi r^2$, where r is the radius of the sphere and π (pi) is a constant approximately equal to 3.14. If a source is radiating energy into the atmosphere, the power of that energy source is the amount of energy radiated per unit time. The *intensity* of an energy source is its power *density*, or the power per unit area.

The intensity of a point source of energy assumes a spherical pattern. Therefore, its intensity, I, at any distance, r, from a source radiating with power, P, can be written as

$$I = P/4\pi r^2$$

If the intensity is I at a distance r from the source, then at a distance $2r$ the intensity is reduced by $1/(2)^2$ or $(\frac{1}{4})r$. If the distance is trebled, the intensity is reduced by $(1/9)$. Quadrupling the distance results in the intensity decreasing by $(1/16)$, etc.

The exponent of 2 in the denominator of the expression for I indicates there is a decreasing nonlinear relationship between intensity and distance. Appendix A discusses nonlinear relationships in more detail. Figure 4.1 illustrates the geometry of a point source of power and shows the disproportionately increasing area over which the intensity acts as a function of the distance from the source.

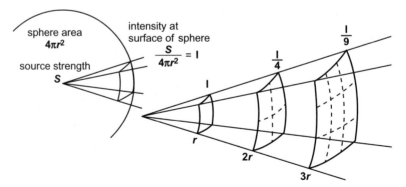

FIGURE 4.1

Intensity from point sources and the inverse square law. *(From Goddard Space Flight Center. "Supernovae." http://imagine.gsfc.nasa.gov/docs/science/try_l2/supernovae.html.)*

It is clear from this figure that the intensity of a point source radiates in an ever-expanding, balloon-like pattern. Notice that the *total* radiated power calculated at any distance from the source remains constant. How could this be otherwise?

The radiated energy is completely encapsulated by an imaginary surface. Therefore, the total power, P_t, at any distance from the source is the intensity (P/SA) times the encapsulating surface area (SA) or (P/SA) $\times SA$. The surface area of the encapsulating sphere is irrelevant if one is calculating the total power radiating from the source.

However, the intensity or power density definitely depends on the surface area over which it acts, and therefore it decreases inversely with the square of the distance. A point source of radiating energy is a recurring physical model that can be applied to certain terrorism threats based on the scenario-specific geometry.

A plot of intensity versus distance for point sources of radiating energy is represented by the $1/r^2$ function in Figure 4.2. A $1/r^3$ function is also shown for comparison. As you would expect, the latter decreases faster than the former.

If the source of energy is a chunk of radioactive material, the intensity of the radiated energy is a key factor in assessing the vulnerability to radiation exposure. If the source of energy is an antenna, the intensity of the radiating energy is a factor in determining if the signal can be detected by an adversary.

The minus sign before the exponent implies that the intensity *decreases* as the distance from the radioactive source increases. The implications of this inverse

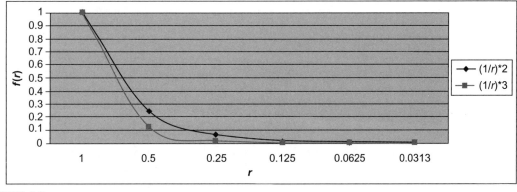

FIGURE 4.2
The functions $1/r^2$ and $1/r^3$.

nonlinear relationship are that disproportionate effects accrue with distance from point sources of radiating energy. Moving nearer or farther from the source will disproportionately impact the vulnerability component of risk and, quite possibly, the resulting mitigation strategy.

To get a more intuitive feeling for the concept of intensity, let's look at a real-life example of radiating objects and observe how the intensity scales with surface area. The human body radiates thermal power in the infrared energy band. This is why humans are quite visible using infrared-detection equipment. It is also why CCTV camera systems are equipped with special technology so they can view living things at night.

Have you ever tried holding a 150-W incandescent lightbulb in your bare hands when it is still glowing or it has just been turned off? My guess is that you could not do so for very long since it is extremely hot. Without getting too personal, what happens when you do the same thing with your significant other? Many responses are possible, but screaming in agony should not be one of them. Do you realize that your partner is radiating a nearly equivalent amount of thermal power as the lightbulb?

The thermodynamic difference between a person and the lightbulb is that the thermal power radiating from a human is spread out over the body's entire surface. Let's be more quantitative.

Assume that the average human and lightbulb surface areas are $1.73\,\mathrm{m}^2$ and $20\times10^{-4}\,\mathrm{m}^2$, respectively. Neglecting the emissivity of human skin (0.97) versus that of a lightbulb (0.26) at infrared wavelengths, the intensity of thermal radiation from humans versus a lightbulb is reduced by about a factor of 1000 because of their respective differences in surface area.

Specifically, the intensity of radiation from the lightbulb is

$$150\ \mathrm{W}/(20\times10^{-4}\ \mathrm{m^2}) \sim 75\ \mathrm{kW/m^2}\ \text{compared with}$$
$$150\ \mathrm{W}/1.73\ \mathrm{m}^2 \sim 87\ \mathrm{W/m}^2\ \text{for the human.}$$

This illustrates the effect of surface area on intensity and also why you should have no thermodynamic concerns about giving your significant other a hug the next time you feel like it.

4.3   EXPONENTIAL GROWTH AND DECAY

Suppose the vulnerability to a terrorism threat was affected by the rate of change of a certain physical quantity. Furthermore, suppose the change in the magnitude of that quantity with time is proportional to the amount that remains. We could write a simple expression that describes this model in terms of a first order differential equation.

Let's say C is the decreasing concentration of a noxious gas known to be used by a terrorist organization, R is the proportionality constant determining the rate of change of C, and t represents time. The expression that characterizes this process can be written as:

$$dC/dt = -RC$$

This expression should be read as the time rate of change of the quantity C (Note: dC/dt is the first derivative of C with respect to time as you no doubt recall from your calculus days) equals the negative of R times C. R will likely vary according to the specific process, but it will always be expressed in units of "something-per-unit time" for time-dependent exponential processes.

What this expression is really saying is that the time rate of change of C decreases faster for larger amounts of C; the greater the concentration, the faster the rate of decrease. Conveniently, this equation can be easily solved, where the time-dependent solution is given by:

$$C = C_0 e^{-Rt}$$

The letter "e" represents the exponential, and this has a constant value of 2.72. So the concentration, C, decreases exponentially with time relative to the initial concentration, C_0.

R is the proportionality constant determining the rate at which C changes with time. A strikingly similar equation can be constructed that describes a process that changes with distance rather than time. In other words, one could also write the following expression:

$$dC/dx = -KC$$

This looks nearly identical to the time-dependent version except that the rate of change of the quantity C is expressed in terms of distance, x. Implicit in this expression is the fact that the proportionality constant, K, is written in units of "something-per-unit distance." Recall in the time-dependent equation, the analogous quantity is R, and it is expressed in units of "something-per-unit time."

In exact analogy with the time-dependent equation, the solution of the distance-dependent expression is given by

$$C = C_0 e^{-Kx}$$

This tells us that the quantity C decreases exponentially with distance from its original value, C_0, and at a rate governed by K. A graph of this function is shown in Figure 4.3.

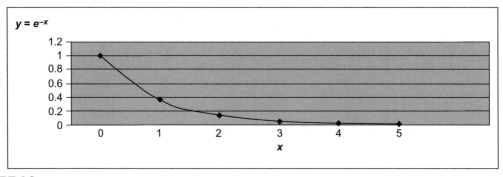

FIGURE 4.3
Decreasing exponential function.

For example, we might want to know the intensity of a beam of gamma radiation as it propagates through a certain material being proposed as a shield. We might hope to calculate its shielding effectiveness and thereby estimate the vulnerability to ionizing radiation. If one plotted the beam intensity versus the thickness of the shielding material it would look like Figure 4.3, a decreasing exponential. The shielding determines the rate of decrease of the intensity from its initial value as the energy propagates through the material.

In this case that rate constant is known as the mass attenuation coefficient of the material. Appendix C provides more details on the exponential function and Chapter 7 discusses interactions of electromagnetic energy with matter.

4.4 HARMONIC MOTION AND THE SINGLE DEGREE OF FREEDOM MODEL

One of the most important physical models in nature is harmonic motion. It describes any situation where a force causes a displacement in proportion to some constant. The deceptively simple expression that characterizes this situation is as follows:

$$F = -kx$$

In this case F is the so-called restoring force applied to a mass, k is the constant of proportionality, and x is the displacement of the mass. This equation states that in the event of a displacement of the mass from its equilibrium position (i.e., the position such that all forces sum to zero), there is a force proportional to k that restores the mass to the equilibrium position. This is also known as Hooke's law.

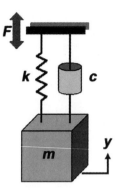

FIGURE 4.4

Harmonic oscillator. *(From FEMCI the Book.* http://femci.gsfc.nasa.gov/random/MilesEqn.html.*)*

Because a force is by definition equal to mass (m) times acceleration (a), or $F = ma$, where acceleration is the second derivative of position with respect to time, the two forces can be equated. The result is that the displacement of the mass can be shown to oscillate with time (in other words, $F = ma = -kx$. So $md^2x/dt^2 = -kx$ so $x(t) = e^{i\sqrt{(k/m)}t}$ or $A\cos\sqrt{(k/m)}t + iB\sin\sqrt{(k/m)}t$).

A mass on a spring is one of the simplest systems that exhibit harmonic motion. Hooke's law can also be stated as: "The extension of a spring is directly proportionate to the load that is applied to it." Figure 4.4 shows a mass-and-spring system.

The model of a mass on a spring naturally leads to the notion of an oscillation period. This is the amount of time required for one complete cycle of mass displacement, and it is inversely related to the frequency of oscillation. For harmonic motion, the angular oscillation frequency is equal to $\sqrt{(k/m)}$.

This simple mass-and-spring system can be used to model a number of physical phenomena including the reaction of building elements to explosives, as will be evident in Chapters 5 and 6. Figure 4.5 illustrates the concept of an oscillation period.

It is well known that the response of a mass on a spring to a transient force is qualitatively different when the natural oscillation period is greater than the force duration versus when the natural oscillation period is less than the force duration.

In the former case, the so-called impulse, i.e., the cumulative effect of the explosive force interacting with the object in question over time, determines the initial velocity of the mass response, while in the latter, the displacement of the mass is practically proportional to the force throughout its application.

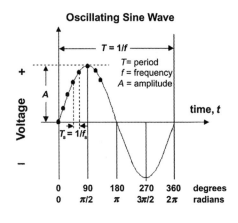

FIGURE 4.5
Oscillation period. *(From NIST.* http://tf.nist.gov/general/enc-p.htm.)

Modeling the window response as simple harmonic motion under explosive loading will be used in Chapter 5 to determine the likelihood that a window design provides adequate protection. The key concept here is that the response of a building element to an explosive force can be crudely modeled as a mass on a spring.

4.5   GAUSSIAN PLUMES[1]

Terrorists are purportedly interested in dispersing nasty stuff into the environment and thereby cause panic, injury, and death. With the exception of one notable incident that occurred in the Tokyo subway in the 1990s, there is not much evidence of an affinity for this attack vector by civilians. However, this may not be due to a lack of desire on the terrorists' part. A simple model of how aerosolized chemicals spread out following their dispersal could be useful in estimating risk if such a threat attack vector was indeed a concern.

Unfortunately, an accurate characterization of the motion of a plume released in air is complicated, especially in urban areas. As with many technical problems, reality is more nuanced than theory, and entire books have been written on the dispersal of aerosols. That said, simple physical models might yield an order of magnitude estimate of risk under certain conditions and thereby point to measures that have a realistic chance of being effective.

The object of the Gaussian plume model is to determine the concentration of a substance released into the air as a function of time and distance. Let's suppose that the substance is a small amount of an unspecified radioactive isotope that is released into the air. The likelihood of a given pathway for the particles in the plume can be described by diffusion. Diffusion is a statistical process, where a probability distribution characterizes particle location as a function of position and time.

Let's examine the spread of a radioactive plume resulting from a dirty bomb. Consider the discharge of Q microcuries (μCi) of this radioactive isotope into a stable atmosphere. The stream mixes with the airstream flowing by at some velocity, v (m/sec). In t seconds, a column of air $v \times t$ meters long will have flowed by and has therefore acquired a contamination loading of $Q/vt \cdot \mu Ci/m$.

The activity along a differential element dx is therefore given by $(Q/vt)(dx)$. The activity will begin to spread out laterally as it is carried along in the airstream. The degree of spreading in the horizontal direction is determined by the shifting wind and in the vertical direction by temperature gradients. Particle motion in this case can be modeled as a "random walk," also known as the "drunkard's walk." This is a well-understood process in physics.

The model consists of fitting the particulate spreading to a normal distribution based on the statistical features of random walks. Using the fact that the area under the normal curve is unity, and the total concentration of radioactivity to be expected at any point downwind (x-direction) will not change (i.e., the total amount of contaminant is conserved, but the density will change as a function of distance in exact analogy with the power density of the point source discussed previously), an expression can be written for the concentration of radioactivity as a function of time and space:

$$C_{y,z} = Q / (2\pi vt\sigma_y\sigma_z)e^{-y2/2(\sigma y)2}e^{-z2/2(\sigma z)2}$$

You might recognize this as the normal or Gaussian distribution in multiple dimensions. What this model tells us, and what is important to remember, is that the concentration of contaminants as a function of distance from the release point can be modeled as a normally distributed random variable. Figure 4.6 illustrates the concept of a Gaussian plume.

Atmospheric scientists have studied this problem extensively since it has many applications that have nothing to do with terrorism, such as the effect of pollutants.

As a final note, variations in wind direction have been accounted for in more detailed versions of the model, since these will be extremely influential in determining downstream concentrations. For more technical details, the reader is referred to *Advances in Biological and Chemical Terrorism Countermeasures*, edited by Ronald J. Kendall, Steven M. Presley, Galen P. Austin, and Philip N. Smith; Boca Raton, FL: CRC Press, 2008.

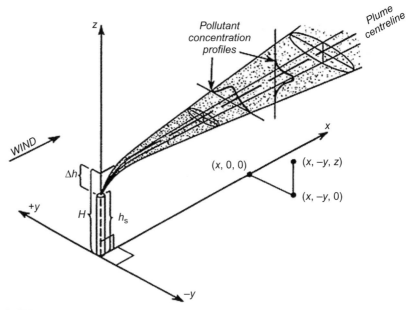

FIGURE 4.6

Gaussian plume. *(From Ministry for the Environment.* http://www.mfe.govt.nz/publications/air/atmospheric-dispersion-modelling-jun04/html/figure2-2.html.)

SUMMARY

Terrorist threats often obey physical laws of nature. These laws can sometimes be used to characterize vulnerability, and quantitative statements of risk can sometimes be developed as a result.

Although exact predictions of the vulnerability to terrorism threats are difficult due to the inherent complexity of physical processes, estimates can be made using simple physical models. Such models are applicable to broad categories of terrorism scenarios.

These models include point source of radiation, harmonic motion, exponential behavior, and Gaussian plumes. A point source of radiation is useful in modeling intensity, harmonic motion can be used to model the response of building elements to explosive loading, and exponential behavior describes many physical processes to include the intensity of radiation as it passes through matter and the concentration of chemical agents in a room as a function of time. Gaussian plumes may be relevant to chemical, biological, and radiological dispersion. Simple mathematical expressions can be used to describe these models, and "back-of-the-envelope" calculations can be used to provide useful if ballpark estimates of risk.

REFERENCE

[1] Shapiro J. Radiation protection: a guide for scientists and physicians. 3rd ed. Cambridge, MA: Harvard University Press; 1990.

Problems

1. Identify one risk factor for the following threat attack vectors against a facility:
   a. Conventional explosives
   b. Chemical agents
   c. Conventional explosives with radioactive material (radiological dispersal device—RDD)

2. A corrosive substance has been released into the air by teenagers who are intent on causing mischief. Unfortunately, local law enforcement officials are not aware of the facts, and they assume it is an act of terrorism. The Department of Homeland Security is called, but sequestration is in effect, and no one answers the phone. Therefore, the local environmental engineer is called in to make some basic calculations on vulnerability. The goal is to notify the local population when it is safe to leave their homes. The engineer assumes that the concentration of the nasty substance decreases exponentially with time.
   a. If the initial concentration is C_0, and the rate of dissipation is R, write an expression that describes the concentration of the corrosive substance as a function of time.
   b. Use the text to specify a solution to the expression in 2a.
   c. Plot the concentration as a function of time using integer units of time.

3. In this chapter we learned that for point sources of energy, the intensity decreases inversely with the square of the distance from the source (i.e., $1/r^2$ where r is distance). Let's say you were able to make an initial measurement of the intensity of a radio signal I at a distance x from the source.
   a. Assuming an open space and no signal reflections or absorptions, what is the signal intensity at a distance $2x$ from the source?
   b. What is the intensity at a distance $3x$ from the source?
   c. Write an expression for the intensity at a distance of $3x$ if the atmosphere attenuated the signal according to exponential decay and the rate constant was $1/x$. (Hint: the intensity decreases as a result of two processes: exponential decay due to the atmosphere and as $1/r^2$ because it emanated from a point source.)

4. An explosion has occurred near your facility, and fortuitously, someone has been operating a video camera that is trained on the window. Even more miraculously, the camera faithfully captures the window displacement in response to the explosive force.
   a. Draw a graph of the window displacement as a function of time if the explosion was due to an M80 firecracker and the force causes the window to vibrate at its natural oscillation frequency of 3 cycles/s. Do not worry about the units

of the graph. The important point is to show the magnitude of the window displacement at its natural oscillation frequency (i.e., its resonant frequency) *relative* to an explosion of greater magnitude (see part b below).

    b. Draw a graph of the window displacement as a function of time if the explosion was due to 10 lb of TNT-equivalent explosive at the same distance as the M80 firecracker. Again, the force of the explosion causes the window to vibrate (but not break!) at the same frequency as in problem 4a above.

    c. What is the period of the natural frequency of vibration of the window?

5. Assume an explosion has occurred near a facility with windows facing the explosion and that the natural oscillation period of the window exceeds the explosive force duration. In that case the impulse dominates the window response as we learned from the text. What would you suggest one could do to the window to reduce the effect of the explosive impulse on the window transient response?

6. A radioactive source is modeled as a point source of energy. The radiation intensity is I at a distance r. What is the intensity at a distance $2r$? $3r$? Plot the intensity as a function of distance for distances of $2r$ to $5r$ from the source.

7. You are a building designer who is concerned about two threats to a new construction project: conventional explosives used by terrorists and high winds. How would the design of the stiffness of the building elements be affected by each threat? (Hint: see the table in supplementary problem 3.)

8. A radiological dispersion device has been detonated and radioactive material is scattered about the area. Each radioactive chunk is assumed to be a point source of radioactive energy.

    a. If you are initially located at a distance r from one chunk, how is the radioactive intensity changed if you move in a circle about the chunk but keep the same separation distance, r?

    b. How could you possibly reduce the radioactive absorption if you could not increase the separation distance from the chunk?

9. The intensity of radiation impinging on your antenna from a local transmitter at a specific location is $1 \cdot W/m^2$.

    a. If you double the distance between the transmitter and the antenna, what is the intensity as seen by the antenna?

    b. What is the change in intensity if you doubled the transmitter power but kept the distance constant?

10. We learned that point sources of energy radiate "isotropically" so that the energy intensity decreases equally in all directions from the energy source. Assuming an open space and no signal reflections/absorptions, what would you expect to happen to the signal intensity of a radiofrequency energy source when you doubled the distance from the source? Tripled the distance from the source? Quadrupled the distance from the source?

11. Discuss the security implications of the effect noted in problem 3 on signal intensity. What mitigation might be applicable if increasing the distance from the source that is radiating company-proprietary information was not feasible?

12. You are the technical security director for a large healthcare facility. You are concerned about the security of radiological materials stored in your facility. A company is trying to sell you a radiological detector, and they show you a graph of the intensity of a radiological source as a function of distance. They then compare the result in the graph with the sensitivity of the detector in an attempt to demonstrate the area of coverage of the sensor relative to a source. They claim to model the radiological material as a point source and show you a graph of radiation intensity versus distance as follows:

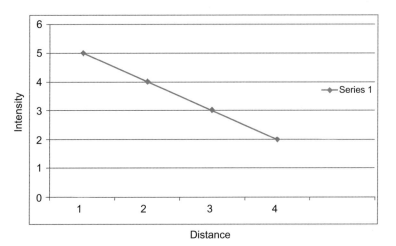

FIGURE 4.7

   a. Is the graph of intensity representative of a point source?
   b. If not, sketch the intensity as a function of distance for a point source. Do not worry about units on the axes. Can you guess the form of the function that is being graphed in 12a above? (Hint: this line is very linear.)
   c. Would you purchase the detector from this company if the sales person's representation about the data was inaccurate?

13. Assume the following Gaussian distributions represent a time sequence of a probability distribution of toxic gas particles in one dimension. The chemical has been released into the air by a terrorist organization that is opposed to the imposition of daylight savings time on the general population. Ignore the caption on the x-axis. Indicate the time sequence of these Gaussian curves. In other words, which curve most likely characterizes the initial or earliest distribution of gas particles, the distribution after some intermediate time interval, and the most recent distribution of particles. Why? Explain your reasoning in terms of the statistics of particle motion in time.

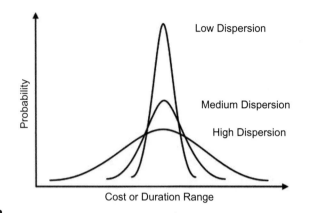

FIGURE 4.8
(From: U.S. Department of Transportation. "Risk Analysis: Objectives of Risk Analysis." http://international. fhwa.dot.gov/riskassess/risk_hcm06_04.cfm.)

14. A terrorist has just detonated an RDD. Fortunately you are at the dentist's office where there are a number of lead aprons available. You quickly wrap these around your body and wait for the coast to clear. A radioactive chunk lands near the office. I_o is the intensity of gamma radiation inside the dentist's office due to the chunk. The intensity of the radiation as it penetrates the lead shield is given by $I_o e^{-kx}$, where I_o is the initial intensity, k is the attenuation rate due to the shield, which we will arbitrarily define as 3/mm, and x is the distance the gamma ray propagates through the lead shield.

   a. By what fraction is I_o reduced after the energy propagates a distance of 3 mm? 6 mm? 9 mm? 12 mm?

   b. Graph the intensity (in units of I_o) as a function of distance for the values noted in part a.

15. Identify a physical, biological, financial, or chemical process that displays exponential decay or growth (i.e., $f(x) = e^{-x}$ or $f(x) = e^x$).

Supplementary Problems

Physical models discussed in this chapter (e.g., the harmonic oscillator and point sources of radiation), along with standard technical machinery such as the concept of a decibel discussed in Appendix D, are directly relevant to the threat of audible information loss.

Although not a threat traditionally associated with terrorism, intelligence gathering and covert data collection could be part of a sophisticated terrorism attack strategy including electronic terrorism. I have therefore included problems related to this topic as a supplement to this chapter. For more details regarding physical threats associated with information compromise, see Young, C. (2010). *Metrics and Methods for Security Risk Management.* Waltham, MA: Syngress.

1. You are the security director for a major U.S. corporation with a significant presence overseas, especially in countries known to provide government support for industrial espionage. Your company has been losing important deals to local competitors and you suspect hanky-panky. However, you also notice that employees are quite lax in handling sensitive information. It is therefore unclear if and/or how information is actually being lost. Outline a high-level but risk-based mitigation strategy that you would communicate to senior management. Note that the corporate culture is loose regarding securing information.

2. Referring to the chart below, and specifically the curve for a stationary source:

   a. What is the effect on barrier attenuation when the Fresnel number is increased from 0.1 to 10? Express your answer in dBs by reading the number directly off the chart.

   b. What is the linear representation for your answer to a? Recall $dB = 10 \log(x/y)$.

   c. Is barrier attenuation linear with Fresnel number in this range? Why or why not? (Hint: if you increase the Fresnel number from x to y, does barrier attenuation increase proportionately?)

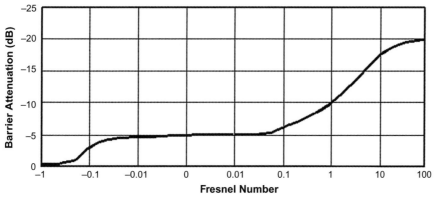

FIGURE 4.9
(From U.S. Department of Transportation. http://www.fhwa.dot.gov/environment/noise/noise_barriers/design_construction/design/design03.cfm.*)*

3. You are the information security director of a major U.S. corporation. Your cheap CEO who is a graduate of a prestigious MBA program has approved moving into an overseas headquarters within a shared facility inside a country known for state-sponsored industrial espionage. To make matters worse, conference rooms

in this facility are contiguous with uncontrolled space. Your CEO is arguing for the conference rooms to be built from the cheapest materials possible.

You are especially concerned about information loss from passersby. Refer to the chart below and answer the following questions:

	Wall/Barrier Acoustic Attenuation Factors
< 100 Hz	Stiffness is predominant in attenuation. Resonances exist.
100 – 1000 Hz	Doubling the mass or sound frequency doubles the attenuation.
1000 – 4000 Hz	Resonances @ coincidence angles

    a. Would you recommend a relatively light or heavy material for conference room wall construction to reduce the vulnerability to speech-borne information loss in the 100 to 1000-Hz frequency range?

    b. Would you recommend a flexible or stiff material to attenuate sound energy in the 0 to 100-Hz frequency range?

    c. What would you do in terms of treating the wall in order to simultaneously reduce the risk of information loss in both frequency ranges?

    d. It turns out that the wall can be modeled as a harmonic oscillator at low audio frequencies. Therefore, the angular frequency of wall oscillation in response to audio vibrations (e.g., speech) is proportional to $\sqrt{(k/m)}$, where k is wall stiffness and m is wall mass. From this expression, would you expect the wall frequency of oscillation to increase or decrease with increasing mass? What about the effect on the wall frequency of vibration with increasing wall stiffness?

4. You have become fed up with the CEO of your previous company and you now work as the security director for a more enlightened firm. You are confronted with the problem that although most of your new company's conference rooms are located in interior space, and are therefore only contiguous with company-occupied offices, a few conference rooms are located adjacent to public space.

    a. Discuss the risk associated with information loss with respect to the conference rooms that are located in interior space versus public space. (There is no right or wrong answer here. The point is to provide a risk-based analysis.)

    b. Sketch out a qualitative argument for the cost effectiveness of installing absorbing material to reduce the vulnerability to audible information loss.

5. Referring to the graph below that depicts transmission loss as a function of frequency for various materials, which material would you recommend and why? Consider the cost of the material (per unit area) as well as practical issues (e.g., weight) in your argument to management.

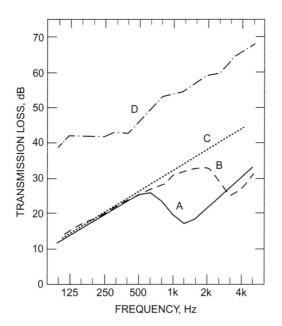

FIGURE 4.10
Transmission losses of typical single-leaf walls, A: 16 mm plywood, 10 kg/m², STC 21; B: 13 mm wallboard, 10 kg/m², STC 28; C: 1.3 mm steel, 10 kg/m², STC 30; D: 100 mm concrete, 235 kg/m², STC 52. *(From http://archive.nrc-cnrc.gc.ca/eng/ibp/irc/cbd/building-digest-239.html. National Research Council of Canada.)*

6. You are the director of information security at a high-profile financial company that deals with sensitive client information. The employees want to utilize "hands-free" telephones that radiate electromagnetic energy to a base station. In the interest of continued employment, you have accepted the fact that you cannot win the argument to prevent their usage. However, you intend to manage the risk to the extent possible and practical. You are aware that there are buildings with unknown occupants within 100 feet of your facility on all sides as well as unknown tenants on other floors within your building.

   a. Discuss the risk factors associated with the use of this product relative to the threat of audible information loss.

   b. What risk-mitigation methods would you consider suggesting to senior management and why?

   c. How might you model the hands-free telephone in order to make simple estimates of the vulnerability to audible information loss as a function of distance? (Hint: the telephone antenna is small compared to the distance from the source and the wavelength of radiated energy.)

CHAPTER 5

Exploiting Terrorism Uncertainty

5.1 INTRODUCTION: ADDRESSING TERRORISM RISK FACTORS

What constitutes "success" to a terrorist? Before 9/11 it typically meant harming or killing as many people as possible *without getting caught or causing harm to oneself*. This is one reason 9/11 was a game-changer, since that model no longer applied. Nowadays suicide bombings are common among certain groups who commit acts of terrorism to achieve their ends. For these individuals, getting caught in the act is of little concern. This is an important consideration in developing an effective risk-mitigation strategy.

Nevertheless, the principle that drives suicidal terrorists is also relevant to other terrorism attack vectors. Namely, terrorists seek to achieve the maximum destructive effect and elicit the most fear as a result of their actions.

In addition to some form of weapon, a terrorist will typically require physical access to the target in order to use the weapon of choice to maximum effect. But the devil is in the details, and in this case that aphorism is particularly apt. What about the target itself?

One of the scariest things about terrorism is the seemingly random occurrence of incidents. As discussed previously, terrorism is anything but random, except that by happenstance the victims are in the wrong place at the wrong time.

The terrorist has near-infinite choices with respect to target selection and timing, but attack parameters are greatly influenced by his or her agenda as well as physical constraints associated with the chosen attack method. The inherent uncertainty associated with precisely where and when an attack will occur gives the perception of randomness.

In fact, there is a definite bias in the terrorist modus operandi. That bias is introduced by the aforementioned cause or agenda. For example, if the maker of fatty fast food is the focus of terrorist enmity, then purveyors of fast food are more likely to be targets than other industries.

In the parlance introduced in Chapter 3, these facilities are said to have a greater potential for attack. If the U.S. government is considered to be the enemy du jour, then entities associated with Uncle Sam are more likely to be in the terrorists' crosshairs.

As a terrorist you likely require three things to conduct your mission: a target symbolizing the cause you are championing, physical or electronic access to that target, and a weapon that maximizes death, destruction, and/or chaos. At first glance it does not seem all that difficult to design a counterterrorism strategy. Of course the difficulty is in predicting what, when, and how a terrorist attack will occur. There are also different varieties of terrorism. In other words, there are different causes in addition to different modes of attack. For example, the strategy to address Charles Whitman's method of terrorism could be quite different than the one used to counter Al Qaeda. The electronic terrorism landscape is a relatively new frontier.

Appreciating the bias introduced by a terrorist group's agenda helps in developing a counterterrorism strategy. This bias is ultimately reflected in the risk factors that drive the likelihood and vulnerability components of risk.

5.2   RISK FACTOR-RELATED INCIDENTS; INDIRECT MEASUREMENTS OF SECURITY RISK

In the absence of statistically significant data on terrorist threats, there is a meaningful way to measure terrorism risk. Incidents associated with a risk factor for a threat or threat attack vector can sometimes be identified. Such incidents provide statistical evidence of risk in the absence of an actual threat incident. *The absence of a threat incident does not imply an absence of risk.* Measuring incidents associated with the risk factors for a given threat was mentioned in Chapter 2 as one of the three food groups worth measuring to assess risk.

From a statistical perspective, risk factor-related incidents typically occur more frequently than the threat itself. The point is that incidents related to a given terrorism threat's risk factors reveal underlying risk.

Let's examine the theft of valuables as an example, although this method could just as easily apply to a terrorism attack vector. The number of theft incidents might be quite low for a particular building or campus. In general, people are honest or are afraid of getting caught. However, the rate of unauthorized physical access, possibly due to piggybacking, could be quite high. The fact that individuals have accessed the premises in this way increases the vulnerability to theft as well as the potential for occurrence due to increased opportunity, irrespective of whether thefts have actually occurred.

So instances of unauthorized physical access can be said to provide an *indirect* measurement of risk with respect to theft.

In other words, we can estimate the vulnerability and/or the potential for theft by measuring instances of a risk factor for theft. Specifically, these represent instances of increased opportunity to commit an act of terrorism by virtue of unauthorized physical access to the space of interest.

Note that despite such indirect measurements, one cannot make the following statement on risk: "There is a 20 percent likelihood of a theft of valuables as a result of 100 people being granted unauthorized physical access to this space during the previous reporting period." However, one can say something like the following: "There is a significant increase in the potential for theft of valuables due to a 50 percent increase in incidents of unauthorized physical access from the previous reporting period."

In other words, although one has successfully made a quantitative statement on risk by indirect measurement, this does not say anything about the precise likelihood of a future threat incident. It does allow one to make qualitative statements on the increased potential for a future threat incident based on a statistical characterization of risk factor-related incidents.

It is important to measure only meaningful risk factor artifacts. For example, one might make the valid claim that nighttime is a risk factor for certain types of violent crime. Yet it is probably not particularly instructive to count the number of hours without daylight and hope to learn anything meaningful about risk.

On the other hand, it might be quite informative to count the number of crimes of violence that have occurred in close proximity to your facility at night versus the number that occur during daylight hours. Such a statistic might drive a requirement for visual monitoring of the immediate environs at night, which would likely initiate research into appropriate CCTV systems with an infrared capability or external illumination with a specified luminosity. If statistics regarding one's own environment do not exist, obtaining statistics regarding risk factors for comparable scenarios can be instructive.

The fact that a risk factor for a given threat is nighttime activity could certainly affect one or more operational requirements of relevant security controls and methods. To belabor the obvious, if criminal activity occurring close to your facility at night is a risk factor for crime committed at your facility, then an operational requirement for security controls being contemplated should be nighttime functionality.

Let's discuss a more concrete example of risk factor measurements. I did some consulting work for a large healthcare organization with a number of member hospitals. They deployed metal detectors in some of their emergency rooms but omitted them in others. They also did a very intelligent thing: they kept accurate statistics on weapons confiscations at each metal detector.

Historically, emergency rooms are the most likely venue for physical violence in a hospital setting. I did a simple statistical analysis of the data relating to confiscated weapons at each metal detector. Note that this did not involve counting incidents of violence, which were very low in number. But I was counting the number of confiscations of concealed weapons.

The possession of a weapon in that setting represents a significant risk factor for lethal violence. I suspect most law enforcement professionals would agree with me, especially those who have worked in an urban hospital emergency room on a Friday or Saturday night.

Importantly, and in addition to the *hundreds* of confiscated weapons per month, the statistics showed a nearly constant ratio of weapons confiscated to the number of people screened. Surprisingly, the ratio was nearly the same for the suburban and urban locations. Table 5.1 reveals the actual numbers as well as the weapons-to-inspections ratio.

Counting the number of confiscated weapons is an indirect measurement of the potential and vulnerability components of risk. The results argued strongly for the installation of metal detectors (and possibly X-ray units) in every hospital emergency room under that organization's aegis, a recommendation I made based on this simple analysis. I suspect it would be good practice for any hospital emergency room based on this compelling if limited data.

This raises a key question regarding security and the organizational culture. A security professional will be required to assess the components of risk as well as gauge the general tolerance for recommended security measures relative to the culture of the organization being evaluated. It is always worth remembering that such measures will invariably cause inconvenience for

Table 5.1 Weapon Confiscations at Emergency Room Metal Detectors

	Total Number of Weapons Confiscated (2010)	Average Number of Weapons Confiscated Per Month	Monthly Fluctuation (Standard Deviation) of Confiscated Weapons	Total Number of Inspections (2010)	Weapons Confiscated Per Inspection (to Three Significant Figures)
Hospital 1	3654	305	38.9	105,045	0.034
Hospital 2	7391	616	64.4	208,646	0.035
Hospital 3	3720	310 (7 months)	24.0	133,802	0.028

the people being protected. This is not to suggest that one must change the methodology if measures prove to be unpopular. The juxtaposition of security and convenience is at the heart of any risk management strategy, and this sometimes requires difficult trade-offs. But the inconvenience factor actually reinforces the need to justify such decisions, which translates to rigorously evaluating the components of risk for each impactful threat and attack vector. This is especially the case if an inconvenient measure does not comport with the organization's culture.

5.3 THE "PROBABILITY OF PROTECTION" METHOD

What about making a direct measurement of the likelihood component of risk? This can be tricky, and as noted in Chapter 3, we must be careful to interpret the word "likely" correctly. The comparison between terrorism and games of chance relative to the likelihood of their respective outcomes is illustrative.

One cannot hope to know the number of possible outcomes in a terrorist threat scenario in the same way we know the outcomes in a game of chance such as dice. With a game of dice, all outcomes are known before the dice are even thrown. Specifically, there are a total of 36 outcomes, and therefore everyone seated at the craps table knows the probability of any single outcome. Importantly, everyone at that table also knows that a throw is definitely about to occur.

What kind of meaningful statement can be made about likelihood and terrorism, if any? It turns out that one can use the threat risk factors to make a quantitative statement about likelihood. The road to salvation involves a bit of a fudge, although it is a well-known technique employed by physicists to model many physical systems.

It works by essentially throwing up our hands and admitting that the magnitude of identified risk factors is unknown. In fact, they are *unknowable*. However, this leads to an assumption that the relevant risk factors are normally distributed random variables with scenario-specific limits. It is these limits that connect the specific scenario to reality.

We then plug this normal distribution into a physical model that characterizes the threat, and the result is a distribution of terrorism/security risk scenarios. We can then determine the probability that the proposed mitigation addresses the spectrum of scenarios. This technique yields the probability of protection offered by a specific risk-mitigation measure.

Although this author and my colleague David B. Chang were apparently the first to apply this method to security problems, it is actually a variant of the famous Monte Carlo technique, a well-known method with application to many fields.[1]

Specifically, it exploits the statistical uncertainty inherent in terrorism scenarios. In the following sections several examples of its application to specific security problems will be described.

5.3.1   The Minimum Number of Required Security Officers

The probability of protection method is first applied to a seemingly pedestrian (no pun intended) security problem. The reasons for using this example are twofold. The first is that the appropriate number of security officers is a key parameter in a security risk-mitigation strategy. Interestingly, a literature search did not identify a single analytic method that might be applied to this problem despite the significant use of security officers.

The second reason this example has been chosen is that it is a relatively simple problem and therefore demonstrates the applicability of the probability of protection method to general security issues. It is admittedly not an optimal physical model, since the identified risk factor, hallway population, might not be the driving risk factor associated with the "threat" of inadequate response time. The point here is mostly to demonstrate the relevance and mechanics of the technique. Refer to problem number 8 at the end of this chapter to see another potential application of this technique to another security problem.

Because of the importance of security officers in implementing key physical security controls (e.g., incident response and visual monitoring), a calculation of the required number of security officers could represent a crucial security risk metric. Furthermore, if the number of security officers dropped below some specified figure, this might signify an unacceptable level of risk, which is precisely the point of a security metric.

Of course there are many variables that might influence the number of required security officers. We saw in Chapter 1 that museums use their own model, which by necessity differs from other organizations with different business models. For museums, the paradigm is to saturate the premises with security technology and security officers in order to compensate for a lack of other controls, which are impractical in a museum setting.

A potential driver of the number of required security officers in a more traditional setting is the ability to respond to security incidents in a timely fashion. The operational word here is "timely," and this is a matter of judgment combined with the tolerance for risk. In this model, it is assumed that security officers on foot would be required to arrive on scene in 1 min or less from the time of incident notification. This is a stringent requirement, but it could easily be adjusted according to the assessed risk.

The 1-min response time represents an upper bound (i.e., the maximum) on timely response, which translates to a lower bound (i.e., the minimum) on the required density of security officers. This is clearly not the only criterion that should be applied in making this determination. But it might be useful in confirming intuition about resourcing and thereby provide a "rule of thumb" on staffing during various shifts.

Ideally the model also enhances security officer visibility during business hours. Visibility is an important feature for some security resources, and one where the benefits are not necessarily measurable or even tangible. Fortunately, the requirement for increased officer density occurs with greater hallway populations, so this model is in keeping with that requirement.

Once the maximum response time is agreed, two risk factors affect the vulnerability component of risk (note: the "threat" is not responding in a timely manner as alluded to previously): (1) the varying density of the hallway population, which is likely to be strongly correlated with the time of day, and (2) the speed of the individual security officers.

First, how do we account for the uncertainty in the hallway population density? The number of individuals in the hallway is modeled as fixed points in a lattice. It is assumed that they are fixed because their speed is much less than the security officers rushing to an incident. Moreover, the points in the lattice are assumed to be staggered so that a security officer walking briskly or running through the hall must follow a zigzag pattern. The rate of zigs and zags is dependent on the population density. Figure 5.1 is a cartoon illustrating the difference in the security officer's path in responding to an incident when there are people in the hallway and when no such obstacles are present.

**Security Officer Paths
and Hallway Population**

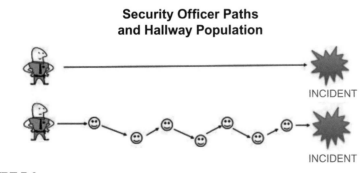

FIGURE 5.1
Security officer responding to an incident with and without a hallway population.

Of course, this pattern is physically unrealistic because the spacing between individuals is merely fixed and people in hallways are not statues. However, it is intended to be indicative of the obstacles that affect the incident response time. If there were no people in the hallway as exemplified in the top scenario of Figure 5.1, and the officer's rate of speed was constant, his or her arrival time is given by a simple expression:

$$\text{distance traveled} = \text{officer speed} \times \text{time of officer travel}$$

However, if there are people present, the officer will presumably zig and zag, where each zig and zag is assumed to be a fixed length. Therefore, we can use simple geometry to calculate the additional distance needed to move around each individual in the hallway. This is simply given by the Pythagorean theorem, which you no doubt recall from junior high school geometry class. Here we assume that each diversion around a human obstacle is approximated by a right triangle. If each leg of this triangle is 3 ft in length, the extra distance traveled per zig or zag is 1.4 ft.

The number of zigs and zags that occurs between the officer's starting point and the incident location results in extra travel distance for the security officer. The inverse of this effective distance yields the required security officer density to ensure the maximum response time is not exceeded. The hallway population distribution combined with the officer's speed determines the probability of achieving the required security metric, i.e., arriving within 1 min of incident notification.

As noted above, and in the limit of zero hallway population (e.g., late at night and on weekends), the maximum response time is set exclusively by the officer's speed. If the maximum permitted response time is 60 s, and the officer can run at 10 mph or 15 ft/s, this implies that the maximum distance an officer can travel to achieve the minimum response time is 900 ft.

Using the limit dictated by the assumed maximum response time and guard speed, the equation that describes the officer density, S, is dictated by the added distance and can be shown to be the following expression:

$$S = \{vt[1 - 1.4\,\rho]\}^{-1}$$

In the expression for S, v is the officer speed, t is the maximum response time that is arbitrarily set equal to 60 s, and ρ is the population density in the hallway.

The significant parameters or risk factors in the model are ρ, the hallway population density, and v, the officer speed. Both will strongly influence S, although I suspect that officer speed will in general vary over a narrow range. Therefore, three representative values have been chosen within that range pursuant to estimating the effect on the minimum required guard density, S.

Ideally one might conduct an experiment where a security officer runs a gauntlet using various hallway population densities. Repeating this many times would indeed yield a distribution of response times. One could then make statistically significant statements about the likelihood of "success," which we know is defined as responding to an incident in 1 min or less. Unfortunately, conducting such an experiment is not practical.

However, one could easily perform a computer simulation of that experiment. Such a simulation was performed using a Monte Carlo technique with an open-source version of Octave. Monte Carlo simulations are also possible in other popular commercial software products such as Excel. Specifically, 1000 points from a normal distribution of population densities was randomly selected. To reiterate, the hallway population density, a risk factor for not achieving an on-time security officer response, is assumed to be a normally distributed random variable.

The procedure is illustrated at a high level in Figure 5.2. A normal distribution of hallway population densities is plugged into the expression for S, the model, for the required number of security officers.

Reasonable values of the mean and standard deviation of hallway population densities have been selected in order to construct the model. The mean and standard deviation completely determine the shape of the normal probability distribution.

A more rigorous study would run multiple simulations using different distributions based on a better understanding of the mean and dispersion of

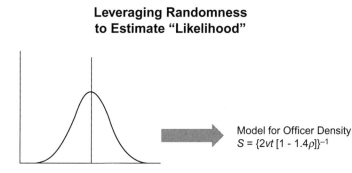

**Leveraging Randomness
to Estimate "Likelihood"**

Normal Distribution of Hallway Population Densities, ρ

Model for Officer Density
$S = \{2vt\,[1 - 1.4\rho]\}^{-1}$

FIGURE 5.2
Probability of protection method applied to the minimum number of security officers.

hallway population densities. This could be accomplished by observing hallway dynamics over various time periods. Such estimates would yield more educated assumptions and would therefore lead to more accurate estimates.

In this case, the mean hallway population density is assumed to be 0.15 individuals/linear foot with a standard deviation of 0.04. Each simulation was run using three representative officer speeds, v: 10 ft/s, 7.5 ft/s, and 5 ft/s, respectively. These results are shown below in Figures 5.3A–C.

The results show the logarithm of the guard density (guard/foot) versus their respective probability of occurrence. To convert to a linear and therefore more intuitive representation of officer density, one must exponentiate the values on the x-axis (i.e., 10^{-x}) and multiply the results by 1000.

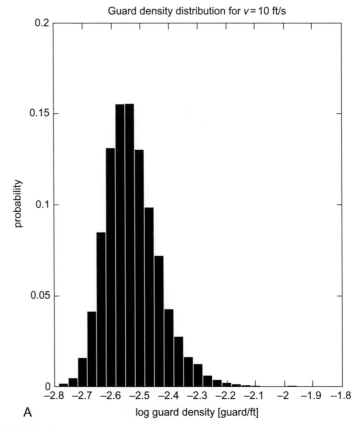

FIGURE 5.3A–C

Probability distribution of a required security officer density for three security officer speeds. *(Simulation results courtesy of Jean Gobin, Stroz Friedberg.)*

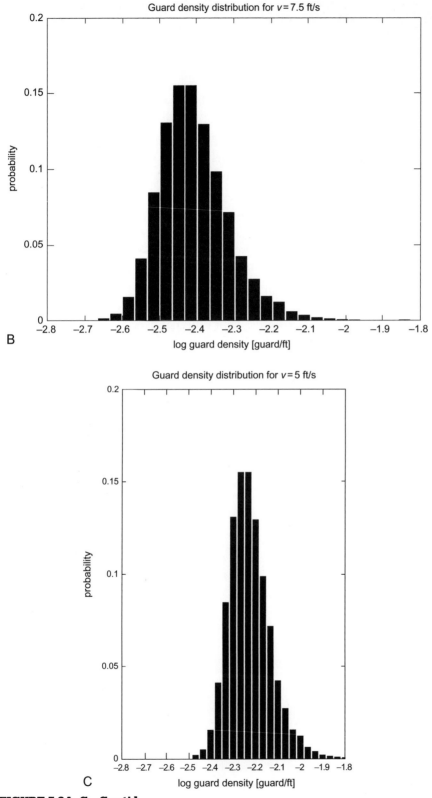

FIGURE 5.3A–C—Cont'd

Cumulative distributions have also been computed as shown in Figure 5.4. These specify the guard density required to achieve a 95 percent or greater probability of an on-time journey for a given officer speed.

From these graphs one can quote a confidence interval for exceeding the maximum allowed response time for a given security officer speed. This can then be used to specify an appropriate security metric for the minimum number of security officers in a facility.

For example, to achieve a 95 percent confidence (i.e., 1.96 standard deviations from the mean) that a security officer running at 7.5 ft/s will arrive at a security incident within 1 minute of notification requires a security officer density of 0.008 officers/linear foot (i.e., 8 officers/1000 ft).

This seems a bit high, but recall that this figure was calculated for horizontal trajectories only, so the security risk metric actually could be applied to multiple floors in parallel. In other words, eight officers can cover 1000 ft horizontally

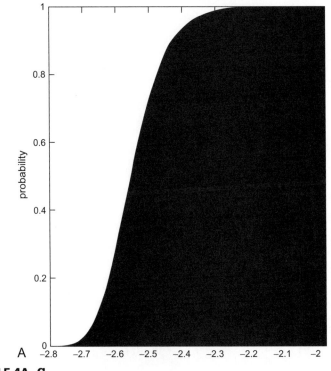

cumulative distribution for $v = 10$ ft/s

FIGURE 5.4A–C
An on-time arrival of 95 percent or greater probability in responding to an incident for three security officer speeds. *(Results courtesy of Jean Gobin, Stroz Friedberg.)*

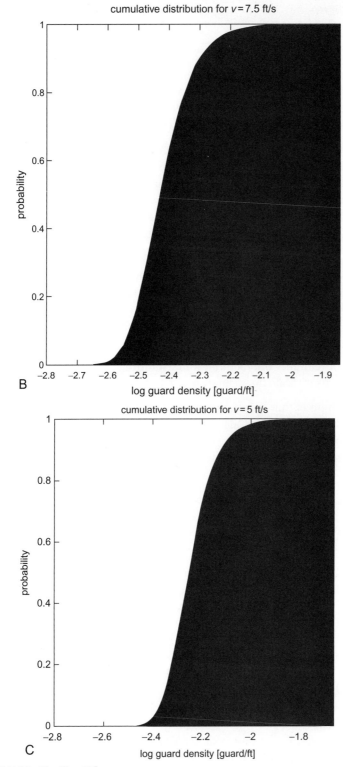

FIGURE 5.4A–C—Cont'd

across multiple floors simultaneously. If one assumes a 10-ft vertical separation per floor (i.e., one story), this represents a relatively small distance compared to the total horizontal floor length. Therefore, a single set of officers could reasonably be expected to cover multiple floors.

Also, my colleague Chris Briscoe pointed out after the simulations were performed that this figure is actually double the required number of officers since two officers running in opposite directions toward the same incident need only cover half the distance as a single officer running to the same event. So the more precise expression for S includes a coefficient of 2 in the denominator when considering the linear hallway scenario.

This highish estimate for the required density of officers might also suggest that unrealistic values have been assumed for the mean and standard deviation of the normal distribution of hallway population densities and/or distorted ranges of officer speeds. I note that the maximum officer speed of 10 ft/s equates to 6.8 mph, which is hardly breakneck speed.

Finally, the maximum 1-min response time might be aggressive. The previous discussion highlights the fact that understanding scenario-specific conditions will lead to more realistic simulations.

The point here is that this methodology provides a means of analyzing current security practices and also yields a method for quantitatively assessing risk. In this case the risk is the likelihood not achieving the 1-min response time by security officers. Refining the model over time is essential to making it useful.

Figure 5.5 uses the previous data to display the sensitivity of security officer density as a function of security officer speed in order to achieve a minimum 95 percent confidence of not exceeding the maximum allowable incident arrival time of 1 min.

We see from this curve that the required officer densities are approximately 11 officers/1000 feet, 8 officers/1000 ft, and 6 officers/1000 ft for officer speeds of 5 ft/s, 7.5 ft/s, and 10 ft/s, respectively. Again, these numbers should not be considered immutable for the reasons previously cited.

5.3.2   Explosive Blasts and the Probability of Window Protection

Let's consider a more complicated application of the probability of protection method. Here it is used to examine the vulnerability of windows to vehicle-borne explosives, a problem with great relevance to counterterrorism. Debris from shattered glass is the biggest contributor to injury and death in explosive

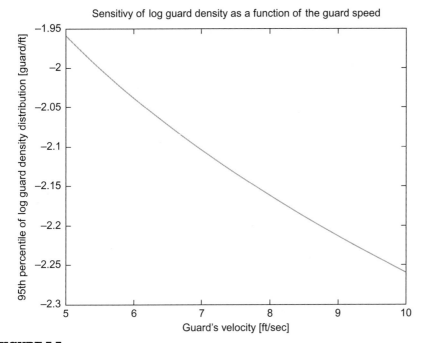

FIGURE 5.5

Sensitivity of guard density to a 60-s incident response time. *(Graphic courtesy of Jean Gobin, Stroz Friedberg.)*

incidents. The following discussion is based on the results of a paper by this author and David B. Chang.[1]

As in the security officer response scenario presented in the last section, a statistical characterization of the vulnerability component of risk has been created using scenario-driven conditions. However in this case, the statistical method is applied to a simple model for window-explosive response. This enables the generation of confidence limits for window behavior under explosive loading.

As with the security officer problem, this entails accepting the inherent uncertainty of several risk factors for the vulnerability to this threat. In this case, the explosive payload and the distance from the explosive source are the risk factors and, importantly, are assumed to be normally distributed random variables. These will be used to determine the likelihood of window protection relative to the spectrum of possible distance-payload scenarios.

It is also important to appreciate that the prescribed limits on the risk factors are scenario-specific. These limits are what couple the problem to the real world. Uncertainty does not confer the right to ignore reality.

These models yield probability distributions for payload, $F_m(m)$, and distance, $F_r(r)$ as shown in Figures 5.6 and 5.7:

It is now possible to establish a joint probability distribution. This is the product of the individual distributions for payload and distance: $F_{mr}(m,r) = F_m(m) \, F_r(r)$ using the numerical values specified in $F_m(m)$ and $F_r(r)$ as shown in Figure 5.8.

The joint probability distribution function has a single maximum at (m_0, r_0) with a spread in the TNT-equivalent mass m, determined by the dispersion in

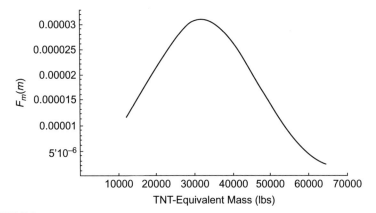

FIGURE 5.6

Probability distribution for payloads.

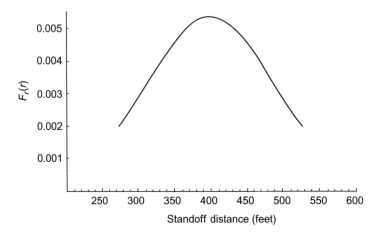

FIGURE 5.7

Probability distribution for distance.

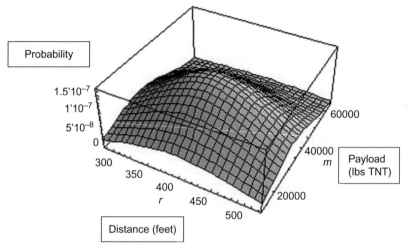

FIGURE 5.8
Joint probability distribution for explosive payload and distance.

payload values δm, and a spread in the standoff distance r, as determined by the dispersion or spread in distance values δr.

A two-dimensional contour plot of this three-dimensional joint probability distribution is shown in Figure 5.9. All combinations of explosive payload and distance on a circle have the same probability.

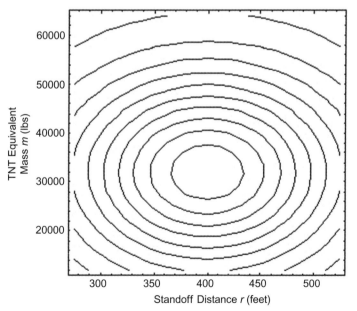

FIGURE 5.9
Contour plot-joint probability distribution for payload and distance.

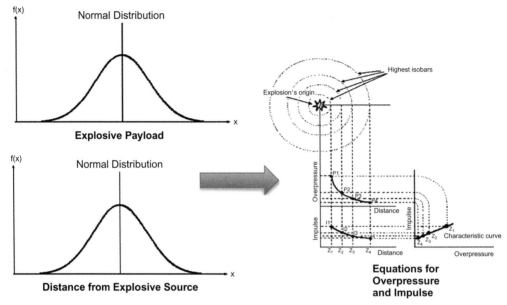

FIGURE 5.10

The probability of protection method and explosive loading.

Figure 5.10 illustrates the probability of protection procedure applied to windows relative to vehicle-borne explosives. In summary, we have assumed explosive payload and distance from the source are normally distributed random variables. These are combined to yield a joint probability distribution, and they are applied to equations that describe the window response as follows.

Recall that the goal is to develop confidence levels that a particular window design will provide adequate blast protection. This is accomplished by applying the joint probability distribution for distance and explosive payload to a model for the window response to explosive loading.

The response of the window system can be modeled as a single-degree-of-freedom (SDOF) system. This is equivalent to viewing the window system as a simple mass on a spring with a force constant and driven by a forcing function (i.e., the explosion).

The physical model is illustrated in Figure 5.11. Recall this diagram was introduced in Chapter 4 when harmonic motion was first discussed. The force F in this case is the explosive blast, the window is the mass m, k is the window

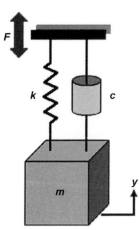

FIGURE 5.11

Single degree of freedom system. *(From FEMCI the Book.* http://femci.gsfc.nasa.gov/random/MilesEqn.html.*)*

stiffness, c represents any internal damping of the force, and y is the window displacement in response to the force.

The conditions that determine the response of the mass to a force were also previously recounted in Chapter 4, but these bear repeating.

Differing elements of the building will vary in their natural period of oscillation in response to a force, i.e., the duration of one complete cycle of its natural frequency. The response of each building element to an explosion is a function of its natural period of oscillation relative to the duration of interaction with the blast.

Specifically, the response of a mass on a spring to a transient force is qualitatively different when the natural oscillation period is greater or less than the force duration. In the former case, the impulse determines the initial velocity of the mass response, while in the latter the displacement of the mass is practically proportional to the force throughout its application.

Since it is the impulse and overpressure that determine damage to a facility as a result of an explosive force, understanding how these quantities behave with distance and time is critical to analyzing explosive blast scenarios. In the language of risk, physical proximity to the explosive source and the magnitude of the explosive payload are risk factors for damage by explosive-type threats.

A unique design curve can be generated for specific values of pressure, impulse, and the system natural oscillation frequency and such graphs are generally

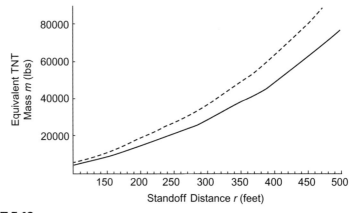

FIGURE 5.12
Design curves for window blast protection.

referred to as pressure-impulse (P-I) curves. This P-I curve can be parameterized in terms of payload and distance as shown in Figure 5.12. The solid curve has been chosen to pass through a design specification corresponding to pressure and impulse values of 8 psi and 170 psi-ms, respectively, where the natural period of oscillation for the particular window under evaluation is 0.11 s (i.e., $57 \, s^{-1}$ angular frequency).

The dashed curve has been chosen to pass through design specifications corresponding to pressure and impulse of 16 psi and 185 psi-ms, respectively. Again, $57 \, s^{-1}$ is the window natural oscillation period. When considered monolithically (i.e., the window is analyzed as a unified entity rather than examine individual components of the window), the window will withstand combinations of distance and explosive payload that lie below these values of the design curve.

Superimposing these design curves onto the contour plot of the joint probability distribution of explosive scenarios and integrating the probability distribution $F_{mr}(m,r)$ with respect to r and m reveal the probability of maintaining window integrity under explosive loading.

The results are shown in Figure 5.13. All points (i.e., payload-distance combinations) below the solid and dashed lines are protected by the respective window designs. Specifically, there is 80 percent confidence that an 8 psi/170 psi-ms window design specification will withstand the spectrum of scenario-specific payload-distance combinations. There is 91 percent confidence that the window will withstand the same distribution of payload-distance combinations if a 16 psi/185 psi-ms window design specification is used.

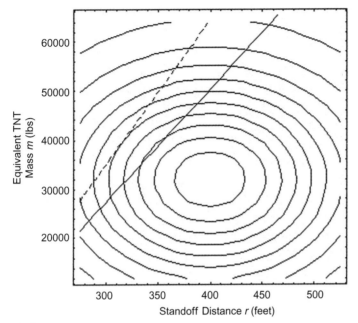

FIGURE 5.13

Confidence limits for explosive blast protection for two window designs.

5.4 THE PROBABILITY OF PROTECTION METHOD SUMMARY

A qualitative summary of the probability of protection method is provided below. Listing the steps in this way might be helpful in recognizing when this procedure is applicable in addition to demonstrating how to apply it:

- Identify a risk metric for a specific threat (e.g., limits on window breakage under explosive loading, minimum number of security officers, bollard kinetic energy rating).
- Establish a model/equation for the risk metric in terms of a risk factor(s) of unknown magnitude.
- Assume the risk factor is a normally distributed random variable with scenario-specific limits.
- Plug the normal distribution into the model/equation.
- Calculate the confidence interval (i.e., likelihood) in achieving a specific value of the risk metric.
- Estimate the probability of protection based on the conditions dictated by the model.

Note that this technique has limitations. Many risk factors might affect the components of risk for a given threat. For example, for the security officer response, a timely response does not guarantee protection from threats, and the response time of security officers does not solely depend on the population in the hallway.

In addition, recall that ranges of values for key parameters in the security officer model were established by guessing. With respect to the window protection model, this method does not examine the performance of specific window components, but treats the window as a monolithic structure. Therefore, a failure of one of these components under explosive loading could occur and not be accounted for using this technique.

Significant assumptions often have to be made to make the problem tractable. An example is specifying that the security officers run around fixed objects in the hallway without changing speed.

However, the aforementioned do not undermine the overall viability or applicability of the method. Despite its limitations, it can be useful in estimating the likelihood of achieving a successful risk mitigation strategy.

5.5   PHYSICAL ACCESS CONTROL SYSTEM RISK STATISTICS

One approach to measuring security risk is to invoke statistical processes that are applicable, assuming risk factors are random variables. I often take a cue from Mother Nature, where examples of statistical processes abound (e.g., evolution and Brownian motion). With respect to a security risk, the probability of a protection method enables one to model the vulnerability component of risk as a statistical process.

In this section an attempt is made to examine the risk associated with the threat of physical access system enrollment errors. The following is admittedly a very simple model with significant assumptions. However, despite its simplicity, it highlights the complexity associated with physical access system administration and the associated risk of unauthorized physical access.

This approach might take some work to be appreciated. The formalism is presented here in the hope that it will highlight issues associated with large/complex environments, and thereby lead to a broader examination of physical access risk.

As has been mentioned numerous times, a risk factor for numerous security threats is unauthorized physical access to restricted space. Measuring a risk factor like the number of unauthorized physical access incidents represents an indirect measurement of the risk associated with a threat like theft or electronic terrorism where the latter would be affected by physical access to a network port. So, one indicator of risk for both physical and electronic threats might be the likelihood of a programming error in assigning access privileges as part of the physical access control system enrollment process.

It is important to point out that using a completely statistical approach to address physical access risk has limitations, particularly for smaller environments. However, this approach becomes increasingly relevant for more complex physical environments, and this is also where automated enrollment systems could add the most value as a security control.

For companies with thousands of employees, and that use a unified global physical access control platform, maintaining proper access control across disparate groups with varying access privileges can be challenging. The key operational issue is the assurance that employees are assigned appropriate physical access privileges as part of the system enrollment process. The following definitions and assumptions apply to this model:

1. A role is characterized by a unique set of physical access privileges.
2. There is a unique set of card readers that facilitates physical access to all individuals assigned to that role.
3. Employees are granted physical access privileges based on their assigned role.
4. A physical access error occurs when an employee is granted a physical access privilege that is not consistent with his or her assigned role.
5. A card reader that erroneously denies access to a restricted area is not considered an error.
6. Each employee must have a role.
7. Each employee can only be assigned one role.
8. Every physically restricted space has a card reader.
9. Enrollment errors occur at random.

If there are N roles in an organization, the probability that an individual is randomly selected for an incorrect role is $1/(N-1)$. Note that the denominator is $N-1$ rather than N because one of the N roles is the correct one. Random enrollment errors probably do occur as a result of distractions, complexities, and/or miscommunications.

But note that knowing the rate of errors in a physical access enrollment process does not address the important question on risk. What we seek is the probability that an individual is afforded physical access to a restricted space due to a mistake in the enrollment process.

Even though each role is unique, and therefore has a correspondingly unique set of card readers linked to that role, some subset of card readers will belong to multiple roles. Therefore, even if a person has been erroneously assigned to a role, some of the card readers in the erroneous role could in fact be appropriate, and therefore he or she should legitimately have access to those restricted spaces.

So the probability of having unauthorized physical access to a restricted space is given by the probability of being assigned to an incorrect role times the fraction of nonauthorized readers within that erroneous role.

Let N be the total number of roles, T is the total number of card readers, and M is the number of authorized card readers within an erroneously assigned role.

Previously it was explained that the probability of being assigned an incorrect role at random is $1/(N-1)$. The probability of having access to an unauthorized card reader in that erroneously assigned role is $(T-M)/T$. Therefore, the probability of being granted unauthorized physical access to a restricted space equals the probability of being assigned an incorrect role times the probability of having access to an unauthorized card reader in that erroneously assigned role. This expression is given by $1/(N-1) \times (T-M)/T$.

Plugging in some numbers, if $N = 100$ roles, $T = 1000$ card readers, and $M = 50$ card readers, we get that the probability of randomly granting unauthorized physical access to an individual at one or more readers is 0.0096 or approximately one in a hundred.

Note that this calculation applies to one individual enrollment. Let's assume we have a 10,000-person organization. What is the probability of at least one individual having unauthorized access to at least one card reader given 10,000 enrollments?

That probability is given by $1 - (0.01)^{10,000}$, which is close to unity, and therefore the likelihood of a single incident is a near certainty. The larger the number of enrollees, the greater is the probability of an enrollment error across the enterprise.

It is important to note that this model represents a near-worst case scenario. Presumably the enrollment process implemented at an organization has checks in place to ensure such errors do not occur. An even worse case would be the intentional misprogramming of the system. The discussion herein is a purely statistical analysis of risk. The calculations of risk are facilitated by randomly occurring enrollment errors. Intentional enrollment errors are examples of the threat posed by insiders, a very different and more vexing security risk problem.

SUMMARY

The likelihood of a future security incident is often unknowable. However, some security scenarios can be modeled in terms of expressions that govern the behavior of identified risk-factors. These risk factors can be assumed to be normally distributed random variables with scenario-specific limits. Calculating confidence intervals corresponding to the distribution of security scenarios relative to a specific risk-mitigation measure specifies the probability of protection afforded by that measure.

In general, statistical models can be invoked when security-related processes, features, or risk factors are assumed to be random variables. In that vein, a statistical analysis of physical access control system enrollment errors can reveal the likelihood of unauthorized physical access to restricted space.

REFERENCE

[1] Chang D, Young C. Probabilistic estimates of vulnerability to explosive overpressures and impulses. J Phys Secur 2010;4(2):10–29.

Problems

1. You are the Director of Security at a large international corporation. The CEO is an impatient creature with whom you manage to get a brief audience whenever his golf date is unexpectedly cancelled. You need to describe the probability of protection method of analysis to him since you are basing part of your strategy on this type of analysis. Provide a "junior readers edition" explanation of the methodology and its objectives.

2. Discuss how the probability of protection method characterizes the vulnerability component of risk in terms of likelihood.

3. Provide another security scenario (terrorist-related or not) that might lend itself to a probability of protection-type risk analysis.

4. If the distribution of values for a key security parameter used as part of a security model is a normal distribution, what is the effect on a probability of protection model if the distribution is narrow versus wide? How might that affect a risk-mitigation strategy that is based on this model?

5. As the Director of Security at a prestigious five-star hotel, theft from patrons is the highest priority threat. There are two modes of theft: those committed by insiders (i.e., hotel employees) and thefts committed by external parties. The number of thefts has historically been quite low, but you are determined to stay on top of this issue since it is highly correlated with the bottom line and, hence, your future in this job. What risk factors would you track in order to indirectly measure the vulnerability to theft for each mode of theft?

6. You are the Director of Security at a large medical center in an urban setting. Reducing violent crime on campus is the number one priority of your security department as mandated by hospital management. You have read this book from cover-to-cover and have recommended it to all your friends. Importantly, you

are a convert to the strategy of measuring the risk factors to address security threats. However, the medical center is a business, and therefore attempts to turn the institution into a fortress would not be appreciated by either the community or management. You have determined that possession of a lethal weapon is a significant risk factor for the threat of violent crime. Describe what methods you would employ to *indirectly* measure the risk of violent crime on campus and, importantly, specify where in the hospital you would deploy these methods. Explain your reasoning in precise, risk-based language.

7. You are the head of the Transportation Safety Authority (TSA) within the Department of Homeland Security. You have been mandated by the President to develop a more sophisticated approach to counterterrorism based on public frustration with your department.

   a. Identify three risk factors for terrorism on airplanes.

   b. Specify a strategy to measure those risk factors.

   c. Discuss the "cost" associated with those measurements relative to the introduction of passenger delays, personal invasiveness, etc.

   d. "Profiling" is defined as the selective identification of specific human characteristics, affiliations, or ethnic/religious backgrounds in addressing risk. Discuss profiling as a method of addressing risk factors for terrorism. Would you support the use of profiling to counter terrorism? Why or why not?

8. You are the Director of Security for an iconic U.S. company with significant brand name recognition. You make a risk-based decision to install bollards around the perimeter of your headquarters facility and you receive the backing of the CEO. However, you decide to first implement the probability of protection method to understand the likelihood that the selected brand of bollards will provide the required protection. Using the expression for the kinetic energy of an attacking vehicle, $1/2mv^2$, where m is vehicle mass and v is vehicle velocity, sketch out how you would use this expression in conjunction with the probability of protection method to determine the appropriate bollard energy rating. You need not be quantitative here. The point is to provide a qualitative discussion that illustrates your understanding of the technique.

9. Two hospitals are being evaluated for certification. Hospital A treats the standard spectrum of illnesses and injuries, and Hospital B is a hospital that treats patients with special needs and rare diseases. The rate of mortality and readmission is much higher at Hospital B than Hospital A. You are the Director of Risk Management at Hospital B. How would you justify your hospital's performance in terms of its mission and risk management efforts relative to the competition? What statistics would you use to bolster your argument?

10. You are the principal of a large urban high school and are concerned about the potential for violence on campus. Although to date there have been relatively few incidents of violence involving weapons, you are determined to be proactive in addressing a threat with a high impact component of risk.

   a. Identify risk factors for intraschool violence with weapons.

b. What controls would you introduce to address these risk factors?

c. What statistics might provide insight on the magnitude of risk and the effectiveness of controls?

d. There have been recent press reports of a lone gunman who has no affiliation with schools using automatic weapons on students in those schools. How would you distinguish between this threat and the threat of intraschool violence with respect to a risk-mitigation strategy (i.e., what are the differences in the risk factors for each threat attack vector)?

e. What controls would you implement for a lone gunman threat attack vector? Are these controls substantively different than the controls implemented for intraschool violence?

11. You are the head of security technology for an international company headquartered in Europe. You maintain unified, global physical access control and CCTV systems and you keep statistics on system performance. In addition, security officers maintain logs of risk-relevant incidents for analysis.

a. What system outputs might be relevant to examining the vulnerability to theft?

b. Are there any system features that might be useful in addressing/measuring the risk factor of unauthorized physical access?

12. You are the global head of security technology for a major U.S. corporation. Your 10-year-old physical access control system is continuously breaking down. Because you understand that the number of failures represents an important security metric, you keep accurate records on failure rates. Most recently these failures are occurring at a rate of two readers per day. It costs $500 per unit to fix. There are 1000 card readers on campus and each new card reader costs $1000, which includes a five-year warranty. Provide a risk-based and cost-effective strategy for continuing to replace individual card reader versus replacing the entire system. Note: there is no right or wrong answer. The goal is to demonstrate risk-based and fiscally sound reasoning.

13. Unauthorized physical access to restricted space is a risk factor for numerous security threats including terrorism. Describe in quantitative or qualitative terms why the "indirect risk" for these threats is enhanced with increasing numbers of randomly occurring access control system programming errors that facilitate unauthorized physical access to restricted space.

Measuring Terrorism Risk

CHAPTER 6

Conventional Explosive Threats and Risk Mitigation

6.1 INTRODUCTION

Explosive threats are a significant problem in an era of increasing concern over terrorism. Conventional explosives are relatively easy to obtain, and there are numerous examples of major damage caused by small amounts of highly energetic materials. Vehicles in particular offer opportunities to conceal and deliver substantial explosive payloads.

Such payloads are capable of causing tremendous physical destruction and loss of life. The truck bomb that leveled the U.S. Marine Corps barracks in Beirut, Lebanon, in 1986, the Khobar Towers in Saudi Arabia, and the bombing of the Alfred R. Murrah building in Oklahoma City, in 1995 are three prominent examples.

Many books and technical articles have been written on conventional explosives. It is beyond the scope of this book to delve deeply into the chemistry or physics of explosives. An excellent technical reference on conventional explosives can be found at the following website: *http://www.nps.gov/history/history/online_books/npsg/explosives/Chapter2.pdf.*

The purpose of this chapter is to analyze the key physical parameters that affect the vulnerability component of risk for conventional explosive incidents. The ultimate objective is to estimate how these parameters scale with distance and payload, two risk factors for this threat. Significant simplifications will admittedly be made in modeling this risk. But even simple physical models can be helpful in estimating risk and, importantly, in providing insight into effective risk mitigation.

Unfortunately, terrorism incidents using conventional explosives are commonplace in some parts of the world. Attacks such as the Khobar Towers bombing, shown in Figure 6.1, leave an indelible mark on the affected countries as well as the victims and their families. Hence, conventional explosives are attractive as terrorism weapons.

FIGURE 6.1
Khobar Towers, Dhahran, Saudi Arabia, 1996. *(From* http://www.nyc.gov/html/nypd/downloads/pdf/
counterterrorism/engineeringsecurity_030_guidlines_on_perimeter_security.pdf.*)*

We will explore the parameters that affect the vulnerability to explosive attacks
in some detail. On a qualitative and highly intuitive level, it is easy to appreciate
that moving as far as possible from the source of an explosion is an eminently
reasonable risk-mitigation strategy.

However, assessing vulnerability as a function of distance with more precision
is more challenging. A few additional feet of separation between the explosive
source and the target structure can make a significant difference in the resulting
damage. So a setback from the street might be an important factor in selecting
a site for a new facility if terrorism using conventional explosives is a threat
attack vector of concern.

The problem is that in urban settings, additional real estate can be a scarce commodity. Enforcing a physical separation between publically accessible streets
and the building façade through the use of barriers might be a top security
priority as part of the overall security strategy. But it might also represent a significant expense. Therefore, rigorously assessing the vulnerability component
of risk as well as the requirements for risk mitigation might assume a special
importance for organizations deemed at risk and for whom real estate is a
prized commodity.

In the case of the Oklahoma City bombing, U.S. domestic terrorists were
responsible for destroying a government facility. It is instructive to have some
idea of the destructive power that is possible using a bomb made with relatively common materials. In this case, 4000 lb of a TNT-equivalent mixture of
ammonium nitrate and fuel oil or ANFO was detonated 14 ft from the building

FIGURE 6.2
The Alfred R. Murrah Building, Oklahoma City, Oklahoma, April 19, 1995. *(From Oklahoma.gov.* http://
www.ok.gov/homeland/Interoperable_Communications/index.html.*)*

at a height of 4.5 ft above an 18-inch thick pavement. The damage to the structure is shown in Figure 6.2.

Understanding the basic physics of explosions is helpful in our quest to understand how damage to a building scales with the risk factors for vulnerability:
explosive payload, and distance.

When an explosion first occurs it creates a shock wave that causes a pressure
condition that exceeds the ambient atmospheric pressure (i.e., 14.7 lb/in^2).
The extent of any ensuing wall collapse and/or window breakage will depend
on the magnitude of that "overpressure" as well as the duration of the shock
wave relative to the vibrational characteristics of individual building components. Therefore, the interaction of explosive forces with affected building elements demands further examination.

6.2   APPLYING THE SINGLE DEGREE OF FREEDOM MODEL

When the probability of protection method was discussed in the last chapter, individual building components were modeled as a mass on a spring. This was one of the fundamental models of terrorism discussed in Chapter 4 also. As noted previously, the mass-on-a-spring system is referred to as the single-degree-of-freedom (SDOF) model. We note in passing that this model is called single degree of freedom because the mass is constrained to travel in a single direction.

Harmonic motion results from the explosive force applied to the building components. In other words, these components vibrate in response to this violent stimulus. The SDOF model is a greatly simplified version of reality, but it yields useful results.

In Chapter 4 we also learned how the time history of the force affects the response of the mass to the explosion. The resulting damage depends on the magnitude of the overpressure and the impulse. The latter is the duration of the explosive force in interactions with building elements.

More specifically, the impulse is the integral of the pressure with respect to time. In other words, the impulse is the cumulative effect of the overpressure with respect to time and is mathematically represented by the area under the pressure curve. Figure 6.3 shows the time history of overpressure following detonation.

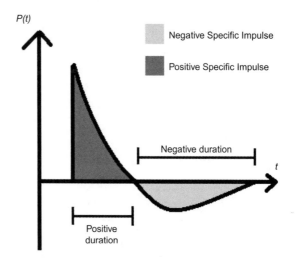

FIGURE 6.3

Time history of an explosive blast pressure. *(Used with permission from Ngo, T., P. Mendis, A. Gupta, and J. Ramsay. 2007. "Prediction of Blast Loading and Its Impact on Buildings: An Overview." eJSE International.)*

Following detonation, the pressure wave radiates away from the explosive source and the dynamic pressure decreases with increasing distance. As one can observe from Figure 6.3, the explosive pressure wave actually becomes negative relative to atmospheric pressure following the positive pressure phase. Importantly, dynamic pressure in fluids such as air that is caused by explosions is a function of direction. This is in contrast to static pressures, where the pressure is the same in all directions.

As previously noted, you do not need this book to tell you that it is best to avoid being in proximity to an explosion. However, estimating a safe distance from that explosion and/or whether a building will be resilient in the face of an attack is more difficult. Such an estimate is the essence of a terrorism risk assessment and is a central theme of this chapter.

6.3   EXPLOSIVE OVERPRESSURE AND IMPULSE PARAMETRIC SCALING

There are a number of scenario-dependent parameters that affect the vulnerability component of risk in response to explosive forces. It is a combination of the explosive overpressure and impulse in conjunction with structural details of the building that determine the damage from an explosion. It is therefore a logical question to ask how pressure and impulse scale (i.e., change) as a result of changes in distance from the explosive source and the magnitude of the explosive payload. The distance from an explosive source to a specific point in space, and the magnitude of the explosive payload are two risk factors for the vulnerability component of risk for conventional explosive threats.

Perhaps surprisingly, there is not complete agreement on the precise answer to this question. In the technical literature, four distinct scaling laws have been mentioned for pressure and two for impulse. In one commonly cited work, pressure, p, and impulse, i, scale with payload, m, and distance, r, as follows:[1]

$$p(\text{megapascals}) = 0.085(m^{1/3}/r) + 0.3(m^{2/3}/r^2) + 0.8(m/r^3)$$

$$i(\text{pascal} - \sec) = 200(m^{2/3}/r)$$

The important point is that impulse scales inversely with distance (i.e., $1/r$), and the dominant pressure term scales inversely with distance cubed (i.e., $1/r^3$). Therefore, increasing the distance between the explosive source and the target is clearly beneficial in reducing the vulnerability component of risk. Importantly, these expressions specify the rate at which such benefits accrue.

A little math adds insight to these scaling relations. With respect to pressure changes, if one doubles the distance from the point of detonation, the pressure is reduced by 1/8. Trebling the distance from the explosive source reduces the pressure by 1/27, etc. Similar scaling arguments are found throughout this book and with respect to a number of terrorism attack scenarios. Curves depicting general functions that scale as $1/r^2$ and $1/r^3$ are shown in Appendix A.

Because of the role of the overpressure and impulse in determining damage, pressure-impulse (P-I) curves are often calculated for structural elements. These specify the combination of pressure-impulse values that affect the response to explosive loading.

The TNT-equivalent model is the principal method for characterizing the effects of explosions. The model calculates the TNT equivalent mass, W_{TNT}, which is the mass of TNT that would produce the same effects as the amount and type of explosive involved in the actual incident.

The TNT equivalent mass describes the effect of the explosive material at a certain distance when it detonates, and it can be calculated from the quantity of explosives W_{exp} and the equivalency factor, f(kg TNT/kg explosive substance), where $W_{TNT} = f x W_{exp}$.

Equivalencies for explosives and otherwise unstable substances can be found in the literature, but TNT equivalences often vary with distance. The authors in the cited reference present a more efficient method of determining the effect of explosives in one step, and without the use of scaled parameters, although we in fact will use such parameters later as part of a specific analytic technique.[2]

Moreover, the relationship between overpressure and impulse can be shown to depend only on the TNT-equivalent mass. The greater the TNT-equivalent mass, the higher the impulse is for the same overpressure. The authors use pressure-impulse (P-I) curves to generate so-called characteristic curves. These are parallel lines whose position depends only on the TNT-equivalent mass. Recall that in Chapter 5 a P-I curve was used to determine the probability of protection for windows under explosive loading. P-I curves have general applicability to analyzing the effects of blasts on building structures.

Characteristic curves specify the pressure-impulse-distance relationship in a single curve and thereby facilitate estimates of overpressure and impulse at each distance from the explosion. If the points corresponding to the same distance on different characteristic curves are joined, so-called iso-distance lines are obtainable.

To quote the authors, "Using characteristic curves simplifies the approach, as both overpressure and impulse can be determined in one step, avoiding any calculation of scaled magnitudes. This model, based on characteristic curves, allows an overview of the evolution and relationship of all variables involved in the detonation of explosives ..." Figure 6.4 illustrates the characteristic curve concept.

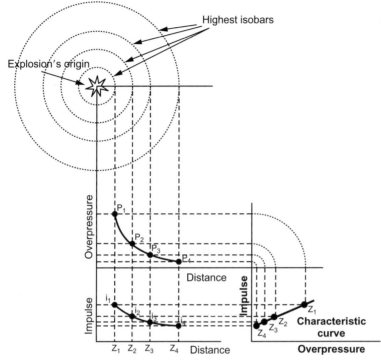

FIGURE 6.4

Explosion characteristic curves. (Journal of Hazardous Materials. *Volume 137, Issue 2, 21, pages 734–741.*)

6.4   BLAST EFFECTS: A QUALITATIVE DESCRIPTION

Following an explosion, the resulting shock wave expands outward and enters facilities in the path of the radiating wave. It simultaneously pushes upward and downward on the floors. Floor failure is common due to the large surface area it presents to the shock wave relative to the floor thickness. Progressive collapse, i.e., the failure of critical building supporting structures that produces a cascading effect as the structure falls in on itself, can occur within seconds after the explosion.

If the exterior building walls are capable of resisting the blast load, the shock front penetrates window and door openings, subjecting the floors, ceilings, walls, contents, and people to sudden pressures and fragments from shattered windows, doors, etc.

Building components that are not capable of resisting the blast wave will fracture and be further fragmented as well as abruptly moved by the increase in dynamic pressure that immediately follows the shock front. Building contents and people will be violently displaced in the direction of blast wave propagation. The blast wave will propagate throughout the building, causing similar effects throughout.

When the overpressure shock wave radiates away from the explosive source, its magnitude decreases with distance and time. As noted previously, it actually becomes negative as shown in Figure 6.3. This negative pressure causes suction forces on the building and the generation of a high-velocity wind. The net result of this wind is to propel particles and debris, thereby causing extreme risk of injury. In addition, and as time progresses, the pressure wave spreads out and is reduced in magnitude but affects a wider area. Figure 6.5 illustrates the magnitude of the pressure wave as it evolves with time.

Finally, nearby buildings are subject to violent ground motion caused by the explosion. The duration of explosive forces is typically significantly less than it is for earthquakes, a point that is especially important when designing a building to withstand both of these threats.

It is well known that the effect of explosive blasts is much different in confined spaces than in open areas. Confined explosions are accompanied by shock wave reflections off the confining surfaces, thereby amplifying the explosive effect. The typical result is more devastating for a confined scenario, all other parameters being equal. This has significant implications for urban areas.

Explosive effects can be quite complicated. Developing a more precise picture would require computer modeling. To that end, commercial programs using

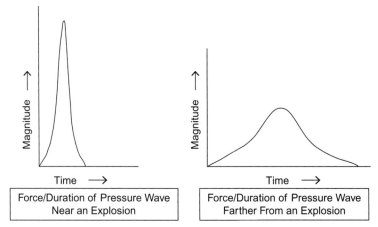

FIGURE 6.5

Time history of an explosive pressure wave. *(From Department of Transportation.* http://transit-safety.fta. dot.gov/security/SecurityInitiatives/DesignConsiderations/CD/sec6.htm.*)*

numerical techniques exist (e.g., ConWep), and only very rough estimates are presented here. However, even approximate results can be useful for estimates of the vulnerability component of risk.

6.5   THE EFFECTS OF DISTANCE AND PAYLOAD

As noted in the previous section, two significant risk factors for the vulnerability to explosive threats are the distance from the explosive source and the explosive payload. Table 6.1 provides the magnitude of explosive payloads relative to specific delivery methods. This information can be used to identify physically realistic attack scenarios.

Although the effects of nearby structures and the ground are ignored, Figure 6.6 is useful for estimating vulnerability to explosive threats since it shows explosive damage in terms of both distance and payload[3].

Specifically, Figure 6.6 specifies what I choose to call the "lines of constant damage" for combinations of explosive payload and distance. In other words, each curve shows those combinations of a TNT-equivalent explosive[a] and the distance between the explosive source and target that produce the same damage to a structure. Although the data represent approximations, this chart is useful in developing a ballpark estimate on the vulnerability to conventional explosive threats.

Since it is the pressure wave in excess of ambient atmospheric conditions (i.e., the overpressure) caused by detonation in combination with the explosive impulse that inflicts damage, it is instructive to examine the direct effect of distance on these parameters with respect to an explosion.

Figure 6.7 shows the magnitude of the overpressure as a function of distance from 500- and 5000-lb-equivalent TNT payloads. One can see the dramatic falloff in overpressure with distance for both payloads[4].

Table 6.1 Explosive Delivery Methods and Payloads

Explosive Delivery	Method Approximate Payload (lb TNT)
Pipe bomb	5
Suitcase bomb	50
Automobile	500 to 1000
Van	1000 to 5000
Truck	10,000 to 30,000
Semi-tractor trailer	40,000

[a]The U.S. reference for an explosive payload is equivalent pounds of trinitrotoluene (TNT).

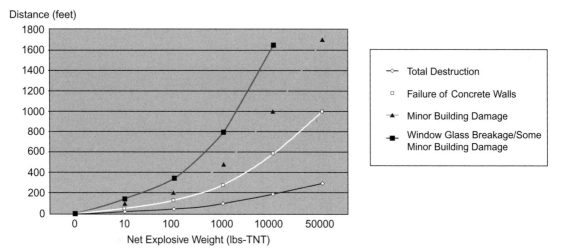

FIGURE 6.6

Explosive effects on structures. *(From U.S. Air Force, "Installation Force Protection Guide."* http://www.wbdg.org/ccb/AF/AFDG/ARCHIVES/afinstal.pdf.*)*

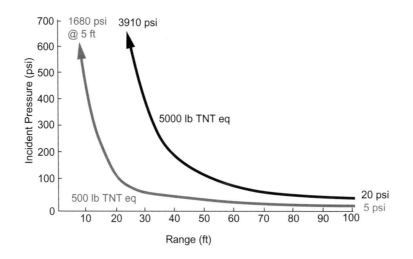

FIGURE 6.7

Explosive pressure as a function of distance. *(Reproduced with permission from the National Institute of Building Sciences as it appeared in the Whole Building Design Guide.* http://www.wbdg.org/resources/env_blast.php.*)*

The data in Figure 6.7 shows the effect of separation distance on overpressure and therefore provides an explicit connection between building damage and separation distance. Notice that the magnitude of the overpressure associated with the smaller payload is initially smaller and also decreases much more rapidly with distance.

6.6   VEHICLE-BORNE EXPLOSIVES

The use of vehicle-borne explosives is an all-too-familiar scenario. The principal reason why this attack vector is popular as a weapon of terrorism is the ability to deliver relatively large, concealed payloads in proximity to the target. Figure 6.8 depicts the pressure resulting from the detonation on the various building surfaces.[5]

If there is concern about the vulnerability of a building to total destruction from a vehicle-borne explosive, the bottom curve of Figure 6.6 plots the combinations of distance and explosive payload that will produce this level of damage. Clearly the closer the bomb is to the target, the less of a payload is required to produce the same effect.

However, the salient question is how the damage scales with distance and payload for a given destructive scenario. In other words, how sensitive is building damage to the separation between the explosive source and the target as well as to the magnitude of the explosive payload?

To get a feel for the answer to that important question it is useful to revisit Figure 6.6. Notice that all four curves of constant damage are increasingly "curvy" for greater

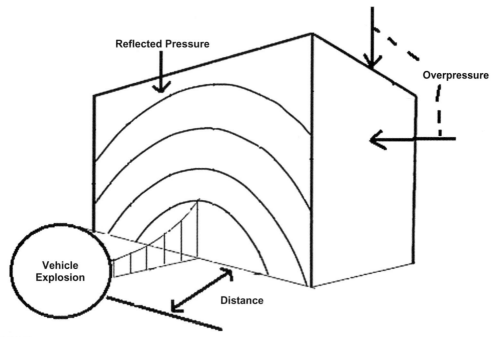

FIGURE 6.8

Vehicle-borne explosives scenario. *(Adapted from Ngo, T., P. Mendis, A. Gupta, and J. Ramsay. 2007. "Prediction of Blast Loading and Its Impact on Buildings: An Overview."* eJSE International.*)*

separation distances. This is an example of a nonlinear effect, and it has important operational implications. Namely, the damage induced by an explosion for a given destructive scenario (e.g., window breakage, total building destruction, etc.) is disproportionately reduced with increasing distance from the explosive source. These curves provide an approximate answer to the important operational question of how much the damage is reduced with distance from the explosion.

For example, and referring once again to Figure 6.6, 100 lb of TNT-equivalent payload detonated at a distance of almost 400 ft will produce the same damage as 1000 lb at 800 ft. In other words, an explosion caused by a payload x that is detonated from a distance y will yield the same damage as a payload of magnitude $10x$ and separation distance $2y$. So merely doubling the distance between the explosive payload and the target requires a 10-fold increase in payload to produce the same effect.

This explains in quantitative terms why terrorists using conventional explosives are determined to get as close to their intended target as possible. It also poignantly illustrates why security professionals should be equally determined to restrict physical proximity to authorized individuals and vehicles, and to keep unauthorized vehicles as far from a facility as possible.

The aforementioned discussion is indicative of the type of analysis that is critical to rigorously assessing vulnerability and the formulation of a risk-based counterterrorism strategy. It also demonstrates the value of a simple graphic in developing and illustrating ballpark estimates of risk.

Let's examine a familiar corporate scenario. We encountered the same scenario in Chapter 1, but now we assume the security director can be more specific in his or her discussions with management.

Suppose you are the security director of a high-profile international corporation whose headquarters are in the United States. You have been asked to weigh in on the location of a parking area for your posh new company headquarters facility. This is the area that cars, taxis, limousines, etc. will use to pick up and drop off company executives and other big shots.

The senior managers of the firm, i.e., the people who pay your salary, are arguing vigorously to have the vehicle waiting area as close to the facility as possible. As the security director, you have serious concerns about the wisdom of such a move. However, you must make a compelling argument in order to win the hearts and minds of individuals who are used to getting their way. Unfortunately, the bosses view security as an annoyance if it interferes with their perquisites.

Table 6.1 and Figure 6.6 together are useful in establishing the requirements for explosive risk mitigation. By now we are familiar with Figure 6.6. Let's reexamine the line of constant damage corresponding to "total destruction." We can observe another interesting fact from this curve that hopefully will get senior management's attention.

Increasing the separation distance between the explosive source and the facility façade from 10 to 20 ft would force a bomber to increase the payload from 100 to 1000 lb of TNT-equivalent explosive. Referring to Table 6.1, this would likely force an attacker to use a truck rather than a car to achieve an objective of total building destruction. This analysis provides quantitative support for restricting physical access by vehicle type, and thereby offer, risk-based operational recommendations to management.

A security professional's responsibility is to *manage* risk, noting that eliminating risk is not possible in most scenarios. But what does this mean more precisely? With respect to most threat scenarios including this one, managing risk means decreasing the vulnerability component of risk through the imposition of security controls.

This is precisely what increasing the standoff distance from the building using a barrier (e.g., the control) accomplishes. Furthermore, we can be more exact in estimating the vulnerability for each unique scenario since we have real data. The point is that such analyses have operational implications.

Figure 6.9 is a reformulation of Figure 6.6. In this version, the vulnerability to building damage as a function of distance to a vehicle carrying 1000 lb of

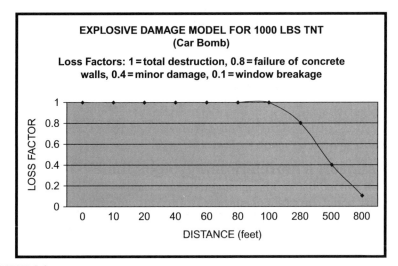

FIGURE 6.9
Damage from 1000 lb of TNT-equivalent explosive.

TNT-equivalent explosive is presented. We see that a separation distance of 800 ft is required to limit the damage to window breakage.

Unfortunately, adversaries have the luxury of dictating the magnitude of the key risk factors of an explosive attack. This does not mean the defense is powerless in making reasonable estimates of vulnerability. Although in theory there are an infinite number of attack scenarios, careful consideration of site-specific constraints, an adversary's objectives, and an analysis of relevant risk factors can narrow the spectrum of reasonable attacks. Recall such an analysis was part of the probability of protection method discussed in Chapter 5.

The shape of a building can also affect the extent of damage caused by the explosive shock wave[4]. Reentrant corners, i.e., corners with angles less than or equal to 90 degrees and pointing inward, as well as overhangs, are likely to trap the shock wave. This may amplify the effect of the air blast. Large or gradual reentrant corners have less of an effect than small or sharp reentrant corners and overhangs. In general, convex shapes are preferred for the exterior of the building. The reflected pressure from the surface of a round building decays more rapidly than a flat or U-shaped building.

It is recommended that the lobby and loading dock areas are placed exterior to the main structure to limit the potential for progressive collapse. Figure 6.10 illustrates some shapes that dissipate and accentuate air blasts.

6.7 VEHICLE-BORNE EXPLOSIVE RISK: A SIMPLE CALCULATION

A precise determination of the damage caused by explosions requires sophisticated civil engineering methods. The approximate techniques provided in this book cannot supplant numerical methods used to calculate explosive loading of specific building elements.

However, it has been shown that under certain conditions, a simple method can be used to determine the peak reflected overpressure and reflected impulse, the major contributors to building damage from explosive loads.[6]

This method can be applied to a point on the building above the ground for the elevation directly facing the explosive source and when the angle of incidence between the vehicle and the point on the building is less than 45 degrees. The geometry is shown in Figure 6.11.

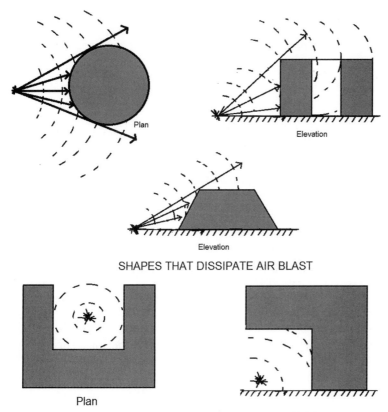

FIGURE 6.10

The effect of building shape on the damage from explosive blasts. *(Reproduced with permission from the National Institute of Building Sciences as it appeared in the "Whole Building Design Guide."* http://www.wbdg .org/resources/env_blast.php.*)*

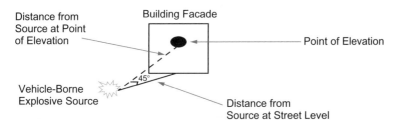

FIGURE 6.11

A blast scenario associated with a simple risk calculation method. *(Adapted from Remennikov, A.M. 2003. "A Review of Methods for Predicting Bomb Blast Effects on Buildings,"* Journal of Battlefield Technology.*)*

A step-by-step recipe for this method is included here. It provides a simple if approximate (estimated to be ~20 percent accurate) means of analyzing vehicle-borne explosive scenarios without resorting to computer programs.

For scenarios where there is an appreciable standoff, the 45-degree condition will almost certainly be satisfied based on simple geometry. If the point on the building to be analyzed is at ground level (i.e., at the same level as the explosive), the analysis is even simpler.

The technique involves the concept of a scaled range. It turns out that by using a parameter of a scaled ground distance, $\lambda = R/W^{1/3}$, where R equals the distance in feet or meters of the explosive source to the target and W equals the equivalent TNT explosive weight in pounds or kilograms, the building damage can be related to this scaled range. Scaling laws provide parametric correlations between a particular explosion and a standard charge of the same substance.

The procedure for analytically determining peak-reflected pressure and impulse when the aforementioned geometric conditions are satisfied is given by the following recipe:

1. Determine the explosive charge weight, W, and assume a hemispheric burst model. Select a point-of-interest on the exterior vertical wall of the building at height h above the ground.
2. For the point-of-interest, calculate the standoff distance at height h (Pythagorean theorem), R_h, scaled standoff distance, Z_h, and angle of incidence, a, as follows:

$$R_h = (R_g^2 + h^2)^{1/2} \quad (\text{note}: R_g \text{ is the distance from the} \\ \text{explosive source to the building at ground level})$$

$$Z_h = R_h / W^{1/3}$$

$$a = \tan^{-1}(h / R_g)$$

3. Read the peak reflected pressure and scaled positive reflected impulse, $i_r/W^{1/3}$, from Figure 6.12 (i.e., Figure 2-15 in the cited reference).
4. Multiply the scaled impulse by $W^{1/3}$ to obtain the absolute value of the peak reflected impulse.

Table 6.2 shows calculated peak reflected overpressures (in units of megapascals (MPa)) for various payload-distance (i.e., W-R) combinations.

Using the computed value for overpressure obtained via the technique just described, or using estimates from Table 6.2, one can refer to Table 6.3 to estimate the damage caused by an explosion.

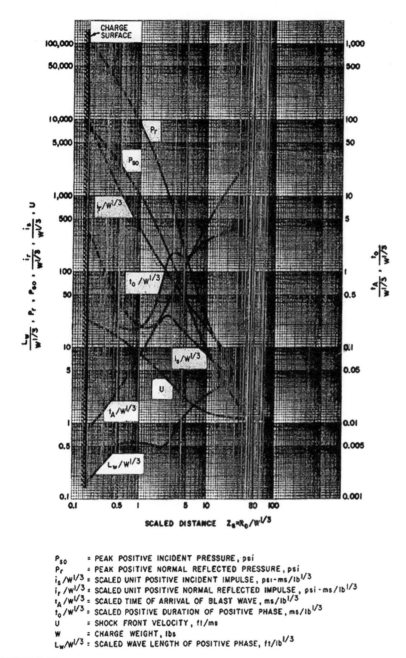

FIGURE 6.12

Positive-phase shock wave parameters for a hemispherical TNT explosion on the surface at sea level. *(From U.S. Department of Army. November 1990. "Structures to Resist the Effects of Accidental Explosions." Technical Manual. 5– 1300.)*

Table 6.2 Peak Reflected Overpressures for Various Payload-Distance Combinations

R \ W	100 kg TNT	500 kg TNT	1000 kg TNT	2000 kg TNT
1 m	165.8	354.5	464.5	602.9
2.5 m	34.2	89.4	130.8	188.4
5 m	6.65	24.8	39.5	60.19
10 m	0.85	4.25	8.15	14.7
15 m	0.27	1.25	2.53	5.01
20 m	0.14	0.54	1.06	2.13
25 m	0.09	0.29	0.55	1.08
30 m	0.06	0.19	0.33	0.63

(From Ngo, T., et al. 2007. "Prediction of Blast Loading and Its Impact on Buildings: An Overview." eJSE International. With permission.)

Table 6.3 Explosive Shock Wave Effects

Overpressure		Expected Damage
kpa (kilopascals)	psi (lb/in^2)	
1.0 to 1.5	0.15 to 0.22	Window glass cracks
3.5 to 7.6	0.51 to 1.1	Minor damage in some buildings
7.6 to 12.4	1.1 to 1.8	Metal panels deformed
12.4 to 20	1.8 to 2.9	Concrete walls damage
Over 35	Over 5.1	Wooden construction buildings demolition
27.5 to 48	4.0 to 7.0	Major damage on steel construction objects
40 to 60	5.8 to 8.7	Heavy damage on reinforced concrete buildings
70 to 80	10 to 11.6	Probable demolition of most buildings

(From TB 700-2 Department of Defense (DoD). "A&E Hazard Classification Procedures.")

6.8 BARRIERS AND BOLLARDS

The threat of conventional explosives is significant in some areas of the world. A study of historical data would yield abundant information on the use of this technique by extremist groups. Conventional explosives are relatively easy to acquire, and small amounts can cause major damage.

We previously learned how explosive effects scale with distance between the explosive source and the target: $1/r^3$ with respect to overpressure and $1/r$ for impulse, where r is the distance between the explosive source and the target.

The situation gets more complicated in spaces crowded with large structures, but these scaling relationships are a reasonable approximation to reality in open spaces. In all cases, ensuring adequate separation between the explosive source and a potential target is critical to protecting physical assets from this threat.

The use of physical barriers and bollards to enforce this separation has increased dramatically in recent years based on concern for vehicle-borne attacks. Bollards are designed to prevent moving vehicles from breaching a prescribed boundary and are rated according to their ability to absorb the energy of a moving vehicle. This energy rating will vary based on the bollard type and installation details. Bollards must be appropriately anchored to the ground in order to achieve the designated energy rating. A set of bollards is typically ganged together while connected to a heavy underground mass that provides the inertia to resist impacts.

The U.S. Department of State has established performance ratings for barriers. These ratings are useful in determining the appropriate barrier for a scenario of interest[7]. They specify the maximum kinetic energy (i.e., combination of vehicle weight and speed) a barrier can withstand such that it will not allow a vehicle to penetrate the barrier following impact. Table 6.4 lists the results.

In cases where deep excavations in the ground are precluded, surface-mounted bollards may be used. Where deep surface excavation is possible, and vehicle access is intermittently required, retractable bollards are used to facilitate physical access to restricted spaces by authorized vehicles. These are hydraulically lowered below grade to allow vehicles to pass as required.

As a practical matter, the raising and lowering of retractable bollards should ideally be performed at a location remote from the bollards themselves. An individual hoping to destroy a facility and kill its occupants would not hesitate to kill or at least threaten the bollard operator and thereby force him or her to lower the bollards or do so himself.

Comparing the performance specifications for barriers against estimates of vehicle weight and run-up speed is critical to developing a successful defensive

Table 6.4 U.S. Department of State Crash Ratings for Bollards

Department of State Impact Rating for Barriers			
Barrier Rating	Vehicle Speed	Vehicle Weight	Vehicle Kinetic Energy
K4	30 mph	15,000 lb	0.6 MJ (megajoules)
K8	40 mph	15,000 lb	1.1 MJ
K12	50 mph	15,000 lb	1.7 MJ

strategy for vehicle-borne explosive threats. The objective is to mandate that the barrier energy rating exceed the kinetic energy of an attacking vehicle.

Let's assume a security professional has done his or her homework and has estimated the required separation distance between the bollards and the building. This estimate is based on determining the effects of distance and explosive payload on building damage as discussed in the previous section.

Once barrier placement is determined, the type of barrier must be specified. That is, one needs to figure out its performance specification relative to the maximum kinetic energy that can be achieved by an attacking vehicle. The maximum energy is determined by plugging the vehicle's weight and speed of approach into the formula for kinetic energy.

The kinetic energy of an object is the energy acquired through motion. The formula for kinetic energy is a linear function of its mass, m, and a nonlinear function of its velocity, v. Once again we see the importance of understanding the scaling of key physical parameters in estimating the vulnerability component of risk. Vehicle velocity has a disproportionately greater effect on kinetic energy than does mass, so limiting the run-up velocity would have a disproportionately larger effect on risk mitigation.

Specifically, the kinetic energy of an object is equal to $\frac{1}{2} \times mass \times velocity \times velocity$ (i.e., velocity squared), written compactly as $\frac{1}{2} mv^2$. Therefore, if one doubles the object mass, the kinetic energy is doubled. However, if one doubles the velocity, the kinetic energy is quadrupled. Because of the strong dependence of kinetic energy on velocity (note: to be technically precise, we should speak of speed rather than velocity since velocity is a vector quantity and therefore has both magnitude and direction), it is instructive to focus on calculating the maximum velocity of a vehicle that could breach a barrier in a given scenario.

There are many examples that demonstrate the nonlinear effect of velocity relative to mass in scenarios where kinetic energy is important. I am sure football and rugby players intuitively understand this concept quite well. Tackling a big but slow man might be difficult, but it is less onerous than tackling a somewhat smaller man running at a higher speed. In another example, high-velocity rifle rounds are more penetrating than slower bullets of a larger caliber.

The velocity achieved by an accelerating vehicle is given by

$$v = v_o + at$$

v_o is the initial velocity before acceleration, v is velocity, a is acceleration, and t is time. In this analysis, the initial velocity is assumed to be 0. In other words, an attacking vehicle is presumed to charge the building from a dead stop.

The total distance traveled by a uniformly accelerating vehicle is easy to determine from the expression for velocity by integrating with respect to time. The distance, x, is given by

$$x = \frac{1}{2}at^2 + v_o t$$

In order to assess vulnerability and establish a mitigation strategy for this threat, it is important to know the maximum possible run-up distance by an attacking vehicle. If this run-up distance, x, is known, one can solve for t in the expression for distance. Once the time for an accelerating vehicle to reach a building is established, its velocity on impact can be determined since we have an expression relating velocity, acceleration, and time.

We now know that the kinetic energy of a moving object is given by $\frac{1}{2}mv^2$. It is sometimes useful to specify various combinations of vehicle velocity and mass that are necessary to achieve a barrier or bollard energy rating. If physically realistic combinations of vehicle mass and velocity fall below this energy rating, then the barrier should prove resilient in an attack.

Such a plot is shown in Figure 6.13 for a kinetic energy specification of 5.8×10^6 J (5.8 MJ). This value has been selected because it represents a midrange value

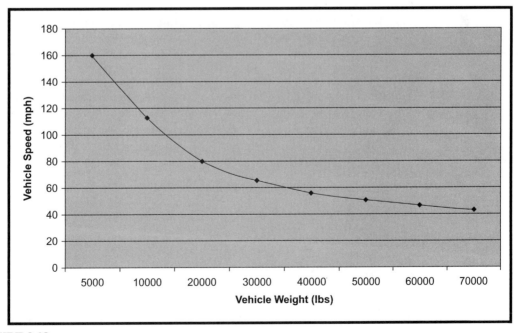

FIGURE 6.13
Vehicle mass-velocity combinations to achieve 5.8 MJ kinetic energy.

for one well-known, high-performance bollard, the Delta Scientific DSC720 (i.e., between 15,000 lb at 81 mph and 30,000 lb at 68 mph).

We see that a 5000-lb vehicle must travel at a breathtaking 160 mph to achieve a kinetic energy of 5.8 MJ. However, a 70,000-lb truck need only achieve a speed of 43 mph to develop the same kinetic energy. Heavier vehicles typically accelerate more slowly than lighter vehicles. Anyone who has ridden a motorcycle can attest to its exceptional acceleration due to the combination of a relatively powerful engine and low vehicle weight. Vehicle acceleration will profoundly affect the required run-up distance to achieve a specific impact velocity. The greater the acceleration, the shorter is the required run-up speed.

A mitigation strategy must be designed to ensure a vehicle cannot develop sufficient kinetic energy to exceed the performance specification of the proposed barrier make and model. Published vehicle acceleration data for a Ford F-150 pickup truck has been used to determine the required run-up distance to achieve 5.8 MJ.[8] That calculation is shown in the next section.

6.9 ASSESSING BOLLARD EFFECTIVENESS

Using our knowledge of kinetic energy and vehicular motion we can easily calculate the required run-up distance for a given scenario. In this example we use 5.8 MJ as the kinetic energy limit and examine the motion of a popular U.S. pickup truck, the Ford F-150. We will assume that this is the terrorist's vehicle of choice. Performing this calculation will determine whether a 5.8 MJ-rated barrier is sufficient in this scenario.

Published data indicates that this vehicle can accelerate from 0 to 60 mph in 8.96 s. This works out to a rated acceleration of 3.0 m/s^2 assuming uniform acceleration. A Ford F-150 weighs about 5500 lb or 2.48×10^3 kg.

Since the maximum kinetic energy of a vehicle should not exceed 5.8 MJ if we want our bollards to be effective, the vehicle velocity, v, required to achieve this energy is a robust 68 m/s or 153 mph.

We know that final vehicle velocity = vehicle initial velocity + (acceleration × time), or written compactly as $v = v_o + at$. So $t = 23$ s by direct substitution. Since it is assumed that the vehicle begins from a dead stop (i.e., the initial velocity $v_o = 0$), $x = (1/2)at^2 = 794$ m is the distance required to achieve the kinetic energy limit of this bollard.

Therefore, if an empty Ford F-150 or equivalent vehicle was denied 794 m of runway to accelerate, it could not breach 5.8 MJ-rated bollards, assuming they were installed correctly. Of course a loaded truck would weigh more, but it would also require a longer run-up distance.

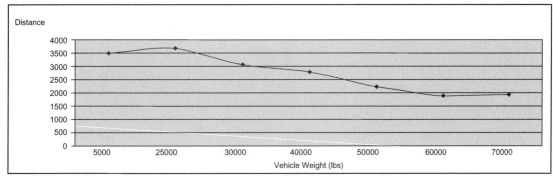

FIGURE 6.14
Run-up distance required to achieve 5.8-MJ kinetic energy.

Figure 6.14 depicts the run-up distance for various vehicle weights relative to a 5.8-MJ kinetic energy limit, using the method described above and publically available data on truck acceleration.[9]

Even if the chosen barriers are deemed adequate based on kinetic energy limits, consideration should be given to seeding the run-up route with obstacles that force a vehicle to deviate from a straight path. In Britain such obstacles are known as chicanes, a word that interestingly shares the same root as "chicanery."

The theory is that a circuitous route will force vehicles to slow their speed or risk tipping over and/or sliding off the road before reaching the target. Figure 6.15 illustrates the concept of a chicane minus the obstacles.

FIGURE 6.15
A chicane. *(From* http://www.fhwa.dot.gov/publications/research/safety/09061/02.cfm.*)*

FIGURE 6.16

Double layer of bollards at Shoe Lane looking south (Central London, UK). © Copyright Colin Park and licensed for reuse under this Creative Commons License.

Chicanes are not necessarily as effective as other barrier configurations, and the specific scenario should be carefully analyzed for its effectiveness in slowing approaching vehicles. An example of an alternative configuration is a double layer of retractable bollards. In addition to providing significant defense against vehicle penetration, a double layer of bollards has the added benefit of minimizing the risk of piggybacking by following vehicles.

Figure 6.16 is a photograph of Shoe Lane in Central London, where such a strategy has been deployed. If you look carefully between the buildings, there are two parallel sets of retractable bollards that extend across the width of Shoe Lane. Shoe Lane terminates to the south at Fleet Street.

The operational principle is simple. Vehicles approaching from the north (i.e., behind the reader) are stopped at the north set of bollards. These are retracted to allow the vehicle to move forward. The vehicle moves forward, and the north set of bollards is raised behind the vehicle. The driver and vehicle are inspected while the vehicle is physically confined between the two sets of bollards.

Once the inspection has concluded, the south set of bollards is lowered and the vehicle is allowed to continue to its destination. Vehicles traveling behind the first vehicle cannot physically move forward until the first vehicle has moved out of the way, thereby preventing piggybacking. I am particularly proud of this solution, as this author posited it in 2006 while working for Goldman Sachs in London. It not only solved an operational problem for the firm as discussed below, but it also satisfied the City of London authorities who were not thrilled with the aesthetics of the proposed chicane design.

This configuration replaced a proposed chicane that was intended to slow traffic approaching from the north in conjunction with a single layer of bollards placed at the northern end of Shoe Lane. It was clear from the analysis, which was similar to the one provided below, that the proposed chicane would do little to slow shorter-length trucks (a.k.a. "lorries") as well as cars.

Chicanes can indeed be effective in slowing vehicles. But as always, the physical details of a given scenario determine the success in achieving the stated security objectives. As noted above, the act of turning will affect a vehicle's maximum speed if it is to remain upright and/or maintain a constant turning radius. The purpose of a chicane is to force a vehicle to limit its speed to avoid tipping and/or slipping at higher speeds.

A simple relation governs the maximum velocity such that the vehicle will not slip out of its turning radius. Perhaps you've experienced anxiety in a related scenario when exiting a highway? Because the individuals who design roads have anticipated such excesses, off-ramps are often banked to leverage the force of gravity and thereby maintain a constant turning radius.

When turning a vehicle, three forces are acting on the vehicle: the weight of the vehicle, the centrifugal force due to motion, and the centripetal force exerted by the tires in contact with the road in the form of friction. Centrifugal force is a so-called "apparent force" since it is generated only through motion. This is the force that causes the vehicle to stray from its turning radius, and is equal to the vehicle mass m, times its velocity squared, divided by the turning radius r, or $F = mv^2/r$.

The combination of these three forces will determine if the vehicle can negotiate a turn without slipping. Friction resulting from the weight of the moving vehicle's tires in contact with the road surface is required to counter the centrifugal force.

We are interested in knowing the maximum velocity for which a vehicle can still maintain its turning radius without slipping. It is clear that the bigger the turning radius r, the greater the velocity v that will satisfy this condition. However, if the centrifugal force exceeds the force due to friction, the vehicle will slide laterally or flip over if enough torque is applied to the vehicle about its center of mass.

Expressed as an equation, the condition for nonslipping on a flat surface while turning is written as follows:

$$mg\mu = mv^2/r$$

m is the vehicle mass, g is the acceleration due to gravity or $9.8\,\text{m/s}^2$ (i.e., $32\,\text{ft/s}^2$), μ is the coefficient of friction, and r is the turning radius.

Solving for the velocity, v, we get $v = (g\mu r)^{1/2}$. The first thing to notice is that the vehicle mass does not enter into the solution, as it cancels from both sides of the equation. If the vehicle in question uses quality tires, then we can assume the coefficient of friction, μ, is 0.9 on a scale from 0 to 1.

If the entrance to a facility requires a turning radius of 10 meters, then the maximum velocity it can maintain without slipping is $v_{max} = (9.8\,\text{m/s}^2 \times 0.9 \times 10\,\text{m})^{1/2} = 9.4\,\text{m/s}$, or 21 mph.

Increasing the turning radius by a factor of 3 (i.e., 30 m) increases the allowable speed to 36 mph. We see that v_{max} scales as the square root of the turning radius.

Therefore, imposing a small turning radius on vehicles entering a facility will limit the maximum velocity it can achieve without slipping. This in turn limits the maximum kinetic energy that can be imparted to barriers intended to stop an attacking vehicle. This translates to less-expensive barriers, which reinforces the importance of analyses like this in estimating risk.

As usual, certain simplifying assumptions have been invoked. First, it is assumed that the road surface is flat. Second, the vehicle weight is concentrated at its center of mass. This avoids the real-life complication of a torque that could tip the vehicle as it turns. That torque about the center of mass would be more pronounced for those vehicles with a higher center of gravity (e.g., SUVs) since the effective "lever arm" is increased. Presumably extremists prefer to use larger vehicles since these allow for larger payloads.

As noted above, highway exit ramps are often banked so that vehicles can leverage the force of gravity and the vehicle maintains its turning radius. The condition for constraining the vehicle to a given radius without slipping on banked surfaces is given by $\tan(\theta) = v^2/rg$, where θ is the angle of the banked surface, v is velocity, g is the acceleration due to gravity, and r is the radius of the curved path. Figure 6.17 is a diagram illustrating the forces involved in the banked road scenario.

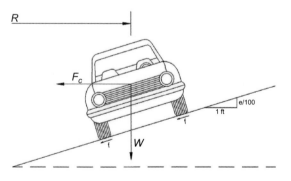

FIGURE 6.17

A force diagram for a vehicle on a banked surface. *(From U.S. Department of Transportation. "Speed Concepts: Information Guide."* http://safety.fhwa.dot.gov/speedmgt/ref_mats/fhwasa10001/.)

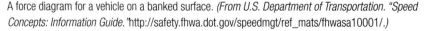

The aforementioned analyses, albeit elementary, are important in determining ballpark estimates on barrier performance for a given scenario. However, a qualified engineer should be consulted to determine the effectiveness of actual barriers under operational conditions. Proper installation of the barriers is critical to meeting the desired performance specifications.

6.10   ANTIBLAST FILM

The application of anti-blast film is a traditional method for preventing the splintering of glass when subjected to explosive loads. The application of anti-blast film is a well-known technique, and there are many online references to such products.

Injuries or death sustained by shards of broken glass is one of the most common effects resulting from explosions. Following a detonation, sharp pieces of window and/or decorative glass are propelled at tremendous speeds, thereby exposing anyone in the vicinity to severe injury.

Antishatter protection in the form of polyester film is sometimes applied to the glass surface with the intent of preventing splintering. Typical values for film thickness range from 175 μm to 300 μm (1 μm is one millionth of a meter or 10^{-6} m), depending in part on the glass surface area and level of protection required.

In addition, the glass must be appropriately anchored to its frame in order for the glass-frame system to maintain its integrity and withstand the effects of the explosive-induced overpressure.

The British government has provided detailed performance standards for anti-blast film. In particular, the Centre for Protection of National Infrastructure is a useful source of information on general window treatments to mitigate the risk of explosive threats.[10] Note that specifications will vary depending on the magnitude of the threat, the area of the glass pane, and the location within the facility of interest.

Test results conducted by a commercial vendor have demonstrated significant performance enhancements for treated versus untreated glass.[11] For example, untreated quarter-inch glass subjected to a 38.9-psi-ms impulse experienced extensive damage when tested. However, when 4 mil anchored film was subjected to a similar impulse (39.2 psi-ms), the glass proved to be sufficiently resilient.

These tests demonstrated a factor of three increase in the tolerance to peak pressures for windows that were both anchored and glazed versus those that were glazed only. Specifically, tests on 14 mil anchored film versus 14 mil daylight (i.e. glazed but unanchored) glass showed a pressure tolerance improvement from 3.0 to 9.1 lb/in^3, a significant enhancement.

The effectiveness of window glass and its treatments has been analyzed relative to both explosive blasts and projectile-type threats.[12] Window treatments are typically used to address explosive threats, and their efficacy with respect to projectiles is not often examined. It is useful to consider this mitigation measure relative to both attack vectors.

The following are the practical recommendations that have resulted from a theoretical analysis of window performance under blast and projectile-type loading:

1. Recommendations for increasing window blast resistance only:
   a. Use glass that has been heat-treated to obtain a greater tensile strength.
   b. Increase tensile strength with one or more layers of film.

For example, if the heat-treated glass has a tensile strength that is larger than that of untreated glass by a factor of 3, then heat-treated glass could be used in conjunction with a single layer of film.

2. Recommendations for both blast and projectile-resistant windows:
   a. Use a plastic-like material that has a relatively low Young's modulus (i.e., make the stiffness similar to the film material) but has a thickness similar to a standard glass window.
   b. Stiffen the glass by adding layers of tempered glass with a larger Young's modulus and of comparable or less thickness.

The film and tempered glass would both have tensile strengths of the same order of magnitude, but the lower effective Young's modulus for the system would result in a smaller induced stress on the window and therefore reduce its vulnerability to shattering.

Finally, useful technical specifications on windows have been extracted from the cited reference, and these are listed in Appendix E.

6.11 EXPLOSIVE DETECTION

Explosive-detecting canines are often used to detect the presence of explosives. Dogs can definitely be effective in such scenarios, depending on the operational requirements. However, there are alternatives or at least complementary methods in the form of portable explosive-detection devices. These might be effective depending on the scenario and are much less expensive than canines over the long term.

Although not nearly as cuddly as a dog, these devices do not get tired, require no messy cleanup or dog food, and are also capable of detecting a range of explosive types.

One operational limitation is that surface contact (i.e., swabbing the surface) is necessary to detect nonvolatile (i.e., low vapor pressure) explosives, although the devices are advertised as being capable of detecting vapors when they appear in sufficient concentration (See "Devices Go Nose-to-Nose With Bomb Sniffer Dogs," *New York Times*, October 15, *http://www.nytimes.com/2012/10/16/science/explosives-detectors-aim-to-go-nose-to-nose-with-sniffer-dogs.html?pagewanted=all&_r=0*).

Although the initial expense of a unit may be relatively high, one should compare this cost with the recurring expense of canines and handlers over time. Explosive-detection canines are definitely an effective risk-mitigation measure. But it is important to assess their effectiveness in specific scenarios of interest and compare this to alternative methods.

One such alternative is the Sabre 5000, a portable explosive-detection unit manufactured by Smiths Detection. The company website indicates the device can detect both particulates and vapor, weighs 7 lb with a 4-hr battery, has a detection time of 10 sec, and yields a complete analysis in 20 s. The device uses ion mobility spectrometry (IMS) to detect the explosives RDX, PETN, TNT, Semtex, TATP, NG, Ammonium Nitrate, "and others" as well as chemical warfare agents.

This device is compact and relatively easy to use. Figure 6.18 is a photograph of the device taken from the Smiths Detection website

Assuming explosives are a threat of concern, this device and a representative sampling of competitors should be tested in simulated scenarios. It is also important to learn about available training, maintenance agreements, and rates of false positives/negatives. The required sensitivity to vapors should be investigated, and this can be evaluated as part of the testing protocol. A list of customers who have operational experience with this technology in similar risk scenarios would be invaluable in the decision process.

FIGURE 6.18
The Sabre 5000 handheld trace detector.

6.12   X-RAY INSPECTION TECHNOLOGY

Screening for explosives has become commonplace in today's society. Anyone who has flown on a commercial airplane in the last 30 years has had baggage subjected to X-ray imaging prior to departure. Commercial facilities sometimes screen the bags of visitors (and even employees!) in order to manage the risk of hand-carried explosive devices and other weapons.

X-ray inspection technology applied to security scenarios is nearly ubiquitous, but many security professionals do not appreciate how these work or their operational limitations. To facilitate a deeper understanding of the science of X-rays, the fundamentals of X-ray and gamma-particle physics are discussed in Chapter 7 in connection with the threat of radiological dispersion devices.

The intensity of X-rays (and gamma rays, the nuclear analog of X-rays) becomes attenuated as the energy propagates through various materials. X-ray technology is based on the fact that X-ray absorption in matter varies with the energy of the incident beam and the density of the absorbing material. This produces a contrast that appears on a monitor as areas of light and dark shading. Alternatively, this contrast is artificially colored on the viewing monitor to indicate differences in material density.

The three modes of interaction of X-rays with matter are introduced here, with more details provided in Chapter 7: the photoelectric effect, Compton scattering, and pair production. Figure 6.19 shows the regions of energy where each

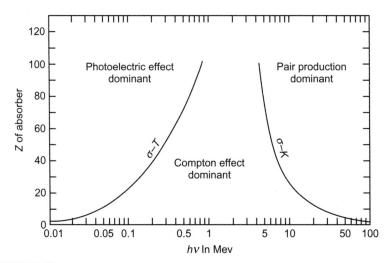

FIGURE 6.19

The interaction of gamma or X-ray energy with matter. *(Used with permission from Advanced Laboratory, Physics 407, University of Wisconsin; Madison, Wisconsin. 1999.* http://www.hep.wisc.edu/~prepost/407/ gamma/gamma_html.html.*)*

mode dominates as a function of the absorber atomic number, i.e., the number of electrons/protons.

Many X-ray devices used for security and other things are based on the photoelectric effect. How does this work in practice? The X-ray energy impinges on the item to be inspected (e.g., your carry-on bag, your teeth, etc.) and a detector is located on the far side of the inspected item. The intensity of the energy as sensed by the detector will vary according to the density of the material being imaged.

To illustrate the point, let's examine what happens when your dentist wants to investigate the source of pain in your tooth.[b]

All human teeth are made up of relatively dense material that contains numerous protons and an equal number of electrons (e.g., calcium, $Z =$ atomic number $= 20$). Because of the large number of electrons in calcium, that element interacts preferentially with the X-ray energy compared to the lower density material in your cavity, e.g., air. Recall air consists of 78 percent nitrogen and 21 percent oxygen, where each of those elements contains many fewer electrons ($Z = 7$ for nitrogen, $Z = 8$ for oxygen) than calcium. Again, details of the photoelectric effect are given in Chapter 7.

The interaction of the X-ray energy with the material in your tooth via the photoelectric effect results in a preferential absorption of energy relative to the air-filled cavity. That is, the portion of the beam that interacts with air (i.e., it is assumed that the hole in your tooth is at least partially filled with air) is relatively unaffected, as it traverses the same distance to the detector as the portion of the beam that interacts with the electron-dense calcium.

Therefore, most of the X-ray energy that interacts with air reaches the detector. The solid portion of the tooth appears as a dark shadow on the film. This is because the electron-rich calcium has attenuated the intensity of that portion of the X-ray beam. By contrast (no pun intended), the cavity shows up as a light, wispy streak. Seeing that wispy streak confirms your dentist's suspicions as he reaches for his high-speed drill along with a merciful injection of Novocain.

The X-ray in your dentist's office is probably a transmission-type machine. The carry-on bag inspection method deployed in airports works in the same way but with a twist. Like your teeth, a weapon's metal components preferentially absorb X-ray energy. Therefore, a gun's characteristic silhouette is readily

---

[b]I am indebted to my dentist, Dr. Arnold Mars, for stimulating technical discussions that prompted deeper thinking about X-ray inspections. Moreover, his approach to cavity detection and resolution is superb and pain-free.

apparent on the monitor when stuffed among clothes, books, and other lower-density materials.

But what happens if an electronic device such as a radio is packed within that suitcase? Moreover, suppose that the radio is actually an explosive device and the bomb's electronic components are interspersed among similar components found in a radio. It is quite possible that an X-ray inspector might have difficulty discriminating an explosive device from a radio. This is precisely what occurred in the case of Pan Am 103 that exploded over Lockerbie, Scotland, in 1988.

Fortunately, there are several X-ray technologies that can deal with this scenario and thereby more effectively highlight suspicious packages in general. The first such technology is known as dual-energy X-ray inspection.

The theory of operation for dual energy X-ray inspection is relatively simple. The impinging X-ray beam consisting of a spectrum of energies in the 140- to 160-kVp (peak kilovolts) range passes through the inspected material and hits the first detector. The energy is filtered, and the higher-energy portion of the spectrum is removed before it impinges on a second detector.

Because the X-ray intensity attenuation is a function of the beam energy and the density of the material, it is possible to distinguish between higher-density objects like electronic components containing copper wire and silicon-integrated circuits and lower-density organic materials such as nitrogen, an element found in many explosives. This is accomplished by comparing the results of the two detectors. A computer artificially colors higher- and lower-density material based on the relative intensities as seen by each detector.

The second X-ray inspection technique that is used to detect lower-density material such as explosives is X-ray backscatter. It is based on the phenomenon known as Compton scattering, as described in Chapter 7. In this case, energy is selectively scattered by the material, and the intensity of scattered energy is a function of the X-ray energy and the material density.

At typical X-ray inspection energies in the 100-keV range, lower-density materials scatter the X-ray beam preferentially relative to higher-density materials like metals. Therefore, the explosive material concealed within an electronic device shows up as a bright image on the monitor. Backscatter machines can be used to scan humans, since each image results in extremely low-energy absorption.

In this case the lower-density human scatters X-ray energy preferentially relative to the higher-density gun. Figure 6.20 shows a backscatter X-ray image of an individual with concealed weapons.

What if a handgun is plastic and it is put through a transmission-type X-ray machine? In theory it would be transparent if it were concealed among items

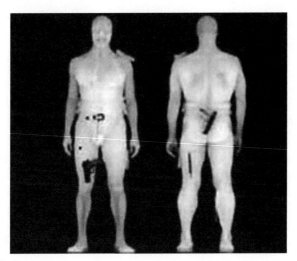

FIGURE 6.20

X-ray backscatter images. *(From NIST. "2.1 Personel X-ray Anomaly Imagers."* http://www.nist.gov/mml/mmsd/security_technologies/dietimage.cfm.*)*

with a similar density. Recall some years ago there was concern that the Glock pistol could defeat traditional X-ray machines. However, even the Glock has some metal parts and is therefore vulnerable to detection using this technology and others.

One last comment on X-ray inspections is worth mentioning. This actually applies to any inspection technology or process. That is, the quality of the inspector is as important as the quality of the technology. This is exemplified by the following true story.

I was flying to London from Washington, D.C., in the 1990s in my official capacity as an FBI agent. I was not authorized to carry a firearm in the UK, but inadvertently left a pouch of .38 rounds in my carry-on bag. This pouch went undetected during the X-ray inspection prior to my outbound flight at Washington Dulles Airport.

However, I was summarily pulled out of line following the X-ray inspection at London Heathrow Airport on the return flight. Needless to say, I had quite a bit of explaining to do. Fortunately I had my government credentials to bolster my credibility. As a security professional, I was impressed by the attention to detail demonstrated by the British authorities.

In the end, I made my flight, and I was allowed to keep the leather pouch. Not unexpectedly, I was required to donate the bullets to Her Majesty before being allowed to embark for home.

6.13 THE DANGLING CRANE: TERROR WITHOUT TERRORISTS

At this point it may be slightly therapeutic to divert our attention away from terrorism for just a moment. This does not mean it is safe to relax. Although terrorism is a genuine concern these days, there are dangers that rival such threats, and they can occur where you least expect it. These are poignant reminders that terrorists are not the only purveyors of death and destruction.

One such threat recently emerged in proximity to my apartment in New York City. Consider the crane that had famously been dangling precariously 90 stories above the city at the 1 W. 57th Street construction site in midtown Manhattan. This was not a scenario perpetrated by terrorists but was in fact caused by Mother Nature. Figure 6.21 shows a photograph of the beleaguered mechanism after it was partially dislocated from its platform by Hurricane Sandy.

FIGURE 6.21
A crane dangling above New York City. *(From Wikipedia.* http://en.wikipedia.org/wiki/Effects_of_Hurricane_Sandy_in_New_York.*)*

It is a sobering exercise to calculate the energy generated by the crane upon impact if it had hit the ground from that height. It is also relevant that the likely impact zone was a stone's throw from Carnegie Hall as well as some very high-priced commercial and residential real estate in midtown Manhattan.

The first thing to determine is the velocity of the crane upon impact with the earth. This is quite straightforward, but it is not obvious that one can neglect the effect of the air on the crane as it falls through the atmosphere. Is neglecting air resistance a reasonable assumption in this case?

In the absence of air resistance, an object falling to earth continues to increase in velocity due to the force of gravity until it hits the earth. In fact, all objects falling to earth accelerate at a rate of 9.8 meters per second (i.e., $9.8\,m/s^2$ or equivalently $32\,ft/s^2$). So with every passing second, a falling object increases its velocity by $9.8\,m/s$ if the medium in which it is falling does not slow it down. All objects subjected to the force of gravity accelerate at the same rate.

But fluids such as air do indeed act as a drag on falling objects, as every sky-diver knows. This limits an object's velocity in free fall. This limit has a name and is known as the "terminal velocity." The interesting thing is that an object's terminal velocity is directly proportional to the square root of its mass; the heavier an object, the greater its terminal velocity. That is why people who weigh more require larger parachutes than their skinnier counterparts.

If the effects of this resistance can be neglected, an object's mass will not influence its velocity as it is accelerated by gravity. This may seem counterintuitive, but it is true, and it follows from the principle of conservation of energy (see below). For the skeptics among you, recall Galileo's experiment at the Leaning Tower of Pisa.

If we approximate the shape of the crane as a cylinder, and we are to believe published reports that it weighs 80 tons, it is possible to calculate its terminal velocity in air. The point is to determine if the air significantly affects the crane's velocity during its descent.

As noted above, an object's mass plays a crucial role in determining its terminal velocity. However, other physical parameters are important, and these are listed below with estimated values:

- Mass $\sim 72575\,kg$[c]
- Cylindrical drag coefficient ~ 0.82
- Crane cross section $\sim 3.2\,m^2$
- Air density $\sim 1.2\,kg/m^3$

---

[c]The weight of the crane was listed in one local newspaper as 80 tons. However, weight is actually a force (i.e., mass × acceleration) and is therefore not a unit of mass, although it is often incorrectly viewed that way.

After plugging these numbers into the formula for terminal velocity[d] we see that the crane would achieve a maximum velocity of 672 m/s or 1502 mph if it was dropped from a sufficient height. Note that the speed of sound in air is 762.8 mph at a temperature of 15° C (i.e., 59° F). So the 80-ton crane is capable of reaching a velocity of nearly twice the speed of sound! Note that the weight of the crane seems a bit excessive, and the quoted figure probably includes its base plus the tower. However, even if this is an overestimate, it will not affect the stated result too much.

For example, if we assume the crane weighed 40 tons, or half the weight quoted in the paper, the terminal velocity would be reduced by the square root of 2, i.e., to a mere 1073 mph. For comparison, a commercial jet can cruise at approximately 600 mph.

Recall the statement that the velocity of a falling object is independent of its mass assuming we can neglect air resistance. How do we prove this?

The potential energy of an object with respect to the force of gravity is equal to the product of its mass, m, the acceleration due to gravity ($g = 9.8\,\text{m/s}^2$), and its height above the ground, h, before release. Its maximum kinetic energy, or the energy acquired through motion following being dropped, is given by $1/2mv^2$, where v is the maximum velocity. Recall the same formula was encountered when discussing the kinetic energy specification for bollards.

According to the principle of conservation of energy, the potential energy of a hovering object at a given height above the earth must equal the kinetic energy developed while it falls to earth from that height. Gravity is referred to as a "conservative" force precisely because energy is conserved. It is not a statement about political orientation.

The principle of conservation of energy for gravity can be expressed mathematically as $mgh = \frac{1}{2}mv^2$. Those who know a little algebra will see immediately that the mass, m, cancels from both sides of the equation. Therefore, after rearranging terms, the velocity of an object upon impact with the earth equals the square root of the product of 2, g, and h. This is written compactly as $v = \sqrt{(2gh)}$. Notice that the object's mass is nowhere to be found in this expression.

What would be the maximum speed of this dangling crane upon its impact with the ground? Assuming the crane is 900 ft or about 274 m above the ground, it is easy to show that the velocity, v, is a measly 73 m/s or 163.3 mph.

---

[d]The terminal velocity is given by $\sqrt{(2\,mg/(dCA_c))}$, where d is the density of air, C is the crane drag coefficient, and A_c is the crane cross sectional area.

Therefore the velocity of the crane as it hit the ground from this height would not even come close to its terminal velocity.

So it seems that we are justified in neglecting the effect of air resistance if the crane had fallen to the street below. Using the velocity calculated through the principle of conservation of energy, the kinetic energy of the crane at the moment of impact with the earth equals 193.4 MJ.

It turns out that 1 kg of the high explosive trinitrotoluene (TNT) releases 4.68 MJ of energy. Therefore the kinetic energy of the crane upon hitting the ground is roughly equivalent to the energy released in detonating nearly 91 lb (~41 kg) of TNT.

To give some crude feeling for the effect of an explosion of this magnitude, the following is a link to a website that simulates the destruction of a factory using 50 kg of TNT: *http://www.youtube.com/watch?v=TXAZxyVNuMo*.

The lesson here is that threats come in many shapes, sizes, and heights. Furthermore, accidents can be comparable to terrorist incidents in terms of their potential for causing death, destruction, and general mayhem.

SUMMARY

Understanding how overpressure and impulse scale with distance and explosive payload is relevant to estimating the vulnerability to conventional explosive threats. Back-of-the-envelope calculations can be effective in developing practical if high-level risk management strategies, although computational methods are required for more exact solutions.

In that vein, a simple analytic method can be used to calculate the reflected pressure resulting from an explosion and thereby estimate building damage.

Various methods of risk mitigation exist and are routinely deployed. These include X-ray technology to visually detect the presence of concealed guns and bombs, portable explosive detection devices to chemically sense the presence of explosive elements, and bollards to restrict physical access and enforce a minimum standoff distance.

Understanding their respective performance specifications with respect to identified operational requirements contributes to the development of an effective terrorism risk mitigation strategy.

REFERENCES

[1] Jeremic R, Bajic Z. An approach to determining the TNT equivalent of high explosives. Scientific-Technical Review 2006;56:58–62.

[2] Alonso F, et al. Characteristic overpressure–impulse–distance curves for the detonation of explosives, pyrotechnics or unstable substances. J Hazard Mater 2006;137(2):734–41.

[3] U. S. Air Force. Installation force protection guide.

[4] Hinman E. Blast safety of the building envelope. WBDG. http://www.wbdg.org/resources/env_blast.php.

[5] Ngo T, Mendis P, Gupta A, Ramsay J. Prediction of blast loading and its impact on buildings: an overview. eJSE International 2007.

[6] Remenikov AM. A review of methods for predicting bomb blast effects on building. Journal of Battlefield Technology 2003.

[7] SD-STD-02.01 (latest revision). Specification for vehicle crash test of perimeter barriers and gates, and 12 FAH 5. In: Foreign affairs handbook—physical security handbook.

[8] Pick-up Trucks.com. www.pickuptrucks.com.

[9] Poplin WM. Acceleration of heavy trucks. W. Poplin Engineering. http://www.wpoplin.com/acceleration_of_heavy_trucks.pdf.

[10] Centre for the Protection of National Infrastructure. http://www.cpni.gov.uk/.

[11] BlastGARD. http://shattergard.com/blastgardhome.html.

[12] Chang D, Young C. Comparison of window stresses from explosions and projectiles. J Phys Secur 2012;6(1):46–58.

Problems

1. We know that the overpressure caused by an explosive shock wave scales *nonlinearly* with distance from the explosion. Namely, it scales as the inverse of the distance cubed (i.e., overpressure $\sim 1/r^3$).

   a. If the distance were doubled from the explosive source, what would be the effect on the overpressure relative to the original position from the source? (Hint: plug 2 into the above expression.)

   b. What would be the effect on the overpressure if the distance is trebled?

   c. What would be the effect on the overpressure if the distance is quadrupled?

   d. Plot the overpressure versus distance for a to c above. Don't worry about the units, as it is the relationship between the two quantities that matters.

2. We know that the explosive overpressure scales linearly with payload, m (i.e., overpressure $\sim m^1$).

   a. If the payload is doubled, what is the effect on the explosive overpressure?

   b. What would be the effect on the overpressure if the payload is trebled?

   c. What would be the effect on the overpressure if the payload is quadrupled?

   d. Plot the overpressure versus payload for a to c above and compare the results to the plot in Problem 1d.

3. Based on the scaling relations for overpressure noted in problems 1 and 2 above, if you could somehow either halve the explosive payload or double the distance from the explosive source, which would represent a more effective risk-mitigation strategy for your facility? Why?

4. Referring to Figure 6.6 from the text showing the lines of constant damage, answer the following questions:

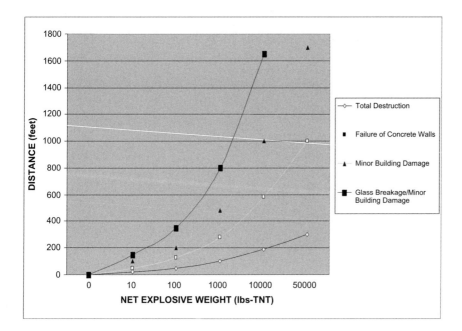

a. Refer to the curve corresponding to total building destruction. If the distance from the explosive source was 100 ft, by what factor would the net explosive weight have to be increased to cause the same damage?

b. Refer to the curve corresponding to window breakage. If the distance doubled from approximately 400 to 800 ft, by what factor would the net explosive weight have to be increased to cause the same damage?

5. You are the security director of a high-profile international corporation. Because of this profile, you are particularly concerned about terrorists using vehicle-borne explosives against your facility. You are attempting to determine the required specifications for bollards, and your physics-trained security consultant is otherwise occupied. Vehicle A is a 10,000-lb truck that can achieve a velocity of 30 mph at the bollard line. Vehicle B is a 5000-lb truck capable of achieving 60 mph at the bollard line.

a. We know the kinetic energy of a moving vehicle is given by $1/2mv^2$. Which of these trucks should be used to determine the appropriate bollards for installation, and why?

b. If the velocity of a vehicle could be halved by installing a chicane, what would be the effect on each of the vehicle's kinetic energy and hence the required bollard rating?

6. Referring to Table 6.1 and Figure 6.6 from the text.

  a. What does increasing the standoff distance from 100 to 300 ft do to limit the attack scenarios available to terrorists with respect to causing total building destruction?

  b. Answer the same question for window damage.

Explosive Delivery Method	Approximate Capacity (lb TNT)
Pipe bomb	5
Suitcase bomb	50
Automobile	500 to 1000
Van	4000
Truck	10,000 to 30,000
Semi-trailer	40,000

7. The graph below specifies the explosive-induced stress on a glass window as a function of both glass thickness (Lower Curve) and stiffness (Upper Curve). It is the explosive-induced stress exceeding the tensile strength of the glass that causes the window to shatter under explosive loading.

Effect of Window Stiffness and
Thickness on Explosion-Induced Stress

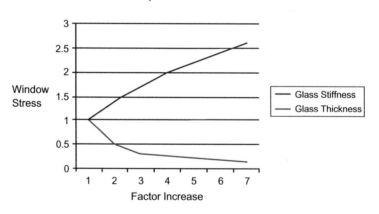

  a. What is the approximate effect on explosively induced window stress if the glass thickness is increased by a factor of 2 to 4?

  b. What is the approximate effect on the explosively induced window stress if the glass stiffness is increased by a factor of 2 to 4?

8. You are the security director of a major international corporation. Your company occupies a multistory facility in Europe that has iconic status and therefore is a potential target for anti-Western elements. The building has no mitigation for the threat of vehicle-borne explosives. Use the risk assessment framework provided in Chapter 1 to develop a risk-based mitigation strategy to address this threat.

9. The chart below shows peak sustainable pressure of tempered glass panels versus the duration of the blast for panels of varying dimensions.
   a. What do these curves say about the relation between blast resistance and panel design?
   b. Why would the larger area panels be less resistant to the blast duration than smaller area panels? (Hint: over what area does the explosive force act?)

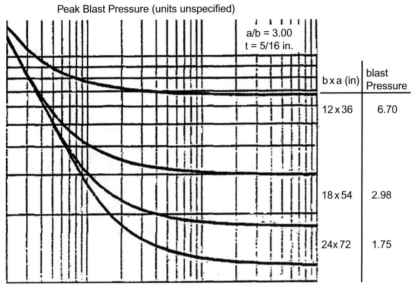

Peak Blast Pressure (units unspecified)

a/b = 3.00 t = 5/16 in.		
b x a (in)		blast Pressure
12 x 36		6.70
18 x 54		2.98
24 x 72		1.75

Duration of blast pressure (ms)

(Reproduced from the U.S. Department of Defense TM15-1300.)

10. Which of the following vehicles would have greater kinetic energy:
   Vehicle a = weight of 5000 lb traveling at 50 mph.
   Vehicle b = weight of 2500 lb moving at 50 mph.
   Vehicle c = weight of 2500 lb moving at 100 mph.

11. Referring to Figure 6.19 in the text, which process would you expect to dominate in the interaction of X-ray energy with a material of atomic number (Z) = 40?
   a. E = 0.1 MeV (i.e., 100 KeV)
   b. E = 1 MeV
   c. E = 100 MeV
   d. What do the results of a-c above say about the interaction of X-ray energy with materials if anything?

12. What operational scenarios might it be preferable to use a portable explosive detection device versus a canine and vice versa?

13. You are redesigning the security infrastructure for your company's corporate headquarters. As the Director of Security, you are concerned about vehicle-borne explosives as an attack vector. You have the opportunity to install a chicane in front of the facility to slow approaching vehicles.

    a. If the vehicle run-up speed was initially calculated to be 50 mph, what would the speed be if you could decrease the allowed turning radius by a factor of 4?

    b. What would the speed be if you could decrease the turning radius by a factor of 8?

    c. What would the speed be if you could decrease the turning radius by a factor of 16?

    d. Plot the speed versus turning radius for a-c above.

14. What is an operational limitation of an X-ray inspection device that only exploits the photoelectric effect?

CHAPTER 7

Nontraditional Terrorist Threats and Risk Mitigation

7.1 INTRODUCTION

In the last several decades the types of threats appearing on the radar screens of security professionals have broadened. It was not so long ago that issues like vandalism, theft, robberies, and general harassment dominated the security landscape. Accordingly, locks, alarms, and security officers essentially covered the gamut of required mitigation. Those traditional threats have not gone away, but the list of security concerns has expanded.

Although the potential for threats like radiological, biological, chemical, and electromagnetic weapons may or may not have increased, the public is definitely more aware of their existence. In addition, the abundance of dangerous materials that are housed in civilian facilities increases the risk. Importantly, the impact component of risk is high for all these attack vectors.

It is necessary to understand the vulnerability component of risk, even for incidents with a low potential for occurrence. In addition, fear counts for a lot in the terrorism business even if the facts do not always support the accompanying hype. This is one of many reasons why it is important to apply science to assessing terrorism risk.

So-called weapons of mass destruction have been deployed against civilian and military targets since World War I. A number of countries still maintain active research and development programs. The government of Syria appears to have recently used chemical weapons on its civilian population, a good example of state-sponsored terrorism.

Although there is little history of terrorist organizations utilizing the types of weapons discussed in this chapter, this might not be due to a lack of interest. The possibility that these weapons might find their way into the hands of terrorist groups is concerning.

From a strictly technical perspective, one of the most terrorizing aspects of these types of attacks is that such weapons can be difficult to spatially confine. The anticipated mode of delivery often involves dispersal, so even if a particular facility is targeted there is a significant risk of collateral damage.

However, although the vulnerability to such attacks may be significant, this does not imply that a specific organization should implement defensive measures. As discussed in Chapter 1 and elsewhere, a counterterrorism strategy involves analyzing multiple components of risk for a given threat or attack vector. Therefore, both the vulnerability and potential for such threats must be evaluated while balancing the cost of risk mitigation against the cost of addressing spectrum of competing security priorities.

At this juncture it would be prudent to say something about two important risk factors for nontraditional terrorism threats: distance and time. The effect of distance on the vulnerability to explosive threats was discussed extensively in Chapter 6. The vulnerability to both traditional and nontraditional terrorist threats is generally enhanced with a decreased separation between the threat source and the target and/or an increased time of exposure.

The effect of separation between a threat source and a target as well as the time of threat exposure can be profound. You do not need to study a textbook on counterterrorism to appreciate that it is best to remain as far as possible from explosive threats and to limit the time of exposure to toxic agents such as biological, chemical, and radiological materials. Common sense dictates as much. But providing estimates on acceptable limits for risk factors such as time and distance requires a deeper understanding of terrorism threats. Analyses that facilitate such estimates represent key elements of this book.

Some of the more prominent nontraditional terrorist threats are analyzed in detail in this chapter. Of course, a specific attack scenario is likely to be somewhat unique but at a high level, basic physical phenomena apply and can be used to provide estimates of the vulnerability component of risk. Understanding the scientific facts is required to justify putting potentially costly risk mitigation in place.

Finally, a prudent course of action would be to determine an order of magnitude estimate of vulnerability to these threats and then develop a plan based on approximations so derived. Of course the likelihood component of risk (i.e., the potential in this case) needs to be assessed as well, and this should be factored into decisions involving competing priorities as noted above.

This is the essence of rigorous security risk management. As a result of this analysis, the optimal defensive strategy might actually be to do nothing. However, it would be unwise to ignore the problem or merely guess at an appropriate mitigation strategy, as this would essentially be leaving the outcome to chance.

7.2 RADIOLOGICAL DISPERSION DEVICES (RDDs)

7.2.1 The RDD as a Weapon

This chapter begins with what is probably the simplest nontraditional attack vector, the radiological dispersion device or "dirty bomb." In this scenario, a conventional explosive is detonated with radiological material included with the payload. The explosion causes the radioactive material to break up into smaller radioactive chunks that are dispersed over an area dictated by the amount of radiological material, the size of the explosive payload, and local ambient conditions such as wind.

An RDD is not the same thing as a nuclear bomb. The latter functions in a completely different manner, and are typically much more powerful in terms of explosive force. Nuclear bombs work as a result of nuclear fission or fusion to release tremendous amounts of explosive energy equivalent to thousands or even millions of tons of TNT. Nuclear bombs were dropped on the Japanese cities of Hiroshima and Nagasaki during World War II by the United States.

In contrast, an RDD combines the deleterious effects of conventional explosives with a radioisotope as part of the mix. The isotope itself does not contribute to the force of the explosion. However, the device does give the terrorist a twofer in terms of harmful effects based on the direct impact of the explosion and the potential exposure to radioactive material.

7.2.2 Dentists, Bananas, and the Natural Radiation Background

It is a fact of life that humans are constantly being exposed to nuclear radiation despite our best efforts to do just the opposite. Some radiation derives from primordial sources in the earth and others rain down on us from extraterrestrial sources such as the sun. There are also commercial devices that utilize radioactive sources. These include smoke detectors, certain types of gauges, and sources used for medical therapy.

Radioisotopes produce energetic particles as part of the natural process of nuclear decay. These inherently unstable materials typically emit radiation in the form of alpha, gamma and beta particles and/or neutrons. Unfortunately, such particles are invisible and can be very deleterious. This is especially true if they are inhaled, come in contact with the skin, or there is sufficient exposure via a combination of the radioactivity of the source, physical proximity, and time of exposure. In addition, the biological effects of exposure to radiation are cumulative.

The number of neutrons in their respective nuclei is what distinguishes the isotopes of a given element. This number is designated by a superscript next to the element symbol (e.g., ^{60}Co), where the superscript denotes the sum of the protons and neutrons.

The first important concept is that of nuclear activity. The activity refers to the number of times the nucleus of an unstable isotope decays and thereby produces a radioactive particle such as a gamma (γ) particle, a neutron, and/or a beta (β) particle. These emissions are what cause health problems based on the radioactive flux (i.e., the number of particles hitting a specified area), the type of particle, its energy, and the part of the anatomy where the particle is absorbed.

These particles cause damage to tissue by ionizing the atoms of the material with which they interact. There are two types of ionizing particles: direct and indirect. Directly ionizing particles carry an electrical charge with sufficient kinetic energy to produce ionization through collisions. Recall kinetic energy of any object equals the product of its mass and velocity squared, as we learned in Chapter 5 in the discussion on bollard effectiveness. Therefore, it is the particle's mass and velocity that cause ionization. The charged particles that are emitted by radioisotopes have a limited energy range and are stopped in a relatively short distance upon contact with a material (e.g., a few millimeters in the human body). Directly ionizing particles include beta particles, electrons, protons, and alpha particles.

Indirectly ionizing particles are uncharged but act by liberating directly ionizing particles or by initiating a nuclear transformation. For both indirectly and directly ionizing particles, it is the action of charged particles that cause damage to tissue. In one case it is done directly by energy transfer, and in the other, it occurs as a second order effect. Indirectly ionizing particles include gamma rays and neutrons, and these are much more penetrating than their directly ionizing counterparts.

The modern unit of activity is the Becquerel (Bq), and it is defined as one nuclear disintegration per second. The traditional unit of measurement of activity is the Curie (Ci). A Ci is defined as 3.7×10^{10} nuclear disintegrations-per-second. Therefore, $1\,Ci = 3.7 \times 10^{10}\,Bq$. The amount of radioactive material that is present is often specified by the so-called specific activity or activity per mass.

$1000\,Ci$ of substance A and $1000\,Ci$ of substance B are equivalent in terms of their activity, but they do not necessarily have the same mass. In addition, the radioactive decay products of dissimilar isotopes will likely have different energies, and this profoundly affects their interaction with matter.

Gamma rays, beta particles, and neutrons all have damaging biological effects on human tissue if certain thresholds of absorption are exceeded. The mean absorbed dose in a localized area of tissue is determined by dividing the energy imparted to the matter in that region by the mass of the matter in the same region.

Absorbed doses and harmful levels of radiation are expressed in units of rads. For example, over 100 rads must be imparted in a short period and over a substantial portion of the human body before individuals will show clinical symptoms.[1] A useful fact is that the amount of energy deposited by 1 rad of energy absorption equals $6.24 \times 10^6\,\text{MeV/g}$.

Determining the deleterious effects of an absorbed dose of a given quantity and type of ionizing radiation can be a complicated issue. This is because the absorption often varies with the body part as well as radioactive particle type. However, basic absorption calculations can be made nonetheless and are useful in determining vulnerability to RDDs.

Because of the complexity of radiation absorption, biophysicists have established a term called the linear energy transfer (LET) to measure the relative effectiveness of equal-absorbed doses from different particles in producing injuries. The higher the LET the more injurious is the radiation for a given absorbed dose.

The factor expressing the relative effectiveness of a given particle based on its LET is known as the quality factor (QF). In an effort to normalize the effect of an absorbed dose across particle types, biophysicists have incorporated the QF and the rad and thereby produced another unit known as the Roentgen equivalent man or rem. This unit of radioactive absorption should not to be confused with the sleep cycle or the rock group.

For all practical purposes, radiation doses expressed as rads may be compared to limits given in terms of the rem when dealing with beta particles, X-rays, and gamma particles.[2]

To make things even more confusing, the modern equivalent dose unit is known as the sievert (Sv). $1\,\text{Sv} = 100\,\text{rem}$. For no particularly good reason except force of habit, the rem will mostly be used in this book to specify equivalent dose.

The U.S. Health Physics Society has specified that clinical effects are not observable in humans for whole body equivalent dose levels below 35 rem. Serious short-term effects occur at 70 rem, and death results from exposure to about 400 rem. The 35-rem threshold will be used to assess the risk of radiological exposure to RDDs. It should be noted that 50 rem (0.5 Sv) is sometimes cited as the minimum threshold for radiation poisoning.

Another measure of the risk associated with excessive exposure to radioactivity is an increase in the rate of cancer among a population. This figure is listed as 5.5 percent/Sievert.[3] This means that if 100 people were exposed to a 1-Sv equivalent dose of radiation one could expect to see 5.5 additional cancers in that population.

At this juncture the reader might be getting concerned about what this means to his or her personal health. Specifically, you might be unnerved while contemplating the full set of X-rays you received during your last trip to the dentist. Let's estimate the risk more precisely. One dental X-ray produces an equivalent dose of approximately 0.003 rem. Compare this with 0.4 rem/year that is contributed by the natural radiation background. For example, while reading this page you have absorbed between 1 and 2 μrem of radioactivity. A little arithmetic reveals that 133 dental X-rays is equivalent to 1 year of absorption of the natural background radiation.

At the risk of disappointing the nonmeat eaters among you, plants, vegetables, and fruits are a natural source of radioactivity, principally in the form of potassium-40 (^{40}K). Let's examine one fruit where its virtues are extolled precisely because it is a high source of the element potassium, denoted by the symbol "K" in the periodic table.

In addition to its nutritious components, bananas also contain trace amounts of the isotope of potassium, ^{40}K. ^{40}K has a half-life of 1.25 billion years, so it has been around a long time, and it will continue to persist long after you have finished reading this book unless you are a phenomenally slow reader. The concept of half-life is discussed later in this section as well as in Appendix F. One gram of ^{40}K has an activity of 0.001 μCi or, equivalently, 1 nCi (i.e., 10^{-9} Ci).

The equivalent dose of absorbed radiation due to the ^{40}K in a single banana is 7.8 μrem or, equivalently, approximately 0.1 μSv. Therefore, the absorbed radiation resulting from eating 40 bananas is equivalent to the absorbed dose resulting from one dental X-ray.

If 8 Sv represents a threshold for a lethal dose of absorbed radiation, one would need to ingest 8 million bananas to die from the radiation due to bananas! I suspect the gastrointestinal effects would take effect long before the absorbed radiation. Even eating can be an exercise in risk management.

Living and/or working at high altitudes increases the exposure to radioactivity. The source of this radiation is secondary cosmic rays (i.e., decay products from primary cosmic radiation interacting with the atmosphere). The contribution to the natural background radiation increases with altitude, from 0.3 mSv per year for sea-level areas to 1.0 mSv per year for higher-altitude cities. Airline crews flying long distance, high-altitude routes can be exposed to extra radiation each year due to cosmic rays, nearly doubling their total ionizing radiation exposure. What is the measured absorption during a typical airline flight and cumulatively over the course of a year?

According to the Health Physics Society, the average effective dose rate of all flights of Xinjiang Airlines from 1997 to 1999 was 2.38 μSv/h, and the average annual cosmic radiation dose for flight personnel was 2.19 mSv. The good news is that the annual individual doses of all monitored flight personnel appear to be well below the limit of 20 mSv/y recommended by the International Commission on Radiological Protection (ICRP).

Some secondary cosmic rays are charged particles and so they are deflected by the Earth's magnetic field as a result of the Lorentz force. Therefore, the cosmic ray intensity will vary according to altitude and latitude. In general, radiation shielding by the geomagnetic field is greatest at the equator and decreases as one goes north or south.

Again, according to the Health Physics Society, at typical flight altitudes of 9,000 to 12,000 meters, the difference between the cosmic ray dose rates at the equator versus the north or south poles is about a factor of two to three, depending on the point in the 11-year sunspot cycle.

The lesson here is that each person on earth is continuously being exposed to low levels of nuclear radiation and we remain blissfully unaware of the experience. We will leave this section by acknowledging the somewhat unsettling fact that humans continuously irradiate *themselves* due to the presence of trace amounts of radioactive material in our own bodies (about 0.24 µCi for a 75 kg human). Figure 7.1 indicates the relative contributions to radioactive absorption for various sources.

7.2.3 Radioisotopes as Weapons

An accurate assessment of the vulnerability to an RDD would require knowing the exact radioisotope being used by the terrorist. There are about 3800 radioactive isotopes, and in theory, many of these could be used in an RDD. However, the features of availability, toxicity, and radiological persistence are factors of key importance to anyone considering their use for terrorism. These operational issues drive reasonable assumptions about candidate weapons.

Radiological persistence means that the substance continues to undergo nuclear decay for a sufficient period of time and thereby causes ongoing angst among the target population. A measure of this persistence is the so-called radioactive half-life. This is defined as the time required for the population of continuously decaying radioactive nuclei to be reduced by half.

Three radioisotopes that are relatively easy to obtain and might have attractive features for terrorism are ^{60}Co, ^{192}Ir, and ^{137}Cs. Each produces gamma radiation, but at different energies. The biological effect of radiation as a function of activity is measured in units of rem/Ci-hr at 1 m (RHM).

This is a very useful parameter in estimating the risk from an RDD since it takes into account the deleterious biological effects due to the time of exposure,

RELATIVE DOSES FROM RADIATION SOURCES

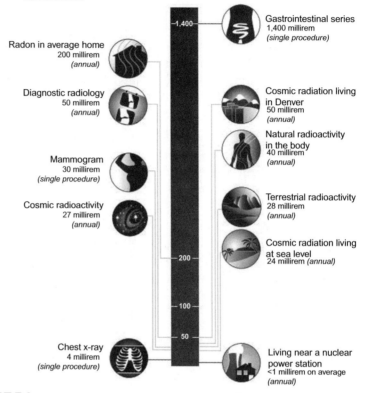

Millirem Doses

Gastrointestinal series
1,400 millirem
(single procedure)

Radon in average home
200 millirem
(annual)

Cosmic radiation living
in Denver
50 millirem
(annual)

Diagnostic radiology
50 millirem
(annual)

Natural radioactivity
in the body
40 millirem
(annual)

Mammogram
30 millirem
(single procedure)

Terrestrial radioactivity
28 millirem
(annual)

Cosmic radioactivity
27 millirem
(annual)

Cosmic radiation living
at sea level
24 millirem (annual)

Chest x-ray
4 millirem
(single procedure)

Living near a nuclear
power station
<1 millirem on average
(annual)

FIGURE 7.1

Equivalent doses from radiation sources. *(From U.S. Environmental Protection Agency. "Radiation Doses in Perspective." http://www.epa.gov/rpdweb00/understand/perspective.html.)*

distance from the source, and source quantity. The RHM values for ^{60}Co, ^{192}Ir, and ^{137}Cs are 1.35, 0.59, and 0.38, respectively.

The Health Physics Society has established another useful metric that has applicability to RDDs. They specify that 1000 Ci or ~11.4 g of ^{137}Ce spread evenly over a circular area with a radius of 100 m (~7.8 acres) could produce observable clinical effects after 100 hr of unshielded exposure.

Recall the 35 rem equivalent dose figure cited as the threshold for significant health concerns from absorbed radiation. That figure combined with the metric specified immediately above tells us that roughly 4 days of exposure to an exploded 1000-Ci ^{137}Cs source spread evenly about an area would be required before one would expect to see clinical effects from the radiation.

In the next section we estimate the risk associated with exposure to a small chunk of unshielded radioisotope relative to the 35-rem equivalent dose threshold. The vulnerability is estimated as a function of distance from the source. Of course this would probably not be an entirely accurate RDD scenario since the radioactive source would be dispersed due to the explosion, but it is instructive nonetheless.

7.2.4 Radioactive Flux, Absorption, and Shielding
7.2.4.1 Radioactive Flux
Now that we have been introduced to some of the fundamental concepts that affect estimates of RDD risk, it is necessary to explore additional factors that influence radioactive absorption. Specifically, these factors include the substance activity (i.e., the number of Curies), the type of emitted radiation, the attenuating effect of any intervening material, the time of radioactive exposure, and the distance between the radioactive source and the affected individual.

Suppose a 1000-Ci radiotherapy source of ^{60}Co (about 0.9 g) was left unattended in an unshielded container. This is not a good situation, and you should definitely *not* try this experiment at home or elsewhere! As noted previously, the RHM value of ^{60}Co is 1.35.

A 1000-Ci source of ^{60}Co would result in the absorption of a 1350-rem equivalent dose in 1 hr at a distance of 1 m. That means that in about 1.6 min, a human would be exposed to the suggested subclinical threshold for an entire lifetime. ^{60}Co is particularly nasty stuff. Note that for a 2000-Ci source of ^{60}Co, the time required to absorb the same equivalent dose would be cut in half. This tells us that absorption scales linearly with activity all other factors being equal.

However, and as we know from the discussion of point sources, the intensity scales nonlinearly with distance. Specifically, the intensity of radiation from a point source decreases inversely with the square of the distance from the source. It is useful to once again conjure up the image of the expanding sphere of intensity for a point source of energy as depicted in Figure 4.1.

The flux of radioactivity hitting a human body from a chunk of ^{60}Co is by definition the number of gamma particles hitting the body surface area. The flux decreases as one gets further from the source since the area over which it acts increases with distance from the source.

This has significant implications for calculations of risk since the number of particles that come in contact with a target directly affects the number available for absorption. Importantly, the benefits of separation between a source and target accrue disproportionately with increasing distance.

7.2.4.2 Radioactive Absorption

But separation distance and the activity of the source are not the whole story with respect to understanding the vulnerability component of risk for an RDD. Thankfully we are surrounded by an envelope of air that is an absorber of radiation at radioactive energies of concern. The two coincident gamma rays emitted from the chunk of ^{60}Co that result from each nuclear decay immediately interact with air consisting of nitrogen (78 percent), oxygen (21 percent), and other elements in lesser quantities following ejection from the nucleus.

The interaction of radiation with materials is well understood by physicists. This interaction is a function of the energy of the ionizing radiation as well as the atomic number of the material with which it interacts.

The attenuation of electromagnetic energy as it traverses through a material can be calculated using a parameter that accounts for all three types of interactions with matter. These interactions are discussed individually in the next section on radiation shielding. This parameter, the mass attenuation coefficient, can be used to calculate the rate of decrease in intensity as the radiation plows its way through a given material.

More precisely, the mass attenuation coefficient is defined as the probability of photons interacting with matter per unit distance. The mass attenuation coefficient for each of the two coincident decay products of ^{60}Co in air is approximately equal to 0.1 cm^2/g.

Figure 7.2 is a useful graphic that indicates both the mass attenuation and mass energy-absorption coefficients (see the discussion below for an explanation

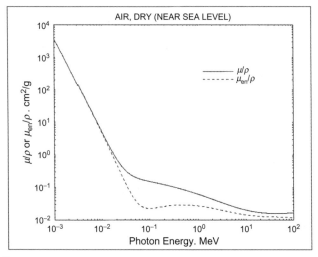

FIGURE 7.2

Mass attenuation and mass energy-absorption coefficients for X-rays and gamma rays in air. *(From NIST. http://physics.nist.gov/PhysRefData/XrayMassCoef/ComTab/air.html.)*

of the latter) for gamma rays and X-rays propagating in air over a range of energies. Similar curves exist for many other substances, and one such curve is used to calculate the shielding effect of concrete later in this chapter.

The decrease in intensity of this ionizing energy as it passes through a material obeys simple exponential decay as described in Chapter 4 and is explained mathematically in Appendix C. More specifically, the loss in intensity of a beam of radiation as a function of distance, r, as it moves through the material is reduced at an exponential rate.

Assume photons with a flux, N, are incident on a very thin absorber of thickness, dx, and photons with a flux, dN, that emerge from the absorber in the forward direction. The number of photons removed per unit time by a unit area of the absorber is then dN. The number of photons removed in encounters with atoms in the absorber, dN, is proportional to the photon flux, N.

The number of atoms the beam of energy encounters is directly proportional to the thickness of the absorber. So dN is also proportional to dx. Therefore, $dN = -\mu N dx$, where the constant of proportionality is called the attenuation coefficient, μ.

The solution to this equation is the exponential function discussed in Chapter 4. Specifically, the number of photons, N, can be shown to be $N_o e^{-\mu x}$, where N_o is the initial number of photons.

It is common to use the mass attenuation coefficient in calculations of radioactive attenuation. This parameter consists of the linear attenuation coefficient divided by the density of the absorber, ρ. The mass attenuation coefficient, μ/ρ, has units of cm^2/g.

In general, energy absorption and scattering result from three phenomena: the photoelectric effect, pair production, and Compton scattering. The relative contribution of each process depends on the beam energy and the material atomic number. Pair production only occurs at energies exceeding ~1 MeV or twice the rest energy of an electron.

We can now describe the attenuation process more quantitatively and thereby determine the radiation intensity as a function of distance as the energetic particles travel through air, or any material for that matter.

The intensity of the gamma energy as a function of distance traversed in a material is given by

$$I = I_o e^{-(\mu/\rho)pr}$$

I_o is the initial intensity, e is the exponential (~2.72), μ/ρ is the mass attenuation coefficient of the material, and r is the distance the gamma energy travels through the material. Since the mass attenuation coefficient incorporates

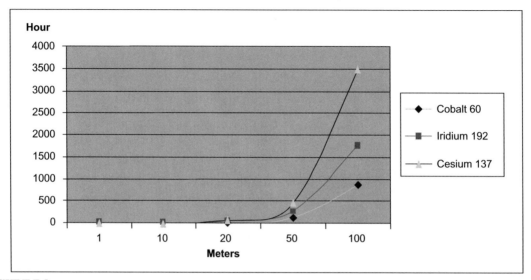

FIGURE 7.3

Time required for a 35-rem equivalent dose absorption as a function of distance from a 1000-Ci point source.

density in the denominator and has units of cm^2/g, one must multiply by the density of the material (e.g., air) in the exponent.

Using this expression combined with the $1/r^2$ decrease in intensity from a point source, the attenuation of gamma energy can be calculated to estimate the vulnerability to radioactivity due to an RDD.

Figure 7.3 shows the time required for a 35-rem equivalent dose absorption of radiation as a function of distance through air as a result of exposure to 1000-Ci point sources of ^{60}Co, ^{192}Ir, and ^{137}Cs.

We see from the curves that the required time to absorb 35 rem increases dramatically for distances greater than 50 m for all three isotopes. We also see that the exposure time required to absorb the threshold dose of ^{60}Co is much less than the other two radioisotopes. To repeat the previous admonition, ^{60}Co is particularly nasty stuff.

However, it is clear from these curves that the 35-rem threshold is not reached except for exceptionally close encounters with a 1000-Ci source and for a significant time of exposure. Therefore, one can conclude that *the acute vulnerability associated with the threat of an RDD derives principally from the initial explosion rather than from the radioactive emissions*. Extended exposure to the isotope would be required to cause significant health problems.

That said, the health effects could be significant if the radioactive material makes contact with the skin or is ingested. Any exposure to an RDD would not be a particularly welcome experience for individuals so affected.

7.2.4.3 Radioactive Absorption in Human Tissue

As the radioactive intensity decreases so should the absorption by any target that happens to be in the path of the radioactive flux. However, quantifying the radioactive absorption in humans can be complex since it depends on the organ that is being irradiated and other biological factors.

Recall from the previous section that radioactive attenuation in matter is a result of three different interactions: Compton scattering, photoelectric effects, and pair production. However, not all of the energy of the incident photons that interact with the material is absorbed there. Absorption is the process that results in tissue damage. The unit specifying the rate of absorption at a distance, RHM, discussed in the previous section, accounts for those radioactive processes that contribute to human tissue absorption.

Recall that the attenuation coefficient, μ, is used to characterize the rate of photon attenuation as energy travels through matter. It accounts for all physical processes in the interaction of energy with a given material.

On the other hand, the energy-absorption coefficient, μ_{en}, determines the rate of absorption of radioactive energy in matter as its name implies. It is defined as the fraction of the incident energy that is locally absorbed per centimeter.

In exact analogy with the mass attenuation coefficient, the mass energy-absorption coefficient, μ_{en}/ρ, is the energy-absorption coefficient divided by the density of the material.

Table 7.1 shows differences in the mass attenuation coefficient and the mass energy-absorption coefficient for photons in water (i.e., human tissue) and in the energy range associated with particles emitted by candidate RDDs. It can be concluded from the data that not all of the energy of these incoming photons that interact with the tissue is actually absorbed there. Therefore, the mass energy-absorption coefficient is the appropriate coefficient to use in calculating radiation absorption (i.e., vulnerability to RDDs) in human tissue.

Absent data specifying RHM values, one must calculate the flux of photons impinging on the tissue surface and the energy imparted per gram of tissue. A sample calculation is illustrative since the RHM for a particular radioisotope may not always be available.[2]

Table 7.1 Mass Attenuation and Mass Energy-Absorption Coefficients in Water for Likely RDD Photon Energies

Photon Energy (MeV)	μ/ρ (cm²/g)	μ_{en}/ρ (cm²/g)
0.01	5.33	4.95
0.10	0.171	0.0255
1.0	0.0708	0.0310

Consider a beam of gamma photons impinging on 1-cm² area of human tissue that is conveniently assumed to be perpendicular to the beam. Assume also that 100 photons of 1-MeV energy are crossing the area each second.

These photons will impart a fraction of their energy per unit distance as they travel through the tissue. This has been calculated to be 3 percent of the energy per centimeter in soft tissue. Therefore, the total energy imparted through 1 cm of tissue with an area of 1 cm² is (i.e., a volume of 1 cm³) is given by

$$(1.0 \text{ MeV} \times 100/\text{cm}^2 - \text{s}) \times (0.03/\text{cm}) = 3.0 \text{ MeV}/\text{cm}^3 - \text{s}$$

The density of human tissue is assumed to be the same as water or 1 g/cm³. Therefore, the energy imparted per gram of tissue is

$$(3.0 \text{ Mev}/\text{cm}^3 - \text{s})/(1 \text{ g}/\text{cm}^3) = 3.0 \text{ MeV}/\text{g} - \text{s}$$

Using the fact that that the amount of energy deposited in 1 rad of energy absorption equals 6.24×10^6 MeV/g, (or 62,400 MeV/g-mrad), we see that the absorbed dose rate in this scenario is equal to the following:

$$(3 \text{ Mev}/\text{g} - \text{s} \times 3600 \text{ s}/\text{hr}) / 62,400 \text{ MeV}/\text{g} - \text{mrad} = 0.172 \text{ mrad}/\text{hr}$$

Therefore, at this rate of exposure, it would take 664 years to absorb 100 rad.

Since radioactive nuclei are continuously decaying, one might be tempted to just hang around until the radioactivity diminishes to a harmless level. Unfortunately, Mother Nature is not particularly helpful here. In fact, a thoughtful terrorist might choose a specific isotope in part because of its radioactive persistence in order to maximize disruption and chaos for as long as possible.

The half-life of ^{60}Co is roughly 5.4 years. This means that we must wait 5.4 years for half of the radioactive nuclei to decay. This isotope produces two coincident gamma rays with energies of 1.17 MeV and 1.37 MeV for each nuclear decay.

It seems we must wait a long time for the intensity to diminish sufficiently to be safe. But what if an educated adversary chooses a different isotope? For example, the half-lives of ^{137}Cs and ^{192}Ir are 30.1 years and 74 days, respectively. Let's say ^{192}Ir is the isotope du jour, and you therefore elect to follow a strategy of waiting out the decay process.

One gram of ^{192}Ir has an activity of between 550 and 600 Ci. Let's assume the activity is 575 Ci. In 74 days the chunk will be at half that activity according to the definition of half-life. In 10 half-lives or 740 days, the activity would be reduced by a factor of $(½)^{10}$ or 1024. Therefore, the activity of the remaining radioactive chunk would be approximately 0.56 Ci or 560 mCi after 2 years. How dangerous is this radioactive chunk after waiting a period of 2 years?

The average gamma energy emitted by Iridium-192 is 0.37 MeV, and we use this as the activity level, noting that a more rigorous calculation would use the fractional contribution from each emitted gamma particle energy.

The exposure rate in mrem/hr at 1 meter is approximately (within 20%) given by $(5000 \times 562$ mCi $\times 0.37$ Mev$)/(100$ cm$)^2 = 103.9$ mrem/hr. Recalling our 35 rem threshold, it would require about 14 days to observe significant health effects from Iridium-192 at this distance.

We conclude from this exercise that having patience in physically approaching short half-life isotopes might pay off. However, it's important to note that exposure to one gram of Iridium-192 at this distance while anticipating its inevitable decay would definitely produce harmful effects.

In case you are a remarkably patient person, you should know that some primordial radioisotopes have a half-life of over a billion years. That is why they are still around. Recall we encountered this issue when we contemplated the effect of eating bananas, since each banana contains trace amounts of ^{40}K, an isotope with a half-life of 1.248×10^9 years.

From the terrorist's point of view and as alluded previously, it is important to use a radioisotope of sufficient longevity since the principal goal is to cause maximum chaos. But as we observed, close and sustained proximity to the chunks of dispersed radioactive material is required to cause significant biological damage. It therefore bears repeating that the explosion itself is the most dangerous feature of an RDD.

There is legitimate concern over the radioactive detritus that would linger in the streets following an explosion. This could find its way inside buildings and generally infiltrate the environment. This analysis is not meant to trivialize the cleanup effort that would be required as a result of the detonation of an RDD. But it is important to appreciate the near-term risks to individuals in the vicinity of the explosion.

Later in this book we will also see that contaminated air can enter buildings through the façade, complicating matters from a health and safety perspective. This is a potential problem for a building population seeking refuge from an RDD attack. Of course the building air intakes represent an obvious concern since these are designed to suck in large volumes of potentially contaminated air.

7.2.4.4 Radioactive Shielding

There are essentially three ways to mitigate the effects of a radioactive substance following its release into the air: increase the distance between the source and the absorber, provide shielding from the source, or minimize the time of exposure. The time required to absorb a 35-rem equivalent dose of ^{137}Cs, ^{192}Ir, and ^{60}Co as a function of the distance from the source was shown in Figure 7.3. These times are based on the published RHM values.

It was also shown that at a distance of 50 m or more, and with only air between the source and target, multiple days of exposure would be required before any clinical effects from the radiation would be observable for these three radioisotopes. In a previous section we observed that air does act as a shield to radioactive emissions, but typically a more effective material is required.

It was posited that ^{60}Co, ^{137}Cs, and ^{192}Ir might be ideal candidates for radiological dispersion devices because of their availability, toxicity, and persistence. For the information of the inquisitive reader, 1000 Ci of these substances weigh 0.9, 11.4, and 1.7 g, respectively. Note there are 454 g in a pound, so a little of this stuff goes a long way. The principal radioactive emissions from these materials are gamma rays in the 0.5- to 1.5-MeV range.

In some scenarios it would be reasonable to assume that shielding could be an option for reducing radiation intensity. However, the highly energetic form of electromagnetic energy emitted from radioisotopes is very penetrating. Typical metal enclosures used to shield radio frequency energy will do little to block gamma rays or neutrons.

We learned that the three mechanisms that determine the attenuation of X-rays and gamma rays in matter are the photoelectric effect, pair production, and Compton scattering. The mass attenuation coefficient, μ, accounts for the attenuating effects of all three processes. Let's now investigate each process in more detail.

Recall we encountered the photoelectric effect when we discussed X-ray-detection equipment. Photoelectric absorption occurs when the incoming photon of gamma radiation is absorbed by an electron and results in the ejection of the electron from its orbit. This process is graphically illustrated in Figure 7.4.

Compton scattering occurs when the incoming photon of radiation is absorbed by an electron and then reradiated at a different energy by the affected electron. In this process, standard physical principles of conservation of energy and

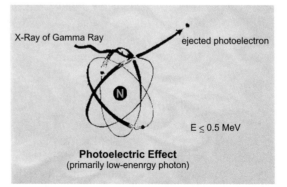

FIGURE 7.4
The photoelectric effect. *(From Occupational Safety and Health Administration.* http://www.osha.gov/SLTC/radiationionizing/introtoionizing/slidepresentation/slide9.html.)

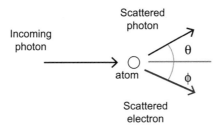

FIGURE 7.5

Compton scattering. *(From Goddard Space Flight Center. "Compton Scattering." http://imagine.gsfc.nasa .gov/docs/science/how_l2/compton_scatter.html.)*

momentum determine the distribution of energies of the scattered photon and recoiling electron. Figure 7.5 illustrates the process of Compton scattering.

Finally, when the incoming radiation is sufficient (i.e., twice the rest energy of the electron or $2 \times 0.511\,\text{MeV} = 1.02\,\text{MeV}$), another absorptive process takes place. This process is called pair production because of the electron-positron "pair" creation. Figure 7.6 illustrates the process.

Lead is often used as a radiological shield in part because it is relatively cheap. For example, your dentist probably drapes a lead apron over you when imaging your teeth in the search for cavities and other anomalies. If he or she does not take such precautions, you might consider switching dentists.

This is nice to know, but lead is not a typical building material. Therefore, it might be difficult to find a convenient lead shield in the event of an RDD attack unless you happened to be visiting your dentist at the time of the attack.

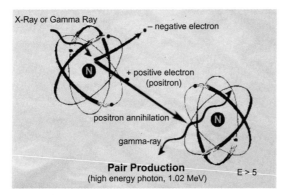

FIGURE 7.6

Pair production. *(From Occupational Safety and Health Administration. http://www.osha.gov/SLTC/ radiationionizing/introtoionizing/slidepresentation/slide11.html.)*

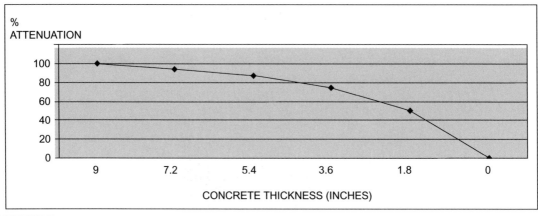

FIGURE 7.7
One-MeV gamma radiation attenuation through concrete.

By contrast, concrete structures are often in abundant supply, and although they are not as effective as a lead shield, they are more effective than air at energies of concern. How much more effective is concrete than air at shielding energy from an RDD?

Figure 7.7 shows the percent attenuation of a 1-MeV energy gamma ray as a function of concrete thickness (in inches). You can see from this graph that even a few inches of material has a substantial effect on shielding from gamma radiation. Nine inches of concrete effectively provides sufficient insulation from this energy.

With respect to the detection of radiological threats, portable commercial products are available that will identify the energies of radiological decay products. The good news about radioactive detection is that such readings are relatively unambiguous. Moreover, background levels for gamma radiation and/or neutrons would presumably be significantly less than those encountered during a radioactive release. A significant spike in detected activity would definitely be cause for concern.

However, it is also true that certain medical treatments that use radiological isotopes can trigger false positives in these devices. In addition, I have personally observed leakage from X-ray-inspection machines trigger them as well. Such sources of false readings should be appreciated before deploying these devices in a counterterrorism strategy to address RDDs.

7.2.5 Radiation from an Extended Source

Up to this point we have conveniently assumed a point source as the model for radioactive emissions. Therefore, the intensity of the radiation scales inversely with the square of the distance. How would the intensity differ if we assumed physically larger sources of radiation?

Radiation from an RDD will probably be scattered quasi-evenly over some area. We might approximate the shape of that area as a disc. The intensity of radiation from a disc-shaped source of radius R at a point p located a distance x from the disc is given by the following expression.[4]

$$I = (S/4) \times ln(1 + R^2/x^2)$$

S is the flux of photons/gamma rays emitted. Figure 7.8 shows how the relative intensity varies as the ratio of the source radius to the distance to the source (i.e., R/x), neglecting the attenuation due to air.

It turns out that when the distance to the disc x is much less than the radius of the disc R, the intensity is given by the following expression, where ln is the natural logarithm [4].

$$I = (S/2) ln(R/x)$$

Note that when $R = x$ the intensity is 0, since $ln(1) = 0$.

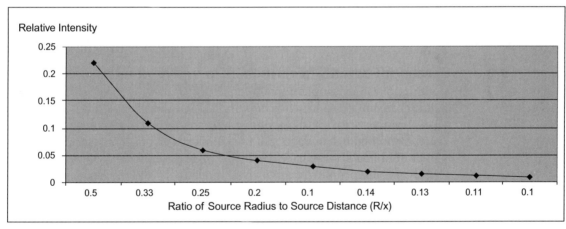

FIGURE 7.8
Radiation intensity from an extended radioactive source.

7.2.6 Theft of Radiological Material from a Hospital

Let's utilize some of our newfound knowledge about radioactive threats to analyze a scenario that is concerning to homeland security types. The reader is referred to the following article in the public domain: "Hospitals with Radioactive Materials Expose Weakness in Anti-terror Rules," *New York Times*, Matthew L. Wald, March 14, 2012.

For this risk-assessment exercise, we assume that someone has stolen radiological material from a hospital, and the government suspects that terrorists are behind the theft. In this case the alleged perpetrators managed to obtain ^{137}Cs, another highly active radioisotope that is used for medical applications.

Upon investigating further, law enforcement officials discovered that the chunk of ^{137}Cs was stolen from a special storage facility within the hospital. Unfortunately, this room had not been outfitted with appropriate physical security controls. These controls will be discussed in more detail in Chapters 10, 11, and 12. At a high level, such controls include authentication of identity, physical access restriction, access auditing, and visual monitoring.

In this case the hospital installed a radiation detection system in the loading bay. The strategy was that the detector would alert hospital security personnel in the event radioactive materials were removed from the premises.

How effective would such a detection system be in defeating a terrorist plot to steal radioactive material from a hospital? Assuming reasonable detection system parameters, it will be demonstrated that an easily transportable lead container could effectively shield a therapeutic dose of ^{137}Cs, thereby emphasizing the requirement for compensating physical security controls to address the theft of radiological material.

Indicative numbers are used to calculate the vulnerability of ^{137}Cs to covert removal from the facility based on a hypothesized, but not physically unrealistic, detection system. This is admittedly a "back-of-the-envelope" calculation in the spirit of many such calculations that are useful in addressing counterterrorism risk problems.

In this scenario the thief/terrorist is an employee who has access to internal hospital areas. In my experience patients and visitors often have liberal physical access privileges in hospitals. This employee is capable of replicating information encoded on the low coercivity magnetic stripe of the hospital's access cards. The security of ID cards and physical access control systems is discussed in Chapters 9 and 10.

Our terrorist is able to use this bogus card at the card reader on the front door leading to the Nuclear Medicine area. He guesses correctly that hospital security types do not review physical access control system logs for anomalous activity. As a last resort, he plans to piggyback into this area of the hospital and wait for an opportune moment to steal material from the radiologic storage room.

Crucially, our terrorist also knows there are no cameras to record his covert entry into that storage room. This individual also knows where the shared mechanical key to that room is kept. He has heard anecdotal stories of a radiological detection system somewhere in the hospital, but he does not know its location. Therefore, he designs and constructs a shield to covertly transport the illicit goods off the premises without detection. What are the design parameters for such a shield?

We first indulge in a bit of introductory physics to fully appreciate the terrorist's challenge. ^{137}Cs is an isotope of the element Cesium and has a half-life of ~30 years. The nuclear decay of ^{137}Cs results in gamma particles with an energy of 0.661 MeV per nuclear decay that is highly penetrating through matter.

It is assumed that this terrorist is well versed in the principles of nuclear physics. Therefore, he knows that lead is an excellent shield for gamma radiation at this energy, and he proceeds to design a lead box with the intent of sneaking the material past the detector, wherever it may be located. The first task is to calculate the reduction in intensity of the gamma radiation as a result of the lead box.

For simplicity, the linear dimension, x, of lead required to reduce the gamma intensity by a factor of 10 is first calculated. This means the terrorist must solve for x in the following expression:

$$I/I_o = 1/10 = e^{-\rho \mu x}$$

The mass attenuation coefficient μ/ρ was introduced earlier in this chapter and is an experimentally determined parameter with units of cm^2/g. It is used to calculate the reduction in intensity as electromagnetic energy propagates through the material. In this case the energy is 0.661 MeV, as noted above.

Recall the mass attenuation coefficient accounts for all interactions of electromagnetic energy with matter. The mass attenuation coefficient for 0.661-MeV photons in lead is $0.13 \, cm^2/g$, based on the chart in Figure 7.9.

Our nuclear physics-enlightened terrorist is interested in reducing the intensity of radiation so that the detection system is incapable of distinguishing the gamma radiation source from the background. The density of lead is given by ρ and is equal to $11.34 \, g/cm^3$. Solving for x in the expression for I/I_o, the gamma energy intensity is reduced by one-tenth after traversing 1.56 cm of lead.

He further assumes that the small quantity of ^{137}Cs secreted inside the shield is a point source of radiating energy (i.e., small compared to the distance from the source. Note that 1000 Ci of ^{137}Cs weighs about 11.5 g). Therefore, the intensity of radiated gamma energy is given by

$$I = S/4\pi r^2$$

S is the activity of the source, and r is the distance from the source. $1000 \, Ci = 3.7 \times 10^{13}$ nuclear disintegrations/sec since $1 \, Ci = 3.7 \times 10^{10}$ disintegrations/sec.

If the distance from the source to the detector, r, is estimated to be 3 m, the intensity, I, at the detector is $0.03 \times 10^9 \, cm^{-2} s^{-1}$. It is assumed that there is a single detector with a surface area of $100 \, cm^2$ (i.e., $10 \, cm \times 10 \, cm$). Furthermore,

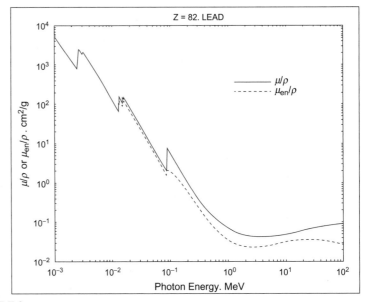

FIGURE 7.9

Mass attenuation coefficient for lead. *(From NIST.gov.* http://physics.nist.gov/PhysRefData/XrayMassCoef/ElemTab/z82.html.)

the terrorist traverses the detector at right angles to its surface and takes approximately 10 s to do so; this terrorist is in no hurry. Approximately 10 counts are needed to discriminate a legitimate signal from the background intensity. Contributions to the background are principally from cosmic rays and primordial sources of radiation.

In 10 s, the 100 cm² detector registers approximately 3×10^{10} counts of ^{137}Cs from a point source. In order to stay below the 10-count minimum, the terrorist must reduce the intensity by 3×10^{9}. Therefore, a 14.5-cm-thick lead shield is required that is enclosed on all six sides if it is a cubic container.

The terrorist assumes the thickness of each side of the lead cube is approximately 15 cm. The volume required to stash the radioisotope inside the cube can be quite small since it is only required to hold 11.5 grams (i.e., 1000 Ci) of ^{137}Cs. He assumes the area of one side is 5 cm × 5 cm = 25 cm² just to make things easier. The weight of the lead cube is calculated as follows:

$$\text{Cube Weight} = (6 \text{ sides/cube}) \times (25 \text{ cm}^2 \times 15 \text{ cm})/\text{side} \times 11.34 \text{ g/cm}^3$$
$$\sim 25{,}515 \text{ g}$$

Therefore, the weight of a lead cube required to remove the ^{137}Cs source without detection is estimated to be ~56 lb. This is easily transportable using a dolly. Note that the calculation was the weight required for a lead cube. If the terrorist manufactured a spherical container, this would result in a smaller and hence lighter container. The key point is that a physically fit terrorist could carry a 56-lb container for a considerable distance with the concealed radioactive material, and no one would be the wiser.

7.3 BIOLOGICAL THREATS AND RISK

7.3.1 Assessing Biological Risk

In the interest of full disclosure, a full treatment of biological weapons would require considerable background material on viruses, bacteria, and toxins. This is also true of chemical weapons. Such treatments are beyond the scope of this text. Therefore, the problem will be approached from a strictly operational perspective but will be supported by relevant scientific principles. What that means is that the science related to defensive measures will be examined in light of likely modes of attack rather than analyzing the various weapons themselves and their effects.

Specifically, the biology or chemistry of these weapons will not be examined, but instead we will look at the effectiveness of various security risk-mitigation methods. All biological weapons will produce unacceptably horrific effects, and there is little point in quantifying the relative magnitude of human misery. Therefore, all biological-threat attack vectors are assumed to be equally bad, although various features will affect the vulnerability component of risk differently because of specific features (e.g., diameter).

For example, considerable attention is devoted herein to analyzing the mechanical effects of filtering as a function of pathogen size to estimate removal rates from air intakes. Air intakes in buildings will draw massive amounts of contaminated air in the event of a biological attack. Issues such as contagiousness that will clearly affect the vulnerability component of risk (as well as likelihood and impact) are not addressed in favor of examining the susceptibility to mechanical filtering. The same strategy is used in discussing chemical threats, where the focus is on the efficacy of sorbent filters.

Pursuant to understanding the operational limits of standard risk mitigation, the flux of aerosolized biological agents across a building façade must be analyzed. A key by-product of this analysis is the effect on a shelter-in-place strategy. The so-called "stack effect" is an operational reality in most buildings, and this is a key factor in determining the rate at which external contaminants enter a building via the façade and exterior walls. The stack effect will be studied in some detail given its effect on the vulnerability to the dispersal of biological, chemical, and radiological agents.

As usual, the appropriate questions to ask in advance of developing a risk management strategy for any impactful threat are as follows:

- What is the potential for a biological attack to occur?
- What is the magnitude of the vulnerability to such an attack if it does occur?
- What is the cost of mitigating the vulnerability to the attack relative to the potential and vulnerability to occurrence?

7.3.2   Aerosolized Biological Agents

Biological weapons are a relatively new concern to the civilian security sector. These threats come in three basic types: bacteria, viruses, and toxins. The delivery mechanism envisioned for these threats is via an aerosol spray.

The spray's atomized particles are released into the air to be inhaled by those who come in contact with the toxic plume or picked up through contact with surfaces upon which the pathogen has settled following droplet evaporation. An analysis of surface contact versus inhalation has shown the former to be a more effective mode of transmission than inhalation.[5]

For some pathogens the disease might be preferentially contracted from those infected by the original plume. However, for viruses this will not typically occur until later in the incubation period. Symptoms may not be manifest in individuals until days after the attack has been initiated, thereby complicating response options.

A reasonable assumption about a biological attack is that it would be initiated at ground level. As noted above, another operational assumption is that biological agents would likely be dispersed using some form of an aerosolizing mechanism rather than with explosives. Biological material delivered by an explosive device might be possible, but this mode of delivery could be tricky to implement since the high temperatures of detonation could kill the pathogens.

Therefore, a significant building mitigation feature for the dispersal of biological threats is elevated air intakes. This is based on the previously noted assumption that an aerosolized attack is likely to be initiated at ground level and that the material so dispersed would be heavier than air. Physical access to air intakes, especially those located at street level, represents a risk factor for this threat since these afford direct access to the air circulating within a building.

The vulnerability of building occupants to biological agents will be affected by the defensive measures deployed within a building's heating, ventilation, and air conditioning (HVAC) system. These systems constantly pull in large volumes of air from the outside before being heated, cooled, and/or filtered. External air in the vicinity of an attack should be considered contaminated following an attack.

The Gaussian plume model introduced in Chapter 4 offers a simple if highly approximate model for estimating the concentration of a contaminant that is released in open spaces as a function of position and time. In keeping with the hypothesized aerosol-based attack mechanism, it is reasonable to postulate that some form of nebulizer would be used to produce the aerosol itself. These devices generate droplets of liquid material and are familiar to those who water plants, clean the house, etc. Presumably terrorists would use a more powerful instrument than the handheld version I use in my apartment.

For such an attack it might be important to know how long the droplets remain in a liquid state. In other words, we would want to know the droplet evaporation time since the effectiveness of mitigation methods could depend on whether the toxin is a liquid or a solid. In addition, a mitigation strategy might be preferentially oriented to suppress infections contracted by either inhalation or surface contact.

Biological material that has been dispersed via liquid droplets sprayed into the air would presumably exist as a salt upon droplet evaporation. Droplets sprayed inside a building would be subject to the inertial forces exerted by the building air circulation system.

Therefore, lower system air velocities would have a more-limited effect in terms of risk from inhalation since droplets would be carried over a shorter distance and, therefore, evaporation would take place over a smaller area.

A calculation to determine the droplet evaporation time as a function of droplet size has been performed, and the results are quoted from the cited reference.[6]

A spherical droplet of water or other material with a vapor density, C_o, was assumed for this calculation. This is the density of the saturated vapor in g/cc at 20 ° C. and a vapor pressure of 17 mm Mercury (Hg) so that the water vapor density is equal to 1.8×10^{-5} g/cc. In addition, the vapor has been assumed to have a binary diffusion coefficient of D in air, and the liquid is assumed to have a density ρ, which in the case of water is 1 g/cc. A reasonable handbook value for D is 0.2 cm²/s.

The scaling relation for the droplet radius relative to the time-to-evaporation is as follows:

$$r^2 = 2DC_o(t_o - t)/\rho$$

Therefore, the time-to-evaporation, t, scales as the square of droplet radius. Below a 0.1-μm droplet radius, where free-molecule flow dominates, the evaporation rate was shown to be simply proportional to the product of the vapor density and the free-molecule speed.

Time-to-evaporation (milliseconds)	1	3	10	30	100
Droplet radius (microns)	0.85	1.47	2.68	4.65	8.49

A 17-μm-diameter droplet would last 0.1 s. In an airflow of 500 cm/s, the droplet would be carried 50 cm downstream. A 3-μm-diameter droplet would be carried for 3 ms or a distance of 15 cm in that same airflow. Therefore, the diameter of the droplets in question has implications for the probability of airborne versus surface-borne infection and the effectiveness of building filtration.

The vapor pressure of a very small droplet is enhanced because of the capillary pressure (i.e., the difference in pressure across the interface of two immiscible fluids). It is reduced by the electric tension of the surface charge. The tension cannot exceed the capillary pressure without destabilizing the droplet.

Capillary pressure is important for droplets in the few-nanometer size range. Moreover, charge tension can be comparable with capillary pressure only for droplets far larger than those of concern in biological threats. Figure 7.10 graphically depicts the evaporation time for larger droplet radii, which is the size region of concern for biological threats.

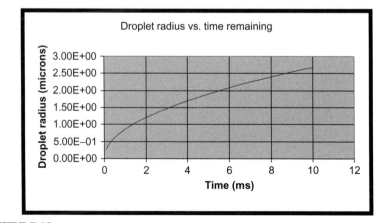

FIGURE 7.10
Droplet radius versus time remaining as a droplet for an aerosolized spray.

7.3.3 Sheltering-in-Place

Although air intakes enhance the vulnerability to the threat of internal building contamination, shutting the system down and closing the vents will not necessarily be effective as a mitigation strategy. Ultimately the effectiveness will depend on parameters like the building design, wind speed, and external versus internal temperature gradients.

The effectiveness of filtering in managing the risk associated with biological agents, a topic discussed in Section 7.3.4, is also a function of the airtightness of the building skin. If a building is porous to outside air, the effectiveness of filtration used in-line with the air intakes will be negated since unfiltered air will likely bypass these intakes.

The rate of airflow across the building façade is driven by temperature differences between the inside of the building and the outside environment. This is a well-understood phenomenon and it is known as the stack effect. Section 7.3.7 explains the stack effect in more detail.

Buildings will require insulation, filtration, and positive pressurization relative to the external environment to reduce the vulnerability to the dispersal of biological agents. A combination of these mitigation methods is required to facilitate a successful shelter-in-place strategy.

But positive pressurization requires that clean air be supplied from somewhere, and in these scenarios the outside air must be considered contaminated. Therefore, positive pressurization using clean air will likely require extensive filtering.

It is also important to recognize that commercial buildings are never completely airtight. In fact, many buildings are poorly insulated – especially older ones. Internal and external air is exchanged across small fissures in the building façade. Airtightness is determined by conducting a pressurization test on a floor-by-floor basis. One technical specification of airtightness is the room air exchange per hour (ACH).

ACH is the rate at which outside air replaces inside air within a room, assuming artificial forces that affect air exchange are not present. In the absence of an active HVAC system, the inside and outside air will ultimately achieve equilibrium. Exchange rates range from 0.25 room ACH for tightly constructed buildings to 2.0 room ACH for leaky facilities.[7]

Examining filter effectiveness relative to pathogen diameter yields an estimate of the vulnerability to the spectrum of biological attack vectors as explored in the next section. However, even if air filtration is present, the HVAC system should be shut off in the event of external air contamination because of the tremendous flux of external air being pulled into the facility and the probability that some contaminant particles will not be captured by the filtration system.

Building occupants would typically be advised to shelter-in-place in the event of an external contamination incident. This is intended to provide a place of relative safety for a minimum period of time. Buildings theoretically do offer some degree of protection from external contaminants when the windows, vents, doors, etc. are closed relative to the external environment. But do buildings offer significant protection from such attacks? More precisely, how much time do building occupants have before those sheltering inside are exposed to significant levels of external contaminants?

An estimate of the vulnerability to external contaminant dispersal can be calculated based on the airtightness specifications quoted above. This assumes the exchange of air as a function of time across the building façade obeys a simple exponential model such as the one that was introduced in Chapter 4.

Let's assume there is a concern over an external contamination and the HVAC has been shut off. Therefore, no air is being pulled into the building by the ventilation system. Initially there is no contaminated air in a room that is contiguous with the outside environment. The outside air is initially assumed to be 100 percent contaminated, and the inside air is assumed to be 100 percent clean.

The contaminated external air will eventually seep into the room until the air inside the room is replaced by outside air. It is also assumed that when the inside room air consists of 50 percent outside air, it is no longer safe for occupancy. Of course the accuracy of this supposition depends on the particular biological agent in use. However, and as usual, the objective is to develop an order of magnitude estimate of risk.

According to the exponential growth and decay model, the change in concentration of contaminated room air with time is proportional to the concentration of contaminated room air, which in this case increases with time, and the expression governing this process is written as follows:

$$dC/dt = RC$$

C is the concentration of contaminated room air and R is the rate governing the change in concentration of contaminated room air with respect to time.

We know from Chapter 4 that the solution to this equation is an increasing exponential where $C = C_o e^{Rt}$ and C_o is the initial concentration of contaminated air in the room.

Using this model, and assuming two room exchanges per hour (i.e., ACH = 2) or a leaky building rate constant, 50 percent of the inside room air consists of contaminated outside air in about 21 min. Another 50 percent of the room air is exchanged with external air in the next 21-min interval. It follows that

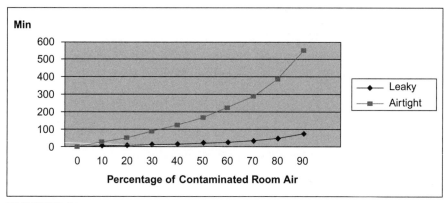

FIGURE 7.11
Room air contamination using an exponential model of exchange with outside sources of contamination.

for each successive 21-min interval, half of the remaining inside room air is exchanged with the outside environment.

If $R=0.25$ ACH corresponding to an airtight building (i.e., ACH $=0.25$), then the time required for half of the room air to be exchanged with external air is calculated to be 2.8 hr. Consider how varying rates of air exchange might affect a shelter-in-place strategy if the building was subjected to an externally dispersed biological threat. Figure 7.11 graphically illustrates the rate of room contamination for leaky and airtight buildings based on a simple model of exponential air exchange.

7.3.4   Particulate Filtering

Particulate filters are an important mitigation method for biological threats and are also used to maintain the general health of the building population. Particulate filters use fibers to remove particulates from the airstream. These fibers utilize three capture mechanisms: impaction, interception, and diffusion.

Interception works as a result of the size of the particle relative to the size of the fiber, which blocks its path. Impaction is where the particle departs from the airstream and by virtue of its momentum hits the fiber. Diffusion occurs when the particle trajectory oscillates about the airstream, thereby exhibiting random motion (i.e., Brownian motion).

Larger particles are affected more by impaction and interception. Diffusion is actually a more efficient capture mechanism for smaller particles.[8] When air with contaminating particles such as biological or radiological agents are incident on the fibers of a filter, air will flow around it. However, the particles will tend to continue in a straight line because of their inertia. Filters consist of closely packed fibers in a mat, and the filtering action for small particles is the result of the action of individual fibers.

After impact, the particles are held in place by the fibers as a result of physical, short-range forces (i.e., van der Waals forces). However, as the particle size decreases, their inertia is reduced, and they are more prone to follow the airstream. At even smaller sizes, the particles stray from the airstream motion as a result of collisions with air molecules (Brownian motion/diffusion). This increases the probability of interaction with filter fibers and removal from the stream. This is why diffusion is more efficient for smaller particles as noted above.

An unambiguous relationship exists between the fineness of particulate filters used in HVAC systems and building vulnerability to infiltration by pathogens based on their size. Filters are installed in-line with HVAC systems to trap incoming airborne particulates before they can enter a building's ventilation system. It is worth mentioning that such filters could also help mitigate the vulnerability to RDDs by trapping radioactive dust, thereby reducing the possibility of inhalation or skin contact.

HVAC filters are rated for different diameter particle sizes, and their effectiveness against the spectrum of likely pathogens will vary based on the match between filter quality and particulate size. This can be gleaned from Table 7.2 in conjunction with the data provided in Figure 7.12. The latter reveals filter performance as a function of filter size for various filter types.

Notice the dramatic dip in filter effectiveness in the 0.1- to 0.3-μm particle diameter range. This corresponds to the virus-size particle regime. We would therefore expect that some fraction of an aerosol-containing virus would penetrate these filters and circulate throughout the building courtesy of the HVAC system.

The vulnerability of the building population to infection via inhalation versus surface contact will in part be related to the length of time the virus remains in droplet form. Also, infection rates will depend on whether the viruses are

Table 7.2 Diameter of Pathogen Types

Diameter (microns)	Pathogen Type
< 0.3	Viruses
0.3 to 1.0	Bacteria, dust, legionella
3. to 10	Dust, molds, spores

(From U.S. Department of Health and Human Services, Centers for Disease Control and Prevention, National Institute of Occupational Safety and Health (NIOSH). (April 2003). "Guidance for Filtration and Air-Cleaning Systems to Protect Building Environments from Airborne Chemical, Biological or Radiological Attacks.")

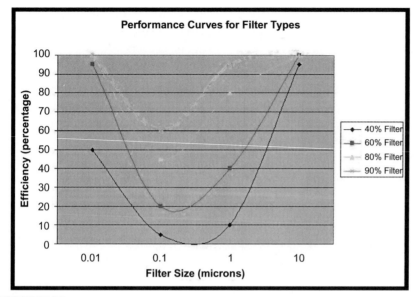

FIGURE 7.12

Performance curves for particulate filter types. *(From Ensor, D.S., J.T. Hanley, and L.E. Sparks. 1991. Healthy Buildings. Indoor Air Quality. "Filter Efficiency," Washington, D.C.)*

released within the building or originate externally. The external scenario is operationally similar to the biological agent dispersal scenario discussed in the previous section.

The virus should be more prone to being inhaled while still in droplet form since these are being carried along in the airstream and supported by the buoyant force of air. As noted previously, and following droplet evaporation, the virus would likely be deposited on surfaces in the form of a salt. The risk of infection in that case results mostly from surface contact, a more likely mode of transmission to humans than inhalation, although filters could reduce airborne dispersal.

Solid material would also be subject to the force exerted by the internal air circulation and other physical disturbances. A building mitigation strategy must consider the relative risk of infection for each mode of interaction (i.e., surface contamination versus inhalation).

For so-called high efficiency particulate air (HEPA) filters, the particle removal rates are in the 0.1- to 0.3-μm ($1\,\mu m = 10^{-6}\,m$) diameter range, and peak filter performance occurs at 0.3 μm. However, HEPA filters can be costly due to required increases in fan and duct size to compensate for restricted airflow across the filter barrier.

7.3.5 Ultraviolet Germicidal Irradiation (UVGI)

A technology that has been used to enhance the quality of internal building environments is ultraviolet germicidal irradiation. Readers who keep tropical fish might be familiar with this technique as a means of reducing algae in the fish tank.

UVGI involves subjecting incoming building air to ultraviolet light (C Band or 253.7-nm wavelength) for sufficient time and with a minimum intensity. Recent research has shown UVGI to be effective on pathogens of concern in biological attacks.[7,9]

The use of UVGI as a mitigation method can complement particulate filtration by expanding the number of biological weapons that are susceptible to capture or destruction before they enter internal building areas. The goal is to obviate the need for HEPA filters, which are typically necessary if the objective is to eliminate submicron-size particles such as viruses. Even 90 to 95 percent efficiency filters are reduced in efficiency to 60 percent and below for particles in the 0.07- to 0.3-μm-diameter range (e.g., smallpox and tuberculosis).[10]

The potential utility of UVGI is twofold: provide a healthy internal building environment and complement the protective capabilities of HVAC particulate filters in the event of an external dispersal of biological agents. Such filters could also be installed in internal ductwork to reduce the risk of contamination due to internal contaminants.

Appropriate intensities of UVGI for a sustained exposure time in conjunction with filter efficiency (i.e., removal rate) have been shown to produce significant reductions in the concentration of harmful pathogens.[11]

Particulate filtration in HVAC air intakes will address biological and other contaminants to varying degrees depending on the filter size relative to the particulate diameter. However, such filters will have a limited effect on chemical releases except for certain aerosols such as tear gases and low-volatility nerve agents (e.g., VX).[12]

Figure 7.13 in conjunction with Table 7.3 illustrates the effects of particulate filtration for pathogens considered to be prime candidates for biological weapons and that are also the least affected by low efficiency-rated filtration.

The minimum efficiency reporting value (MERV) designation is used to characterize particulate filter performance. The efficiency of particulate filters for submicron particles as specified in the ASHRAE Standard 52.2 is listed in Table 7.4. MERV 17 and above-rated filters are equivalent to HEPA-type filters in performance. Although MERV 13 filtration efficiency can be rated >90 percent, this rating applies only to pathogens larger than 1 μm.

The mean size of some candidate biological weapons is of submicron proportions. Table 7.4 indicates that MERV 13 filters have less than 75 percent

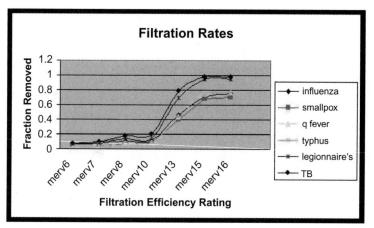

FIGURE 7.13

Particulate filtration rates. *(From Kowalski, W., W. Bahnfleth, and A. Musser. 2003. "Modeling Immune Building Systems for Bioterrorism Defense."* Journal of Architectural Engineering, *9 (2).)*

Table 7.3 Pathogen Mean Sizes

Influenza	0.098 microns
Smallpox	0.22
Q Fever	0.283
Typhus	0.283
Legionnaire's Disease	0.520
Tuberculosis	0.637

(From Kowalski, W., W. Bahnfleth, and A. Musser. 2003. "Modeling Immune Building Systems for Bioterrorism Defense." Journal of Architectural Engineering, *9 (2).)*

Table 7.4 Removal Rates for Submicron Particles as a Function of Filter Rating

MERV 13	< 75%
MERV 14	75–85%
MERV 15	85–95%
MERV 16	>95%
MERV 17	>99.97%
MERV 18 and Above	>99.99%

ASHRAE Standard 52.2

efficiency for pathogens of this diameter. Pathogens and toxins near or above 1 μm (e.g., *R. rickettsi*, also known as Rocky Mountain spotted fever, *Bacillus anthracis* (anthrax), and botulism) are removed at rates equal to or greater than 90 percent using MERV 13 filters alone.

The operational question is, can UVGI provide enhanced removal/kill rates for submicron pathogens and thereby eliminate the need for HEPA filters?

7.3.6 Combining Particulate Filtering and UVGI

The pathogen kill rate from UVGI is given by[11]

$$KR = 1 - e^{-Ik/t}$$

Here k is an experimentally determined rate constant with units of cm²/microwatt-second that will differ for each pathogen, I is the average UV intensity ($\mu W/cm^2$), and t is the pathogen transit/exposure time (seconds).

The overall kill rate resulting from the combination of filtering and UVGI cannot simply be added since the second method in the sequence of elimination methods operates only on the surviving population of pathogens. This is consistent with an exponential rate of pathogen population decay.

The overall kill rate is therefore given by the following expression:

$$KR = 1 - \left(1 - KR_1\right)\left(1 - KR_2\right)$$

KR_1 and KR_2 are the kill/removal rates for filtration or UVGI, respectively, depending on the sequence of implementation. This expression was used to determine the set of curves shown in Figure 7.14 that denote the total kill rates using a combined UVGI and particulate filtration system.[11]

These curves indicate improvement in submicron pathogen reduction when UV and filtration methods are combined relative to the use of particulate

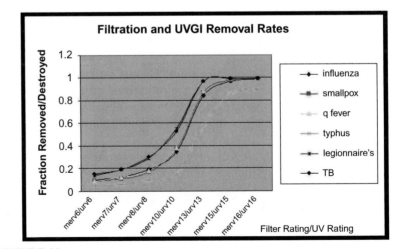

FIGURE 7.14

Combined particulate filtration and UVGI removal rates.

Table 7.5 URV Ratings

URV6	75 microwatts/cm²
URV7	100 microwatts/cm²
URV8	150 microwatts/cm²
URV10	500 microwatts/cm²
URV13	2000 microwatts/cm²
URV15	4000 microwatts/cm²
URV16	5000 microwatts/cm²

filtration (non-HEPA) alone. Specifically, greater than 84 percent removal rates can be achieved for a MERV 13/URV13-rated system and above, for all listed pathogens except typhus. The UV intensity ratings (URV) are shown in Table 7.5.

The pathogen removal rates shown in Figure 7.14 assume particle velocities of 2.54 m/s within the HVAC intake chamber. They also assume a 0.5-s exposure time. The 2.54-m/s figure is posited as an average HVAC air velocity value and might be a good approximation if one assumes laminar flow (i.e., uniform distribution of air velocities and low turbulence) within the HVAC chamber.

If it is assumed that the average air velocity is 2.54 m/s and a 0.50-s exposure time, [13] this imposes a minimum path length requirement for UV exposure of at least 1.27 m since path length = 2.54 m/s×0.50 s. UVGI installations could be affected by this parameter since the required path length might be constrained by the available air intake real estate in a building. Variations in the required path length for sufficient UVGI exposure might result from turbulent HVAC airflow as a result of diffusion-like processes.[14]

Developing an effective building defense against nontraditional threats can indeed be difficult, and this discussion is meant to introduce some of the salient issues associated with addressing the problem. Qualified building engineers should be consulted in conjunction with security experts to recommend an appropriate defense against particulate-based building contamination.

7.3.7   The Stack Effect

For most buildings, the benefits of sheltering-in-place in response to external contaminants are problematic even with the HVAC operating unless positive pressure can be maintained relative to the ambient external pressure. This is because building façades exist in varying states of leakiness, as noted in Section 7.3.3. This feature makes buildings susceptible to the stack effect, which can vitiate the effectiveness of filters or sterilization methods installed downstream of the HVAC air intakes.

The stack effect results from the creation of internal vertical temperature gradients that produce pressure differences with the outside environment. [15] If the density of air inside the building as a function of height above the ground is different than the pressure outside the building at the corresponding elevation, air will flow in or out of the building depending on the relative pressure difference (i.e., greater inside the building than outside or vice versa).

The distribution of holes in the building exterior as well as the unobstructed vertical flow of air within the building interior are major factors that affect the magnitude of the stack effect. This in turn will affect the rate of unfiltered air entering the building in spite of the best efforts of any HVAC filtration/sterilization systems. An illustration of the stack effect is shown in Figure 7.15.

In winter months in the northern hemisphere, air is being heated inside the building and the warm air rises to the upper levels. This is because the buoyant force of the heated air exceeds the gravitational force exerted on the same air volume. This in turn causes an increase in air pressure at higher elevations and reduced pressure at lower elevations. Air at the upper levels is therefore "pushed" out of cracks in the exterior since the pressure is greater than it is on the outside of the building at that height above ground.

In the absence of other sources of pressure, the volume of air exiting the building at upper levels exactly balances the volume drawn in at lower levels.

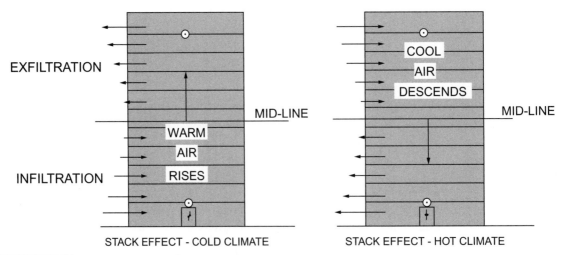

FIGURE 7.15
The stack effect. *(From* http://homeenergypros.lbl.gov/photo/stack-effect-reverse-stack?context=album&albumId=6069565%3AAlbum%3A9465.)*

In summer months the effect is reversed. The air is cooled and descends to lower levels because the buoyant force exerted on a volume of air is less than the gravitational force exerted on the same volume. The air at the lower levels exits the building through cracks and pores. Outside air is drawn in through similar cracks in the façade at the upper stories.

Clearly the pressure gradient in the vertical direction is greatly affected by the distribution of openings in the façade. If we assume a uniform distribution throughout the exterior, then the outside pressure and inside pressure will be equal at some point in the building structure. The height where this occurs is referred to as the midline or neutral zone.

Table 7.6 lists equivalent orifice specifications for other building elements.[16] To illustrate the meaning of this data, 100 ft² of 13-in porous brick wall (no plaster) is equivalent to an opening in the façade with an area of 3.1 in².

The actual pressure across cracks and openings will roughly correspond to the algebraic sum of the separate effects of pressure gradients caused by wind action, the stack effect, and the building air supply and exhaust systems. It is sometimes assumed that with the HVAC fan system functioning, buildings could maintain positive pressure relative to the outside and thereby minimize the vulnerability to external contaminants. This is not necessarily true.

As a result of the stack effect, leaky structures would be susceptible to some contamination, irrespective of mitigation implemented as part of the HVAC system. As noted previously, this is because some of the air that enters the building will bypass the HVAC filters. The magnitude of the effect is highly dependent on the structural details of each building.

One possible method to minimize the stack effect might be to shut the heating or air conditioning off and close the vents. This would reduce the temperature gradient between the inside and outside environment. But this will not happen instantaneously, and the stack effect would continue to operate until the temperature of the outside and inside air achieved equilibrium.

Table 7.6 Equivalent Orifice Areas (in²)

13-in porous brick wall, no plaster, 100 ft²	3.1
Wall as above, 3-coat plaster, 100 ft²	0.054
Frame wall, wood siding, 3-coat plaster, 100 ft²	0.33
Door, tight fitting, 3 ft × 7 ft	7.6
Window, double-hung, loose fitting, 3 ft × 4 ft	0.93

It is estimated that a 1000-ft^3 room would be filled with outside air in about 12 min under leaky façade conditions and assuming there is no internal air pressure generated by the building HVAC system. Again, the engine for the stack effect is a temperature gradient between the internal and external air.

Another potential solution might be to use fans and filtering to develop an overpressure condition and thereby protect fire stairwells by selectively pressurizing one compartment of the building. Filtering the external source of air would be essential since this scenario assumes that the outside air is contaminated. In any case, any proposed strategy should be vetted with a qualified building engineer before implementation.

7.4 CHEMICAL THREATS AND RISK

7.4.1 Chemicals and Chemical Weapons

Chemical weapons have been used as weapons of terror, although their historical use has mostly been confined to the battlefield. Such weapons were widely implemented in World War I. Wilfred Owen referred to the horrors of chemical warfare in his dramatic poem, *Dulce et Decorum Est*.

Some of the background material mentioned here regarding the types and production of chemical weapons was obtained from a single source [17]. In addition, the "Chemical Weapons" write-up in Wikipedia provides an excellent summary of the technology and history of their use in warfare.

Toxic industrial chemicals such as chlorine or phosgene are easily available and do not require great expertise to be modified into chemical weapons. Nerve agents are more difficult to produce and require a synthesis of multiple precursor chemicals. They also require high-temperature processes and create dangerous by-products. This makes their production unlikely except by an advanced laboratory. Blister agents such as mustard can be manufactured with relative ease but also require large quantities of precursor chemicals.

Aerosol or vapor forms of chemical weapons are the most effective for dissemination, which can be carried out by nebulizers or an explosive device. However, such agents are vulnerable to temperature, moisture, and wind and would therefore be most effectively used on an indoor population.

The Aum Shinrikyo incident is often cited as an example of the limited effectiveness of chemicals as terrorist weapons. Although the cult was able to produce the nerve agent sarin and release it in a closed environment, the Tokyo subway, the attack resulted in only 12 fatalities. Of course, this is not much consolation for those victims, but the limited number of deaths does seem surprising to anyone that has been in a crowded Tokyo subway station.

Contrast this with the hundreds who have died in some of the more catastrophic terrorist incidents where "traditional" weapons such as conventional explosives were used. It makes one wonder why a terrorist would go through the bother of deploying a chemical weapon. However, the specter of a horrific death from an invisible but highly toxic weapon might inspire terrorists to try their hand at this particular attack vector. Recall the earlier discussions on the importance of fear relative to the magnitude of the actual threat posed by non-traditional weapons.

That said, perhaps you recall a fatal incident at a chemical factory in India in 1984. On December 2 to 3, 1984 in Bhopal, India, a gas leak occurred at the Union Carbide India Limited pesticide plant. An estimated 500,000 people were exposed to methyl isocyanate and other toxic chemicals. The number of confirmed deaths was stated as 3787, but other estimates range between 8000 and 16,000 immediate and subsequent deaths. The Indian government stated that the number of injuries resulting from the release was 558,125.

The point is that toxic chemical releases can clearly result in mass carnage whether such releases are intentional or not. Therefore, the argument about chemical weapons being ineffective for terrorism is not entirely persuasive. However, the real point is that although the efficiency might vary, the inevitable panic could more than compensate for a relatively low kill rate in the minds of terrorists.

In the previous section particulate filters were discussed in some detail in connection with trapping biological contaminants (note: particulate filtering could work for radiological contaminants as well). Unfortunately they are not generally useful in capturing vapors resulting from chemical attacks. The exceptions are tear gases and low-volatility nerve agents such as VX, although a vapor component could exist for these agents. In general, mitigating the effects of chemical agents in vapor form requires the use of so-called sorbent filters.

Inhaled chemical vapors could have an immediate and profound effect on an individual. In addition, chemical vapors are likely to suffuse into the clothes of victims and thereby affect others in contact with those originally impacted for some time after the initial attack.

There are numerous harmful chemical agents. This issue frustrates the development of a comprehensive risk-mitigation strategy. However, phosgene and mustard gases are prime candidates as terrorist weapons because of their significant impact on victims and the fact that these agents are stockpiled and therefore are potentially at risk of theft.

Leaky buildings would be particularly vulnerable to external releases of chemical agents. Wind conditions would tend to both disperse and dilute the vapors.

As discussed in Section 7.3, the temperature gradient-driven stack effect would play a prominent role in the vulnerability of a specific building to a dispersed chemical attack.

Consistent with the presumed modus operandi for dispersed biological attacks, it seems reasonable to assume that chemical attacks would be initiated at ground level. Therefore, the vulnerability to external contaminants increases during the winter months in tall buildings relative to summer because of the stack effect.

For wartime applications, increasing the density of delivery systems has been a principal goal of weapons designers. Vapors so modified would tend to linger on the battlefield and thereby amplify their effect. Local atmospheric conditions will play a significant role in the effectiveness of a chemical attack. Fortunately, an effective chemical attack is believed to be difficult to execute since proper dispersal is key to maximizing exposure before the agent evaporates or becomes too dilute.

It is interesting to note the operational differences between biological and chemical attack vectors. A relatively low number of infectious biological particulates can have the desired deleterious effect since individuals become ill from a relatively small infecting dose and then spread it to others. Terrorists using biological attack vectors hope to disperse their wares through contagious mechanisms.

Therefore, the biological attack strategy is to avoid redundant contacts of the pathogen with the same individual in order to infect the maximum number of individuals using a finite amount of material. In this case, dispersal of the material via dilution is suggested since more people are likely to become impacted if there are lower concentrations of particulates for the same quantity of infecting material.

In contrast, a chemical attack requires a minimum threshold concentration to perform the desired effect. Therefore, excessive dilution of a chemical agent would negate the effect of a chemical attack. Chemicals released into the external environment must overcome the effects of evaporation and/or dispersal in order to ensure sufficient concentrations.

7.4.2   Sorbent Filters [2]

As noted previously, and consistent with the approach taken in addressing biological threats, detailed discussions of individual chemicals will be avoided here. There are an unlimited variety of noxious chemicals that would be highly disruptive if not lethal to those so exposed. An entire book could be devoted to addressing all of these chemicals in detail.

Instead, the focus will be on the effectiveness of mitigation measures that have general applicability. I believe this approach will be most useful to security professionals who are seeking general knowledge as well as basic guides to security risk management. Important background material is included to establish a familiarity with the threat, and examples of risk scenarios relative to mitigation methods provide a more textured view of risk.

So-called sorbent filter beds are used in hospitals and other buildings to remove vapors and pollutant gases. Sorbent filters are one of the principal mitigation methods to address chemical threats, so it is worth a discussion on how they operate and their operational limitations.

Commercial facilities that have deployed sorbent filters for the purpose of mitigating the threat of chemical weapons are not common. However, this is not to suggest that such filters are not being used by some commercial entities, and I suspect they may be deployed in certain government facilities. Sorbent filters utilize *adsorption*, where the pollutant molecules actually stick to the surface of the adsorbing substance, oftentimes in the form of a charcoal bed.

Specifically, the molecules of the chemical vapor reach the interior surface of the charcoal grains by diffusion from the airstream. Recall diffusion was mentioned earlier in this chapter when discussing the filtration of dispersed biological threats. The charcoal surface is very irregular with many tiny cavities and convoluted channels. These present a huge surface area to the diffusing chemical agent. For example, a high-quality activated charcoal can have a surface area as high as $1500 \, m^2/g$. The contaminants are adsorbed at sites on the surface by an essentially irreversible mechanism. Note that adsorption is a surface phenomenon and should not be confused with *absorption*, in which molecules are taken up by the entire volume of the absorbing material.

At low-mass concentrations, the concentration of the contaminant decreases exponentially with distance down the charcoal bed. The determining factor for removal of vapor particles is the time, t, that it is in contact with the charcoal bed.

If V = the bulk volume of the sorption material and v = volumetric flow rate of the contaminating gas, then $t = V/v$ for a constant flow rate. The ratio of the effluent and influent (i.e., outbound and inbound) concentrations $c/c_o = e^{-Kt}$ is known as the decontamination factor, where K is creatively referred to as the K-factor or performance index.

The K-factor itself depends on many factors and must be determined experimentally for each batch of sorbent material. Here again the exponential model communicated in Chapter 4 comes into play since one can work backwards from the solution to state the governing equation for the inbound and outbound concentrations of gas, c.

$$dc/dt = -Kc$$

Over time, the sites that are available for adsorption will decrease and thereby become immobilized in the filter bed. As the number of available adsorption sites is exhausted, the contaminant will break through and be transported through the bed at the speed of the airstream.

The performance of a charcoal bed could be affected by trace impurities in the air as well as humidity. Rapid decreases in removal efficiency can result from the adsorption of solvents (e.g., cleaning agents) and oil vapors (e.g., painted surfaces). Therefore, beds must be periodically tested. Such tests consist of passing a labeled contaminant through the bed. The influent and effluent contaminant volume is measured and the bed retention is computed. The test should be conducted with the relative humidity set at various levels up to 95 percent.

Sorbents are rated in terms of adsorption capacity for the specific chemical of interest. The adsorption capacity is the quantity of the chemical that can be captured by the filter. The efficiency of the filter decreases as the amount of captured contaminant increases. This implies that saturation can occur at some point in the adsorption process. Sorbent beds are sized on the basis of the specific chemical agent, air velocity and temperature, and the maximum downstream concentration.[11]

As stated previously, there are a wide variety of potential chemical agents at the terrorists' disposal. Unfortunately, a specific design will not be effective against all of them. In addition, sorbent filters could dramatically increase the load on an HVAC system. As always, the risk versus gain (i.e., the cost of remediation relative to the magnitude of the components of risk) must be carefully assessed.

Deploying separate air handling systems and establishing negative pressure relative to the remainder of the building might be considered for areas deemed at high risk. In the event of an internal chemical release, fresh air can be brought in from uncontaminated parts of the building to dilute the effects of the contaminant without polluting unaffected areas. If the area is at negative pressure with respect to the other portions of the building, but positively pressurized relative to the outdoors, the risk of contaminating other areas is reduced.

7.5   ELECTROMAGNETIC PULSE THREATS AND RISK

7.5.1   Basic Electromagnetic Theory and Attack Vectors

Concerns about the threat of nonnuclear electromagnetic pulse (EMP) weapons directed against commercial facilities have emerged into the public consciousness. These weapons generate a high amplitude and broadband electromagnetic pulse. This spike in energy is intended to inductively and/or capacitively (i.e., due to magnetic or electric fields) couple to electronic circuits with potentially disruptive or even catastrophic results.

A number of mechanisms exist for delivering high-intensity electromagnetic energy in scenarios of concern. These include explosively pumped flux compression generators (EPFCG), explosive and propellant-driven magneto-hydrodynamic generators, and high-power microwave sources.[18]

This crude analysis focuses on EPFCG as the weapon of choice. However, the generation of an electromagnetic pulse is common to all EMP devices, and it is this pulse that is the source of damage to electronic circuitry independent of its mode of generation.

In order to discuss the risk associated with electromagnetic weapons, it is useful to review some background information on electromagnetic energy. Electromagnetic waves from a variety of sources are propagating all around us. We are continuously awash in a veritable bath of electromagnetic energy. This energy is comprised of many types of signals, man-made and otherwise. Electromagnetic waves are so-named because they have both an electric and magnetic field component. These components oscillate at right angles to each other in a sinusoidal pattern as depicted in Figure 7.16.

Electric fields originate from static charges and electric currents (i.e., moving charges) that generate magnetic fields. The behavior of *all* electromagnetic phenomena is characterized by four equations formulated by James Clerk Maxwell in 1864. Not surprisingly, these are known as Maxwell's equations, and every college physics major learns these as part of the core undergraduate curriculum.

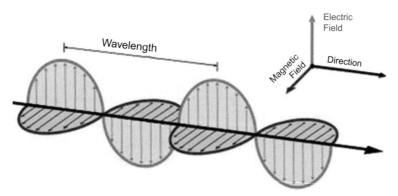

FIGURE 7.16

An electromagnetic wave. *(From NOAA. National Weather Service. "Remote Sensing."*http://www.srh.noaa.gov/jetstream/remote/remote_intro.htm.*)*

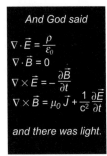

FIGURE 7.17

Maxwell's equations T-shirt. (http://mstatic.mit.edu/nom150/items/maxwell.jpg.)

When I was an undergraduate, a popular T-shirt at my alma mater paid homage to Maxwell by displaying the four famous equations shown in Figure 7.17 in differential form.

The spectrum of electromagnetic energy is vast and includes wavelengths of tens of meters down to a fraction of a picometer (i.e., 10^{-12} m). Examples of electromagnetic energy include X-rays, radio waves, microwaves, visible light, and cosmic radiation. Figure 7.18 reveals important elements of the electromagnetic spectrum.

EPFCG devices operate by using a conventional explosive to rapidly compress a magnetic field, thereby transferring energy from the explosive to the magnetic field. The collapsing magnetic field will induce huge voltages in metal objects thousands of feet from the explosive source. These devices are reportedly capable of producing peak power levels of tens of terawatts (i.e., 10^{12} W).

For reference, the peak power level of a lightning strike is on the order of a terawatt. Figure 7.19 shows the rapid evolution of a magnetic field resulting from the detonation of an EPFCG developed by Los Alamos National Laboratory (note: the tesla (T) is a unit of magnetic flux density. $1\,\text{T} = 1\,\text{Wb/m}^2$ (the symbol for weber is Wb)).

An EPFCG is capable of delivering electromagnetic pulses that are comparable to those produced by nuclear weapons and lightning. Therefore, EPFCGs have the potential to be formidable weapons in their own right, although their purpose is not to cause loss of life.

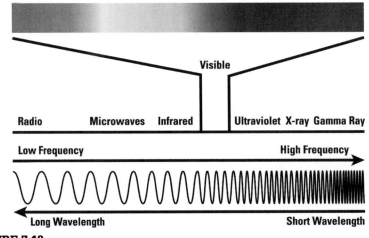

FIGURE 7.18

The electromagnetic spectrum. *(Source U.S. Geological Survey.* http://earthshots.usgs.gov/earthshots/about.*)*

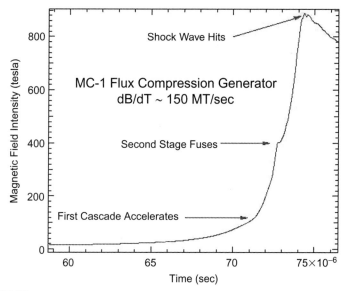

FIGURE 7.19

The magnetic field profile of an MC-1 flux compression generator. The jump from 100T to 850T takes place in ~3.5 μs. *(Source Mielke, C.H. Los Alamos National Laboratory. Flux Compression Generator.* http://www.lanl.gov/orgs/mst/nhmfl/mielke/MC1.html.)

Consider the scenario where a vehicle detonates an EPFCG in the vicinity of a data center. Upon detonation, a powerful electromagnetic pulse is generated that consists of a broad spectrum of frequencies. In theory, an appropriately constructed Faraday cage (i.e., a sealed metal box) could effectively shield circuits from damaging sources of external electromagnetic energy.

However, it is important to appreciate that electronic devices, especially in data centers, require long leads for power and information transfer that preclude complete physical isolation from the external world. As a result, complementary methods are required to establish an effective mitigation strategy relative to the threat of an EPFCG.

7.5.2   Unshielded Data Centers

In this scenario it is assumed that no shielding exists around servers, routers, and other technical equipment and that underground cables feeding data centers are not affected by the EMP. Specifically, an electromagnetic pulse generated by an EPFCG directly interacts with the internal circuitry of key electronic components in digital devices. Such circuitry is comprised of metal oxide semiconductor (MOS) devices that are sensitive to high-voltage transients.

Power cables and interconnections between electronic circuits will develop electric potentials in response to the changing magnetic flux (i.e., through magnetic induction). This voltage will cause arcing through the insulation that separates the gate from the drain/source elements of field-effect transistors (FET). These are the components that make up electronic circuits on computer boards.

This arcing will inevitably result in the breakdown of the device since voltage levels so induced would be applied to the gates of the FET and others. Such devices have maximum operating voltages of about ± 20 V. Other electronic components have even smaller breakdown voltages.

Consider an EPFCG that generates a terawatt (TW) of electromagnetic power detonated in the vicinity of a data center. A rough calculation of the electric field and induced voltage caused by a hypothesized weapon at a distance of 1 km from the pulse source is shown immediately below.

The energy of the pulse will propagate with equal intensity in all directions unless specifically designed to do otherwise. The energy density in free space for fields produced by a dipole charge is given by the following expression:

$$(1/2)(\varepsilon_o E^2 + 1/\mu_0)H^2$$

ε_o is the electric permittivity of free space, μ_0 is the magnetic permeability of free space, E and H are the electric and magnetic field intensities, respectively.

The total energy is divided equally between the electric and magnetic fields so the intensity can be expressed as twice the electric field component alone. The electromagnetic field intensity, I_o, caused by the pulse traveling at the speed of light has units of watts per square meter (W/m²) and is therefore equal to the following expression:

$$I_o = c\varepsilon_o E^2$$

c is the speed of light in free space.

As noted above, the power of the electromagnetic pulse following the explosion is 10^{12} W. Based on the point source model introduced in Chapter 4, the intensity of the electromagnetic pulse as a function of distance for a wave propagating isotropically is $P/4\pi r^2$, where r is the distance from the explosive source.

Equating the intensity of the propagating pulse with the intensity of the electromagnetic field yields

$$P/4\pi r^2 = c\varepsilon_o E^2$$

The electric field, E, at a distance of 1 km from the source is now easily calculated. This will yield insight into the effectiveness of physical separation between the vehicle and the target facility. Note that it might be difficult to establish even 1 km of physical standoff for most facilities in urban areas. This might severely affect the proposed risk-mitigation strategy. Moreover, this rough calculation suggests that even this distance does not offer much protection from this type of threat.

The distance, r, is 1 km or 10^3 m. Plugging this value into the above expression and using $c = 3 \times 10^8$ m/s and $\varepsilon = 8.9 \times 10^{-12}$ F/m, the electric field is calculated to be 5.5×10^3 V/m. Therefore, a cable of any significant length interfaced to a rack of electronics would be vulnerable to kilovolt-level potentials. This greatly exceeds the breakdown voltage of digital components of computers.

Even if the calculation were in error by an order of magnitude based on poorly chosen parameter values or erroneous physical assumptions, such voltage levels would still exceed the typical operating specifications of electronic components.

7.5.3   Shielded Components in Data Centers

Now it is assumed that the target facility or components within the facility are electromagnetically shielded using an appropriate metal enclosure. The effect of metal shielding is to create eddy currents (in response to magnetic fields) and charge motion (in response to electric fields) that cancel the effect of the electromagnetic radiation. In this scenario, a Faraday cage is deployed that is designed to protect electronics from the effects of an EMP.

EMP-type events actually occur every day throughout the world. These simulated EMP incidents can be used to better understand the effects of a pulse so initiated. Namely, cloud-to-earth lightning strikes will be examined to gain an appreciation for the effects of an EMP. A strike of lightning during a thunderstorm can produce peak currents ranging from 1000 to 100,000 A (amperes) with rise times of 1 μs.

Figure 7.20 shows the induced voltage from a lightning strike as a function of distance from the strike. At 1000 ft from the strike the induced voltage is nearly 1000 V. The intense electric and magnetic fields surrounding a typical 20,000 amp lighting strike will induce a voltage of around 2000 V at a distance of 300 ft in just 3 ft of wire and will induce hundreds of volts at a distance of ½ mile! This serves as a good model for the voltages that could be induced by an EMPG.

Despite the presence of shielding, it would be nearly impossible to defend against a direct hit by a lighting strike of this magnitude. An EPFCG source might produce electric currents equal to or exceeding those expected from lightning, so similar caveats apply.

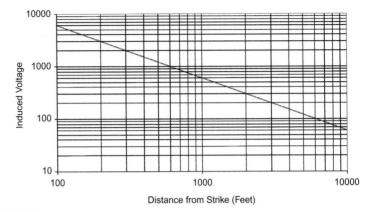

FIGURE 7.20

Induced voltage from a lightning strike. *(From SurgeX. "Lightening Surges."* http://www.surgex.com/library/12001.html.*)*

Buried cables are most vulnerable to an EPFCG attack against a shielded facility. Induced voltages on these distributed elements are common in lightning scenarios. Experiments have been conducted that yield estimates of peak voltages at varying distances from a cable.

In one test, lightning-induced voltages caused by strokes in ground flashes at distances of 5 km (i.e., 3.1 mi) were measured at both ends of a 448-m, non-energized power distribution line. The maximum induced voltage was 80 V peak-to-peak.[19]

Tens of volts presented to input gates of FET devices would exceed its breakdown voltage. Eighty volts exceeds published operating thresholds, although commercially available surge protection would provide some protection relative to this threat.

The point is that shielded devices within data centers are also susceptible to detonated EMP devices because of underground cables that are required to provide power. An EMP generated at distances of a few miles from a facility could in theory be defended using surge protection and/or isolation transformers.

Even if it is assumed that electronic devices are contained within shielded enclosures, small openings such as those surrounding wires entering the enclosure will pass electromagnetic energy at wavelengths shorter than the diameter of the opening.

This phenomenon is the same one that allows you to peer inside your microwave oven while electromagnetic radiation cooks your turkey burger. That is, the shorter wavelengths associated with visible light can pass through the shield, which blocks the longer wavelength microwaves, and therefore prevents you from getting cooked along with the turkey.

Although information on the bandwidth of EPFCG-derived pulses could not be located, presumably a short duration pulse could produce energy at wavelengths of a few tenths of a millimeter (i.e., microwaves), but this admittedly requires confirmation. This is small enough to allow energy to leak into the gap created by wire insulation. The moral of the story is that robust electromagnetic shields are required in mitigating this threat.

The required standoff distance between an EMP source and a target facility could be considerable. This is based on the vulnerability to voltage and current surges generated by direct irradiation and/or electromagnetic signals coupling to underground cables and generating voltages by induction.

A combination of distance, shielding, and surge protection might provide effective mitigation for EMP scenarios. As usual, a cost-benefit analysis is required that boils down to an analysis of the potential for such an attack relative to the assessed vulnerability and the cost of required risk mitigation. Standard lighting protection would fortuitously add value to an anti-EMP strategy. However, a qualified power systems engineer should be consulted to scope the problem for a specific facility, as well as to determine the efficacy of proposed solutions.

SUMMARY

It is important to understand the properties of radioactivity when assessing the risk of an RDD. Moreover, assessing the health risks associated with relevant scenarios is essential to developing an effective risk management strategy.

The physical parameters that affect the vulnerability to RDDs are: (1) the distance from the radioactive source; (2) the energy and type of the emitted radiation; (3) the amount of radiological material in the device; (4) the time of exposure to the radioactive source; (5) the explosive payload and anticipated dispersal; (6) local weather conditions; and (7) the attenuating effects of any intervening material.

Specific radiological isotopes might be more attractive to terrorists because of their persistence and activity. However, a close examination of the risk associated with RDDs suggests that the most harm from these devices irrespective of the chosen isotope is likely to result from the effects of the explosive rather than the radiological component.

The variety of available biological and chemical agents is diverse. However, effective risk mitigation for these attack vectors is relatively few. Specifically, mechanical filtering and ultraviolet germicidal radiation are effective means of managing the risk to facilities from externally dispersed biological contaminants. A combination of these methods applied to elevated building air intakes can be effective across the spectrum of biological pathogens and toxins. The stack effect could reduce the effectiveness of both these measures because of externally contaminated air seeping through the building façade and thereby bypassing the building air intakes.

Chemical weapons require the use of sorbent filters that function through adsorption of chemical molecules along the filter surface. However, sorbent filter effectiveness will vary according to the specific chemical agent. There is no silver bullet that can attenuate the deleterious effects of every chemical. In addition, sorbent filters are affected by dirt and solvents, as well as being susceptible to saturation. Sorbent filters also require ongoing testing and maintenance.

Devices that generate significant electromagnetic pulses (EMP) can produce destructive levels of electromagnetic energy that are similar to cloud-to-ground lightning strikes in magnitude. The electromagnetic energy radiated from an EMPG device would likely couple to electronic components in data centers through distributed power and data lines.

Calculated levels of induced peak-to-peak voltages across electronic component inputs and resulting from EMP-generated surges exceed published limits for electronic components. A combination of standoff distance, shielding, and surge protection could be effective in addressing the risk associated with some EMP-type scenarios, but a rigorous cost-benefit analysis relative to the estimated vulnerability should be conducted before implementing solutions.

REFERENCES

[1] Saenger EL. Medical aspects of radiation accidents. Washington, D.C.: U.S. Government Printing Office; 1963.

[2] Shapiro J. Radiation protection; A guide for scientists and physicians. Harvard University Press; 1990, pp. 46.

[3] The 2007 recommendations of the international commission on radiological protection. Ann ICRP 37(2–4) 103.

[4] Lamarsh J. Introduction to nuclear engineering. 2nd ed. New York: Addison Wesley; 1983.

[5] Young C. Metrics and methods for security risk management. Waltham, MA: Syngress; 2010.

[6] Garwin R, private communication.

[7] Bricker PW, et al. The application of ultraviolet germicidal irradiation to control transmission of airborne disease: bioterrorism countermeasures. Public Health Rep 2003;118.

[8] Oberta AF. The truth about HEPA filters. The Environmental Consultancy; 2004. http://www. asbestosguru-oberta.com/hepa.htm.

[9] Kowalski WJ, Bahnfleth WP. Immune building technology and bioterrorism defense. HPAC Engineering 2003.

[10] Ensor DS, Hanley JT, Sparks LE. Healthy buildings. Indoor air quality. Filter efficiency; 1991, Washington, D.C.

[11] Kowalski W, Bahnfleth W, Musser A. Modeling immune building systems for bioterrorism defense. Journal of Architectural Engineering 2003;9(2).

[12] U.S. Department of Health and Human Services, Centers for Disease Control and Prevention, National Institute of Occupational Safety and Health (NIOSH). Guidance for filtration and air-cleaning systems to protect building environments from airborne chemical, biological or radiological attacks. April 2003.

[13] Kowalski W, et al. Mathematical modeling of ultraviolet germicidal irradiation for air disinfection. Quantitative Microbiology 2000;2:249–70.

[14] Chang DB, Young C. Effect of turbulence on ultraviolet radiation. Journal of Architectural Engineering 2007;13(3).

[15] Wilson AG, Tamua GT. Stack effect in buildings. Canadian Building Digest, 1968 (CBD-104).

[16] Wilson AG. Air leakage in buildings. Canadian Building Digest-23. National Research Council of Canada; 1961.

[17] Bowman S. Weapons of mass destruction: the terrorist threat. Congressional Research Service Report for Congress; 2002.

[18] Kopp C. The electromagnetic bomb—a weapon of electrical mass destruction, http://www.globalsecurity.org/military/library/report/1996/apjemp.htm.

[19] Schneider K. Lightning and surge protection. Telebyte USA.

Problems

1. You are the security director of a major international corporation headquartered in the United States that manufactures doughnuts. There is disturbing news about the increased potential for biological agents being used by groups that oppose the exportation of doughnuts to developing nations by U.S. companies. Design a risk-based and cost-effective mitigation strategy to address the threat of biological agents. As always, this should begin with a precise statement of the distinct and impactful threats and attack vectors and conclude with mitigation specifications that satisfy stated operational requirements. Reference the risk assessment framework discussed in Chapter 1.

2. You are the head of business continuity for an international pharmaceutical company. There is concern over the potential use of "dirty bombs" by groups that oppose your company's experimentation on animals. You embark on developing a strategy that incorporates "shelter-in-place" in conjunction with evacuation for your "leaky" (i.e., nonairtight) headquarters building, which houses about 10,000 employees. Articulate this strategy to senior management, noting the pros and cons associated with recommended actions based on your knowledge of the threat and building issues/limitations.

3. You are the security director of a U.S. corporation with a prominent facility in a developing country that is known to be the target of anti-Western elements. You have a finite security budget and must prioritize spending based on risk. Generate a risk-based argument on the efficacy of installing chemical filters in this facility. If you recommend against this form of risk mitigation, what security strategy would you pursue instead, if any?

4. You are the newly appointed security director of a high-rise facility that is currently under construction. You are participating in senior-level meetings with management to provide input on proposed security measures. The subject turns to building filtration, and the facility manager (your counterpart) is making the argument to use low-efficiency air intake filters to reduce costs and HVAC system loading. You are concerned with increasing the vulnerability component of risk for the building occupants with respect to biological and radiological weapons as attack vectors.
   a. Develop a risk-based argument for or against installing an air filtration system/method to address biological threats.
   b. Develop a similar risk-based argument to address a chemical attack vector.
   c. Develop a similar risk-based argument to address a radiological attack vector.
   d. Suggest alternatives to the use of building filtration. Be specific regarding recommended alternatives relative to a particular threat/attack vector.

5. Below are graphs of the mass attenuation coefficient (i.e., μ/ρ) for gamma rays in water, lead, and concrete. Recall that the mass attenuation coefficient determines the rate at which a material attenuates radiation intensity as the energy travels through the material. The greater the value of the mass attenuation coefficient, the more energy is removed from the incident beam of energy per unit distance of propagation. Use the graphs to compare the effectiveness of shielding for water, concrete, and lead as follows:
   a. Which material represents a better shield at 0.1 MeV?
   b. Which material represents a better shield at 10 MeV?
   c. Extra credit: estimate the distance where the intensity of a 0.1-MeV beam is reduced by half the initial value for each material.

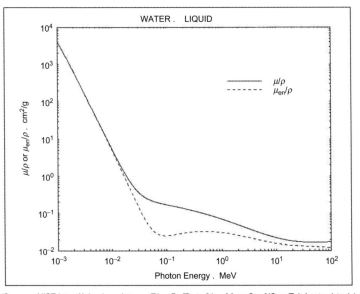

(Source: NIST. http://physics.nist.gov/PhysRefData/XrayMassCoef/ComTab/water.html.*)*

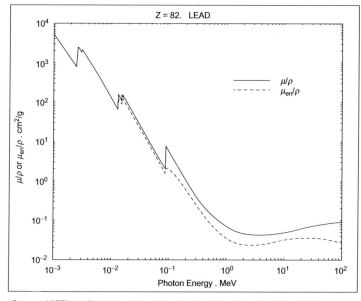

(Source: NIST http://physics.nist.gov/PhysRefData/XrayMassCoef/ElemTab/z82.html.*)*

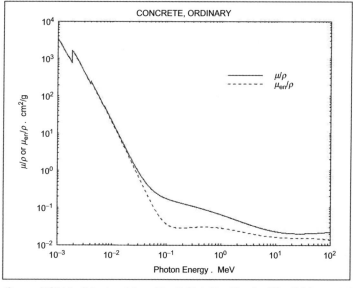

(Source: NIST. http://physics.nist.gov/PhysRefData/XrayMassCoef/ComTab/concrete.html.*)*

6. Qualitatively describe the intensity of a point source versus an extended source of radioactivity as a function of distance. What effect would each have on the requirements for shielding?

7. You are the security director of a large international corporation. One of your important satellite offices is moving into new space that is contiguous with

farmland, where crops are periodically sprayed with insecticide. You are asked to provide advice on the vulnerability of the offices to the insecticide leaking into the building via the façade. The insecticide is sprayed in close proximity to the building. Use the exponential model for air exchange to estimate how long it will take for half the room air volume to consist of external (i.e., contaminated) air and half the internal (i.e., clean) air volume under the following conditions:

a. The building façade is leaky (i.e., 0.5 room air exchanges/hr).

b. The building façade is airtight (i.e., 2 room air exchanges/hr).

8. The American Cancer Society has specified a health risk metric of 5.5 percent additional cancers per sievert of equivalent dose. As the security director of a major U.S. corporation, and anticipating questions from senior management, you perform a calculation to ascertain the real risk of exposure in the event of a radiologic dispersion device incident. Let's say 1000 Ci chunks of the radioisotope ^{137}Cs is sitting 10 m from 10,000 people. The RHM (i.e., rem/hour-Ci at 1 m) value of ^{137}Cs is 0.59. Neglecting the attenuating effects of air, specify the additional cancer rate expected from 1 hr of exposure to this isotope at this distance. Assume the intensity of radiation decreases as $1/r^2$, where r is distance from the radioactive source. This calculation is straightforward if slightly involved, so let's set up the problem. If the RHM for ^{137}Cs is 0.59, then the RHM is 1/100th that figure at 10 m. Why? 0.0059 rem/hr-Ci × 1000 Ci × 1 hr of exposure = 5.9 rem (note: how many rem/sievert?). Recall that the American Cancer Society states that 5.5 additional cancers will result if 100 people are exposed to 1-Sv equivalent dose. We just determined that the equivalent dose for these 100 people in this scenario is 5.9 rem. Therefore, how many additional cancers will occur in the population?

9. You are the director of security at a large corporation located in the downtown area of a major U.S. city. There has been an emergency alert issued by the Department of Homeland Security, and they suspect a radiological dispersion device has been detonated near your facility. No other details are available, and you are essentially on your own to develop a response. You opt for sheltering-in-place rather than risk exposure outdoors. Fortunately there two large areas within your facility, and each can accommodate the entire population of the company. One room is lined with lead, and the other is lined with concrete.

a. Assume the material completely encapsulates each room. If the dirty bomb contains ^{137}Cs, what thickness of lead is required to reduce the incident radiation (i.e., gamma) intensity by half?

b. What thickness of concrete is required to reduce the incident radiation intensity by half?

10. We learned that the ratio of the effluent and influent (i.e., outbound and inbound) concentrations given by $c/c_o = e^{-Kt}$ for sorbent filters is known as the decontamination factor. As noted in the text, K is referred to as the K-factor or performance index. Write down the first order differential equation that describes the relationship between influent and effluent concentrations (Hint: see Chapter 4 and the model for exponential decay).

11. Fundamental differences between mechanical and electromagnetic energy cause differences in their respective requirements for wave propagation. Information-carrying signals exist in either one form of energy or the other. Although both electromagnetic and mechanical signals are affected by ambient conditions, a big difference between the two is that mechanical energy requires a medium for transmission such as air, and electromagnetic signals do not. Explain how the physical form of a signal might affect the vulnerability component of risk for information loss and the associated mitigation strategy. Which form of energy would you think carries more risk and why (note: there is no correct answer here. Your reasoning about risk is what is important)?

12. You are the Chief of Diplomatic Security for an embassy. Following a rigorous assessment of physical security risk, you decide to investigate mitigation for the threat of chemical weapons. You consult a building engineer regarding the installation of sorbent filters to be used in conjunction with the building HVAC system. She reviews some of the technical features with you, and you decide to do some basic calculations to familiarize yourself with product performance.

   a. For one particular sorbent filter being considered, the K-factor is 0.5 and t is 1 sec. Calculate the decontamination factor for this filter.

   b. Is the decontamination factor better if the K-factor is larger or smaller? Why or why not?

   c. Explain why the decontamination factor is a ratio and what are the implications in terms of sorbent filter performance.

13. Refer to figure 7.20 for induced voltage due to a lightning strike.

   a. Is the induced voltage linear with distance?

   b. If the DC resistance is 50 ohms for a particular unshielded electronic component, what would be the induced current in that component at a distance of 100 feet from a lightning strike (Hint: Ohm's Law states that Voltage = Current × Resistance)?

   c. 1000 feet?

   d. 10,000 feet?

14. If the relationship between wavelength and frequency for electromagnetic radiation in a specific material is given by frequency = speed of light/wavelength, would you expect wavelength to increase or decrease with increasing frequency? Is the relationship between frequency and wavelength linear in this case?

15. Explain why the Stack Effect is different in summer than winter. How might this affect a shelter-in-place strategy?

16. Refer to the expression for the UVGI pathogen kill rate given on page 198. Calculate the kill rate for all URV intensity ratings listed in Table 7.5 (i.e., URV 6 through URV 16) using $t = 1$ (second) and $k = 1$ (cm squared/microwatt-second). Is the relationship between kill rate and ultraviolet intensity linear?

CHAPTER 8

Electronic Terrorism Threats, Risk, and Risk Mitigation

8.1 INTRODUCTION TO ELECTRONIC SECURITY

If all security threat scenarios have identical components of risk, why do electronic threats seem different than their physical counterparts? Most prominently, in electronic terrorism there is no direct threat to human life. Certainly an attack against IT services that support life-saving activities such as the 911 or 999 infrastructures could put lives in jeopardy and sabotage is sometimes a motive (e.g., Stuxnet), but the point of electronic terrorism is in general not to kill people.

The scale of electronic and physical terrorism threats are different. Electronic terrorism, and attacks via the Web in particular, have the potential for wide-scale damage because of the sheer number of Internet users. There are millions of individuals who rely on the same communication circuits, shared infrastructure, and common forms of equipment that perform an increasing number of personal and business functions. Therefore, the potential impact of a successful terrorist incident is increasing proportionately.

Figure 8.1 shows the increase in the number of Internet hosts from 1981 to 2012. The rate of growth is truly remarkable, as evidenced by the logarithmic scale on the vertical axis (see Appendix B for details on logarithms).

It is difficult to imagine a world without the Internet, but individuals who can remember when John F. Kennedy was the president of the United States can vividly recall a much less-connected world. The Internet is responsible for profound changes in our global perspective, in part because it has erased distinctions based on physical location. This network has effectively eliminated distance-related barriers to communication, and it affords near instantaneous access to global information resources. On an electronic level, the Internet has homogenized the globe and its inhabitants.

The Internet is precisely what its name implies: a network. Its very purpose is to facilitate communication via connectivity. The problem is that connectivity is itself a risk factor for information compromise. In fact, certain security controls must be included in any modern network design or it cannot be considered a

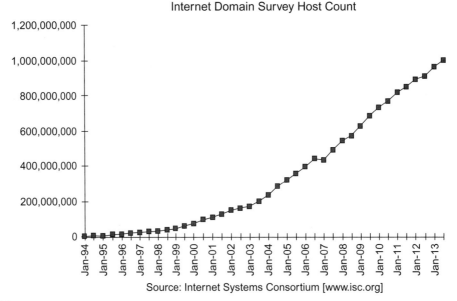

FIGURE 8.1

Global Internet users. *(Reprinted with permission from Internet Systems Corporation, www.isc.org).*

practical network. In other words, the absence of security controls could be considered a risk factor for the threat of information compromise.

Strictly speaking, this is not true for physical security threats. The absence of a lock on a door to an office is not a risk factor for theft. All doors are not created equal in terms of risk. The proximity of an office to public areas, the storage of valuables, etc., are all examples of risk factors for theft. A lock, or more precisely a physical restriction, is one method to address those risk factors.

In addition, physical security threats sometimes lend themselves to quantitative estimates of vulnerability. Physical models can be used to estimate vulnerability, as first noted in Chapter 4. This is not typically the case for electronic security risk, but the increasing convergence of electronic and physical security drives an increasing interdependence among these areas.

To understand electronic security risk it is important to appreciate Internet usage as well as the "standard" vulnerabilities associated with Web-based communication. The canonical Web application architecture is shown in Figure 8.2. Variations on this theme probably exist at a majority of organizations.

Although Web-application architectures are definitely similar across organizations, each of these environments is inherently complex. This complexity contributes to their vulnerability to a variety of attack vectors. For example, a few errant lines of code can create a vulnerability to SQL injection with devastating

Web Application Architecture

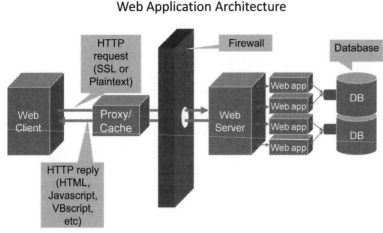

FIGURE 8.2

Web application architecture. *(Graphic courtesy of Steve Doty, Stroz Friedberg.)*

Web Application Vulnerabilities

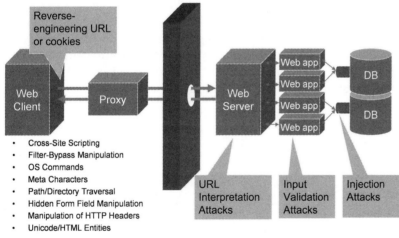

- Cross-Site Scripting
- Filter-Bypass Manipulation
- OS Commands
- Meta Characters
- Path/Directory Traversal
- Hidden Form Field Manipulation
- Manipulation of HTTP Headers
- Unicode/HTML Entities

FIGURE 8.3

Web application vulnerabilities. *(Graphic courtesy of Steve Doty, Stroz Friedberg.)*

consequences. Figure 8.3 lists some of the vulnerabilities associated with various elements of the canonical Web-application architecture.

To make matters worse, there are a significant number of individuals who have nothing better to do than to attempt to compromise information technology (IT) networks and reap significant economic, publicity, or terror-related benefits by doing so. Moreover, these individuals can do their dirty work remotely and therefore are not required to take physical risks.

In the case of electronic threats, the potential for information compromise is a unifying theme for almost all attack vectors. It is essential to understand what constitutes critical data, where that data is located on the network, and what controls are in place to protect it. Understanding what constitutes critical data is a necessary precursor to evaluating the impact component of risk, and it is therefore an important undertaking in an information security risk assessment.

Figure 8.4 is an indicative risk "heat map" for various information security attack vectors. Its purpose is to prioritize risk in terms of impact and vulnerability. This is a useful way to compactly display risk to an organization, recognizing that such evaluations are subjective and represent a relative ranking.

There are many good references on computers and computer security, and it would not be a good use of space to attempt to review this very broad topic here. Instead, an overview of the vulnerability of facilities and computers to specific electronic terrorism threats is provided along with specific methods of risk mitigation.

A principal focus is on risk monitoring, and specifically on providing recommendations to examine risk-relevant traffic between zones of a network. This is a form of measurement, loosely speaking, and therefore comports with the general spirit of this book in measuring security risk. Moreover, and using the language of risk used throughout this book, the specific items being monitored/measured across network zones represent risk factors for information compromise via malware and other exploits.

There is also considerable attention given to network configurations that are designed to stymie classic malware behavior. These ideas derived from my

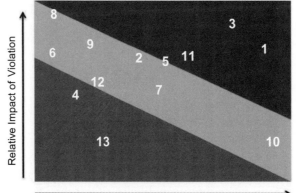

FIGURE 8.4
Security risk heat map. *(Graphic courtesy of David Dalva, Stroz Friedberg.)*

colleague, Jean Gobin, who also had significant input to many sections of this chapter as well as Chapter 9.

The methods and recommendations provided in this chapter have applicability to the general threat of information compromise, not just electronic terrorism. Although there is a focus on attack vectors that might particularly appeal to terrorists, much of the discussion is relevant to other information security-related threats.

In that vein, although electronic terrorists probably hope to do as much damage to their targets as possible, hacktivists and other miscreants relish the thought of doing exactly the same thing. The motivations of each threat actor might be different, but the modes of implementation by adversaries targeting electronic resources will likely be similar. In part, this is because of the inherent similarity among network environments, as noted previously.

If there is a quantifiable difference in various electronic attacks, it is manifest by the sophistication and level of resources one group can muster relative to others. In fact, it is sometimes instructive to characterize electronic threats in terms of the estimated cost and level of effort required to mount a specific attack.

For example, there is likely to be a significant and quantifiable difference in the cost of developing a state-sponsored electronic attack than one launched by a script kiddy. Characterizing the risk in terms of the level of resources required to mount an attack represents a tangible security risk metric that can be useful in developing and prioritizing risk management efforts.

The complexity of IT can seem intractable. There is no single reference that could possibly delineate all the vulnerabilities and risk-mitigation options associated with modern electronic network environments. The complexity of networks and applications resident on servers in a network is another risk factor for electronic terrorism that is inherent in all electronic networks to varying degrees.

As always is the case with complex problems, it is helpful to organize electronic security risk into food groups. It is also important to keep in mind that the ultimate objective is to protect information.

Identifying the spectrum of distinct and impactful information security threats and attack vectors and their respective components of risk is a fundamental part of evaluating electronic security risk. This is identical to risk assessments in physical security. In theory, the problem should be simpler than it is in the physical security world since one is principally concerned with protecting information and information assets.

Unfortunately this is not usually the case. The number of electronic attack vectors can be vast and varied, and different adversaries have completely different motivations that affect the risk profile. Some nonterrorist-related groups want to cause damage just because they can, thereby making evaluations of likelihood/potential-type risk factors more challenging.

Moreover, the intricacy and complexity of individual applications offer numerous opportunities for exploitation. The standard network framework for protocols in an IT environment is complex. Electronic attack vectors typically exploit a vulnerability that exists in a given layer of the open system interconnection (OSI) layer (see below), and sometimes multiple layers.

The standard network framework, represented in seven layers, is a high-level characterization of network functionality. Vulnerabilities with respect to the attack vectors noted herein can be evaluated relative to these layers.

A security control is passed from one layer to the next, starting at the application layer on one workstation, and proceeding to the bottom layer, over the channel to the next workstation, and back up the hierarchy. Figure 8.5 illustrates the OSI model.

Because of the distributed nature of electronic devices and applications, as well as the layering of processes within a network environment as described above, it makes sense to evaluate IT risk by mapping electronic controls against processes, applications, and device types. This generally helps avoid a redundant specification of controls.

In contrast, in the physical security world it is often advantageous to assess physical security risk by location within a facility. As noted numerous times, this entails examining the components of risk with respect to the identified threats and then scrutinizing the controls needed to address the risk factors associated with those threats. I note in passing that some of these physical controls are devoted to protecting electronic assets, a point that is emphasized in Chapter 9.

This chapter is organized into three sections to align with three significant food groups of electronic attack vectors that might appeal to terrorists: (1) denial-of-service (DoS) attacks; (2) advanced persistent threats (APT) and malware; and (3) attacks facilitated by physical security vulnerabilities. Of course the same controls sometimes apply to all three threats, but it is important to see how each is applied to a specific threat type.

An alternative to organizing this chapter by threat would be to organize it by control and then analyze how each control addresses one or more threats. However, a threat-based analysis showcases the direct applicability of controls. It also facilitates easy reference in terms of identifying and assessing useful controls on a per-threat basis.

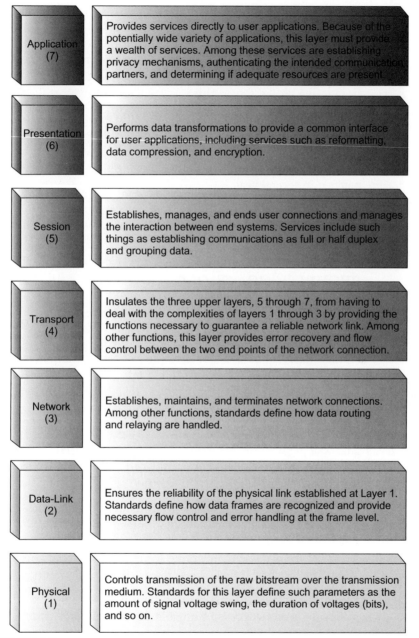

FIGURE 8.5

The OSI model. *(Source: Federal Communication Commission. "Public Safety Tech Topic #2—Internet Protocol (IP) Based Interoperability."* http://www.fcc.gov/help/public-safety-tech-topic-2-internet-protocol-ip-based-interoperability.*)*

The physical security of IT devices and vice versa is an area of increasing importance, especially as the proliferation of virtual machines tends to concentrate electronic risk within Cloud environments. For example, consider the potential damage if a technology-savvy electronic terrorist armed with a portable flash memory device was afforded unescorted access privileges to the back-end storage of a virtual server. This topic will also be explored in Chapter 9.

Next imagine if the same terrorist was able to physically access an electronic port on an IP camera or IP encoder in a public space. Suppose further that this attack vector facilitated access to a network server running Windows, the attacker gained local administrative privileges, and the machine had not been patched in several years.

Each of these scenarios highlights the importance of understanding the increasingly close relationship between physical and electronic security risk.

8.2   DENIAL-OF-SERVICE (DOS) ATTACKS AND SECURITY CONTROLS

A denial-of-service (DoS) attack is the deliberate attempt to make a computer resource unavailable to legitimate users. DoS attacks are a relatively "popular" means of disrupting services provided via the Internet. Several electronic attack vectors stand out in terms of their likely appeal to terrorists, and DoS attacks would likely be high on the list. This admittedly subjective view is based on the fact that DoS attacks can paralyze an organization, and there is no defensive silver bullet, merely varying degrees of preparedness.

These attacks deserve special discussion in view of the historical precedent for such attacks along with the inherent vulnerability of devices with external (i.e., Web-facing) IP addresses. A checklist is provided later in this chapter that summarizes the high-level controls across the spectrum of potential DoS attack subvectors.

It is important to be generally aware of threats publicized on the Internet. Sometimes individuals signal their intent in the form of a call to arms. Organizations should be focused on their Internet risk profile in terms of "who" is saying "what" in online forums such as chat rooms, social media, and paste bin sites. If such clues appear, they should not be ignored.

Preparedness is exceptionally important in the case of DoS attacks. Awareness of hostile information is invaluable in ensuring that reasonable precautions are taken. It is unclear that electronic terrorists would resort to these modes of communication, but the requirement for preparedness applies nonetheless.

It helps to know a little bit about computer architecture to understand DoS attacks. The main part of a computer's operating system is the kernel. As Figure 8.6 illustrates, the kernel establishes a link between the applications

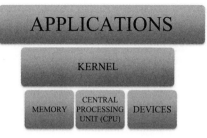

FIGURE 8.6
High-level computer architecture.

and the data processing performed at the hardware level. The kernel is responsible for managing the system resources that consist of the central processing unit (CPU), memory, and input/output (I/O) devices.

A DoS attack aims to overwhelm a computer's resources such that the kernel is not able to manage the standard CPU, memory, and/or device-related functions. There are four general types of DoS attack vectors, and we will examine each of these in sequence:

1. Abuse of administrative commands (e.g., format, delete, or drop a database).
2. Exploitation of a bug (e.g., application crash).
3. Abuse of a lengthy or resource-intensive process (e.g., forcing full-text searches).
4. Overwhelming a service with requests (e.g., a distributed DoS (DDoS) attack).

8.2.1 Abuse of Administrative Commands

In this category of DoS attack, an attacker will gain access to a system with sufficient privileges to execute a command that has destructive results. These privileges can include deleting files or file systems, altering the system configuration, dropping a database, etc.

The attacker could be a person external to the company or merely a system administrator with "fat fingers." Avoiding the risk of a fat finger is usually accomplished through the use of complementary controls or possibly by dieting.

Two important classes of defensive measures for DoS attacks include protecting the system administrator accounts and restricting privileges. These should be implemented as follows:

1. Ensure that accounts with administrative privileges are rare and difficult to compromise. The latter requirement is usually achieved by requiring strong passwords, two-factor authentication, instituting a secure mechanism to request elevations of privileges, and/or by

annexing potentially dangerous commands with commands that require confirmation. Of course limiting the number of accounts with administrative privileges is of paramount importance.

2. Confirm that users with administrative privileges have the proper training and can focus on the tasks at hand (i.e., they are not distracted when doing critical tasks and they receive proper training for their respective domains).

3. Provide a comprehensive and formal change management policy, and require that system administrators describe implementation, backup, and test procedures in detail.

4. Restrict access to administrative interfaces from certain devices or networks within the organization, e.g., filtering secure shell/remote desktop (SSH/RDP) sessions on the servers themselves and by limiting the number of users with the ability to access the device through a remote connection.

5. Restrict privileges for accounts used in conjunction with applications. For example, if a database account is needed for an externally facing application, the account should not also have "grant," "delete," "drop," or "create" privileges.

Recovery from this type of DoS attack usually involves restoring missing files, databases, and/or restarting machines.

The risks associated with privileged accounts are profound and transcend DoS attacks. I quote from the Lieberman software website, a company that has developed a solution to manage administrative accounts (*http://www.liebsoft.com/privileged_identity_management/*):

1. Privileged identities aren't controlled by your identity access management (IAM) system, so in all likelihood:

   a. You do not know of all the privileged logins that exist on your network.

   b. You have no record of which privileged credentials are known to different individuals.

   c. You have no proof of who has used privileged logins to gain access to any of your IT resources, when, and for what purpose.

   d. There is no way to verify that each of your privileged account passwords are cryptographically strong, are sufficiently unique, and are changed often enough to be secure.

   e. You have no reliable list of privileged logins stored within your applications, and no way to know which in-house and vendor personnel can use these credentials to access sensitive information.

Specifically, Lieberman Software offers a privileged identity management tool that facilitates tighter controls over privileging across the enterprise. One feature is the ability to temporarily "check out" administrative privileges for a finite time period and with proper authentication, thereby limiting the risks associated with persistent local administrative rights.

8.2.2 Exploitation of a Software Bug

Certain bugs in software may not lead to a full compromise of a device but could result in a system crash or reboot. In this case, an attacker might leverage this interruption in service. Prevention in this case also includes measures that are generally applicable to a broad range of electronic threats such as implementing effective patch management.

Specifically, it is critical to patch identified vulnerabilities in a timely fashion. In addition, it is important to leverage the firewall or intrusion prevention system (IPS) functionality to block all connections where the content, based on application-level inspections, seems suspicious or is known to be malicious.

Since the result of this type of attack is an application or system crash, the typical remediation is to restart the machine. However, it is important to make sure that the machine is not compromised in some way before initiating the restart.

Often a host intrusion detection system (HIDS) is able to detect the crash through system logs and report it to a central console. From there, alarms and alerts can be sent to system administrators. Intrusion detection and interzone monitoring in general will be discussed more thoroughly in Section 8.3.

8.2.3 Abuse of a Lengthy or Resource-Intensive Process

Certain operations performed on a computer require longer times to execute or they consume appreciable machine resources. An attacker might exploit that condition to make the system appear unresponsive. For example, a site may allow a search within its database, and that operation might be a CPU-intensive process. In that case, an attacker could search for a common term such as "the," "or," "a," or "is," which is likely to return many results.

An attacker could also search for a combination of terms or a query that is known to be memory-intensive such as "the" followed by "the" within a million words or other regular expressions. In such cases, the system would allocate resources for the request and might run out of disk space or memory. It might also occupy enough of the CPU to slow down or prevent other users from gaining access.

For example, a certain session or request would be allotted a specified CPU time and memory allocation. If the request attempts to obtain additional resources it will fail and return an error message. Being attentive to such messages is key to reacting quickly to evidence of an impending threat.

Preventing these incidents requires a combination of measures to include designing clusters of servers rather than individual units. This will also increase infrastructure fault tolerance by distributing the load across multiple machines.

In addition, implementing resource allocation on a per-user and/or per-session basis can effectively mitigate the risk.

In order to expeditiously recover from this attack, the system administrators must be able to detect a situation as it is occurring. This is typically accomplished through use of a monitoring solution that generates alarms based on measurements of high system usage. Upon receiving an alarm, an administrator should investigate the cause and suppress it by killing the offending process or by aborting the transaction.

8.2.4   Link Saturation by Overwhelming a Service with Requests

This is a classic distributed denial-of-service (DDoS) attack. In this case, multiple machines generate valid requests, each consuming finite resources: bandwidth, CPU, memory, etc. Many variations of this attack vector exist such as SYN flood, Internet Control Message Protocol (ICMP) flood, and others.

Consider that the average home digital subscriber line (DSL) e.g., DSL3, bandwidth is around 5 Mb/s. If we assume that all other latencies are small compared to the DSL latency, it takes 20 machines simultaneously sending data at maximum speed to saturate a 100-Mb/s link on the target side. This scenario is admittedly unrealistic since intermediate systems will inevitably drop packets, the latency is not zero, and the source systems must sustain an elevated frame transmission rate.

Each transmission control protocol (TCP) session consumes a small amount of kernel memory on both the client and the server. By connecting enough clients, and depending on the specific operating system, a server may have its kernel memory depleted and would therefore be unable to process additional requests.

The effect may be amplified if each TCP session is used to perform a simple request, such as initiating a Secure Socket Layer (SSL) negotiation or a hypertext transfer protocol (HTTP) request. User memory consumption is added to the kernel memory consumption, and this amplifies the problem.

A successful link saturation denial-of-service attack was mounted against the SCO Group Web server and their FTP (file transfer protocol) server[1]. The following is a blow-by-blow account of the attack, which yields insights into the link saturation attack vector[2]:

Wednesday, December 10, 2003
> **3:20 pm (PST)**—USCD Network Telescope begins to receive backscatter traffic that suggests denial-of-service attack is being distributed against the SCO Group, targeting the servers with approximately 34,000 packets/s.

Thursday, December 11, 2003

2:50 am (PST)—Attacks against SCO's FTP (file transfer protocol) servers begin in addition to the continued Web server attack at over 50,000 packets/s.

9:00 am (PST)—Attack rate is reduced to 3700 packets/s, though the ftp server continues to bear a high-intensity attack (though for a shorter time than the Web server attack).

10:40 am (PST)—SCO removes Web servers from the Internet and stops responding to incoming attack traffic, filtering all Web and FTP traffic until they come back online.

5:00 pm (PST)—Servers back online.

Over the course of 32 hr, SCO responded to more than 700 million attack packets, which consumed computing resources on both the servers themselves and the network connecting the servers to the Internet. Figure 8.7 shows the number of attack packets/second as a function of time for the FTP and Web servers. It is interesting to note the precipitous rise in activity over a relatively short time interval.

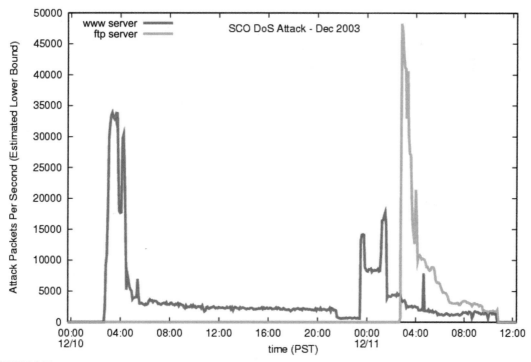

FIGURE 8.7

Time history of denial-of-service attack packets. *(Used with permission from The Cooperative Association for Internet Data Analysis.* http://www.caida.org/research/security/sco-dos/. *Copyright © 2003 The Regents of the University of California.)*

8.2.4.1 Risk Mitigation for Link Saturation

There is no guaranteed method of successfully defending against a link saturation DoS attack. However, some potentially effective controls include the following:

1. Use the firewall functionality to limit the number of sessions from each client and to each server. Ideally, the number of sessions that are allowed to reach a server should be less than or equal to the figure used to size it during its design.
2. Leverage firewall/network features to control the bandwidth used by each application and to leave "space" for other business applications such as emails and hosted applications. This may require coordination with an Internet service provider (ISP) to implement the same configuration.
3. Deploy load balancing for critical communication servers.

Understanding risk with respect to this DoS attack vector will generally require detecting abnormal increases in network traffic volume as well as any increases that persist over time. The following are a few high-level recommendations for network traffic monitoring:

- Use IDS/IPS to detect an unusual amount of TCP segments with the SYN flag.
- Implement monitoring stations to detect an abnormal increase in the number of bytes sent or received at an interface.
- Deploy a log analyzer to detect large volumes of similar requests being made to applications or services.

A useful discussion of the various types of denial-of-service attacks as well as a recounting of some of the more famous incidents can be found on Wikipedia[3].

8.2.5 Collateral Effects of a DoS Attack

With the increase in Cloud computing, which is a cartoonish name for aggregated IT resources in a public or private domain with remote electronic access to those resources, one can fall victim to a DoS attack irrespective of the intended target. This highlights the broader vulnerability to such attacks as well as the need for adequate preparedness.

Let's imagine that the link between the data center hosting Company A's data and the Internet service provider (ISP) was completely saturated with traffic. The saturating traffic was actually aimed at Company B, which shares the same telecommunication link as Company A. The proper response might be to null-route the affected IP range. Assuming this can be accomplished quickly, service can be restored in relatively short order.

The point of this scenario is to highlight the importance of preparedness and the fact that Company A must be vigilant despite the absence of specific risk factors. ISPs can be affected because of the attractiveness of a specific client, which in turn will affect other ISP clients. The effects on collateral targets can be equally disruptive as the intended target. Data centers and hosting services in general are attractive targets precisely because of their potential to affect multiple users with a single attack.

The presence of backup resources is one of the most important controls in mitigating the risk of a DoS attack. Specifically, maintaining an externally hosted data center that is capable of "hot switchovers" should be a priority.

8.2.6 DoS Preparedness Checklist

Given the importance of preparing for DoS attacks, it is useful to summarize key controls in the form of a checklist for easy access and thereby facilitate preparedness:

1. Know the name and contact details (include a phone number in the event email is down) of a person at the relevant ISP who has the authority to make decisions.
2. Ensure all relevant documentation (e.g., circuit ID, IP subnets) are readily available and are up-to-date.
3. Gather information on the appropriate departments within the relevant law enforcement agencies that will be involved in investigating the attack (e.g., FBI, U.S. Secret Service).
4. Deploy an IDS/IPS solution and configure it to detect when the volume of TCP SYN-segments exceeds a set limit.
5. Implement per-client and per-server session limits with respect to SYN flooding, User Datagram Protocol (UDP) flooding, and Internet control message protocol (ICMP) flooding protections on all firewalls.
6. Implement a host-based intrusion detection system (HIDS) solution on all exposed servers.
7. Implement a network and server monitoring solution and define alert thresholds.
8. Collect all relevant documentation on the Internet-facing networks and circuits in order to make these readily available for administrators.
9. Ensure there is an accurate diagram of the network topology (this is related to item number 2 above). The Red Seal application is useful for this purpose and is discussed later in this chapter.
10. Devise and implement a patch management policy and related procedures. Audit this policy and enforce relevant procedures.
11. Restrict the privileges of all users of services and applications to the minimum required to accomplish an individual user's job. This is commonly referred to as the Principle of Least Privilege.

12. Use privilege separation based on a defined security hierarchy.
13. Replace potentially dangerous commands with those that require an interactive confirmation (i.e., a challenge response).
14. Protect all administrative accesses and consoles.
15. Request that ISPs null-route the destination using the border gateway protocol (BGP) if a DoS attack is initiated. This will black hole it from the Internet. This also relieves the line from the attack traffic and allows system administrators to work on a response. However, note that this procedure will cause the destination to be unreachable by legitimate users.

8.3 ADVANCED PERSISTENT THREATS (APT)/ MALWARE, CLIENT-SIDE EXPLOITS, AND SECURITY CONTROLS

8.3.1 Introduction

"Advanced persistent threat" (APT) is a general term that is not particularly helpful to those trying to defend against them. It has as much to do with the types of perpetrators as the attack vector itself. An APT implicitly suggests the workings of a group with resources such as a government that is capable of implementing a sophisticated, targeted, and (of course) persistent electronic attack using malware. An individual or group attempting to commit electronic terrorism would arguably be focused on deploying malware and implementing APTs.

There are potentially infinite versions of malware, but they generally operate in a similar manner. Specifically, malware-type attacks typically attempt to do the following:

- Enter the internal network from external sources (e.g., via externally facing IP addresses or through social engineering/client-side exploits).
- Execute on an internal machine.
- Contact the Internet from within the internal network.
- Move laterally to other networked machines.
- Access protected/confidential information.
- Exfiltrate protected information for indefinite periods without detection.

At a high level, there are four important food groups of controls that attempt to address the aforementioned malware modus operandi:

1. Monitoring interzone network traffic that are risk factors for malware, et al. to detect pernicious lateral movements and/or attempts at unauthorized data exfiltration.
2. Identifying internal network and host vulnerabilities to prevent unauthorized device access and reduce the risk of unauthorized data exfiltration.

3. Exposing expired or faulty identity management privileges to prevent unauthorized electronic access to devices and execution of pernicious code on an internal machine.

4. Configuring networks to segregate information based on "need-to-know" access privileges and to stop pernicious lateral movements between services or functions.

Malware and APTs can be introduced to internal network environments in clever ways. For example, attackers have discovered that they can bypass sophisticated perimeter defenses through deception. Namely, fool a legitimate network user into accepting an email communication or open an attachment that appears to be sent from a legitimate source. A cleverly crafted note might entice an unwitting user to click on an attachment or URL that releases a viral payload or directs the user to a pernicious website. This is an example of a so-called client-side exploit since the attack is perpetrated on/by the client machine, i.e., the "secure" side of the network perimeter.

One might actually be tempted to view the advent of client-side exploits in an optimistic light. Namely, the increasing frequency of these attacks could be interpreted as a sign that IT-perimeter defenses are improving. In this admittedly rosy view of the world, tightening perimeter defenses have caused adversaries to resort to other means to access internal network resources. Electronic terrorists and other miscreants are therefore attempting to exploit the perennial weak link in any security strategy: people.

In the interest of full disclosure, this author fell victim to such an attack, also known as phishing, which is a particular type of client-side exploit that is quite common these days. The circumstances in this case are instructive.

I had recently performed an automatic cash handling (ACH) transfer of money from one of my bank accounts. Although I had also recently checked to see that the money was successfully transferred, I received an email that appeared to originate from a trusted source indicating there was a problem.

I hesitated but then succumbed to temptation and clicked on the hyperlink in the email. I even ignored my own advice to individuals who cannot resist clicking. Namely, click on the attachment using a portable device such as an iPhone or Blackberry. This might limit the impact to the broader network, although the device, and its contents, could be at risk thereafter.

Fortunately for yours truly, the chief security officer (CSO) of my company, our network had an endpoint protection solution in place, which blocked access to the rogue site. In the end, the only damage was to this CSO's ego. But the lesson is compelling: anyone who believes they are not susceptible to subterfuge via the Internet is in for a rude awakening.

Mounting a universal defense against this type of attack is extremely difficult without giving up a significant amount of convenience. An extreme solution is presented later in this chapter that does indeed minimize the risk of information loss but at the expense of business risk. As is often the case, the required trade-off boils down to a decision involving security versus convenience. Education of the user population will help to reduce an organization's vulnerability. But it only takes one individual to make an error in the course of a busy day while answering that 400th email or while shopping online to cause a major calamity.

In fact, even the most technically sophisticated organizations are not immune to client-side exploits. Consider RSA, perhaps one of the most technically mature companies in the world, which practically invented the commercial implementation of cryptography. They fell victim to a social engineering attack and ultimately succumbed to an exploited vulnerability in Adobe Reader.

Although RSA was successfully attacked, the complete lesson here is that they limited the damage by detecting anomalous behavior within their network soon after the attack was initiated. The RSA attack supports the contention that all organizations are vulnerable and that this attack vector in particular argues strongly for ensuring that internal network vulnerabilities are limited.

8.3.2   Content Monitoring

Content monitoring analyzes the network traffic or system activity and matches it against a set of rules describing risk-relevant words, phrases, symbols, etc. This is typically the function of intrusion detection systems (IDS), intrusion prevention systems (IPS), and host intrusion detection systems (HIDS).

Traffic that is allowed by a firewall can be used to carry harmful data or send confidential information to the Internet (see the next section for firewall restrictions). Certain defensive systems are designed to inspect network traffic and either generate alerts or stop suspicious activity.

IDS and IPS work by matching the traffic against a set of rules or signatures. If a match is found, actions can be taken for follow-up. These actions might include generating an alert, flagging the traffic for further inspection, resetting the connection, etc. IDS solutions do not typically distinguish between inbound and outbound traffic. Rather, if a packet matches the inspection conditions (e.g., source, destination, port, and protocol), its content will be compared to the applicable rule.

At an extremely high level, a typical IT network consists of domains that are segmented according to varying levels of risk. The canonical network includes a demilitarized zone (DMZ) segregated by a firewall, possibly even a "secure DMZ" that uses multiple firewalls, and an internal network. The point of a DMZ is to segregate high-risk machines from internal network resources.

This segregation is usually accomplished via the use of one or two firewalls. Figure 8.8 depicts a representative network topology for a commercial entity.

An IDS solution should be installed in each of the major network zones and analyze the traffic specific to that zone. For example, the DMZ IDS would focus on inspecting the http traffic going to Web servers as well as SQL requests between Web and database servers. An internal IDS solution should focus on detecting malware or executables attempting to reach desktop computers, assuming it could recognize the malware signature, a nontrivial issue. In that vein, the next section focuses on behavior monitoring that is intended to address the problem of previously undocumented malware or so-called "zero day attacks."

In addition, the internal IDS could be used as an elementary form of data leakage or data loss prevention (DLP) solution by looking for labels in the network traffic such as "confidential" or "privileged." However, sometimes this is not a particularly fruitful exercise. Consider a law firm that is concerned about a specific form of privileged information. The frequent use of the word "privileged" would likely return many documents so that this specific word might prove useless as a filter.

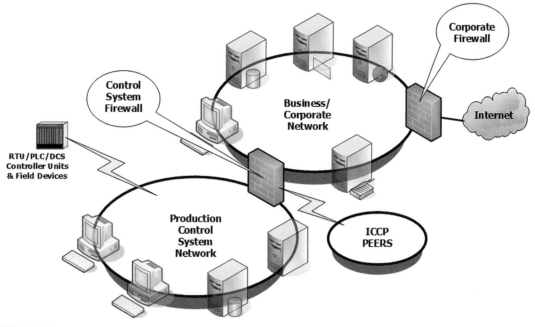

FIGURE 8.8

A high-level network structure. *(Source: Industrial Control SystemsCyber Emergency Response Team.* https://ics-cert.us-cert.gov/content/overview-cyber-vulnerabilities.*)*

Although IDS solutions can be used as a form of DLP technique, it is important to implement a bona fide DLP solution to monitor outbound network traffic. Commercial products exist that not only monitor for risk-relevant packets, but also place strict limits on document transmissions, message forwarding, et al.

Deploying an IDS solution is straightforward and usually requires setting a switch port as a monitor or "span" port. However, although IDS solutions work well in analyzing clear-text traffic, they are powerless in examining encrypted content such as in HTTPS. In that case, other solutions must be designed, such as an HIDS or an HTTPS proxy. Specific recommendations for implementing content monitoring as part of an IDS and/or a DLP solution are as follows:

1. Install an IDS in the DMZ that monitors the following:
   a. Exploits of HTTP and HTTPS and, in particular, Windows and SharePoint-based exploits.
   b. SQL statements and bad requests.
   c. Exploits of File Transfer Protocol (FTP) to include invalid/dangerous file formats and possible intellectual property violations (e.g., audio and/or video files, CD/DVD images, etc.).
   d. Internet control message protocol (ICMP), port scans, Web enumeration, and general TCP exploits or abuses.
   e. Known malicious networks connecting to servers.
   f. NetBIOS exploits, e.g., a "wildcard query" using the *nbtstat-a* command (note: NetBIOS yields information about the computers on a network. This includes the name of the computer, username, domain, et al. The nbtstat command allows for manual interaction with NETBIOS. For example, one can obtain the name of a computer corresponding to a specific IP address using the nbtstat-a command).
2. Install a host-based IDS on each exposed server in the DMZ and program it to report to a central console. The IDS should at a minimum identify:
   a. Failed login attempts.
   b. 404 (page not found) and 50x (server error) HTTP and HTTPS status codes.
   c. Application crashes, core dumps, and illegal operations.
   d. Security log deletion or truncation (i.e., a vulnerability related to SQL injection-type attacks).
   e. Starting and stopping of services.
3. Install an IDS/DLP in the internal network and monitor the following:
   a. Known client-side exploits through HTTP and FTP.
   b. Key words signifying the potential transfer of risk-relevant documents from inside the network to the outside. This could produce large numbers of false positives, so combining key words with behavioral attributes (e.g., transfers late at night, large attachments) would reduce this volume. Note again this method will not work for encrypted traffic.
   c. Connection to known high-risk networks.

d. Transfer of client names from inside the network to outside the network using any clear-text protocol.

e. NetBIOS exploits.

f. Suspicious DNS resolutions (i.e., known bad names or invalid records). There is in fact a product on the market called OpenDNS that blocks suspicious name resolutions before an external connection is made (http://www.opendns.com/). Tests by colleagues at my firm have shown this to be a useful tool, and should be considered as part of a comprehensive defensive strategy against malware.

g. Access to C$ and other administrative shares on servers from non-IT workstations.

8.3.3 Behavior Monitoring

In behavior monitoring, a system or a person analyzes patterns such as destinations, frequency/periodicity of identified risk incidents, and/or volumes exchanged, which indicate whether the behavior exceeds a specified baseline. Of course, determining that baseline can be a judgment call.

Rather than inspecting the content of a connection, behavior monitoring looks at patterns related to the manner in which connections are made. Some parameters for behavior monitoring might include:

1. Frequent connections or connections made in rapid succession to the same host.
2. Periodic communications to the same destination.
3. A source transferring a large quantity of data to the same host, either in one large transfer or in multiple smaller transfers (those familiar with the use of "structuring" in money laundering will recognize this ploy).
4. A source trying multiple usernames against a host, then moving to another host and repeating this activity.
5. A succession of "anomalous" events on a server (Note: this advice might not seem particularly helpful. As indicated previously, one problem with behavior monitoring is the generation of false positives. So careful thinking about genuine risk-relevant behavior is required).
6. An individual changing passwords many times within a short time interval. Note that in general it is not advisable to discourage users from changing their passwords!

A number of tools are available to assist with behavior monitoring. However, a challenging issue is to ensure security logs are regularly reviewed for suspicious events. It is not unusual for a typical firewall log to contain millions of entries, so the sheer volume of information makes it impractical to conduct manual reviews.

In addition to commercial tools that can be used to parse logs based on risk (e.g., Splunk), special scripts can be developed to analyze key parameters such as the following:

1. The volume transferred by each workstation.
2. A set of hosts reporting to the same host.
3. Suspiciously regular activity by a machine (i.e., they occur at regular time intervals). One way to efficiently monitor such activity is to convert a time series to the frequency domain and identify peaks in the transmission spectrum. Such conversions can be implemented by performing a Fourier transform on the time series.

It is sometimes difficult to appreciate subtle anomalies in time series data without viewing the data in both the time and frequency domains. The Fourier transform enables such views and is an important measurement tool that has not generally been applied to security scenarios.

Figure 8.9 shows an indicative Fourier transform of a time series. This data corresponds to pulsar data displayed in the frequency domain, but the principle is

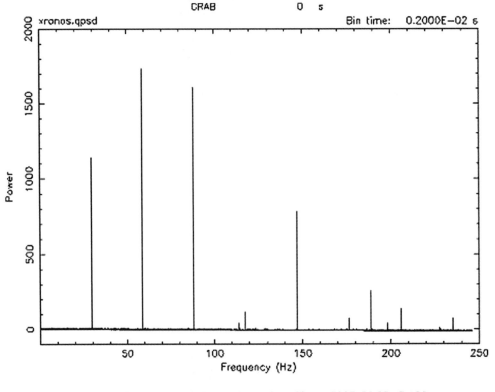

FIGURE 8.9
Fourier transform of a time series. *(Source: Humphreys, J. "Timing an X-ray Pulsar." NASA.* http://heasarc.gsfc.nasa.gov/docs/xte/learning_center/xray_pulsar.html.*)*

the same in all applications of this technique. The Fourier transform is used in many scientific areas in order to evaluate signals in the frequency and/or time domains. The peaks in Figure 8.9 clearly indicate that the signal power is concentrated at discrete frequencies in this bandwidth (i.e., between 0 and 250 Hz).

4. The number of dropped packets at the firewall originating from the internal network.

In summary, the recommendation on behavior monitoring is to parse firewall logs to look for specific patterns of risk such as a large volume of data being transferred, especially during nonbusiness hours, or suspicious patterns of connectivity to the Internet.

8.3.4 Interzone Network Monitoring

The aim of this section is to provide specific recommendations for verification and filtering as a function of communication type and the direction of data flows between zones. The magnitude of risk depends on the direction (e.g., inbound versus outbound) and specific zone (e.g., internal-to-DMZ, internal-to-Internet, etc.) of data flows or electronic access attempt. The following are general subvectors for the threat of information exfiltration or corruption:

1. An attacker could start a service on a machine in the DMZ and bind it to a port, e.g., a proxy, an Internet relay chat (IRC) server, or any other server in order to bypass existing restrictions.
2. An error or issue may lead to an inappropriate service being accessible, such as an HTTPS site that is accessible over HTTP or the administrative share (e.g., C$ and D$) being generally accessible.
3. An internal machine might be used to gain access to IT workstations. Restricting access to management interfaces (e.g., RDP, SSH, and SNMP (simple network management protocol)) will add a layer of protection against an internal machine trying to gain access to these servers.
4. The following subsections include recommendations for monitoring and restricting network behavior to and from the internal, DMZ and external network zones as depicted in Figure 8.8.

8.3.4.1 Monitoring Traffic from an Internal Network to a DMZ

1. Filter traffic so that only known protocols can be implemented (e.g., HTTP, HTTPS, FTP) on a per-server basis.
2. Restrict access to management interfaces (e.g., RDP, VNC (virtual network computing), SSH, SNMP, and Telnet) from workstations.
3. Restrict the use of SNMP.
4. When using clear-text protocols (e.g., HTTP, FTP), use the firewall's inspection capabilities to enforce protocol compliance. Limit the range of available commands (e.g., GET/POST for HTTP). Limit the header size on FTP commands USER/PASS/LIST/STOR/RETR/PORT.

5. Restrict access to the common Internet file system (CIFS) from workstations. CIFS allows users with different platforms and computers to easily share files. CIFS runs over TCP/IP but uses the server message block (SMB) protocol found in Microsoft Windows for file and printer access. CIFS will allow all applications, not just Web browsers, to open and share files across the Internet.

6. If the firewall supports it, disable access to administrative shares from all workstations that do not explicitly require it. The administrative shares are the default network shares created by most Windows NT-based operating systems. Default shares share every hard drive partition in the system. They will grant access to the root directory of every hard drive for anyone who can authenticate as a member of the local Administrators group.

7. Replace all occurrences of ICMP-ANY with ICMP-ECHOREQUEST.

8. Restrict access to the workstations assigned to operators and administrators.

8.3.4.2 *Monitoring Traffic from an Internal Network to the Internet*

The following recommendations are intended to monitor and ultimately block risk-relevant traffic from exiting the network. For example, an individual could covertly change the port for a given application, e.g., run IRC on port 46666 rather than 6666 and thereby circumvent monitoring and filtering activities. The point is to ensure all outgoing traffic is authorized to pass through the firewall.

In addition, if an electronic terrorist does manage to gain access to a server, it is important to make the data exfiltration exercise as tedious as possible in order to give the IT network team time to detect the attack. This is what occurred during the client-side exploit attack against RSA. Although the attack was successfully launched, the attack was detected relatively quickly, thereby preventing more significant problems.

Such measures also help to mitigate the risk of the network being used as a base from which to attack other networks or trusted parties.

1. Block all traffic from internal servers to the Internet, with the exception of known communications (e.g., updates, downloading of signature files, etc.).

2. Block Netbios to the Internet.

3. Allow only known protocols access to the Internet (e.g., HTTP, HTTPS, or FTP). An attacker could easily change the port number for any application to bypass filtering rules.

4. Implement a filtering proxy (e.g., Ironport) to perform additional antivirus scans on the content returned from the Internet.

5. Capture/cache all traffic from routers, e.g., use the Cisco Web cache communication protocol (WCCP) redirect list.

6. Request authentication for all outbound connections.

7. Restrict outgoing simple mail transfer protocol (SMTP) and simple mail transfer protocol security (SMTPS) to internal mail servers.
8. Block outgoing post office protocol (POP), Internet message access protocol (IMAP), to prevent bypassing email monitoring services (e.g., Google Postini).
9. Implement an instant messenger (IM) gateway and deploy a corporate IM client such as Spark/Openfire. This helps to prevent data leakage through IM channels.
10. Replace all occurrences of ICMP-ANY with ICMP-ECHOREQUEST. ICMP-ANY also allows "TIMESTAMP-REQUEST," "NETMASK-REQUEST," as well as other information requests that could be used by an intruder to game your system.
11. Block SSH connections. SSH allows port forwarding and therefore it can be used to circumvent firewall rules by allowing data exfiltration via unmonitored ports.
12. Enforce SMTPS between the internal mail servers and any email monitoring services (e.g., Google Postini).
13. Use the firewall's application level filtering to prevent the resolution of known bad domains (see the list at: *http://www.malwaredomains.com/*) or implement DNS-Black hole.
14. Configure a Layer7 HTTP deep packet inspection policy as part of the application protocol inspection (API).
15. Prevent the movement of certain services (e.g., IRC, Peer-to-Peer (P2P), or Web servers) to unusual ports and thereby reduce the risk of an internal machine sending emails that bypass exfiltration filters.

8.3.4.3 *Monitoring Traffic from a DMZ to the Internet*

DMZs typically host servers, so no user activity should be occurring in this zone. As noted previously, the point of a DMZ is to segregate high-risk services requiring access to the Internet from the internal network. As a result, the set of protocols is usually limited in range and can be filtered on a need-to-connect basis. As a result, the following security restrictions apply:

1. Only servers with external communication requirements should be allowed to send traffic from the DMZ to the Internet. Such communications should only be done via recognized and approved protocols (e.g., HTTP or HTTPS).
2. All servers in the DMZ should be required to use the internal mail server to relay emails.
3. All servers should receive updates/upgrades through an internal server (e.g., WSUS, Altiris, or equivalent) and not retrieve them directly from a vendor.
4. Block all traffic from the DMZ to the Internet by default (see number 1 above).
5. Utilize an addressable proxy server for communication between a DMZ and the Internet.

8.3.4.4 Monitoring Traffic from the Internet to a DMZ or Internal Network

Services exposed to the Internet are at greater risk of compromise and attacks, as discussed previously in this chapter. Therefore, the following security restrictions are recommended for inbound communications from the Internet:

1. For clear text protocols, use the firewall's application-level inspection capability to enforce protocol conformity (e.g., HTTP, FTP) and restrict the set of possible commands (e.g., GET/POST or USER/PASS/STOR/RETR/LIST/PORT/).
2. Implement SYN connection limits on a per-client and global basis in order to mitigate the risk of DoS attacks.
3. Block packets, datagrams, and segments with bad, illegal, and/or insecure options such as loose or strict routing, record route, timestamp, or source route.
4. Prevent the firewall from responding to time-to-live (TTL) 0. An attacker could use the information so derived to detect the firewall.
5. Use SMTPS (i.e., SMTP secured by SSL) between any email monitoring services (e.g., Google Postini) and internal mail servers.
6. Block over-fragmented packets (e.g., fragment size < 20).

8.3.4.5 Monitoring General Interzone Traffic

1. Implement an IDS on all exit points. An IDS will detect activity in and out of the network. Either commercial subscriptions or freeware is appropriate, but both solutions require frequent updating.
2. Implement IDS on all critical/high-risk zones (e.g., DMZs). These should be evaluated relative to baseline levels of traffic volume and patterns in addition to known risk signatures for malware, assuming such signatures exist.
3. Implement IDS on all checkpoints between segments that maintain different security levels. Target a particular machine based on the type of servers/applications located in the higher security zone. This can be a lighter version of the IDS and can be embedded in the checkpoint itself.
4. Implement a DLP capability on proxies with alerting. Implement a data labeling and classification system if possible and practical, noting the caveats specified previously in this chapter.
5. Implement a log correlation system or a security information and event management (SIEM) system. Define and maintain the rules for correlation and alerting.
6. Implement a log searching system, e.g., Splunk. This will facilitate quick searches of a log entry in the log base, although correlations will require additional analyses.

7. Implement mechanisms to detect and report lockouts or frequent unsuccessful login attempts for active directory, remote access, and critical Unix/Linux systems.
8. Implement TripWire or the equivalent to detect when sensitive system files have been altered. Implement such a solution on systems storing and/or processing critical data in order to detect file access.

8.3.5 Enhanced Network Risk Mitigation for APTs

Although interzone monitoring is important to detect lateral network movements and nefarious outbound connections traditionally used by malware/APTs, more active measures can provide additional protection. To that end, the following is a list of key mitigation measures to consider:

1. Force all HTTP/HTTPS traffic to go through Web proxies.
2. Suppress Internet access for all server and printer networks.
3. Enforce authentication for all HTTP/HTTPS connections to the Internet.
4. Suppress Internet access for networks with particularly vulnerable systems. Provide these networks with a few virtual machines so they can use RDP/Citrix to access the Internet.
5. Segregate networks by business function.
6. Implement access control lists (ACL) to restrict cross-communication between networks with different business functions.
7. Implement a network access control (NAC) solution. This will place the machine in its correct virtual local area network (VLAN) based on proper authentication to a portal (note: this could be MAC address-based). It will also enforce the correct segregation of machines. Unknown machines should be put into a guest network. Some NAC solutions (e.g., PacketFence) can even scan the machine and force it into a remediation network if significant vulnerabilities are identified.
8. Block all ports on the firewall except for known services/protocols (e.g., HTTP, HTTPS, or FTP).
9. Implement firewall authentication for ports that are not normally open.
10. If the insecure Windows LanMan hash storage method is used to store passwords, investigate relaxing the character set for the password while porting the minimum number of characters. Utilize passwords that are a minimum of 15 characters. Even if not salted, MD4/MD5 hashes are more difficult to crack than LanMan hashes.
11. Conduct periodic password cracking sessions and require all passwords that do not meet an organization's complexity standard to be changed (see the discussion on password entropy in Chapter 3, Section 3.1).
12. Establish a list of programs that are off-limits. The Nexpose application from Rapid7 maintains a list of every application that is installed on scanned machines. All nonauthorized applications should be immediately uninstalled.

13. Implement time limits for Internet access.
14. Conduct periodic scans for known malware signatures. Note that this is not an antidote to "Day Zero" attacks. See the discussion on behavior monitoring in this chapter.
15. Restrict the list of applications that are accessible via HTTP/HTTPS.
16. Identify and implement an executable blocker on each machine. This will compare the binary to be executed with a white list. Deny access if the binary is not on the list.
17. Periodically force a reimage of all workstations.
18. If practical, use labels/tags on all files to identify the type of information in files and permission the files accordingly. In general, information "owners" (i.e., those who create and control the information) must ensure information is adequately protected and electronic systems have provisions for the secure storage and transmission of information.
19. Suppress all departed users rather than simply disabling their accounts.
20. Implement a periodic audit of privileged accounts and remove any unnecessary privileges. StealthAudit is a useful tool for auditing accounts in Active Directory as discussed later in this chapter.

8.3.6   Identifying Internal Network Vulnerabilities

An important control in addressing malware/APTs is to ensure network devices are properly configured and that internal and outbound connections are appropriately restricted. Recall one of the classic functions of malware is lateral movement within a network and attempting to communicate with external sites for command and control purposes. Therefore, it is critical that internal network vulnerabilities are addressed in the event malware is successfully introduced into the network.

The reality is that IT networks are typically quite complex with many components. They can also be quite dynamic. Attempts at successfully identifying misconfigurations and/or potential vulnerabilities without an automated tool are not likely to be consistently effective.

Attack and penetration tests are often positioned as *the* control in assessing network vulnerabilities. These "black-box" tests scan for external vulnerabilities and, assuming one is found, attempt to perform ethical mischief on the network by escalating access privileges or exploiting other vulnerabilities. In addition, appliances sitting on the network and examining packets whizzing by for malware signatures are advertised as providing protection from APTs.

One problem with these methods is that the development of malware can be a full-time occupation for those engaged in electronic terrorism. Malware signatures are continuously evolving, and no library can adequately keep up with this frenetic pace. In fact, signature-based detection methods are likely to always be behind the curve. In addition, sophisticated malware is often designed to fly below the radar by lying dormant or slowly acting so as not to alert behavior-based monitoring tools.

This is not to say network traffic monitoring cannot be fruitful. Considerable space has been devoted in this chapter to specify methods for monitoring inter-zone network traffic. It should constitute one element of a comprehensive defensive strategy. A truly comprehensive effort to reduce the risk of APTs/malware includes identifying the vulnerability of internal network resources as configured.

One method to effectively and efficiently accomplish this is via a white-box vulnerability test. In this type of test, data from router configurations, VPN gateways, firewall filtering rules, etc. (i.e., Layer 3 devices) are used to build a virtual network model. This virtual network is then used to conduct a methodical analysis of the network with respect to dependencies and threat attack vectors.

In contrast, black-box or standard attack and penetration tests are meant to be conducted as a blind test with no prior knowledge of the system. Traditional black-box penetration tests sometimes use brute-force mechanisms, often targeting specific areas of the global network. This methodology also focuses on individual devices and does not assess the overall security posture. Black-box testing also requires injecting packets into the network that could interrupt normal network operations.

The relative benefit of the white-box vulnerability assesment is that despite complexities in the network, it can more accurately simulate the impact to the entire network and related hosts. Since there is visibility into every Layer 3 network device, this method can specify how attacks to a particular resource will impact the highest priority information assets as well as reveal downstream risks.

How does this work in practice? This approach combines the knowledge gleaned from traditional host vulnerability scans that examine servers and desktops (i.e., via the use of tools such as Nessus, Qualys, or Nexpose) with Layer 3 device configuration files. One consequence of this approach is the creation of a comprehensive security risk heat map that reflects an accurate network topology.

The resulting heat map provides details on mitigation priorities and high value targets that could impact downstream systems. In general this test can be done offline since only the device configuration files are required, assuming host vulnerability scan results are available. If the results of host scans are not available, these must be implemented, and packets must be injected into the system to obtain these results.

Figures 8.10 and 8.11 show a virtual network configuration and critical theats to network devices generated by a particular tool that is used to perform white-box tests.

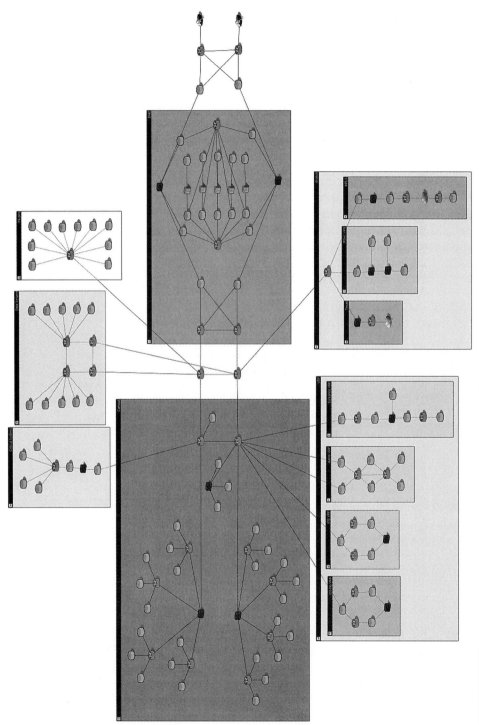

FIGURE 8.10

Virtual network for an organization.

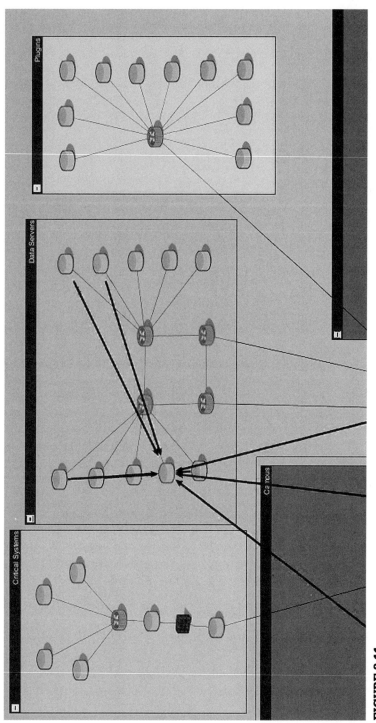

FIGURE 8.11

Threats to critical data servers.

Figures 8.10 and 8.11 were generated using the Red Seal application (*http://www.redsealnetworks.com*), a commercial product that is designed to facilitate white-box vulnerability tests. The data flow analysis results shown in Figure 8.11 graphically illustrate downstream attack routes and highlight areas requiring additional scrutiny.

In one real-life analysis, the white-box test showed that a critical resource physically located inside a client's data center, and presumably isolated via a firewall, was contactable via the Internet. Unfortunately this is not a rare occurrence, especially with more complex networks.

The key questions answered by a white-box test are summarized in Table 8.1.

A black-box penetration test could easily miss internal network vulnerabilities and thereby yield an incomplete picture of risk relative to APTs and malware more generally. A white-box test reveals the spectrum of internal network vulnerabilities plus downstream risks and, importantly, facilitates prioritization of remediation efforts.

An indicative risk matrix that might result from the output of a white-box test is shown in Figure 8.12.

Table 8.1 White-box Vulnerability Testing

Information Security Issue	Key Questions Asked
IT network electronic access	Who can access critical assets? What access is permitted? What is the actual network topology?
Network security policies	Is the network configuration in compliance with security-related requirements?
Access between zones	What access is allowed that could facilitate data loss or leakage?
Firewall and router rule sets	Are there redundant or high-risk rules in place (e.g., IP (any, any))?
Vulnerability of critical assets	What security vulnerabilities can be exploited by an attacker?
Security best practices	How does a device configuration compare to current security best practices?
IT security	What downstream hosts are vulnerable to attack from a given host? What does an IT security heat map look like?

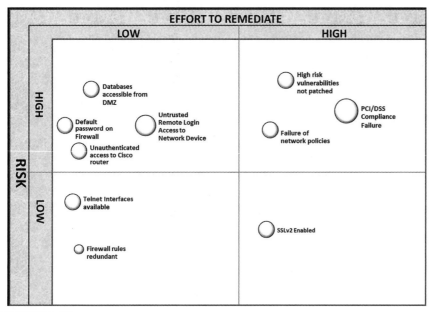

FIGURE 8.12
Indicative risk matrix resulting from a white-box vulnerability test.

8.3.7 Exposing Expired or Faulty Network Identities and Privileges

Electronic access privileges are tied to user credentials based on identity. These credentials allow electronic access to specific devices and information. By design, such privileges can also be of finite duration based on risk. Managing user accounts in Windows for a dynamic population with constantly changing credentials is a continuous process of housekeeping. But this is necessary to maintain a viable security posture. It can be an enlightening exercise to identify the number of stale user accounts that typically persist within large organizations.

Users with local administrative privileges present particular risks, and these accounts should be limited to specific individuals with a genuine business requirement for such privileges. The reader is reminded that software exists to allow individuals to check out such privileges for a specified time period, thereby limiting the risk of unauthorized privilege escalation (*http://www .liebsoft.com/*).

In addition, the white-box tests discussed in the last section can be integrated with electronic audits of the Active Directory to yield an advanced control. Specifically, if host and Windows account vulnerabilities are correlated, any intersections so identified could yield significant insights into enhanced electronic risk. One example of this might be an open share containing sensitive

Table 8.2 Active Directory Assessment

Functionality	Key Questions Asked	Risk
Active Directory—User Accounts	Are there any ACTIVE accounts that have not been used for years?	Assess feasibility of malware or attackers using these accounts to gain access to the environment.
Active Directory—User Accounts	Are there any ACTIVE accounts for users that have never logged on to the environment?	Assess feasibility of malware or attackers using these accounts to gain access to the environment.
Active Directory—Privileged Access	Are there any privileged user accounts violating policy?	Can these accounts be leveraged by an attacker to gain access to critical resources?
Active Directory—Privileged Access	Is the principle of least privileges followed for administrative accounts?	Can these accounts be leveraged by an attacker to gain access to critical resources?

information that has connectivity to the Internet and is also accessible to users with expired access privileges, weak credentials, and/or outdated patches.

Stealth Audit (*http://www.stealthbits.com/*) is a tool that is used to identify risk issues in an Active Directory. Understanding correlations between risk-relevant parameters and/or the intersection of characteristics that enhance electronic risk is a key element of a sophisticated risk assessment. Electronic environments are complex, and programs used to manage security/access privileging are inherently linked to applications that manage sensitive information.

However, more aggressive measures may be required depending on the tolerance for information security risk relative to business risk and modulated by the general concern for APTs. Namely, business and electronic environments might need to be aligned such that access to information and the Internet is highly restricted/segregated based on physical location (e.g., in the office or elsewhere), an individual's role within the organization, and/or information type. In the next section we discuss various electronic configurations that offer varying degrees of security in countering a principal mode of APT behavior, lateral movement. Each configuration offers security resilience at the expense of convenience, the standard trade-off. Table 8.2 summarizes the key questions answered through an Active Directory assessment.

8.3.8 Prevention of Pernicious Lateral Movements and Information Segregation

A high priority of an electronic terrorist launching an APT would arguably be to target the key information assets of a company or organization. The objective would be to either exfiltrate or damage them in some way. Up to this point, the discussion has mostly focused on controls to monitor and detect network traffic for anomalous behavior, identify internal network vulnerabilities, and ensure appropriate identity privilege management. One additional control might be to configure the network a priori to segregate sensitive and time-sensitive information assets as well as reduce the vulnerability to lateral motion.

As is typically the case in security, the tension between convenience and information security is the principal dynamic in refining this control. This is the dialectic that reflects divergent philosophies on information management. On one hand is a liberal (i.e., permit access by default) approach to information sharing, and the other is a restrictive policy on information access based on the principle of "need-to-know (i.e., deny access by default)." In fact, the model used for access privileging is a defining feature of the information security posture of an organization. How might access privileging work in practice?

Organizations maintain information that is stored and accessed as files on servers or drives. These often exist in the form of two distinct file types: active or archived information. Active files are those that have been created relatively recently and therefore are more relevant to current business requirements. These typically mandate immediate and frequent access by numerous members of the user population.

By contrast, archived files contain information in dormant or inactive cases and are likely to require access by a small subset of the user population. In addition, access required by those individuals would typically be intermittent.

Both file types carry risk if unauthorized individuals are afforded electronic or physical access to the information contained therein. In other words, the impact component of risk is significant for both active and archived files. However, each file type requires different controls in the form of access restriction and data leakage protection based on business requirements. The mandate for information security professionals is to facilitate business requirements while effectively managing the assessed risk of information loss to the organization.

What is needed is a means of implementing secure access to both active and archived files according to the need-to-know principle and in a manner consistent with an organization's tolerance for risk versus inconvenience and in consideration of the concern for APTs.

To that end, options are presented here that are principally intended to make unauthorized access difficult but candidly also present varying degrees of access challenges to legitimate users. It is important to appreciate that there is no perfect solution. To invoke a trite but nonetheless appropriate expression, security is about risk management and not about risk elimination.

This section addresses the pros and cons of three general approaches to information security surrounding archived and active file types:

1. **Air gap-type networks**—Active and archived files are on different physical or electronic networks with limited or no electronic or physical connections between them.
2. **Virtual air gap**—Active and archived files are hosted on the same electronic infrastructure with segregation performed by a front-end system.
3. **Application-managed**—Active and archived file segregation is achieved through native security controls in an application.

Security systems such as intrusion detection or intrusion prevention, data loss prevention, and proxies have been discussed earlier in this chapter and would likely be a component of any robust network design strategy. The options discussed here do not obviate the need for vigilant network monitoring and effective response protocols but are intended to provide alternative configurations for enhanced resilience with respect to APTs.

8.3.8.1 The Prime Directive: Restrict Lateral Movement

As noted previously, lateral movement within a compromised network is often a key modus operandi of APTs. The point of the attack feature is to identify the location of the informational crown jewels by moving from device-to-device and then stealing, vandalizing, or destroying the information contained therein.

Such leapfrogging can lead to the compromise of a large number of systems within the internal network. Exposing internal vulnerabilities that might not be exposed to external attacks highlights why white-box vulnerability tests are recommended relative to external penetration tests as noted in the previous section.

To protect against the compromise of systems or devices in this way, an effective strategy is to place as many hurdles as possible and practical between systems that do not need to communicate with each other. This is simplistically illustrated in Figure 8.13.

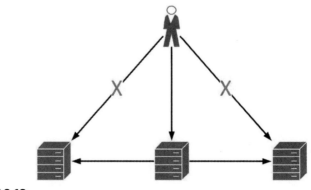

FIGURE 8.13
Denying electronic access to files.

8.3.8.2 *Network Air Gaps*

1. A so-called "air gap" solution consists of two independent systems on different networks that are either physically or electronically isolated. An air gap provides maximum protection from electronic compromise, but it also presents the maximum inconvenience to users. It is important to note that the very notion of "networking" is vitiated by an air gap solution.

2. There are a number of variations on the network air gap theme:
   - Separate internal workstations.
   - Separate internal connections.
   - Internal virtual private network (VPN).
   - Internal Citrix gateway.
   - Dual-headed network.

3. In general, the pros and cons of a network air gap solution are as follows:

   Pros
   - Provides strong segregation between network environments, thereby limiting the vulnerability to nefarious lateral movements.
   - Affords good user access control for both systems and data.
   - Allows for multifactor authentication.
   - Limits the vulnerability to data exfiltration to only keystrokes and screen refreshes.
   - Can be combined with strong encryption for data in transit.

   Cons
   - May require separate databases on active and archived systems that could lead to duplicate searches.
   - Users must choose between accessing either active or archived systems since both cannot be accessed simultaneously.
   - Extending to remote users could be difficult and may lead to decreased productivity.
   - Expensive to implement due to redundant hardware and software.
   - Adds complexity to the archiving procedure.

8.3.8.2.1 Separate Internal Workstations

In this air gap scenario, a number of fixed workstations would be installed in an organization's offices in addition to remote locations as required. These designated workstations will be the only terminals allowed to access the archived environment. This configuration ensures a strict separation between active and archived files. The static nature of this situation also permits additional controls to be applied to various system components (e.g., switches and servers) to guarantee that only designated workstations are granted electronic access to the archived repository.

Citrix is a popular way of gaining access to internal resources without actually granting network connectivity to the client device. Specifically, Citrix presents published applications, e.g., Microsoft Office or even a full desktop that emulates a Microsoft Windows workstation, to a connecting client.

Citrix permits users to access applications from a central server rather than downloading a local copy of the application. Screenshots, keystrokes, etc. are communicated via the Internet so that the user experience is similar to, if a bit slower than, a locally accessed application.

The separate internal workstation solution involves two distinct Citrix presentations to access active and archived environments. Figure 8.14 illustrates this configuration.

An organization's IT infrastructure is often located in a hosted data center that communicates with offices in a remote location. Moreover, such connections, to the user are often based on a Multiprotocol Label Switching (MPLS) backbone, which is a Layer 3 (i.e., the network layer in the OSI model) technology. However, MPLS is actually a Layer 2 (data link layer in the OSI mode) technology from the provider's perspective relative to the use of the high speed networking standard, Asynchronous Transfer Mode (ATM).

While certain techniques exist to carry Layer 2 links over MPLS, such as virtual private LAN services (VPLS) or ethernet over MPLS (EoMPLS), this may create issues such as increased bandwidth requirements since every broadcast will be transmitted over the backbone.

In such a topology, the use of Cisco Virtual Routing and Forwarding (VRF) is recommended, either using multiple VPNs over the MPLS backbone or

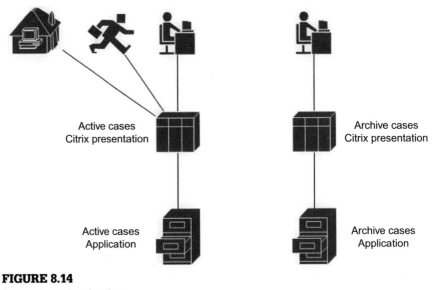

FIGURE 8.14
Separate internal workstations.

by leveraging a virtual tunnel interface in the routing devices present at each location. Different solutions are possible, such as dynamic multipoint VPN (DMVPN) or hub-and-spoke VPNs based on Generic Routing Encapsulation (GRE) or Internet Protocol Security (IPsec) tunnels.

8.3.8.2.2 Separate Internal Connections

In this variation of an air gap solution, each relevant desktop is provided with two network cables. Namely, there is one connecting to the active network and another to the archived network. A user would need to disconnect the machine and reconnect to the other network to access either the archived network or vice versa, but a user would not be able to connect to both networks simultaneously.

This permits a wider audience to have access to the archived network than with the separate workstation solution. However, a geographical limitation exists with this topology. Users in a location with no access to the archived network must request that a user with appropriate access conduct that search. There could be a bottleneck if a significant number of employees do not have access to the archived network relative to the number that do and if the demand for archived information is high.

In the event users are able to download documents on their computer through the Citrix local drive option, the following risks persist: (a) users with access to both systems are able to copy data onto a laptop and thereby exfiltrate the

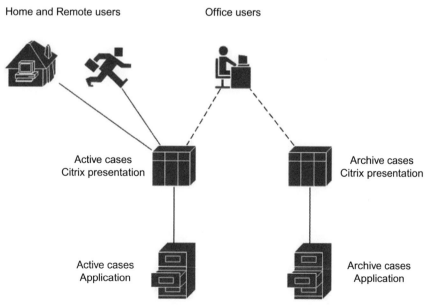

FIGURE 8.15
Desktop with separate internal connections to active and archived networks.

information and (b) if a laptop is compromised by malware, the malicious code may be copying the data and storing it until it can transfer the data to its command and control center, a typical modality of malware. Figure 8.15 illustrates the concept of separate internal connections via Citrix presentations.

8.3.8.2.3 Internal Virtual Private Network Gateway

VPN is a technology used to create a secure remote connection between two systems such as client-to-client, gateway-to-client, or gateway-to-gateway. An indicative if high-level VPN configuration is shown in Figure 8.16.

In this case, the client is a workstation requiring access to the archived network that connects to a VPN gateway that in turn grants access to the "isolated" network. The gateway may perform different security services such as providing two-factor authentication, DLP, and firewalling.

How would this configuration work? A user with a requirement to access the archived environment from within the office would launch a VPN tunnel from an internal workstation to the VPN gateway presented on the active network. The user would then authenticate himself or herself and be permitted to access the archived information.

Remote users would only have access to active files via Citrix. Figure 8.17 illustrates the use of an internal VPN connecting to a Citrix presentation for access to active and archived file information.

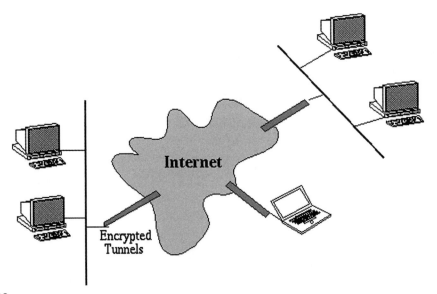

FIGURE 8.16

VPN. *(Source* http://www.csm.ornl.gov/~dunigan/vpn.html.*)*

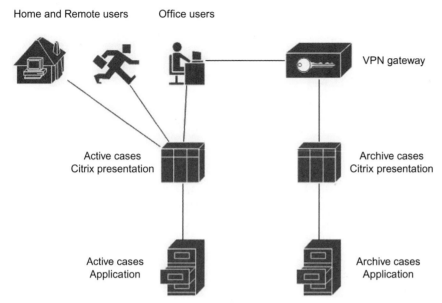

FIGURE 8.17
Use of internal VPN gateway with Citrix presentation.

8.3.8.2.4   Internal Citrix Access Gateway

In this configuration, a user requiring access to the archived environment would first connect to the Citrix Access Gateway for authentication. Once authenticated, the user would be presented with a desktop or the relevant application via Citrix. An illegitimate data transfer could be thwarted if protocols consistent with relevant security policies were not being followed.

However, the bad news is that a workstation that was compromised by malware could be exploited to transmit captured screen refreshes and keystrokes. If this occurred, the attacker would be able to view all workstation activity.

From a convenience perspective, any user with access to the active network, either directly or through a VPN, would be able to connect to the Citrix gateway. Figure 8.18 illustrates the concept of an internal Citrix gateway for active and archived file segregation and access.

8.3.8.2.5   Two-Pronged Network

The first of two types of two-pronged networks presented is a conceptual extension of two physically separate networks. Archived and active environments would each have their own dedicated hardware and Internet access, but access permissions and authentication is co-implemented via a firewall. This will lower the risk of a nefarious lateral movement while preserving key functionalities such as Internet access. Figure 8.19 illustrates this version of a two-pronged network.

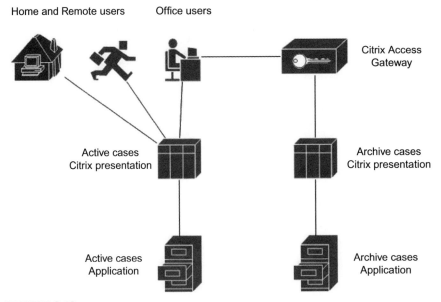

FIGURE 8.18

Use of an internal Citrix Access Gateway.

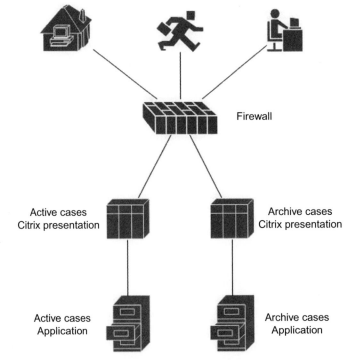

FIGURE 8.19

Two-pronged network: single firewall.

The second variation of a two-pronged network is the use of a double layer of firewalls. This provides greater isolation of the active and archived environments with respect to threats from the Internet while maintaining access to these environments from internal networks. The active and archive domains are effectively equivalent to a DMZ.

External users must either log on to a Citrix Access Gateway present on the first firewall or establish a VPN connection. Once this connection occurs, access will be granted to the second layer of firewalls, and the applications

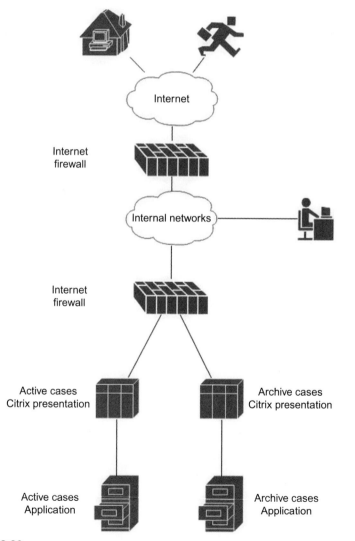

FIGURE 8.20

Two-pronged network: two firewalls.

are presented through Citrix, subject to an organization's access restrictions and policies. The concept of a double layer of firewalls is illustrated in Figure 8.20.

8.3.8.3   *Virtual Air Gap*

In a virtual air gap configuration, the Citrix Access Gateway (CAG) front end presents both active and archive applications to users via Citrix. Figure 8.21 illustrates the concept of a virtual air gap solution.

8.3.8.4   *Variations on a Virtual Air Gap*

- VPN front end.
- Firewalled internal environments.

As noted above, the active and archived environments should ideally reside on different networks with limited or no inter-network electronic access. This will decrease the risk of malware spreading within the network or the facilitation of lateral movements. These are often key objectives of an attacker.

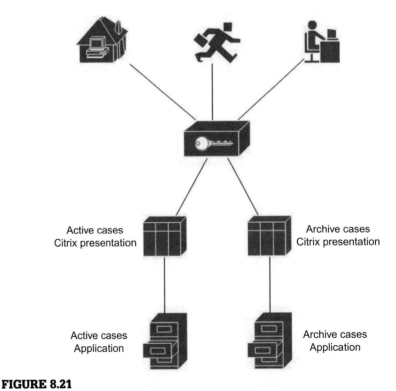

FIGURE 8.21

Virtual air gap via Citrix Access Gateway.

As explained previously, Citrix is a popular method for presenting internal applications to users without actually providing network connectivity. The front end is known as a Citrix Access Gateway (CAG), and it exists as a virtual CAG or the more powerful Netscaler.

In this configuration the CAG performs the initial client authentication and applies access-control rules, e.g., filtering the source of traffic by time of day, whether the user account is in a specific user group, or applying multiple authorization/authentication criteria. Based on the results, user access is either granted or denied.

Also, different applications can be presented according to the particular user group. For example, members of the archived file group will be granted access only to the archived network, whereas members of the active file group will only be directed to the active network environment.

A variation on the air gap solution is to present the CAG behind a VPN gateway. This configuration could definitely increase the security of the archived network. Specifically, it will prevent a computer from accessing the Internet by disabling split tunneling and by only allowing access to keyboard strokes and screen refreshes.

A summary of pros and cons for the configuration of a CAG sitting behind a VPN gateway is as follows:

Pros
- Preserves the segregation between the active and archived environments.
- Permits simultaneous access to active and archived networks.
- Is accessible from internal and external locations.
- Multifactor authentication is possible.
- The vulnerability to data exfiltration can be limited to captured keystrokes and screen refreshes.
- Can be combined with strong encryption to enhance security of data in transit.

Cons
- Separate databases are required for the active and archived networks that could lead to duplicate searches.
- Increased expense due to redundant hardware/software.
- Topology is slightly more complex due to the two Citrix farms with a potential for enhanced maintenance.
- Adds complexity to archiving procedures.

Figure 8.22 illustrates the configuration described above.

The second variation of the virtual air gap configuration is the use of a firewall sitting behind a CAG. Figure 8.23 illustrates the segregation of protected

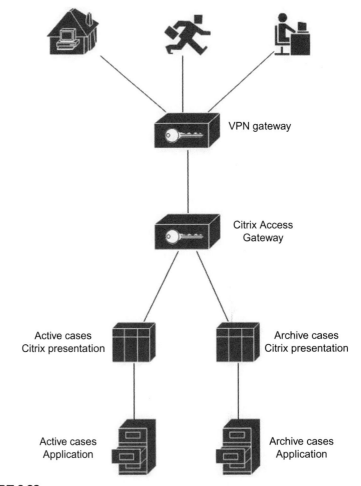

FIGURE 8.22
Citrix Access Gateway behind a VPN gateway.

environments through the use of a firewall. The firewall enhances segregation between the archived and active environments, thereby reducing the vulnerability to nefarious lateral movements while preserving strong authentication via the CAG.

8.3.8.5   Layer 7/Application-Level Security
In this scenario, the application provides the necessary segregation of the data between the active and archived files. Of course, the security will vary depending on the specific application. Protection can be implemented via the use of permissions or Role-Based Access Control (RBAC).

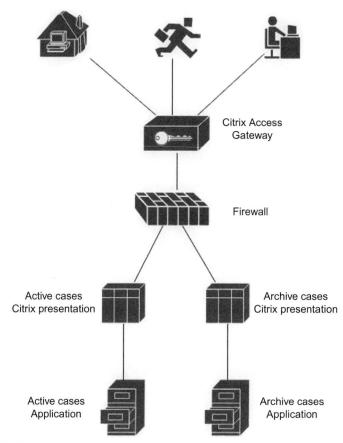

FIGURE 8.23

Firewall segregation and Citrix Access Gateway.

Pros
- Reduced expense.
- Simplified procedure for archiving.
- Single search index for both the active and archived files.

Cons
- Access control mechanisms will vary according to the particular application, and in some instances these could be inadequate.
- Potential existence of "super users" who have access to the entire data set.
- Poor segregation so in the event of a system compromise the entire data set could potentially be accessed.
- Potential for lateral movement by an attacker.

The application-level security option is illustrated in Figure 8.24.

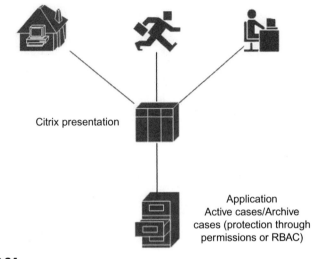

Citrix presentation

Application
Active cases/Archive
cases (protection through
permissions or RBAC)

FIGURE 8.24
Application-level security.

8.3.8.6   Avoiding Death by Spearphishing:
8.3.8.6.1   Strict Segregation of Email, Web Access, and Applications

A popular attack vector of APTs is unauthorized entry into an organization's network through social engineering. In this attack, electronic terrorists and others will trick an internal user into installing or executing malicious code on a computer. This is done by either exploiting vulnerabilities in popular applications such as Adobe Reader or by directing a user to a website in order to download malicious code. The general method of targeting specific users and tricking them in this way is known as spearphishing, a specific client-side attack vector.

One reason this attack vector is so popular is that it exploits an inherent weakness of all networks: human behavior. As noted previously, an optimist might choose to see a silver lining in this cloud, no pun intended. Namely, this technique may signify that network perimeter defenses have become increasingly robust, forcing attackers to utilize other modes of entry.

Notwithstanding such irrational exuberance, client-side exploits have proven to be a very effective attack vector, and successful attacks have been reported against some of the most technically sophisticated organizations (e.g., HBGary and RSA).

Once inside the network, the spearphisher has access privileges equivalent to the local user. That includes access to a local user's machine, other workstations, and internal servers. This will facilitate installation of tools to provide ongoing access to the network or to elevate access privileges. If the user happens to have local administrative rights, life is indeed beautiful for the attacker since installing software for nefarious purposes is now his or her prerogative.

The reader should be forewarned that the configuration offered for consideration here is a radical one. The inconvenience that would result from implementing such a solution would probably not be tolerated by many institutions. Therefore, it is not necessarily being recommended as a viable option. It is merely being posited as a solution that would reduce the vulnerability to spearphishing but at a tremendous cost in the form of convenience. At a minimum it is illustrative to be aware of the significant business risk required in order to reduce the information security risk with respect to this attack vector.

As noted above, spearphishing is so effective because it exploits human foibles and the massive convenience facilitated by email, Web, and application interconnectivity. The following is the standard modus operandi of spearphishing attacks against a network:

- Intrusion/installation.
- Lateral movement/persistence.
- Data gathering/exfiltration.

Intrusion/installation is the phase of the attack when social engineering is used to gain electronic access to the internal network. As noted above, social engineering is frequently successful because it exploits weaknesses in human behavior, and it evades traditional network monitoring/detection methods. It also is a direct means of accessing a smorgasbord of internal network resources. Compare this to attacking a server in a DMZ, which only yields access to peripheral components.

Several techniques are commonly used in this phase of the attack. The most publicized is spearphishing, although this is not the only attack vector. Specifically, this entails sending an email that is addressed to a specific network user (hence the prefix "spear" added to phishing, implying a directed attack). Although not publishing email addresses on the externally facing home page of an organization is indicative of good security practices, realistically it will not result in a significant reduction in the vulnerability to spearphishing given the ease of obtaining such information elsewhere.

After the initial vulnerability is exploited, a second-stage payload is downloaded from the Internet. This will modify the local host to disable any antivirus software, run the malware each time the computer is restarted, and connect back to its command and control server to receive instructions.

One of the key goals of the attacker is to enable unfettered access to the internal network. This is accomplished by either compromising an organization's remote access channel by obtaining a legitimate user's credentials or by installing malware on a server.

In order for the first option to work, the attacker must obtain access to a set of login credentials. This can be accomplished by compromising a local user's password. If the user fortuitously has local administrative rights, passwords can be obtained by dumping Local Security Authority (LSA) secrets. LSA manages a system's local security policy, auditing, authenticating, logging users on to the system, and storing private data. User and system sensitive data is stored in LSA secrets. LSA secrets offers protected storage for important data used by the LSA in Windows.

LSASecretsDump is an application that extracts the LSA secrets from the registry, decrypts them, and dumps them into the console window. The LSA secrets key represents a security vulnerability if compromised, since it may contain the remote access service (RAS)/VPN passwords, Autologon password, and other system passwords or keys.

A condition that facilitates the compromise of user credentials is when the remote access machine utilizes standard Windows authentication rather than multifactor authentication. The importance of using multiple factors for authentication is discussed in Chapter 10.

Planting a remote access tool in a server is often favored by attackers over compromising a remote channel. The former leaves less of a footprint in system logs and can survive a user password change.

Once the attacker has established a presence inside the network, the terrorist's search for interesting data begins. When such information is located, the next task is to aggregate this data for compression and transmission outside the attacked organization's network (i.e., exfiltration). The gathering phase can potentially last for an extended period, thereby substantiating the use of the word "persistence" in the APT acronym.

It is important to distinguish a target from a fortuitous attack. If the attack is fortuitous or nontarget-specific, it is likely that an attacker will move on to the next victim if stiff resistance is encountered. This is analogous to the proverbial burglar shopping around for a soft target in a neighborhood.

The situation is more concerning if an attacker is intent on compromising a specific entity. In that case, and provided the attacker has enough resources, a compromise is almost inevitable. APTs are often state-sponsored, so resources are not an issue. Time is on the side of the attacker, while the victim mounts a defense that is largely reactive.

Since the modus operandi of targeted and untargeted attacks are similar and differ mostly in the degree of stealth, it seems that a successful strategy for directed attacks will also address fortuitous ones.

Recall that the general principles in mounting a defensive strategy for malware were specified previously. In general, these entail making it difficult for malware to do the following:

- Access the internal network.
- Execute on a machine.
- Connect to the Internet.
- Facilitate spreading to other machines.
- Access protected information.
- Transmit harvested information to the Internet.

The network architecture plays a critical role in the overall security strategy. A network security design is often a layered structure. Each layer fulfills one or more roles such as preventing communication or code execution, controlling access to internal or external networks, or limiting the time of day certain actions can take place.

In previously cited examples of network configurations for accessing active and archived files containing confidential or sensitive information, a fundamental security control relative to APTs/malware was network segregation. To reiterate, this means that systems of differing security levels and/or purposes should be isolated from one another, and the principle of least-privilege should be strictly enforced. This translates to restricting communication between network segments to only what is needed to conduct business.

One mistake would be to merely harden the network exterior but to leave the interior relatively soft. The problem with this approach is that once the attacker has cleared an exterior barrier there would be little or no resistance to movement inside the network. Therefore, the entire network must be part of the security solution to restrict an attacker's movement should the perimeter be breached. This is the principle behind deploying white-box internal network vulnerability assessments versus the use of traditional penetration tests, as discussed earlier in this chapter.

Spearphishing is facilitated via connectivity between email and Web services. Recall the earlier description of my personal transgression in clicking on a hyperlink embedded in a targeted email. Accessing the Internet via email or having the ability to open attachments embedded in an email is extraordinarily convenient. Think about the number of times someone transmits a file attached to an email and/or embeds a link to an interesting website.

A simple way to significantly reduce the risk of spearphishing is to simply break these connections, as illustrated in Figure 8.25. The proposed solution contains the following devices and services that are defined as follows:

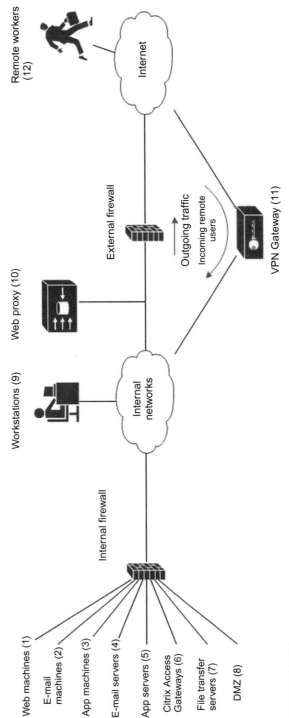

FIGURE 8.25

Antispearphishing solution via segregation of key services.

- **Web machines**—Published desktop of virtual workstations intended to browse the Internet. No other task or work should be done on these machines.
- **Email/office machines**—Published desktop or virtual workstations intended to process email and perform various office tasks (i.e., process Word or Excel documents, facilitate access to internal websites).
- **Application machines**—Published desktop, application, or virtual workstations used to access document management systems.
- **Email servers**—The servers containing email-related infrastructure.
- **Application servers**—Document management servers and related infrastructure such as file servers,
- **Citrix Access Gateway (CAG)**—This is the front-end component of the Citrix solution. The CAG is responsible for the authentication, authorization, and encapsulation of traffic in the HTTPS protocol.
- **File transfer servers**—These servers are used to exchange files between the email, Web, and application zones.
- **DMZ**—All other business-critical servers are located in this zone, such as Intranet, RSA, or backup servers.
- **Workstations**—These are the physical workstations—the machines used by employees. In this configuration they are little more than terminals and should not host any business applications.
- **Web proxy**—Ideally these are set up to transparently intercept all HTTP and HTTPS connections. A Web proxy filters the outgoing requests, performs user authentication and authorization, and scans the returned data for malware.
- **VPN gateway**—External users requiring access to internal resources must establish a secure tunnel to the VPN gateway following successful authentication.
- **Internal firewall**—Electronically segregates network services into separate zones.

The key elements of the antispearphishing strategy and the pros and cons are discussed below.

The isolation of email, office, and Web machines is at the heart of the proposed defense against malware contained in emails. The effectiveness of this approach is based on the strategy of denying email-borne malware the ability to contact its base on the Internet. If malware is obtained through a compromised website, the malware can contact its control center but will not be able to access an organization's information assets.

Pros
- Separates machines with confidential data from those with Internet access, thereby eliminating a path for data exfiltration.

Cons

- URL and hyperlinks provided in emails have to be copied and pasted from the email to the browser. This will represent a major pain to users.
- Online content in emails (images, audio files, etc.) will not display.

The Web proxy will require all traffic attempting to connect to the Internet within a session to be authenticated. This forces the user to take action each time a resource or process is invoked. Based on that authentication, additional rules can be applied, such as restricting what is accessed, when the access can take place, and/or what objects can be transferred.

Moreover, the authentication should be required on a per-browser-session basis. Once the user has authenticated, no further identity check will be performed until either the browser is closed and reopened or the authentication expires. This "session authentication" will ensure that if two processes try to communicate with the Internet, both will be required to authenticate. This is in contrast to machine or IP authentication where a single authentication is sufficient for all processes running on the same computer.

Pros

- Unauthenticated sessions will be blocked and unable to connect to the Internet.
- Increased probability of identifying malware before it contacts a control center.

Cons

- Users may be prompted to reauthenticate at regular intervals, which will inflict more pain.
- Some sites may break.

The file transform platform is a repository where files are dropped from one environment and retrieved from a different environment. Information transfer between zones would be implemented using a file transfer server in this configuration. Enhanced security can be achieved by combining the use of such a platform with automatic file deletion after a specified time interval.

Pros

- Strict control over what information is exchanged.
- Strong auditing capability.
- "Hopping" between the three environments (i.e., Web, applications, or email) becomes difficult for electronic terrorists (as well as users, unfortunately!).

Cons

- Additional steps are required when exchanging files between these three environments, which implies even more pain for users.

Remote users will be required to establish a VPN session to the external gateway prior to accessing internal resources. Figure 8.26 illustrates the process.

A remote user would first initiate a tunnel via the VPN gateway. The latter requires the user to authenticate, ideally using a strong form of authentication (e.g., two-factor). Once the VPN is established, the user has a connection that appears to the user to be functionally equivalent to being in the office. All traffic will be routed through the tunnel and processed by internal network components.

For example, if a mobile device tries to establish an HTTP connection to a website on the Internet, the request will go through the Web proxy. This will require the user to authenticate, proceed through the firewall, and exit via the established mode of corporate Internet access.

This will help reduce the risk of malware recording keystrokes and/or screenshots as well as sending these to a third party since this process requires authentication and applies Web policies to Internet-bound traffic.

In order to access Web servers, email/office machines, and machines housing applications, the user must also connect to the Citrix Access Gateway, creating a second tunnel that will reside inside the first tunnel. This double encryption enhances, albeit modestly, the security of the traffic as it traverses the Internet. In this configuration a compromised host will not be capable of sending key strokes or screen refreshes in real time to its control center. Authorization and auditing of incoming connections are facilitated in this case as well.

In addition to the risk of online compromise, workstations and especially laptops are subject to data breaches through the loss or theft of a device. Notwithstanding the fact that many companies use full disk encryption to protect laptops, an attacker with enough resources and/or expertise could circumvent the encryption and access the data. Successful attacks against full disk encryption solutions have been documented[4].

Citrix virtual desktop infrastructure (VDI) also permits a user to check out a virtual desktop, work offline, and then check the virtual desktop back in with its modified data. However, this raises the issue of protecting the stored data. If the device is lost or stolen, an attacker could compromise the information if he or she has sufficient resources to decrypt the secure container. This risk will be discussed further in Chapter 9 in connection with virtual environments.

In the scheme proposed herein, such machines will be equipped with policies that restrict the programs that can be executed. This will prevent users from

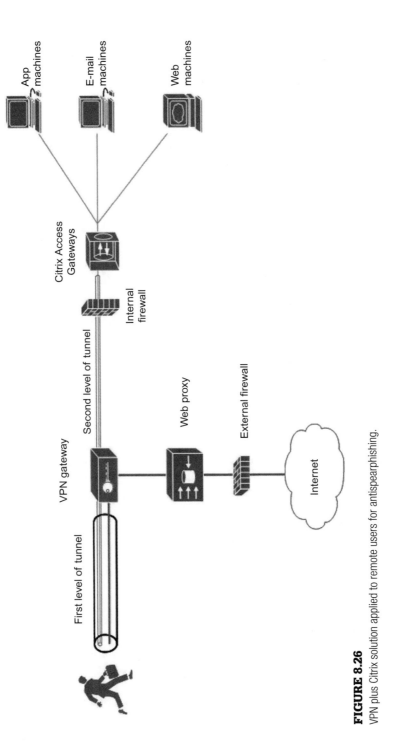

FIGURE 8.26

VPN plus Citrix solution applied to remote users for antispearphishing.

installing or running unapproved applications. Enforcement of this policy will address the threat of executables sent in emails, one of the basic forms of delivering malware. However, it will not prevent exploitation of vulnerabilities within a legitimate application.

Pros
- Data management is simplified since there are only a few data repositories.
- The loss of a device will not necessarily mean there is a data breach.

Cons
- The key advantage of a portable device is weakened since the laptop is merely a terminal with access to the organization's infrastructure. In the event a connection is not possible, the user will be unable to access internal network resources and any data stored therein.
- Users will not be able to install new programs on their machines unless provided with temporary administrator-level privileges.

As noted previously, the CAG is the front end of the Citrix infrastructure. It manages the authentication, authorization and accounting processes, presents applications through a Web browser, and can create SSL VPNs.

Pros
- Requires strong authentication (e.g., multi-factor).
- The traffic to the back-end Citrix servers is encrypted.
- A session can be started inside the network and later resumed over the VPN.

SUMMARY

Electronic terrorism involves similar if not identical attack vectors used in other electronic threats. However, specific vectors might arguably be more attractive to terrorists based on their potential for destruction and/or sensational outcomes. These include but are not limited to denial-of-service attacks and advanced persistent threats via the introduction of malware.

Denial-of-service attacks can indeed be sensational with crippling effects. There are four general food groups of denial-of-service attacks:

1. Abuse of administrative commands (e.g., format, delete, or drop database).
2. Exploitation of a bug (e.g., application crash).
3. Abuse of a lengthy or resource-intensive process (e.g., forcing full text searches).
4. Overwhelming a service with requests (e.g., a distributed DoS or DDoS attack).

Risk mitigation for denial-of-service attacks take the form of specific network designs, monitoring for risk factors associated with denial-of-service attacks, redundancy of resources, coordination with external IT providers, and preparedness via updated response protocols.

Malware/APTs can be equally pernicious albeit in different ways. There are "standard" modes of malware implementation that at a high level involve the following activities:

Accessing the internal network
- Executing on a machine.
- Connecting to the Internet.
- Facilitating spreading to other machines.
- Accessing protected information.
- Transmitting harvested information to the Internet.

Client-side exploits such as spearphishing represent a "popular" means of establishing unauthorized access to internal networks and launching malware. Malware is an attractive attack vector for electronic terrorists and others.

Strategies against malware must recognize and address these standard modes of malicious activity. Therefore, recommendations specified herein focus on monitoring interzone activity (e.g., from internal networks to DMZs, DMZs to the Internet, etc.), exposing internal network vulnerabilities, identifying expired or faulty access privileges and correlating these with identified network vulnerabilities, designing infrastructure to enhance the quality and frequency of required authentication, and preventing lateral movement by an attacker.

Finally, a radical network topology is specified that is intended to significantly reduce the risk of spearphishing. Although this recommendation will likely be impractical, it identifies a potential solution for organizations with extremely low risk tolerance plus equally high insensitivity to inconvenience. It also highlights the extreme measures required to manage the risk associated with this threat.

REFERENCES

[1] Xinuos. http://www.sco.com/.

[2] The Cooperative Association for Internet Data Analysis. http://www.caida.org/research/security/sco-dos/.

[3] Wikipedia. Denial-of-Service Attack, https://en.wikipedia.org/wiki/Denial-of-service_attack.

[4] Schneier.com. http://www.schneier.com/blog/archives/2009/10/evil_maid:attac.html.

Problems

1. Logs of data from suspicious hosts show attempts at connecting to the Internet at a rate of 1000/s. What is the per-connection period (i.e., 1/rate) based on this frequency? If the per-connection period is $1\,\mu s$, what is the connection rate?

2. You are the Chief Information Officer for your organization. The organization has previously provided employees with phones for work, but in the interest of saving money, it is considering allowing employees to use personal phones. You are asked for input regarding this change in policy. Specify potential vulnerabilities associated with personally owned devices and indicate what features would be required for an enterprise security solution.

3. You are the Chief Information Officer at your organization. You are attempting to create a standard for Windows account passwords.

   a. Calculate the difference in entropy (i.e., the number of possible passwords) associated with an 8-character password versus a 16-character password if only lowercase letters and numerals are allowed in each case.

   b. Calculate the difference in entropy between a 15-character password where only lowercase letters are permitted and an 8-character password where lowercase letters, uppercase letters, symbols, and numerals are permitted.

   c. Based on the results of 4b, which password standard would you recommend and why?

4. Specify electronic and physical controls to manage information security risk based on the following:

   a. An IDS solution that is monitoring traffic between the network DMZ and the Internet detects repeated attempts to connect to a suspicious website.

   b. A white-box network vulnerability test in conjunction with an audit of the Windows active directory reveals a shared drive containing sensitive information that is accessible from the Internet that allows weak passwords and has outdated patches.

5. You are the Chief Technology Officer for a large U.S.-based corporation. One day the president and CEO, a graduate of a prestigious business school, stops by your office. He has been reading recent news about successful spearphishing attacks against peer organizations and asks about the company's strategy to address these threats. You explain that you have implemented IDS and other networking monitoring solutions, but he cannot be placated. He gives you marching orders to implement a solution that provides greater immunity to these attack vectors and, specifically, to protect archived and active files from exfiltration.

   a. Briefly describe a potential Citrix solution and how it provides security for network access.

   b. Specify the security versus convenience trade-off of an air gap-type segregation of active and archived files.

   c. Compare and contrast using a VPN gateway versus Citrix Access Gateway as a front end to accessing active and archived files.

   d. Provide a risk-based argument for adding a firewall to further segregate active and archived files in conjunction with a VPN gateway front end.

6. You are the Chief Information Security Officer at your firm. You are concerned about data loss and leakage from the corporate network based on a series of deals that have been lost to your company's chief competitor. You decide to implement a DLP solution that is based on behavioral characteristics such as network activity at "high-risk" times, large numbers of transmissions to competitor email addresses, large attachments to emails, and others. Unfortunately you are inundated with false positives and it is consuming the resources of your analytic team.
   a. Specify what might be implemented to limit the number of false positives.
   b. How could content monitoring be used in conjunction with behavior monitoring if at all?
   c. Sketch out a comprehensive if high-level strategy to address data loss and leakage to complement the aforementioned technical solutions.

7. You are the Chief Information Security Officer at a firm with offices in countries that are known for introducing malware and state-sponsored network attacks. Employees using laptops in those countries are requesting to use VPN for remote connectivity to internal resources since Citrix is slow and does not facilitate file sharing between domains. Would you allow VPN? Why or why not?

8. You are the Chief Information Security Officer at your firm. Your technicians wake you up at 3AM to inform you that they are seeing a precipitous rise in inbound Internet traffic that is threatening Web server functionality. You are immediately concerned that this activity presages a denial-of-service attack. What should you instruct the technicians to do?

9. You are the Chief Information Security Officer at your firm. The CEO has been reading about the devastating effects of spearphishing and client-side exploits in general. He is rightfully concerned about the security of information stored by your company. He is asking you to present options for a strategy and has indicated a zero tolerance for risk. Develop a tiered strategy in varying degrees of inconvenience/disruption to business activities that addresses this threat. Explain the pros and cons as well as macroscopic changes to the network in basic terms.

10. Explain the difference in information security risks presented by Citrix and VPN solutions for remote access.

11. An IDS solution implemented in the DMZ of your IT network detects attempts to connect to FTP servers originating from the internal network. Of course you attempt to address the immediate risk issue, but you are rightfully concerned about the broader information security risk implications. Provide recommendations to remedy potential vulnerabilities that may have been overlooked in previous black-box penetration tests.

12. You are the newly appointed Chief Information Officer at your firm. You are appalled by the state of information security. You decide to implement immediate measures for high-risk services and operations but are rightfully concerned about the reaction from senior executives. You therefore prepare simple "junior readers edition" explanations of the risks associated with information security threats to the firm and your recommendations. To that end, provide explanations for the

following recommendations on enhanced controls. Ensure you communicate the threats or threat attack vectors that are driving these recommendations:

a. Two-factor authentication for remote network access via VPN or Citrix.

b. Increased password complexity from a minimum of 6 characters to 10 for all Windows accounts.

c. Elimination of external webmail at the firm.

d. Enhanced authentication to access specific servers containing confidential information.

e. Development of an information security policy and standards for information technology usage with enforcement.

f. "Bring your own device" restrictions that includes the installation of an enterprise security solution.

13. You are the Chief Information Risk Officer for your firm. You decide that you want to embark on a more sophisticated program of assessing risk by examining intersections and correlations of risk issues. Identify specific items that signify enhanced risk to the firm due to the intersection of vulnerabilities in the Windows and network infrastructure environments.

14. You are the Chief Information Security Officer at your firm. The network administrators have identified specific websites that require an unauthorized application to be downloaded on user machines in order to provide music streaming content. These sites have become increasingly popular with employees. However they consume significant network bandwidth and violate policy regarding the installation of unapproved software. You are concerned about network security and the performance implications of this software, but equally you do not want to adversely affect morale. Craft a brief "to all" communication to the firm advising them of the decision to block access to these sites and suggest possible alternative solutions. It is also important to note that your company provides a guest network that is not electronically linked to the corporate network.

15. You are the Chief Information Security Officer at your consulting firm. This firm employs an internal consulting group that works at client sites and often requires the ability to use special software to conduct their analyses. The solution to date has been to allow local administrative rights on the consultants' machines with attendant risks. The IT department has alerted you to this condition and is looking to you for guidance. Propose a solution that minimizes the information security risks to the firm and does not significantly impact the business. Concisely and briefly explain how the solution minimizes both business and information security risks.

16. You are the Chief Information Security Officer at your firm. You are concerned that there is an increased potential for your firm to be the victim of electronic terrorism. However, a number of the most senior partners are refusing to comply with the password policy, citing excessive inconvenience. In fact, a number of these partners refuse to use any passwords on their Windows accounts. How would you deal with these partners? What would you do or say to convince them of the risks to information loss via APTs and other threats to information security?

CHAPTER 9

The Convergence of Electronic and Physical Security Risk

9.1 INTRODUCTION: CULTURAL AND ORGANIZATIONAL DRIVERS OF SECURITY

Ten years ago security professionals were beating the drum about the integration of electronic and physical security. There was even talk about the need to combine IT and physical security departments to ensure proper coordination.

Looking back, the push to forcibly join two fundamentally dissimilar groups was probably premature. I recall speaking to my colleague Phil Venables, now a partner and global head of information security at Goldman Sachs, about this topic many years ago. He presciently resisted the notion that these two groups must be combined. But he recognized that they must coordinate more closely, particularly in the area of security risk metrics.

Fast-forward 10 or more years and the trend clearly points to the need for an integrated approach to security and a closer alignment of IT and physical security departments. Certainly a cultural divide between physical and IT security practitioners persists, but this can no longer be used to justify security silos.

In general, physical security professionals are often oblivious to the electronic vulnerabilities inherent to the physical security devices they prescribe for risk mitigation. Importantly, they often do not appreciate the implications of electronic vulnerabilities to the physical security risk profile.

Conversely, IT professionals do not always recognize the importance of physical security technology to the security of the network and information assets. Moreover, their decisions on security requirements are often driven by the technology rather than the other way around. Some IT types have a preternatural desire to install an appliance to monitor/detect *something* without understanding how that appliance fits into a broader information security strategy. In addition, even if they do monitor identified security risk parameters, they often do not appropriately analyze the data resulting from such efforts.

Cultural differences plus divergent views of technology and risk contribute to this gulf between two entities with similar missions and increasing interdependencies. It has been said that the difference between IT and physical security professionals can be summarized as follows: in high school, the physical security department members were on the football team and the IT types were in the band.

To complicate matters, multiple departments within an organization, and even technology providers/vendors, weigh in on security decisions. Figure 9.1 depicts the components of a security decision as a vector with three components: the security technology type, the technology provider, and the department that is the beneficiary of the decision. Usually one or more of these components plays a prominent role in the technology decision.

The good news is that the proliferation of computer technology has elevated the technology awareness of the general population. Therefore, the current generation of physical security professionals is typically more tech savvy than its forebears. In addition, the potential vulnerability of information assets to physical attacks is causing IT professionals to recognize the importance of physical security devices. As those devices become increasingly networked, IT professionals are naturally taking more of an interest in physical security.

Anyone who is not convinced of the inexorable link between physical and electronic security need only consider the information shown in Figure 9.2. This is a real example of a set of physical access control records obtained by logging into a server from the Internet. Clearly the owner of the system would not be

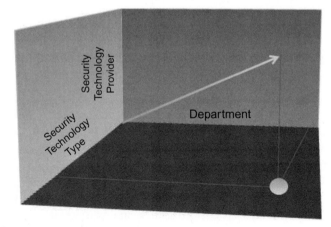

FIGURE 9.1
Security decisions. *(Graphic courtesy of Chris Briscoe, Stroz Friedberg.)*

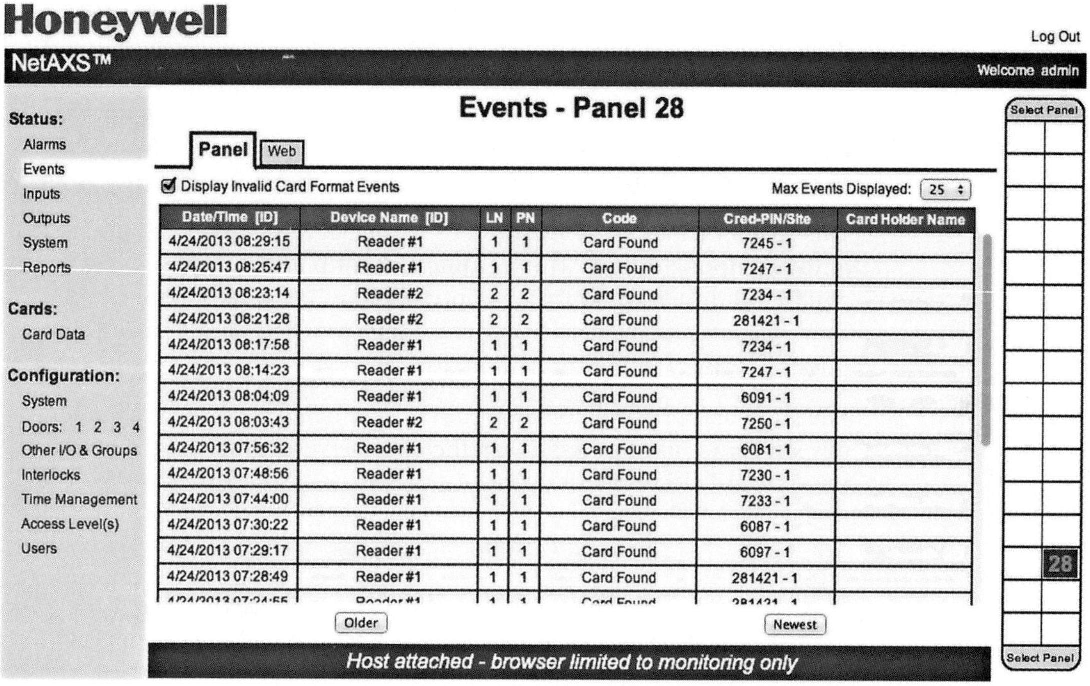

Honeywell   Log Out

NetAXS™   Welcome admin

Events - Panel 28

Date/Time [ID]	Device Name [ID]	LN	PN	Code	Cred-PIN/Site	Card Holder Name
4/24/2013 08:29:15	Reader #1	1	1	Card Found	7245 - 1	
4/24/2013 08:25:47	Reader #1	1	1	Card Found	7247 - 1	
4/24/2013 08:23:14	Reader #2	2	2	Card Found	7234 - 1	
4/24/2013 08:21:28	Reader #2	2	2	Card Found	281421 - 1	
4/24/2013 08:17:58	Reader #1	1	1	Card Found	7234 - 1	
4/24/2013 08:14:23	Reader #1	1	1	Card Found	7247 - 1	
4/24/2013 08:04:09	Reader #1	1	1	Card Found	6091 - 1	
4/24/2013 08:03:43	Reader #2	2	2	Card Found	7250 - 1	
4/24/2013 07:56:32	Reader #1	1	1	Card Found	6081 - 1	
4/24/2013 07:48:56	Reader #1	1	1	Card Found	7230 - 1	
4/24/2013 07:44:00	Reader #1	1	1	Card Found	7233 - 1	
4/24/2013 07:30:22	Reader #1	1	1	Card Found	6087 - 1	
4/24/2013 07:29:17	Reader #1	1	1	Card Found	6097 - 1	
4/24/2013 07:28:49	Reader #1	1	1	Card Found	281421 - 1	
4/24/2013 07:24:55	Reader #1	1	1	Card Found	281421 - 1	

Status: Alarms, Events, Inputs, Outputs, System, Reports

Cards: Card Data

Configuration: System, Doors: 1 2 3 4, Other I/O & Groups, Interlocks, Time Management, Access Level(s), Users

Panel | Web

☑ Display Invalid Card Format Events   Max Events Displayed: 25

[Older]   [Newest]

Select Panel   28   Select Panel

Host attached - browser limited to monitoring only

FIGURE 9.2
Physical access control records visible from the Internet.

thrilled to know that his or her company's physical access system details are visible to the world. Moreover, the system itself might be vulnerable to electronic attack because of its exposure to the Internet.

One likely objective of an electronic terrorist would be to physically access the devices that process information deemed critical to an organization or that might produce maximum damage to its reputation. These days, physical security devices present opportunities for both physical and electronic attacks. Why?

Such devices protect the information assets that store and process critical information. But these devices are also connected to the corporate electronic network. So the key point is that if networked physical security devices are compromised via an electronic attack, the compromise increases the risk to information assets via physical attacks as well. In addition, an electronic vulnerability of a physical security device could facilitate an attack against other devices on the network to which it is connected. For example, an individual with malicious intent and physical and/or electronic access to networked physical security systems could facilitate unauthorized access to protected areas such as a data center as well as compromise the network at large.

It is important to investigate electronic vulnerabilities of physical security devices in some detail. Security articles or texts will correctly point out the rather obvious trend toward physical and IT technology convergence. This is not news. But one is often left starved for details on specific vulnerabilities. Understanding the physical-electronic vulnerabilities of physical security system components is essential to developing bona fide security strategies.

This chapter contains an analysis of a particular physical access control system at the component level. The identification of physical and electronic vulnerabilities and their interrelationship is explored. It is important to appreciate from the outset that an electronic vulnerability of a physical security device has physical security implications.

The particular physical access control system being analyzed here is functionally similar to many others. It can therefore serve as a model in illustrating key physical and electronic risk issues.

9.2 ELECTRONIC AND PHYSICAL SECURITY VULNERABILITIES OF A PHYSICAL ACCESS CONTROL SYSTEM

This section is devoted to examining issues pertaining to the convergence of electronic and physical security risk. These issues are being emphasized for three reasons: (1) they are key to developing holistic and integrated security solutions; (2) identified vulnerabilities are typically not addressed in sufficient detail in traditional treatments of security risk; and (3) identification of specific, interrelated vulnerabilities might actually increase IT and physical security department coordination and cooperation.

Figure 9.3 is a graphic highlighting high-level physical and electronic vulnerabilities of physical security devices and the potential effects on IT assets.

Many physical security systems leverage a local area network (LAN) and a wide area network (WAN) to route signals that grant and deny physical access permissions as well as display CCTV images. These devices utilize the transmission control protocol/Internet protocol (TCP/IP) to send packets of information to their respective destinations.

The CampusWide physical access control system manufactured by Blackboard Inc.[1] has been selected for analysis. This is a system that is commonly used in universities, and it is technically similar to other physical access control systems at the level of concern, so the lessons learned are

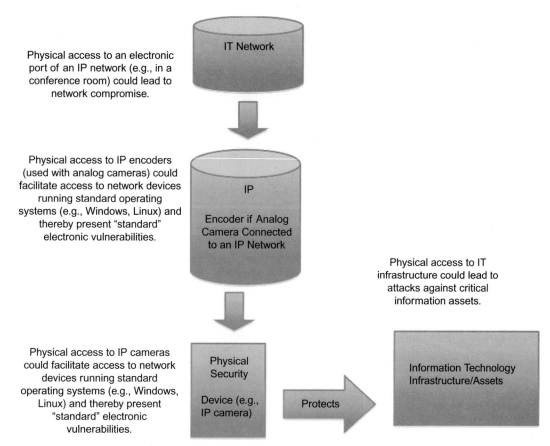

FIGURE 9.3
Overview of physical and electronic vulnerabilities of networked physical security devices.

generally applicable. Note that technical specifications of this system were not publicly available so other sources were used to glean component-level information and thereby identify risks[2].

Physical access to facilities housing IT and other critical resources is typically initiated by the presentation of a credential or ID to a card reader. ID cards will be discussed in some detail in Chapter 10 in connection with authentication and authorization security controls.

At a high level, when an ID card is placed in proximity to the reader, the reader interrogates the card with a radio frequency signal. The information that is encoded and stored on the card is reradiated to the reader, which transmits the information to a local access control panel. The information stored on this panel corresponds to the set of users with physical access privileges at designated doors controlled by card readers.

In this case, the encoded information on the card is stored either on a "smart" chip using "Felica" technology (IBM) or on a high-coercivity magnetic stripe. Although both technologies are present on the card, they are very different in terms of their respective security vulnerabilities, as discussed in Chapter 10.

The access control system signal examined here is fully duplex (i.e., capable of simultaneous bidirectional communication), with two twisted pair drop lines to/from the reader. See Chapter 11 on performance specifications for twisted pair cable. The card readers use the RS-485 standard to transmit/receive data over these lines. RS-485 specifies the electrical characteristics of drivers and receivers associated with data transmission among various components of the system.

Access control data is transmitted by impressing a 5-V potential *difference* across both wires. The configuration increases immunity from common mode electrical interference.

Although the system is transmitting signals to and from the reader over hard wires via a fully duplex, asynchronous 9600 bits per second (bps) signaling protocol, such signals could use any medium (e.g., telephone lines or radio frequency), provided one adheres to the required protocol. At this data rate, the maximum signal transmission distance is estimated to be 4100 ft; but this would decrease at higher data rates. Newer Blackboard CampusWide systems reportedly can handle up to 3072 card readers.

Since the access control signal piggybacks on the local IT network, it must be encoded as TCP/IP packets. Such encoding occurs via a physical device called an IP converter, also known as an IP encoder.

The IP converter has its own IP address, which is most likely static, and there is a daemon or background process running on the device that allows for a Telnet connection pursuant to conducting remote diagnostics, change configurations, etc.

The Telnet service can be selectively activated, but it clearly needs to be managed from a security perspective. Ideally it should be disabled, since this represents a fantastic opportunity for an electronic terrorist and hackers in general.

Up to 16 readers can be used in conjunction with a single IP converter, and there could be multiple IP converters in use. The physical presence of an IP converter affects the security risk profile of any room or facility in which these are housed. Unlike other elements of the physical access system, IP converters are often located near the card reader or local panel rather than in a more secure area such as in a data center.

Two-factor authentication, also discussed in more detail in Chapter 10, should be required for physical entry to any facility that houses IP-based equipment in addition to deploying continuous visual monitoring (e.g., CCTV). A physical access audit trail should exist to record entries into spaces housing IP technology. To reiterate for emphasis, IP converters represent an important physical-electronic security risk interface.

The good news is that data stored on the IP converters in the CampusWide system is encrypted using 128-bit Advanced Encryption Standard (AES). AES is considered by experts (e.g., U.S. government-validated sources) to be high-quality encryption (note: 256-bit AES is commercially available). Absent information to the contrary, this form of encryption is appropriate for commercial scenarios based on trusted government endorsements.

This does not mean such encryption protocols are completely immune to attack. But the magnitude of risk is always a relative measurement. The strength of a particular encryption method should be assessed using experts with respect to the robustness of the algorithm and the resources required to mount a successful brute force attack, i.e., exhausting the key space using computational resources.

Additional details of the encryption implementation are not known, but some basic suggestions are provided. First, the default encryption key for each IP encoder should immediately be changed whenever the system is deployed. Second, each IP converter should have a distinct key, and the key-to-key differences should not be predictable. In other words, one should not be able to derive the key of one IP converter if the key to another converter is compromised.

Although it would admittedly take a sophisticated attacker to identify the key from an inspection of the physical device, the ability to manipulate physical security transactions could result in a big payoff to an electronic terrorist. Therefore, there is a huge incentive to attack these IP devices.

The network processer (NP) is the gateway between the infrastructure and the application processor (AP). It receives the requests from the readers, converts the modes of communication so the AP can interpret them, and transmits the resulting signal. The NP "master" polls all the readers on a regular basis, where the "slaves" (readers) "speak" to the master before the master polls them for data.

The AP manages the stored information and provides an interface for humans to examine logs, run reports, change configurations/privileges, and perform account maintenance. Both the NP and the AP should be physically located in the data center and protected by robust physical and electronic security measures. The presence of such devices provides additional justification for internal physical security controls within a data center.

To that end, enhanced authentication such as multifactor authentication with an audit trail of attempted entries, or the use of biometrics, is recommended for physical access at the entrance to a data center. Other internal and external physical security controls to include CCTV should be instituted. The location of cameras will affect both the physical and electronic risk profiles relative to the threat of information loss and other threats.

With respect to electronic security, the IP converter should be placed behind a firewall with port restrictions that facilitate electronic access to only those IP addresses required for remote diagnostics and management. Appropriate Layer 2 security is also recommended at the switch with the objective of detecting unauthorized changes to the physical connection of the IP encoder[3]. The Cisco product Port Security[4] would be a good candidate technology product for consideration.

Installing dynamic address resolution protocol (ARP) inspection and validating ARP packets at the switch should also be considered. This is intended to reduce the risk of certain man-in-the-middle attacks via ARP spoofing and ARP cache poisoning. The book entitled *Hacking Exposed* by Stuart McClure, Joel Scambray, George Kurtz, Third Edition gives a good exposition on ARP-related attacks.

If unauthorized physical access to the drop lines between the reader and the IP converter can be achieved, these are vulnerable to signal decoding via a RS-485-to-RS-232 converter. Such devices are readily available online[5].

Specifically, an attacker could decode the "OPEN DOOR" signal from the IP converter via the NP and then replay it to a reader at will. Knowledge of the data scheme on the RS-485 drop line is not required. In addition, since the AP would be blissfully unaware of the data interception, there would be no record of any physical access transaction.

One antidote to a replay attack for any physical access control system might be the inclusion of a so-called "nonce" in verifying communications between each "client" (i.e., the panel) and the server. A unique, randomly generated, and encrypted token would be generated for each cardholder at every swipe. The system uses time stamps and/or other methods to verify the authenticity of an access attempt.

Knowing the IP address of the IP converter adds additional risk since one could send bogus packets corresponding to an "OPEN DOOR" command. This could be done remotely without requiring physical access to the drop lines. Therefore, restricting the Telnet service and physical access to the IP converter represent key security controls.

There should also be appropriate physical security provided to the readers as well as the wiring between the reader and the IP converter carrying the RS-485 signal. If possible, all readers should be checked for their vulnerability to unauthorized removal. New reader installations should be installed using wiring that is encased in steel jackets to reduce the risk of physical tampering.

The NP should be electronically isolated from the rest of the network through a virtual local area network (VLAN) or other form of segmentation. However, the particular configuration is important. Three candidate security topologies in descending order of preference are depicted in Figures 9.4, 9.5, and 9.6. Readers are omitted from Figures 9.5 and 9.6 for simplicity, but they are presumed to be present.

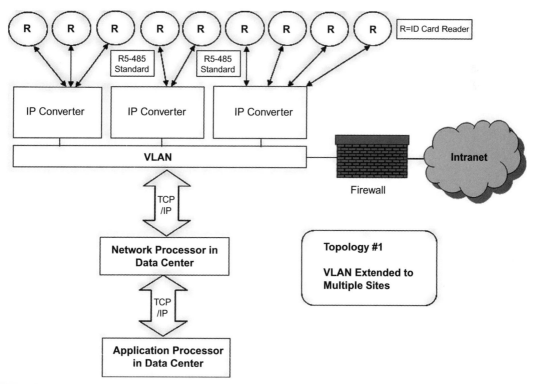

FIGURE 9.4

Physical access control system and a VLAN extended to multiple sites.

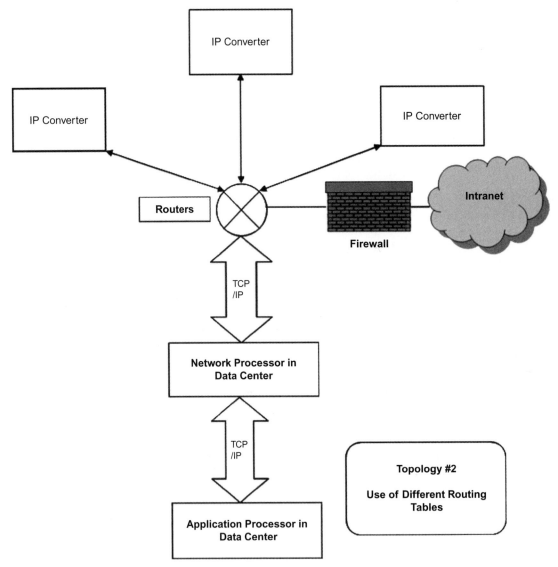

FIGURE 9.5

Physical access control system and the use of different routing tables.

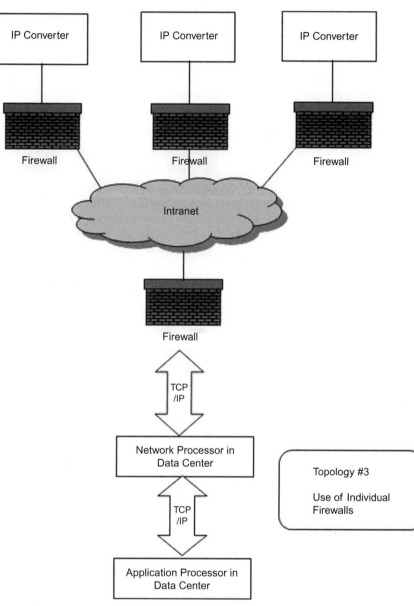

FIGURE 9.6
Physical access control system and use of individual firewalls.

9.3   PHYSICAL SECURITY OF DATA CENTERS

A priority for any electronic terrorist would most certainly be to gain physical access to the IT infrastructure. Hopefully this infrastructure is protected by physical security technology. But as we observed in the last section, networked physical security devices can also have electronic vulnerabilities, thereby increasing both physical and electronic risk.

Critical IT assets are often housed in data centers. When I worked at Goldman Sachs, one of my responsibilities was to develop physical security strategies for data centers in collaboration with information security colleagues. Since these venues were the home of the proverbial keys to the kingdom, the tendency was to embrace a Fort Knox-type security strategy. Such a strategy often entails extreme perimeter hardening and extensive internal controls for authentication of identity and physical access authorization. This is not necessarily an incorrect strategy, but it may be missing the mark in terms of security risk.

One significant attack vector identified by my technology colleagues was the commission of immoral or stupid acts by individuals who were *authorized* for physical entry. Specifically, contractors and vendors with legitimate physical access privileges were responsible for the overwhelming majority of thefts and the destruction of property.

Therefore, the reality is that the most sophisticated biometrics and robust man-traps in the world would have done nothing to address this threat attack vector. This offered a valuable lesson on collaboration and the importance of asking customers about the security issues of most concern.

Of course this does not necessarily mean one should ignore other attack vectors or one's own judgment even if it is in direct conflict with the customer. Providing candid and objective views on risk is what a security professional is paid to do. However, customers tend to understand their environments well, and their input should always be appreciated if not followed to the letter.

Certainly the risk factor of unauthorized physical access must be addressed in data centers. But the spectrum of threats and associated risk factors must be evaluated relative to each other. A rigorous analysis of risk might lead to an emphasis on internal security controls as opposed to external physical restrictions. Most organizations operate on finite budgets, and an assessment of risk provides the only rigorous means of confirming security priorities.

So what is an appropriate defensive posture for data centers?

A digression into the anatomy of data centers is required as part of a fulsome discussion on security risk management. The high-risk area is the so-called data field, where servers and other IT infrastructure reside. This is the location of the high value information assets. All other internal areas exist to support the electronic infrastructure located in the data fields.

Virtualized environments are becoming increasingly popular in data centers since they promote efficiency and cost effectiveness. This technology results in the consolidation of resources by reducing the number of required physical machines. Changes in the electronic environment have physical security risk implications and exemplify the interrelationship between physical and electronic security risk. The security risk associated with physical access to virtual machines will be discussed later in this chapter.

An effective data center physical security strategy should focus on two areas: reducing the vulnerability to unauthorized physical access to the data fields and reducing the vulnerability to malicious or stupid activity by individuals who are authorized to be in the data fields.

One first step might be to assess the required security risk mitigation at the entrance to the data fields. This is in part determined by the nature of authentication and authorization performed at the entrance to the data center facility itself.

A critical issue is whether a single tenant occupies the data center or if it is multitenanted. In multitenanted data centers, the data fields often consist of individual cages, and each tenant is responsible for the physical security of its respective cage. In sole-tenant facilities, the data fields are comprised of racks containing electronic assets, and anyone with access to the data field area has access to all racks, unless they are individually secured. Figure 9.7 is a photograph of data fields in an indicative sole-tenant facility.

FIGURE 9.7
Data center data field (sole-tenant facility). *(Source National Science Foundation. "University of Chicago Launches Bionimbus Protected Data Cloud to Analyze Cancer Data."* http://www.nsf.gov/news/news_ summ.jsp?cntn_id=127935.)

Requirements for enhancing the physical security of individual cages and the racks in data fields will depend on the physical security at the entrance and other key controls. Such controls might include background investigations of contractors and escorting of visitors.

Ideally, physical access to the data fields should always require multifactor authentication, such as biometric data stored on a contactless smart card or an ID card used in conjunction with a PIN pad and associated code.

However, one can mandate 10-factor authentication and it would do nothing to address the risk of piggybacking into the data center. What is the vulnerability to an unauthorized individual following an authorized individual into the facility, and moreover, what can be done about it?

A first response to this question might be to mandate that authorized individuals challenge those who follow closely behind into the facility or other restricted areas of concern. However, this is not a good strategy, especially if one considers how many times people hold doors open for strangers accessing an ATM machine inside a bank vestibule.

Most people are inherently polite and nonconfrontational, and it would be a mistake to base a security strategy on countercultural behavior. This is not to say that people should not be instructed to politely challenge piggybackers. It is just that it would be naïve and ultimately ineffective to base a security strategy on this form of control.

If strict authentication and authorization are performed upstream from the data fields (e.g., at the facility entrance), and strict visitor/contractor control is exercised, antipiggybacking could be superfluous. However, if entry into the data fields is possible after immediately entering the data center, antipiggybacking at the entrance to the data field is recommended. Chapter 12 discusses various antipiggybacking technologies.

In general, it is possible to manage the risk of unauthorized physical access to the data fields via a combination of compensating security controls if the cost of antipiggybacking measures is prohibitive. However, each case must be evaluated on its own merits based on the assessed risk.

What compensating internal controls would be appropriate to reduce the risk of piggybacking? As noted above, these would include authentication and authorization at the data center entrance, escorting of all nonbackground-investigated workers/visitors at all times, and preregistering visitors. In addition, locked equipment cabinets or locked and segregated cages inside the data fields of multitenant facilities would further reduce the requirement for antipiggybacking at the data center or data field entrances.

However, no amount of compensating controls will obviate the need for CCTV coverage. Such coverage should include each row in the data fields of sole-tenant data centers and the entrances to all cages in multitenant facilities. Recall that malicious or clumsy individuals were deemed responsible for the vast majority of security incidents at Goldman Sachs, my erstwhile employer. This is probably not an uncommon phenomenon in general. Deterring and investigating internal risk incidents is optimally accomplished via the use of recorded CCTV images. See Chapter 11 for details on CCTV system performance specifications.

Ideally, authentication and confirmation of authorization for physical access would be implemented at the entrance to each cage. The confirmation process would ideally include an electronic record of all attempted physical access entries for future audits. A card reader linked to a magnetic lock on the cage would serve this purpose, although a mechanical lock with strict key control (i.e., key checkout is electronically audited) could suffice.

Data centers typically have raised floors to allow for the presence of wires underneath. Because of this configuration, individual cages should extend to the floor slab with ports that allow wires to enter the cage. This prevents someone from crawling into a cage from beneath the raised floor.

If this measure seems a bit over-the-top, recall that the impact of a compromise is huge, and the cost of mitigation is relatively inexpensive. In a similar vein, all cages should be enclosed at the top to prevent individuals from gaining unauthorized access by climbing.

Data centers deserve special attention in a security strategy because of the impact of a compromise and its potential effect on the spectrum of information assets. However, that does not mean the strategy implies one has carte blanche with respect to security bells and whistles. As emphasized throughout this book, controls must be proportional to the totality of risk (i.e., all three components) and weighed against the cost of risk mitigation.

An indicative data center standard is provided immediately below. This can be used as a guide in selecting or evaluating a single-tenant or multitenant ("Co-Lo") data center security setup. Although data centers are big business these days, and specifications such as Statement on Standards for Attestation Engagements (SSAE) 16, the successor to Statement on Auditing Standards 70 (i.e., "SAS 70"), are intended to provide security standardization, I have personally observed security lapses in facilities designated as secure by these standards.

For example, in one instance a magnetic lock leading to the cage area was mounted on the insecure side of the door. In another example, cage walls were either insecurely fastened or had no lid. In a number of cases, vendors without validated background investigations had nonescort physical access privileges within the most sensitive areas. Therefore, a security audit designation does not obviate the requirement for a proper risk assessment.

9.4 AN INDICATIVE DATA CENTER PHYSICAL SECURITY STANDARD

9.4.1 Principal Threats and Threat Attack Vectors

The principal threat of concern is the compromise of confidential/sensitive information that is stored and/or processed by electronic equipment controlled by a data center tenant. The most significant threat attack vectors are unauthorized physical access to these resources as well as malicious individuals with authorized physical access. The compromise of devices via remote electronic access to networked devices also represents a significant attack vector.

Refer to "Physical Access Control System Specifications" in Chapter 10 and "CCTV System Specifications" in Chapter 11 for technical details that apply to these security controls and are referenced throughout this standard.

9.4.2 Security Principles

1. Only authorized and appropriately authenticated individuals may be granted physical access to any internal data center space.
2. Data fields and tenant-controlled areas (e.g., cages) contain sensitive/confidential IT resources and are a high risk for information compromise. These areas require enhanced authentication and are to be accessed only by individuals with a specific requirement as determined by the resource owner or its designated proxy.
3. Nonescort physical access privileges within internal data center areas may only be granted to tenants and individuals who have undergone background investigations that comport with individual tenant requirements.
4. All movements of individuals within data fields or immediately external to and within tenant-controlled areas (e.g., cages) must be visually recorded using CCTV. Images so recorded must be securely stored for retrieval only by authorized individuals and stored for a minimum of 31 days.
5. All nonguarded external doors plus high-risk internal areas (e.g., data fields or caged areas) must be alarmed and the alarms must be monitored.
6. All individuals granted nonescort physical access privileges should be issued a data center picture ID to facilitate physical access to internal areas, and this ID must be immediately returned when access privileges have expired.
7. All physical security equipment must be installed and maintained by a reputable firm whose employees undergo background investigations to a standard specified by the tenant.
8. Electronic assets should be protected by electronic controls that are consistent with a risk-based information security policy and accompanying standards.

9.4.3   Facility Security Requirements by Area
9.4.3.1   Perimeter Security Controls

1. CCTV system coverage.
   a. Recognition-level resolution.
   b. 360° perimeter viewing
   c. 20-lux light intensity.
2. Guarding.
   a. Perimeter checks or monitoring of CCTV at regular intervals (24/7).
   b. Updated training and appropriate security certifications.
3. Building façade features.
   a. Low-profile.
   b. Solid construction material.
   c. Set back from the street.
   d. Limited number of exterior windows.
4. Entry door alarm in case of disruptions to the 24/7 guarding operation.

9.4.3.2   Lobby/Reception Area Security Controls

1. Visitor management protocols to include:
   a. Authentication of identity of all visitors via a government-issued or official photo ID (e.g., drivers license or passport).
   b. Electronic and/or written record of visitor access history.
   c. Access control list with quarterly updates by all tenants for confirmation of authorized entry to the facility.
   d. Escorts within internal areas for individuals without tenant-approved visiting privileges and nonbackground-investigated vendors (i.e., those not on the access control list (ACL)).
   e. Issuance and same-day collection of visitor ID badges.
2. CCTV system coverage of entrance- and exit-identification-level system resolution.
3. Physical access control system—single-factor authentication "in" and "out" via card readers linked to a magnetic lock.

9.4.3.3   Data Field Security Controls

1. CCTV system coverage of all entrance- and exit-identification-level system resolution.
2. CCTV system coverage of all aisles such that every cabinet is in at least one camera's field-of-view with identification-level resolution.
3. Physical access control of all entrances to include:
   a. Multifactor or biometric authentication for entry.
   b. Antipiggybacking (e.g., full-height turnstile) optimal but not required if compensating controls are in place.

    c. Single-factor authentication (i.e., data center ID) for exit using a card reader.

    d. Locks on all equipment cabinets if two-factor authentication at the entrance and CCTV coverage of all aisles is not implemented. Strict physical access control and auditing of physical keys.

    e. 24/7 manned monitoring of entryway with preentry sign in if not done at reception.

    f. Proximity-alarmed (e.g., passive infrared sensor) with total area coverage if there is disruption in 24/7 monitoring. Sensors mounted in nonphysically accessible locations.

9.4.3.4 Cage Area Security Controls (Colocation Facilities)

1. 24/7 monitoring of entrance to cage area with written sign-in sheet for individuals not possessing a data center ID.
2. CCTV system coverage of the entire internal area of the cage.
3. Physical access control system restriction.
       a. Single-factor authentication on cage door (dual factor or biometric preferred).
       b. Subflooring physical access restriction (e.g., extend cage to beneath the raised floor).
       c. Top of cage physical access restriction (e.g., slab-to-slab cage or a cage lid/top).
4. Total area coverage proximity alarm (e.g., passive infrared sensor) in case of disruptions in 24/7 monitoring.

9.4.3.5 Loading Bay Security Controls

1. CCTV system coverage of entrance and exit-identification-level system resolution.
2. Physical access control system. Single-factor authentication (e.g., data center ID) to raise shutters installed on the secure side of loading bay.
3. Shutters/portals alarmed after business hours.

9.4.4 General Security Controls
9.4.4.1 Background Investigations

1. Background-investigated security personnel. Minimum of credit check, criminal check, verification of work history (minimum 5 years prior), and the right to work (UK/Europe).
2. Nonbackground-investigated data center vendors and contractors must be escorted by background-investigated individuals at all times when such vendors and contractors are located in internal areas of the data center.

9.4.4.2   Security Incident Response

1. Establish written protocols to respond to alarms and other security incidents.
2. Conduct "red teaming" exercises (i.e., regular testing of incident response protocols).
3. Track incidents and identify trends to assess evolving risk profiles.

9.5   VIRTUALIZED ENVIRONMENTS AND THE CONCENTRATION OF INFORMATION SECURITY RISK

9.5.1. Introduction to Virtualization and Security Risk

In the previous section, the security of data centers was discussed in detail because of their increasing importance in storing information. The potential for electronic or physical compromise of a data center by electronic terrorists is high because of the concentration of electronic assets located therein.

The trend in information storage, management, and accessibility is toward the use of Cloud services. Moreover, the use of virtualization by Cloud services is enhancing the concentration of information security risk within data centers, thereby increasing the vulnerability and likelihood components of risk. Although virtualization has definite security benefits, specific vulnerabilities with a physical security dimension are noteworthy.

In the traditional server architecture, there is one piece of hardware supporting a single instantiation of an operating system (OS) or application. For example, a corporate email server might be running Windows 2008/Microsoft Exchange. Why is this an issue? A software application like Exchange is estimated to use 15 percent of the processing capacity of a server. This leaves 85 percent of the processing capacity unused. Virtualization helps to address this inherent inefficiency.

In a virtualized environment, a layer of software known as a hypervisor is inserted between the hardware and the OS. The hypervisor allows for multiple OS/application servers, also called virtual machines (VMs) or "guests," to exist on that same physical hardware. This facilitates increased processing capacity of the hardware, leading to enhanced resource utilization and efficiency.

The hypervisor does the heavy lifting in terms of allocating CPU time, etc. across the coresident guest operating systems. Figure 9.8 illustrates the architecture of hosted virtualization at a high level (i.e., the hypervisor runs on a host OS that manages the hardware resources).

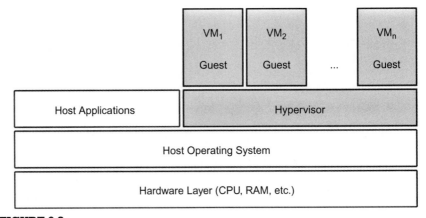

FIGURE 9.8
Machine virtualization.

This configuration requires less hardware to support the same number of application servers. The net result is less money spent on servers and supporting hardware and the colocation of multiple operating systems and applications.

Consider an organization that requires 12 application servers to support its operation. In the traditional model, the organization would purchase 12 physical systems with associated costs including hardware, operating system, and supporting hardware.

Assuming a properly configured virtual server could support four application servers, the organization would purchase three systems to handle the 12 application servers. The organization would need to purchase the operating systems and VMware software and would probably want to purchase shared storage to leverage other benefits of virtualization.

Figure 9.9 shows the virtual infrastructure discussed above. It shows three VMware vSphere servers with shared storage supporting 12 virtual machines. The hardware and software supporting the virtual environment costs significantly less than 12 physical servers handling the same workload.

9.5.2   Virtualization and Physical Security Risk

It is clear that increased efficiency is a by-product of a virtualized environment. However, what are the security implications of a virtualized environment? For the information of interested readers, excellent technical reviews of electronic attack vectors are available online and represent significant sources of information in this discussion.[6,7]

The focus of this review will be on virtual machine attack vectors that are facilitated by physical security vulnerabilities or have some physical

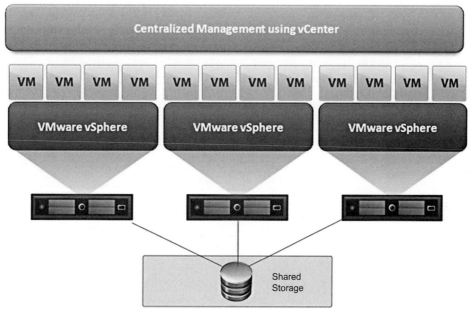

FIGURE 9.9

The virtualized data center. *(Source: Virtual Innovation. "The Virtualized Data Center." http://vi-mw.com/v_infrastructure.htm.)*

dimension. The point is to show how physical security and physical access is particularly relevant to virtualized environments because of a concentration of electronic risk.

The vulnerability to theft of a physical object from a properly secured data center is admittedly low. It is difficult to steal a physical server or other hardware from a physically secured data center. This is especially true if the security controls specified in the previous section are in place. However, information theft does not require anything to be physically missing. Moreover, because of the concentration of information assets in data centers, a condition that is enhanced in virtualized environments, the impact component of risk is increased.

9.5.2.1 Compromise of the Virtual Hard Drive

Physical thefts of information assets can indeed take place in virtual environments. Virtual machines (VM) can be encapsulated into a single virtual hard disk file. A virtual hard disk (VHD) is a disk image file format for storing the complete contents of a hard drive. The disk image/VMs replicate an existing hard drive and include all data and structural elements. It can be stored anywhere that the physical host can access so it is easily transportable, such as on a USB flash memory device.

In fact, an attacker could access a virtual hard disk file without actually entering a data center. Instead, this could be accomplished by accessing devices in the host data store. Attackers can access the host with a "secure copy" program through client management utilities. This would allow an intruder to browse data stores and download files.[8]

It is critical to protect virtual hard disk files as part of the security strategy. In general, such protection requires three elements:

1. Limiting access to the host data stores where the VMs reside.
2. Implementing electronic access logging to know when a breach occurs.
3. Physically isolating the storage network so that only the storage devices and hosts have access.

9.5.2.2 Backup Repositories and Storage Devices

Another attack vector involves access to the backup repositories or network access to VM storage devices. An attacker can simply download the entire virtual disk file from a host to any workstation and copy it to a removable USB storage device. Once the contents of the virtual disk file exist in an external memory device the game is over. An attacker can now mount the disk or power on the VM using the same hypervisor software, and thereby access the VM contents.

9.5.2.3 The Holy Grail: Attacks on the Hypervisor

Attacks on the hypervisor through a guest OS amount to using a guest OS to gain unauthorized access to other VMs or the hypervisor. This is also known as a VM escape or jailbreak attack, as the attacker essentially "escapes" the confinement of the VM into layers that are otherwise unknown to the VM. According to Reference 9, this represents one of the more realistic attacks on the hypervisor, since an attacker can often only compromise a VM remotely because the underlying host OS is invisible.[9]

However, since many VMs share the same physical resources, if the attacker can determine how the VM's virtual resources map to the physical resources, attacks can be conducted directly on the physical resources. By modifying the virtual memory to exploit how the physical resources are mapped to each VM, the attacker can affect all of the VMs, the hypervisor, and potentially other programs on that machine.

Figure 9.10 shows the relationship between the virtual resources and the physical resources and how the attacker could attack both the hypervisor and other VMs. The black arrows indicate the virtual to physical mapping and the grey arrows indicate the direction and resource being compromised.

The hypervisor is clearly the principal target of opportunity on a virtualized machine. However, attacks on the hypervisor through the host OS will likely attempt to exploit vulnerabilities of the host OS on which the hypervisor runs.

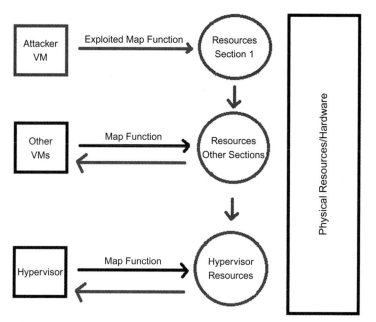

FIGURE 9.10

Attack on a hypervisor through a guest OS. *(Information from Zheng, M. "Virtualization Security in Data Centers and Clouds." http://www.cse.wustl.edu/~jain/cse571-11/ftp/virtual/#randell.)*

Once the attacker has control of the host OS, the hypervisor is essentially compromised since it is merely a layer running on top of the host OS. The inherent administrative privileges of the hypervisor will enable the attacker to perform any malicious activities on any of the VMs hosted by the hypervisor.[9]

9.5.2.4 Virtual Library Checkout

Another potential attack worth noting could occur in connection with virtual library checkouts. This is when a checked-out VM image becomes infected on another virtual machine manager (VMM) or equivalently, the hypervisor, and is later readmitted to its original virtual library. This type of attack exploits the fact that the guest VMM may not be as secure as the original virtual library.

When the VM image becomes infected on the guest VMM and readmitted into the virtual library, the infection can potentially spread through the entire virtual library to other VMs and hypervisors in the data center or Cloud. This could be accomplished by either using a classic inter-machine communication vector (e.g., shared storage, database) or by bouncing off the VMM (i.e., an attacker entering a VM would infect the VMM and from there infect all the machines on the same hypervisor). The latter attack would be catastrophic because this method bypasses all security mechanisms on the network.

What is meant by a virtual library checkout and why is the process vulnerable to attack? A checkout occurs when a VMM fetches a virtual machine's definition and storage from a library and then runs it. When the virtual machine is terminated, the VMM copies the definition and storage back to the library. This allows for preservation of the state and data of the virtual machine.

Let's imagine the following scenario: a virtual machine is stored within a library of virtual machines. It is moved to an infected VMM where it becomes infected. It is later readmitted back into the virtual library. From there, it can be checked out to another VMM, where it may infect other virtual machines, which could be stored in other virtual libraries. This process could continue until the entire virtual infrastructure is compromised.

When the VM image becomes infected on the guest VMM, and is readmitted into the virtual library, the infection could potentially spread through the entire virtual library as well as to other VMs and hypervisors in the data center or Cloud. This is an attack that exploits the abuse of implicit trust that exists between the VMM and the virtual machines. In other words, if the virtual machine is not scanned while it is in the virtual library, it will be run "as is" and therefore become a vector for further compromises.

This vulnerability is particularly acute in organizations that utilize a Virtual Desktop Infrastructure. In that case, virtual machines function as desktops, which either run on their personal computer or on a server.

Let's expand our scenario. The attacker hopes to infect a specific virtual machine, however he doesn't have direct access to it. In order to reach his target, he may attempt to infect another virtual machine, and let his malware hop from virtual machine to VMM to virtual machine, etc., as these are repeatedly checked out and checked in. In order to accomplish this, he gains physical access to an office - not even the data center - and proceeds to check a virtual machine out using a legitimate username and password that has been successfully compromised.

He then carries out his task by infecting the virtual machine now running on a VMM that he controls. When he completes the infection, he checks the virtual machine back into the virtual library, where it will remain dormant until its legitimate user checks it out and infects the VMM being used to run another virtual machine. In fact, any virtual machine run on this VMM will be infected, and the cycle could continue until the attacker's target is reached.

Clearly physical proximity to the employee's machine would facilitate this type of attack, and most notably, without requiring physical access to the data center itself.

9.5.2.5 *Migration Attacks*

Migration attack vectors are similar to the Virtual Library Checkout with one small but important difference. Namely, the virtual machine is not stored in a library during its transfer and execution between two VMMs. Rather, the machine is migrated directly from one VMM to another.

Migration may occur for a variety of reasons to include load balancing and fail-over. This presents opportunities for information compromise if the migration is to machines located in less secure environments (i.e., physical access is afforded to unauthorized or untrustworthy individuals).

Modern VMMs have the ability to globally balance the execution of virtual machines across several VMMs to avoid depleting a single VMM of its resources. While this presents a huge operational convenience, it also represents a security vulnerability as noted above.

In addition, it should be noted that the operational objective here is to minimize the time a virtual machine is not responsive. Therefore, it is migrated while still running. This leaves little opportunity to conduct a security check prior to resuming operation from its briefly interrupted state.

As a result, an infected machine may be migrated to a VMM, where it may infect other virtual machines in operation. That virtual machine may then be migrated to other VMMs, etc., thereby ultimately infecting the entire virtual machine population.

These virtual machines are moved from VMM to VMM, and typically are servers. An attacker would have difficulty accessing them directly - he does not have the opportunity to check a virtual machine out on his own VMM.

However, if he gains physical access to a VMM, he may force a migration of all the virtual machines to other VMMs, and then proceed to infect a specific VMM. When this VMM is again available, the centralized manager will detect a VMM with no load, and it will initiate the migration of virtual machines to it. Those virtual machines will become infected, and these may be migrated to other VMMs over time, which will spread the infection to additional VMMs and virtual machines.

9.5.3 Some Security Benefits of Virtualization

There are definite security benefits associated with virtualization. Indeed, an attack on a VM would likely require significant computer skills. Moreover, merely detecting the presence of a virtual machine might be a significant challenge, although some experts believe it to be a difficult but not impossible challenge.[7,10]

Importantly, virtualization allows for the isolation of resources since each guest OS is encapsulated and abstracted from the hardware. Each user accesses separate file systems and memory blocks. However, it should be noted that modern hypervisors have the ability to share file system and memory blocks in order to limit the resource utilization on the host. In theory, an individual VM compromised by attackers will not affect the host or other VMs on that host unless the VMM itself is targeted from the virtual machine. Note that we posited such attacks in previous sections of this chapter.

Indeed each VM runs without the knowledge of other VMs. Aside from some configurations that allow communication between VMs, when a VM is compromised it is generally difficult for an attacker to access other VMs since only the hypervisor knows the existence of other VMs.

In addition, cost-effective security can result from a physical concentration of assets. For example, perimeter defenses only need to be applied to one physical machine, which reduces the cost. Also, security appliances can be applied to each VM with software.

Virtual machines are known for their ease of use, but this might actually enhance their vulnerability since basic precautions that are routinely implemented on physical machines can be neglected.

This condition seems to be supported by available statistics. It is estimated that 60 percent of virtual machines in production might be considered less secure than their physical counterparts as a result of neglecting to use traditional security measures that would prevent most attacks to VMs.[11]

9.5.4   Virtualization and Denial-of-Service Attacks

From an electronic terrorist's perspective, virtual environments might make attractive targets because denial-of-service (DoS) attacks could be particularly fruitful. The reason for this is that such attacks have the potential to consume resources from all VMs on the host.

In virtual machine architecture, the guest machines and the underlying host share physical resources such as a central processing unit (CPU), memory disk, and network resource. So it is also possible for a rogue guest to initiate a denial-of-service attack against other guests residing within the same system.

A guest machine that consumes all possible system resources would constitute one form of denial-of-service attack in a virtual environment. If this were implemented, the system denies services to other guests that are making request for resources because there is no resource available.[12]

Naively, it would seem that a good approach to prevent a guest from consuming system resources is simply to limit the resources allocated to guests. Current virtualization technologies offer a mechanism to limit the resources allocated to each guest machine in the environment.[13]

Although VMs appear to have additional vulnerability to DoS attacks by virtue of their centralized command and control protocol, this vulnerability actually facilitates another security solution: hypervisors can simply prevent any VM from gaining 100 percent usage of any resource, including CPU, random access memory (RAM), network bandwidth, and graphics memory.

Additionally, the hypervisor could be configured so that when it detects extreme resource consumption it evaluates whether an attack is underway and automatically restarts the VM. VMs can usually be initialized much faster than physical machines because their boot sequence does not need to verify hardware.

9.5.5 Physical Theft of Virtual Machines

As noted above, VMs are not immune to physical theft. The contents of the virtual disk for each virtual machine are usually stored as a file, which can be run by hypervisors on other machines. This allows attackers to copy the virtual disk and gain unrestricted access to the digital contents of the virtual machine. Think about the implications of a nonbackground-investigated individual gaining physical access to the machine when he or she is armed with a portable flash memory device. Hence there should be an emphasis on internal security controls in data centers and the use of background investigations as a condition for unescorted physical access privileges.

Virtual machines are inherently not physical, which implies that a theft can take place without an actual theft of the host machine. To emphasize a point made previously, since the contents of the virtual disk for each VM are stored as a file by most hypervisors, this allows VMs to be copied and run from other physical machines. The bottom line is that the need for appropriate internal physical security controls in data centers takes on added significance in light of virtual technology.

Consider the following scenario: An electronic terrorist, or someone paid handsomely by a terrorist organization, has access to internal data center areas. He or she could copy the VM to portable storage media and then access this data on his or her own machine without physically stealing a hard drive.

Once an individual has direct access to the virtual disk, that individual has all the time in the world to defeat any security mechanisms. These include the use of standard tools such as password cracking and offline attacks. Importantly, the attacker is accessing a copy of the VM rather than the original file. Therefore, the VM will not show any record of intrusion.

9.5.6 Managing Security Risk in Virtual Environments

The aforementioned discussion emphasizes the need for implementing basic electronic security controls such as the timely installation of patches as well as standard physical security controls within data centers. Such controls should include proper background investigations for anyone with unescorted access privileges, CCTV coverage of internal data fields, and physical access restrictions to the data center facility, internal data fields, and individual tenant cages.

9.6   THE INTEGRATION OF PHYSICAL AND ELECTRONIC SECURITY WITHIN ACTIVE DIRECTORY [14]

The advent of IP-based physical security technology creates opportunities for system integration and the leveraging of IT assets to create a holistic security environment. In addition to enhancements to physical security, the use of a unified platform facilitates enhanced electronic security by validating the user's physical presence relative to his or her electronic access history.

Windows Active Directory is a directory service created by Microsoft for Windows domain networks. It is included in most Windows Server operating systems, and it provides a central location for network, computer, service and user management.

Computers that run Active Directory are known as domain controllers. An Active Directory domain controller authenticates and authorizes all users in a Windows domain-type network. It assigns and enforces security policies for all computers. For example, when a user logs into a computer that is part of a Windows domain, Active Directory checks the submitted password and determines whether the user is a system administrator or a user with standard privileges.

The Windows Active Directory structure is a hierarchical framework of objects. Each object represents a single entity such as a user, a computer, a printer, or a group and its attributes. There is no functional difference between an Active Directory object and a physical security object. In physical security, typical entities would be users and devices (e.g., card readers or door-locking hardware).

In Active Directory, an object is uniquely identified by its Security ID (SID) and has a set of attributes. Attributes are the characteristics that the object can possess. These attributes are defined by a schema, which is an organization's structure corresponding to the types of objects stored in Active Directory. The objects and attributes of a physical security device will be contained within a physical security schema extension within Active Directory.

The first advantage of an integrated platform for physical and electronic devices is the elimination of a separate user database for physical security. The physical security Active Directory schema uses the existing electronic schema. Users and groups often share common electronic and physical permissions so the data does not need to be stored in two places, as is the case with physical access control systems that use local panels.

However, the astute reader will recognize that although this integration presents advantages, it also represents a concentration of risk. If a compromise of the Active Directory is achieved in an integrated electronic and physical environment, not only would electronic access be at risk, the physical access resources would also be in jeopardy. If you learn nothing else from this book, you should remember that security decisions nearly always involve trade-offs.

Active Directory can be used in conjunction with a set of printers to designate permissions for users to print from specific printers. A printer is underrated in terms of the threat of information compromise, and a mechanism that can be used to monitor, restrict, and record printing functions across the enterprise is a definite plus.

If Active Directory is used to manage security devices, it can also designate permissions for these same users to activate specific door locks according to defined access privileges. All security functions, alarms, and events can now be hosted within Active Directory. Physical security infrastructure managed by Active Directory can also be configured so that no individual can log into a specific machine unless the authorized user physically swipes in at the appropriate card reader.

For audit and compliance purposes, a unified set of physical/electronic logs and functions has definite benefits. A unified platform allows new types of rules that might significantly enhance on-site monitoring capabilities. For example, an alert can be generated if an employee is not physically present in a facility according to the physical security access control system but someone attempts to login to a desktop within the facility using that employee's electronic credentials. In the event of an electronic breach, an integrated set of logs will reveal that the employee was not actually in the facility when the network was accessed from a specific machine.

Although such capabilities are possible using standard control panels that are IP-enabled, and thereby establish a common architecture, alternate hardware options exist. One such solution is the use of an IP bridge. A bridge is analogous to a Layer 2 switch and allows users to connect readers directly to a network.

Options listed by one vendor (Freedom) include 1-, 2-, or 4-door configurations with all the necessary inputs and outputs to secure each door. Most are power-over-Ethernet (POE)-enabled with a power input provided where necessary. Specialized bridges allow additional security functions within Active Directory including the control of elevators, alarms, and other sensors.

As noted in the discussion of the CampusWide system earlier in this chapter, a card is presented to a reader and the signal is transmitted to a local access control panel. However, in this case, the reader would send a message to the IP bridge rather than to a panel or server.

The message is encrypted and then sent to an Active Directory server for validation, and another message is sent back to the bridge to enable a door opening via activation of a magnetic lock or electric strike. Such a configuration would provide for high availability since synchronized Active Directory servers can potentially enhance resilience and redundancy.

In addition, each bridge is designed with fault-tolerant software that will allow the bridge to connect to any synchronized server on a network. For example, if a particular server fails, the bridge will attempt to contact other servers to find an open path to facilitate lock activation and door control.

Bridges could also reduce requirements for cabling by using the existing IT network with power supplied via Ethernet as noted above. However, it is important to check that power over Ethernet (POE) can satisfy power requirements for magnetic locks. Chapter 12 specifies technical and functional details on magnetic locks.

9.7 PHYSICAL SECURITY RISK AND ELECTRONIC VULNERABILITIES

Because of the increasing number of physical security devices that leverage the IT infrastructure for signaling plus command and control, the requirements for physical security assessments have also evolved. Because most modern physical security devices are increasingly leveraging the IT network for signal transmission, it is not sufficient to merely assess security risk based purely on classical physical vulnerabilities and the status of physical security controls.

We observed that a physical security device with electronic vulnerabilities places physical and IT assets at risk. This is because the compromise of the device could render it ineffective in protecting the facility from unauthorized physical access as well as providing an attack vector to compromise networked information assets.

The risk associated with physical access to components such as IP encoders was specifically highlighted in this chapter. This vulnerability is relatively easy to identify as long as there is a record of the location and types of security devices and components in use. What about identifying the spectrum of electronic vulnerabilities associated with IP-based physical security devices?

Automated network scanning tools that are used for hosts can be used for this purpose. For example, a scan of all physical security devices with an IP address using a tool such as Nessus or Qualys would reveal common IT vulnerabilities such as outdated patches or configuration errors. If the scan is limited to only physical security devices, the time required to complete this scan should be relatively short.

In addition, Layer 3 vulnerabilities affecting downstream physical security hosts can be determined using Red Seal, a vulnerability assessment tool introduced in Chapter 8. For example, IP cameras sitting behind a firewall can be evaluated for potential vulnerabilities based on a misconfiguration of the firewall itself.

It might be quite revealing to know if any physical security devices or other components presumed to be electronically isolated are accessible from the Internet and, moreover, if those devices have updated patches. Red Seal can help identify such information. In general this can be a nontrivial exercise for complex networks without the use of such a tool. Recall Figure 9.2 that showed physical access control system data gleaned from the Internet.

For CCTV systems, the Digital Video Recorder (DVR) or Network Video Recorder (NVR) is typically the vulnerable element relative to an electronic attack. Although an IP camera will have a physical port for networking, and therefore presents a physical connection to effect an electronic compromise, the camera itself does not run software.

Therefore, the cameras themselves are not vulnerable to attack. But the cameras are electronically linked to a DVR or NVR. These recorders are essentially servers that run on standard operating system platforms (e.g., Windows, Linux) and are therefore potential targets for electronic compromise.

These types of network scans should be standard operating procedure as part of a *physical security assessment*. Alternatively, this type of analysis should be included in an electronic security risk assessment and the results communicated to physical security personnel. Traditional physical security assessments that focus exclusively on the placement and functionality of physical security devices are no longer sufficient to identify the spectrum of risk-relevant vulnerabilities. This will mandate nontraditional skill sets. Wherever these skills derive, the days of relying exclusively on guards, guns, and gates have passed, based on ineluctable trends in physical security technology.

SUMMARY

There is an increasing convergence of electronic and physical security risk. This is occurring principally because of the following:

1. The trend toward networked physical security devices.
2. The concentration of risk associated with Cloud computing and virtualized environments.
3. Physical attack vectors that facilitate electronic attacks.

It is important to identify specific physical and electronic vulnerabilities associated with modern physical access control systems in order to understand the relationship between physical and electronic risk. To that end, the anatomy of a representative physical access system is presented here, as well as potential network configurations that are intended to reduce electronic and physical security risk.

Data centers represent a prime target for electronic terrorists because of the concentration of electronic assets. Physical security controls for data centers are provided as well as an indicative physical security standard.

The use of virtual environments is increasing due to the efficiencies and cost savings they provide in public and private Cloud environments. Virtual environments offer opportunities to access significant quantities of information on a single physical machine due to the colocation of numerous electronic resources in the form of multiple virtual machines.

For example, key elements of a virtual environment exist as a file (e.g., virtual disk file). Therefore, illicit copying to portable flash memory devices represents a significant physical attack vector. A discussion of some of the attack vectors in virtual environments with a physical dimension are included in this chapter.

Finally, the assimilation of physical security devices within the Windows Active Directory offers unprecedented opportunities to integrate electronic and physical security risk management activities.

REFERENCES

[1] Blackboard. http://www.blackboard.com/.

[2] Goldstein E. The best of 2600: A hacking odyssey. New York: Wiley; 2008.

[3] Cisco. http://www.cisco.com/warp/public/cc/so/cuso/epso/sqfr/sfblu_wp.pdf.

[4] Cisco. PortSecurity. http://www.cisco.com/en/US/docs/switches/lan/catalyst6500/ios/12.2SX/configuration/guide/port_sec.html.

[5] Smith RE. http://www.rs485.com/pconverters.html.

[6] Murphy A. Security implications of the virtualized datacenter. F5. http://www.f5.com/pdf/white-papers/virtual-data-center-security-wp.pdf.

[7] Ferrie P. Attacks on virtual machine emulators. Symantec. http://www.symantec.com/avcenter/reference/Virtual_Machine_Threats.pdf.

[8] SearchServerVirtualization.com. Virtual security: new attack vectors, new ballgame. http://searchservervirtualization.techtarget.com/tip/Virtual-security-New-attack-vectors-new-ballgame.

[9] Zheng M. Virtualization security in data centers and clouds. http://www.cse.wustl.edu/jain/cse571-11/ftp/virtual/#randell.

[10] Hyde D. A survey on the security of virtual machines. http://www.cse.wustl.edu/jain/cse571-09/ftp/vmsec/index.html.

[11] Brodkin J. 60% of virtual servers less secure than physical machines, Gartner says. Network World. http://www.networkworld.com/news/2010/031510-virtual-server-security.html.

[12] Reuben J.S. A survey on virtual machine security. Helsinki University of Technology. http://www.tml.tkk.fi/Publications/C/25/papers/Reuben_final.pdf.

[13] https://benchmarks.cisecurity.org/downloads/form/index.cfm?download=virtualmachine.100.

[14] Viscount Systems. http://securityspecifiers.com/DImg/Company/800/CID839/FeaturePage/FeaturePagePdf824.pdf.

Problems

1. IP cameras are installed in a publicly accessible space and are used to record activity in and out of a data center.
   a. Identify potential security vulnerabilities associated with these devices.
   b. Indicate what compensating controls could be implemented to reduce identified vulnerabilities.
   c. Explain why analog cameras might be preferable to IP cameras in reducing the risk associated with physical access to these devices.

2. A physical access control system uses an organization's IT network to route signals that permit and deny physical access at turnstiles, doors, etc. based on access control lists (ACL) stored in a database.
   a. Using any one of the three topologies shown in either Figure 9.4, 9.5, or 9.6, describe the vulnerabilities associated with unauthorized physical access to the major system components shown in the selected diagram.
   b. Suggest ways of minimizing the risk identified in 2a above.

3. You are the Director of Information Security for your company. You utilize virtual machines in your IT environment.
   a. Provide some security potential vulnerabilities associated with virtualized machines as noted in the text or elsewhere.
   b. What controls (physical and/or electronic) would you recommend based on the use of virtual machines?

4. You are the Chief Information Officer at your company and are in charge of security for the new data center. The Director of Physical Security is pressuring you to install the latest biometric access control device at the entrance to the data fields. However, security issues at the data center have historically resulted from contractors and vendors. Explain the precise threat and associated risk to your physical security counterpart and suggest an alternative security strategy.

5. You are the Security Officer on duty at a large data center facility. You notice a contractor who is authorized for physical access to the facility discreetly pull out a portable flash memory device (i.e., USB drive) and proceeds to plug it into a machine. After about 10 to 15 min, he furtively looks around and removes the device and places it back in his pocket.
   a. Describe some of the vulnerabilities to information loss associated with the contractor's action.
   b. How is the risk profile different if this is a virtual machine versus a standard server?
   c. How would you react to what you just witnessed?

6. You are the Security Director for a small company that takes security quite seriously. You have recommended that the company purchase IP-based CCTV and physical access control systems, recognizing the power, flexibility, and customization that is possible with these devices, and the budget was approved for these acquisitions.
   a. Indicate what features would be a priority for you in selecting an access control system and why.

    b. Indicate what features would be a priority for you in selecting a CCTV system and why.

    c. Your company uses a Windows-based operating system. Indicate the benefits of integrating CCTV and physical access control with Active Directory and name two security features you hope to implement as a result of a unified platform.

7. You are the Director of Physical Security at a major U.S. manufacturing company. You are in the process of conducting your annual physical security assessment and you decide to evaluate the CCTV system first. This consists of analog cameras that leverage the IT network to route signals.

    a. You first notice that IP encoders are installed in publicly accessible areas. Describe the risk associated with this configuration and indicate possible compensating security controls (physical and/or electronic).

    b. What operational features and performance specifications would you require for cameras installed in the lobby?

    c. What operational features and performance specifications would you require for cameras installed in office areas?

    d. What operational features and performance specifications would you require for cameras installed within internal areas of a data center? Explain your reasoning for items a to d.

8. You are a security consultant hired to assess physical security for the headquarters facility of a major international corporation. You notice one camera is focused on a doorway and is providing too narrow a field-of-view. What parameters could you modify to correct the situation?

9. Specify three attack vectors on a data center. If you were the director of security for a data center, what controls (physical and/or electronic) would you implement to address the risk factors for the identified attacks?

10. You are the Chief Information Security Officer at your firm. You have concluded that there needs to be enhanced security associated with physical and IT infrastructure. To that end, you specify enhanced controls. Provide risk-based justifications for each of the following:

    a. Two-factor authentication for physical access to IT assets.

    b. End point protection for IP-based physical security devices.

    c. Physical access-controlled doors that provide access to panels that control card readers.

    d. Increased password complexity for administrative access to the network video recorder.

11. You are the Director of Physical Security for your firm. In previous years, the IT staff was responsible for providing physical security for the data center housed in your headquarters. You have conducted a physical security assessment of the data center and have identified a number of vulnerabilities. Provide a risk-based argument on whether the following findings require remediation, and if so, why. (Note: there is no right or wrong answer. Your conclusion should be based on the risk and the requirement for compensating controls. Some of these vulnerabilities may be related and thereby jointly affect the risk profile.):

   a. The CCTV system consists of webcams that do not capture images unless a viewer logs in to the system.

   b. Single-factor authentication exists at the entrance.

   c. IT assets housed inside the data center are not physically secured and data at rest are not encrypted.

   d. Visitors are not logged.

   e. No physical security standard exists for the data center.

   f. Portable memory storage devices are used extensively and USB ports on machines are enabled.

12. You are the Chief Information Security Officer at your firm. You presciently recognize that the IT and physical security teams need to coordinate more closely on issues affecting information security. Articulate the reasons why this is so, identify specific areas for closer coordination, and provide suggestions on how this might best be accomplished with specific metrics to measure success.

13. Your company has offices around the world and has decided to invest in a new physical access control system that will be installed in every office.

   a. Specify high-level security features for this system.

   b. In consultation with the IT department, identify specific security risk events or system features that you hope to implement in order to enhance electronic security.

14. You are the Physical Security Director for an international company. You are presciently seeking to work closely with your counterpart in information security. To that end, you approach your colleague about integrating the physical security access system with Active Directory and, specifically, meshing physical and electronic authentication/authorization protocols.

   a. Discuss the security pros and cons of this move.

   b. What security risk scenarios could be addressed by this integration?

15. You have just purchased a network video recorder (NVR) to monitor and control all CCTV activity on campus. Where would you house the NVR (i.e., in what facility), and what physical security controls would you implement to protect this resource?

16. You are the Director of Security at a company that rents space in a large, co-lo data center. The data center requires two-factor authentication at the entrance to the data fields. However, any individual listed on a tenant access control list has unescorted privileges within the data fields. Furthermore, there is no assurance that any of these individuals are background checked.

   a. Explain the benefits and deficiencies of two-factor authentication in this scenario. Be precise in describing how this control does and does not affect the risk of information compromise by electronic terrorists et al.

   b. Describe the controls you would implement in your own cage/rented space to reduce your organization's risk of information compromise.

Counterterrorism Controls

CHAPTER 10

Authentication, Authorization, and Affiliation

10.1 INTRODUCTION

In Part I, a security risk management framework for assessing counterterrorism risk was introduced. Recurring physical security models were also identified, which in some cases can facilitate estimates of the vulnerability component of risk. How uncertainty can be leveraged to estimate security risk was also discussed.

The chapters in Part II focused on analyzing specific terrorism threats. In Part III the science and technology of fundamental physical security controls are explained. These controls are basic to counterterrorism as well as general security risk issues. Electronic counterterrorism controls were included as part of the threat analyses in Chapters 8 and 9.

Part III of this book examines the traditional controls that constitute the core of modern physical security risk management strategies. These controls are quite general and often are used to address multiple risk factors. Specific methods and associated operational requirements are discussed under each major control subheading.

10.2 ORGANIZATIONAL AFFILIATION

If unauthorized physical access to restricted space is a risk factor for terrorism attack vectors, then clearly an important control would be to confirm authorization to physically access restricted space. Moreover, authorized access to a facility or a space within a facility is, at a minimum, predicated on some affiliation with the organization that controls that restricted space.

Specific criteria to qualify for the privilege of affiliation with an organization must be established. These should comport with the organization's culture and tolerance for risk. To cite an extreme example, most organizations with the exception of La Cosa Nostra would consider a history of convictions for violent criminal offenses to be a disqualification for employment. Therefore, a felony conviction for murder would with few exceptions eliminate one's chances for affiliation with a reputable organization.

Authorized physical access is granted or denied based on an individual's status at a specific moment in time. So when authorization to pass through a door, turnstile, portal, etc. is requested by presenting a credential to the access control system, this implies that the individual holding the credential is a member in good standing at the time of the request. It also assumes that the individual presenting a credential is the rightful credential holder. Recognize too that affiliations are ephemeral, and the situation could change over relatively short time scales.

But this begs the question of the exact criteria that should be used to determine suitability for affiliation. In fact, the decision regarding which criteria are most important, and the specific nature of those criteria, can be tricky. Ideally, one would use a risk-based approach and determine those criteria that reflect core company values and that also might affect job performance.

10.3 BACKGROUND INVESTIGATIONS

The privilege of being affiliated with an organization should require passing a background investigation. The theory behind this requirement is twofold: (1) prior behavior is a good predictor of future behavior and (2) confirming that individuals are who they say they are and have done what they say they have done reduces but does not eliminate both security and business risks. There can be some variation in the criteria for affiliation based on job function, but minimum criteria should be established to determine suitability according to a risk-based standard. What might those criteria be?

In fact, such criteria directly relate to the risk factors for criminal behavior specified below. Terrorism is a form of criminal behavior with specific motivations and/or methods:

1. Criminal activity.
2. Extreme indebtedness linked to irresponsible behavior.
3. Lack of permission to work in a country or jurisdiction.
4. Erratic, inconsistent, discontinuous (without satisfactory explanation), or otherwise negative employment history.
5. False statements.
6. Questionable internet profile.

In general, investigating criminal history, credit history, and the right to work is often less resource-intensive than validating employment history since the required information for the former is often accessible via public databases (in the United States). Note that the standard for organizational affiliation is not formulaic. Exceptions should be evaluated on a case-by-case basis. Specific standards associated with each criterion (e.g., criminal offenses that are not disqualifiers for employment) will be organization-specific and should be determined through consensus between business leaders, human resources staff, the legal department, and security professionals.

Checking credit histories can be controversial and may not even be legal in some countries. However, there is a correlation between some criminal acts and a history of irresponsible financial behavior. Although it represents only one example, the CIA spy Aldrich Ames claimed that the primary motivation for his committing espionage was significant indebtedness.[1]

This is another area where judgment is required in order to determine what constitutes "irresponsible" financial behavior. Severe indebtedness because of healthcare costs does not in any way signal irresponsible behavior, but it might tempt people to do dishonest things out of desperation.

In any case, it is much better to be aware of an issue in advance, and thereby make a conscious decision with all the facts, than become aware of a problem after a risky employee is already on board. Once that occurs, the challenge is to identify an errant insider, a more difficult problem that is discussed in the next section.

With respect to the right to work, a commercial product became available when I worked in London that enabled organizations to validate the authenticity of passports issued by many countries. This document checker was able to validate certain embedded security features and thereby detect a phony passport (e.g., *http://www.peoplechecking.com/passport_check*).

The right to work in the UK was obviously an important criterion for a professional affiliation with companies like Goldman Sachs in London. The rather fluid immigration situation within the European Union resulted in numerous foreign workers seeking employment in the UK. This, in turn, translated into confirming the immigration status and associated right to work for individuals from many countries. This confirmation was predicated on holding a valid passport from a specific set of countries.

Prior to the existence of this commercial passport checker, a practical and efficient means of validating the authenticity of passports was limited. When the method was introduced, rechecking all contract employees was initiated. The result was a not insignificant number of rejects, which resulted in termination of employment for identified individuals and notification of the UK authorities. I recall this included one contract security officer who was mildly upset at his newly exposed immigration status. He attempted "a runner" and a wrestling match ensued with security officers. Life before the financial meltdown was a lot more interesting.

A candidate's Internet profile is an interesting risk criterion. Arguably posting risk-relevant material on a Facebook page speaks to issues of judgment at a minimum. Again, part of the decision to hire (or fire!) will be based on the organizational culture and tolerance for risk. However, it is worth conducting an exhaustive search of the Internet to identify such activity prior to employment and then assessing each case individually.

A mentor of mine, and a senior security figure in the UK, James A. King, once told me that he would choose a thorough background investigation over bollards any day of the week. Hopefully a security professional would never be forced to make such a decision. However, his comment was illustrative of the importance of this control in formulating an effective security strategy.

10.4 INSIDER THREATS AND RISK MITIGATION

The theory behind confirming an individual's history with respect to criminal, credit, and employment activities rests on the assumption that past and future behaviors are correlated. The purpose of a background investigation is to preemptively intervene by identifying the risk factors for the threat of "bad" behavior. Sometimes these factors constitute an immediate disqualifier. Other times it involves assessing the risk that an applicant will continue this behavior after organizational affiliation is granted, especially if extenuating circumstances exist.

Once affiliation with an organization is granted, individuals are typically afforded authorized physical and electronic access to internal resources. Their status as full-fledged employees or contractors immediately confers unconditional acceptance and trust. Individuals with malicious intent and who have been granted affiliation with an organization are generally classified as "the insider threat."

This threat is historically a very difficult problem to address as evidenced by the history of successful attempts at espionage, both in corporate and government settings. Importantly, unauthorized physical access is not a risk factor for this threat, and controls designed to address this are quite likely to be useless.

Sometimes background investigations do not identify the correct historical indicators of risk relevant behavior. Alternatively, conditions change such that an individual succumbs to other life forces and their behavior changes for the worse. What tools are available to address these scenarios?

One historically unpopular option is to periodically update background investigations. The government does this for those holding security clearances. This is a relatively extreme measure due to the expense, especially for a large organization. Also, the organization must be prepared to take action when senior executives are shown to have DWI convictions, are behind on their mortgage payments, etc.

There is at least one tool that has been developed specifically to address this problem. This is known as WarmTouch, and it uses psycholinguistic markers in written communications to indicate risk relevant behavior relative to insider-type threats. WarmTouch was developed by a former government psychologist and is based on the results of experiences during interviews as well as scientific research on human behavior under stressful conditions.

In the interest of full disclosure, my current employer, Stroz Friedberg, owns the patents on this product. However, the company actually deploys this software as part of its investigative toolkit if and when it is deemed to be appropriate. An independent review of WarmTouch and/or a comparison of its effectiveness with other commercial techniques used to identify insider threats is encouraged.

The underlying science of WarmTouch is based on the fact that an individual's written language often changes as a result of his or her emotional state. Specifically, the written language of people under stress has specific characteristics, and people who are about to commit illegal/immoral acts are generally under stress. For example, multiple uses of the word "I" in an email communication by those who do not typically speak of themselves in this way has been shown to correlate with a particular state of mind (e.g., self-righteous indignity) that presages risk-relevant behavior such as revenge.

Similar behavioral risk factors have been identified, and the software has been programmed to examine email traffic. Psycholinguistic markers are identified, weighted, and scored for risk. The publicly available emails associated with the Enron investigation have been used to test this tool. It was successful in zeroing in on the bad actors based on the language they used in email traffic.

However, WarmTouch is not a silver bullet for insider threats; no such silver bullets exist. Clearly many people undergo stress, and their language might change with little consequence to the organizational risk profile. Its value is as a filter in focusing investigative resources for counterterrorism, etc. The problem of identifying insider threats is ultimately statistical: separating meaningful outliers of risk from a distribution and thereby prioritizing risk management efforts.

Specifically, WarmTouch is a tool that is programmed to identify insider threat risk factors. It is essentially a "qualitative-to-quantitative data converter." It works by translating qualitative data into quantitative values of risk based on objective features inherent to human communication.

The difference between WarmTouch, and other tools that also purport to quantify risk is that WarmTouch is based on legitimate psychological criteria that have been scientifically demonstrated to correlate with risk-relevant behaviors. Security surveys come to mind as a poor indicator of security risk. To be clear, these are based on a perception of risk. Understanding perceptions of risk can be valuable in its own right, but it does not necessarily correlate closely with more objective risk criteria.

10.5 A MANTRA FOR AFFILIATION

The following mantra describes the necessary connection between the elements of a background investigation and the issuance of an ID that confirms organizational affiliation. It is useful to keep this in mind when formulating a security risk management strategy:

> No physical access will be granted without an ID, no ID will be issued without the creation of individual identity, no individual identity will be created without conducting a background investigation, all background investigations will include criminal, credit, and employment checks.

10.6 CONFIRMING AUTHORIZATION FOR ACCESS TO RESTRICTED SPACE

Once individuals have been properly vetted with a thorough background investigation, the problem reduces to confirming authorization for physical access at any instant in time. By the way, this situation is completely analogous to confirming access to electronic resources.

Confirming authorization for physical access to restricted space is typically accomplished through the use of a system that electronically links the name encoded on an ID or credential to a database. The database contains the names of all individuals currently authorized for physical entry at that location, presumably based on criteria similar to those noted above.

If the name on the credential matches the name in the database, a signal is sent to the mechanism restricting physical access and thereby causing a relay to close. Closing the relay releases a door lock, turnstile, etc., physical entry is granted, and the event is recorded in the system log.

At a high level, a complete system for confirming authorization for physical access consists of the following components:

- ID or credential.
- Credential reader.
- Physical impediment to accessing restricted space.

- Database with encoded credential information linking that credential to an individual with authorized physical access.
- Electronic communications link(s) from the credential reader to a local panel and then to a central computer linked to a database. (Note: This link would likely be over the local area network. This introduces additional risks as discussed in Chapters 8 and 9.).
- Authentication mechanism such as the use of a biometric, PIN pad, or reviewing photographs on IDs.
- Alerting mechanism (e.g., an alarm).

10.7   PHYSICAL ACCESS CONTROL IDS AND CREDENTIALS

The issuance of a unique credential or ID to an individual who has been authorized to physically enter restricted space is a key element of the access control authorization process. Arguably the ID is also the most vulnerable component of the access control system. Clearly mere possession of a credential is not dispositive of authorization to physically enter restricted space. Another individual could find a lost credential, steal a credential, or be spoofing the system.

Credentials to authorize physical access can exist in a number of forms: (1) a contactless smart card containing a monolithic electronic chip with encoded information about the cardholder; (2) a radio-frequency identification (RFID) containing electronic components with encoded information about the cardholder; (3) a stripe with magnetically encoded information about the cardholder; and (4) a proximity card containing an integrated circuit with information encoded about the cardholder. All of these devices with the exception of magnetic stripe technology have an antenna embedded in the card, although cards can have both a magnetic stripe and an electronic circuit.

In terms of security, there is a lot riding on the authenticity of the credential, as well as its legitimate connection to the credential holder. Therefore, it is surprising that the authenticity of the credential holder is often not challenged in the physical access confirmation process.

Based on informal observations, most organizations either loosely verify the identity of cardholders when they present their ID or they simply ignore the ID altogether. It is therefore tacitly assumed that the cardholder is the person authorized to carry the card. It is likely to be true most of the time. The absence of authentication of the cardholder may or may not be the result of a risk-based decision.

The key point is that if the credential is encoded with information that specifies a unique card-cardholder relationship, and that card facilitates physical access to a facility based on that presumed relationship, that credential must be protected.

As noted above, four major technology types are often used as IDs/credentials, and their respective technical features relate to how they are used: RFIDs, contactless smart cards, proximity cards, and magnetic stripe technology.

RFIDs and contactless smart cards are similar in that they both use wireless communication between the card and a card reader to authenticate the card. These will be introduced here but will be discussed in more detail in later sections in this chapter.

A key difference between RFIDs and contactless smart cards is that contactless smart cards have the capability to read at a maximum distance of approximately 10 cm (~4 in) whereas active RFIDs can operate over many meters. RFIDs can operate at 125 KHz, 13.56 MHz, 850 to 950 MHz, and 2.4 to 5.8 GHz, with on-board memory of up to 2 to 4 kB.

Contactless smart cards operate at a frequency of 13.56 MHz, with a memory capacity that is typically between 8 and 64 kB. The higher security capabilities and memory capacity of contactless smart cards make them suitable for applications such as e-passports, payment cards, and identification.

Passive RFIDs are primarily used for tracking and tracing materials, especially within supply chains. As a general rule, while RFIDs are used in applications that identify and track objects, contactless smart cards are used to identify objects or persons as well as to facilitate financial transactions.

Since RFIDs use wireless communication links between the tag/ID and a reader, there is a risk that an unauthorized reader could read the tag details. Contactless smart cards can encrypt the stored information so that only an authorized reader is able to understand the information. The vulnerability to replay attacks is typically foiled in such systems by using a nonce in the handshake between the central server and local processor.

Confusion can sometimes arise between so-called proximity cards and contactless smart cards because both are used in physical access control scenarios. These two ID types are used in similar contexts, i.e., confirming authorization for physical access. However, their differences are manifest in the technology used to store information. A discussion of those differences along with RFID technology is provided next.

10.8   CONTACTLESS SMART CARDS AND PROXIMITY CARDS

10.8.1   Contactless Smart Cards

Contactless smart cards are becoming increasingly common in the commercial world. Smart cards are smart because they are capable of storing a relatively large amount of data and therefore can facilitate the use of strong authentication such as biometrics and public key encryption, as well as provide a secure container for passwords. The relative advantage of biometric-based readers is that they are capable of authenticating the cardholder, not just recognizing the card, which is a key distinction.

The following is a list of specific security features associated with smart cards:

- Secure password file storage
- Generation of asymmetric key pairs and secure public key infrastructure certificate storage
- Secure symmetric key storage
- Secure one-time password seed storage
- Secure biometric template storage
- Two and three-factor authentication

Contactless smart cards contain an integrated electronic circuit/chip that complies with the ISO 14443 standard. Three main communication protocols are supported under the International Organization for Standardization (ISO) 14443 standard series: Type A (MIFARE), Type B, and Type C (Sony-FeliCa IC, mostly in Japan). ISO 14443A is the most widely used contactless smart card standard in the world and is used mainly for transport applications.

ISO 14443 establishes the communication standards and transmission protocols between card and card reader that enable interoperability for contactless smart card products. As noted above, the read/write range of these devices is usually 4 in (10 cm) or less. This figure is generally accepted but is not explicitly stated in the standard.

The integrated circuit embedded in a contactless smart card consists of a capacitor and an inductor connected in parallel in conjunction with on-board memory. As noted above, the reader radiates electromagnetic energy at a frequency of 13.56 MHz. This energy is resonant with the contactless card circuitry, so it excites the inductor/capacitor (LC) coil/antenna embedded in the card. This energy charges the capacitor that powers the integrated circuit.

The information stored in the chip is modulated by the circuitry, and the radiofrequency signal is retransmitted to the reader. Specifically, the integrated circuit transmits the card number via the coil to the card reader. One key feature of some smart cards is that the encoded information is encrypted. This is an important consideration in the selection of a card type since card cloning of proximity cards (discussed below) represents a prominent attack vector. Anecdotal stories from the UK report that mechanical key cutters are being used to clone proximity cards, which add weight to the concern. Figure 10.1 shows a block diagram of the circuitry of a contactless smart card.

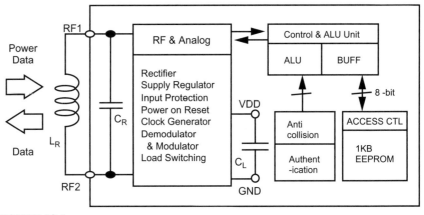

FIGURE 10.1

Contactless smart card anatomy. *(Source: Datasheet Directory.* http://www.datasheetdir.com/ IS23SC4439+Smart-Card-Security.*)*

The following is a hierarchy for the levels of "intelligence" for ID card options:

1. **Dumb:** Simply read the card number or PIN and forward to an access control panel. These often communicate using the so-called Wiegand protocol (discussed in Chapter 12).
2. **Not-so-dumb:** All inputs and outputs exist to control a door, but there is no decision capability. Communication is to a control panel via an RS-485 bus (recall the discussion of the CampusWide BlackBoard system in Chapter 9).
3. **Intelligent:** Inputs and outputs to control a door with memory and processing power on board to make access decisions. Communication is to a control panel via a bus (e.g., RS-485).
4. **Genius:** Communicate to a computer (i.e., not a panel); system network device operating over Ethernet using the TCP/IP protocol.

10.8.2 Proximity Cards

Proximity cards are extremely popular as a credential. If you have a physical access card or ID that is not a contactless smart card, the likelihood is it is a proximity card. The proximity card uses a simple inductor and capacitor to store the cardholder information. The physics of the interrogation process is identical to the contactless smart card.

Aside from the operating frequency, the difference in the two technologies mainly centers on how the information is stored. In the smart card, the information is stored on an integrated circuit. In a proximity card, the cardholder information is stored in the LC circuit described in the previous section.

In exact analogy with the contactless smart card, the simple proximity card circuitry is interrogated by the system transceiver (i.e., combination receiver and transmitter). The interrogating signal couples to the card circuit via the card antenna, and the signal is modulated by the information stored on the card. The modulated signal is reradiated back to the transceiver, and the information stored on the card is evaluated by the back-end system components. The proximity card is interrogated by radiofrequency energy at a resonant frequency (i.e., 13.56 MHz or 125 kHz).

10.9 RADIOFREQUENCY IDS (RFID)

A close cousin of the contactless smart card is the RFID. These are used to identify and track things and sometimes people. As noted previously, the range of RFIDs is typically much greater than contactless smart cards. However, the range among RFID types can vary significantly as well, and that variation is determined by the electronic details of the communication link between card and reader. This has major operational implications since the range among RFID system types can differ by a factor of a thousand.

There are two big food groups of RFID systems: passive and active. Each is discussed immediately below.

10.9.1 Passive RFIDs

Passive RFID systems are called passive because there are no current-draining components on the ID card itself. Therefore, no on-board battery is required in order for the ID to work. But this freedom from power sources exacts a heavy toll in terms of system performance.

Passive systems use the power generated by a transmitted signal to couple to the transponder via magnetic induction (near-field operation) or the transponder senses the transmitted signal's reflection (more precisely the scattered signal) via interaction with the card antenna (far-field operation). The boundary between near-field and far-field regions is approximately equal to $c/2\pi f$, where c is the speed of light and f is the transmitted frequency.

As we observed with other card types, the card stores encoded information that is unique to the user who is hopefully the rightful cardholder. The receive coil on the card is "excited" by the interrogating signal energy, and it reradiates the interrogation signal that is modulated by the encoded information.

How does the signal transfer between the transponder and the reader actually occur? The answer depends on whether the tag is in the near- or far-field of the reader's antenna. Figure 10.2 illustrates the functioning of a near-field RFID system that operates by inductive coupling.

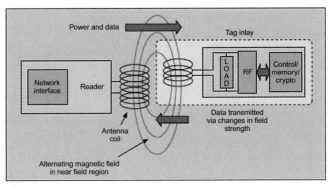

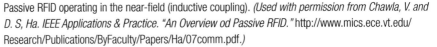

FIGURE 10.2

Passive RFID operating in the near-field (inductive coupling). *(Used with permission from Chawla, V. and D. S, Ha. IEEE Applications & Practice. "An Overview od Passive RFID."* http://www.mics.ece.vt.edu/ Research/Publications/ByFaculty/Papers/Ha/07comm.pdf.*)*

Communication between a reader and the tag (also known as a transponder) for near-field operation occurs through a mechanism called load modulation. Any variation of the current in a tag's coil causes a small current variation in a reader's coil due to the mutual inductance between the two coils. The reader detects this variation in the current. A tag varies the current by changing the load on its antenna coil; hence the name of the mechanism is load modulation.

As a result of the changing magnetic flux due to variations in the current, a voltage is generated in the transponder's antenna coil by inductance. This voltage is rectified and serves as the power supply for the data-carrying device embedded in the card (i.e., a microchip).

With respect to the reader, a capacitor (C) is connected in parallel with its antenna coil. The capacitance of this capacitor in combination with the coil inductance (L) of the antenna coil forms a parallel resonant LC circuit with a resonant frequency that corresponds to the transmission frequency of the reader (by the definition of resonance).

Figure 10.2 illustrates the magnetic coupling mechanism between reader and the transponder/tag. The antenna coil of the reader generates high currents via resonance in the aforementioned parallel LC circuit. It is these currents that produce the requisite magnetic field for near-field communication with the transponder/tag.

A parallel LC circuit tuned to the resonant frequency of the reader exists in the transponder/tag. Maximum voltage of the transponder/tag coil is achieved at the resonant frequency of the transponder/tag parallel LC circuit.

As noted above, variations in the transponder/tag antenna current are caused by data-induced modulation of the antenna load. This creates fluctuations in the reader current due to the mutual inductance between the two coils, and the signal in the reader is ultimately demodulated to yield the baseband (i.e., unmodulated) transponder/tag data signal.

The efficiency of power transfer between the antenna coil of the reader and the transponder is proportional to the operating frequency f, the number of windings n of the transponder coil, the area A enclosed by the transponder coil, the angle of the transponder and reader coils relative to each other, and the distance between the two coils.

As the frequency f increases, the required coil inductance of the transponder coil, and thus the number of windings, decreases (at 135 kHz it is typically 100 to 1000 windings, at 13.56 MHz it is typically 3 to 10 windings). Since the magnitude of the induced voltage is proportional to the changing magnetic flux through the transponder antenna coil, higher frequency interrogating signals require a lower number of coil windings to generate the same inductive effect.

However, and as noted above, there are two types of passive RFIDs: near-field and far-field. Each is designed differently in order to operate within the near and far fields of the electromagnetic signal radiated by the reader. Near-field electric and magnetic fields of an indicative RFID transponder are calculated in Appendix G.

The two most common frequencies used in near-field coupling tags are 128 kHz (LF) and 13.56 MHz (HF). The near- and far-field boundary distances are 372 m for 128 kHz and 3.5 m for 13.56 MHz. For 900 MHz systems, the near-field/far-field boundary is approximately 2 in from the transmitter antenna.

One problem with use of low frequencies is that a large antenna coil is required. Also, the power of the magnetic field of a magnetic dipole loop decreases as $1/r^6$ in the near-field region, where r is the distance between the reader and tag. For far-field RFIDs, the power as detected by the reader decreases as $1/r^4$. Another downside of low-frequency systems is the low bandwidth and, hence, the low data rate.

The electromagnetic field in the far-field region is radiative. In this case, the coupling process works by capturing electromagnetic energy at a tag's antenna as a potential difference via the electric field. Part of the energy incident on a tag's antenna is reflected back due to an impedance mismatch between the antenna and the load circuit. Changing the mismatch or loading of the antenna will vary the amount of reflected energy. This technique is called backscattering.

Figure 10.3 is a graph of the effect of distance on signal intensity for far-field passive RFID systems, where R_o is the initial separation distance between the tag and transceiver and R is a multiple of R_o. In other words, $I = I_o (R_o/R^4)$, where

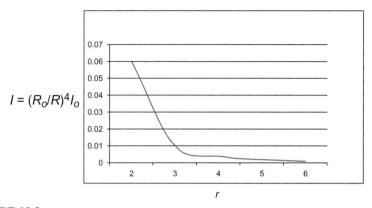

$$I = (R_0/R)^4 I_0$$

FIGURE 10.3
The effect of separation distance on signal intensity for a far-field passive RFID system.

I_0 is the initial intensity. So for example, if the initial intensity is I_0 at a distance, $R_0 = 1\,\text{m}$, then at $R = 2\,\text{m}$, $I = I_0(1/2)^4 = 0.06\,I_0$.

Because of the huge effect of distance on signal intensity, the use of a passive RFID system to track humans will likely require the individual to pass through a prescribed area or portal where the RFID readers are mounted. Figure 10.4 shows the dynamics of signal exchange and power transfer between the reader's interrogating signal to/from the tag in the far-field.

Another significant technical issue that has operational implications is dielectric loading of the ID card antenna. This occurs if the system is used to track humans and the card antenna is brought too close to the skin. Why does this occur?

Antennae are strongly influenced by lossy dielectrics in close proximity. The human body is one such dielectric since it is composed mostly of water. The presence of water adds capacitive reactance to the proximal tag antenna because of the electric fields associated with the water molecule dipoles. Adding reactance has the effect of changing the resonant frequency of the antenna, since the antenna is tuned to be resonant at a specific frequency and impedance ($\sim$10–200J ohms) in air.

In general, resonance occurs when the capacitive reactance cancels the inductive reactance, thereby causing the complex impedance cited above to be entirely real or resistive. Therefore, changing the resonant frequency of the tag antenna effectively "detunes" it and reduces its efficiency. This effect is especially prominent for a so-called high Q (i.e., $f/\Delta f$) element since the bandwidth Δf about the resonant frequency is narrow. For a high Q circuit such as those used in RFIDs to enhance range, a slight deviation from the resonant frequency greatly reduces the effective radiated power.

The solution to this problem is to ensure the RFID tag is sufficiently displaced from the body and thereby not influenced by the electric charges/fields in the dielectric.

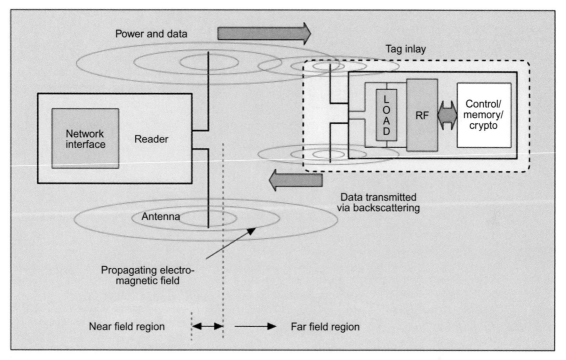

FIGURE 10.4

Far-field RFID system. *(Used with permission from Chawla, V. and D. S, Ha. IEEE Applications & Practice. "An Overview od Passive RFID."* http://www.mics.ece.vt.edu/Research/Publications/ByFaculty/Papers/Ha/07comm.pdf.*)*

Although theoretical calculations can be performed to predict the required stand-off distance, and thereby ensure adequate system performance, this figure will be influenced by clothing, signal polarization, and other factors. Testing is mandated to confirm adequate system performance under operational conditions.

10.9.2 Active RFIDs

Active RFID systems use ID cards or tags/transponders that leverage on-board electrical power in the form of a battery to transmit a signal to a remote receiver. Because passive systems do not generate their own signal, their range is much more limited than active RFID systems. Figure 10.5 depicts passive and active RFID systems in action.

We have observed that for authentication mechanisms between readers and transponders/tags or readers and ID cards, information is exchanged between the card and reader via radio frequency (RF) signals comprised of electromagnetic energy. Such energy obeys well-understood laws of physics. RF transmissions use antennae that radiate electromagnetic energy into the environment. Oscillating currents in these antennae produce fluctuating electromagnetic fields that propagate outward from the antenna to receivers tuned to the signal frequency of interest.

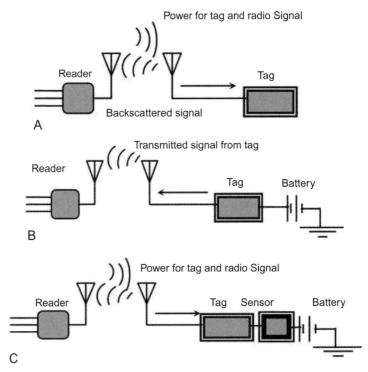

FIGURE 10.5

Passive versus active RFID functionality. *(Used with permission from Turcu, C., Ed. July 20, 2011 under CC BY-NC-SA 3.0 license. "RFID Technology: Perspectives and Technical Considerations of Microstrip Antennas for Multi-Band RFID Reader Operation."* Current Trends and Challenges in RFID. *Chapter 5.)*

Although electromagnetic signals do not require a physical medium to support propagation, the signals are affected by the physical medium with which they interact. In particular, metals have a profound effect on RF transmissions, causing reflections that contribute to spatial differences in signal intensity.

Anyone who listens to a car radio in the city has probably experienced fade-ins and fade-outs. These are caused by reflections, absorptions, and transmissions of RF energy that change the signal intensity as a function of position. If you move the car a few feet (i.e., about a quarter wavelength) from a signal trough, reception is typically restored to health.

The antenna design has an impact on spatial differences in signal intensity. An antenna such as the one on the top of the Empire State Building is essentially a point source, designed to broadcast to as many people as possible within a prescribed radius in all directions. Recall Figure 4.1 provided an excellent pictorial representation of signal intensity from a point source of radiation.

The purpose of an RFID is to provide spatial-temporal information about objects. It is important to recognize that the information being collected as well as the actual deployment conditions will greatly influence RFID system requirements, as well as the appropriate technology to address those requirements. The operational premise for all RFID technology is that a person or an object is linked to a specific card or tag that contains unique identifier information, which is electronically encoded in the card memory.

One might be tempted to think that because of similarities in radiofrequency signaling, all RFID systems are created equal. Googling "RFID systems" yields many varieties, each advertising device-specific operational features and specifications. As with all security strategies, the operational requirements should dictate the chosen system's technical specifications.

It is instructive to contrast RFIDs intended to address counterterrorism scenarios with the requirements of E-ZPass, another well-known RFID system in the United States. This is a useful exercise because it highlights differences in system architecture based on scenario-specific operational conditions.

E-ZPass is used to expedite travel through tollgates. Figure 10.6 depicts the E-ZPass system in action, and the instructions below are from the same government source.

1. As you slowly pass through the toll lane, your E-ZPass tag is read.
2. Instantly, the tag is read by an antenna, and the proper toll is deducted from your prepaid E-ZPass account.

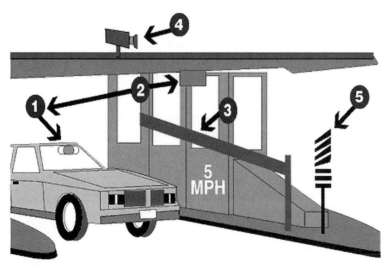

FIGURE 10.6
E-ZPass. *(Source: New York Thruway.* http://www.thruway.ny.gov/ezpass/*.)*

3. At some facilities, there are gates that will go up when a valid tag is read.
4. A video-enforcement system is in place to identify violators.
5. A traffic signal and message is immediately displayed to you just beyond the tollbooth.

So in the E-ZPass scenario, a vehicle is in a known location (i.e., a lane of a prescribed width) and is approaching a tollgate within a limited range of speeds. The tag is specifically designed to transmit only one signal that contains a unique identifier as the vehicle approaches the tollgate.

The E-ZPass system does not require the E-ZPass tag to be transmitting except when it approaches the tollgate. The tag is "woken up" when it receives a transmitted signal from the tollgate. This feature conserves battery life since the E-ZPass tag located in a vehicle only activates when it is required to broadcast.

By contrast, in an envisioned counterterrorism scenario, the RFID tag must broadcast its unique identifier signal continuously if periodically (i.e., once-per-second, once-per-two seconds, etc.), since the point is to determine the position of a meandering tag (i.e., a person) in real time.

Let's compare and contrast the E-ZPass system with an RFID tag used for monitoring the position of individuals as a control to address the threat of terrorism in more detail. In security-related scenarios, one hopes to localize an individual to a specific floor and/or area of a floor in a building. We will examine one system, Elpas (*http://www.visonictech.com/Elpas-Active-RFID-Tags.html*), a division of Tyco, for this purpose. How a specific system operates is important in determining installation details and whether it can be applied to a specific scenario of interest.

The Elpas system uses a low frequency (LF) transmitting beacon (the LF Exciter) that regularly broadcasts a longer-range signal in an omnidirectional pattern (visualize a point source). This is used to detect transitions from zone-to-zone. If a tag comes within range of the LF Exciter signal, the tag broadcasts its exact location to the RF receiver.

Therefore, the system used for counterterrorism includes an LF receiver and transmitter. The LF Exciter is typically deployed in a door or portal and thereby indicates if someone entered or exited a zone of interest, e.g., a particular floor of a building.

After a person with an RFID tag leaves the LF-generated field, the tag will be located by the radio frequency (RF) readers installed on the same floor. A tag's location is then more precisely determined by the relative signal amplitude as measured by the RF reader(s).

If a tag simultaneously registers in multiple LF exciter fields, overlaps between the LF signals generated by tags in response can be used to resolve location as well. The circles in Figure 10.7 depict overlapping LF Exciter signals.

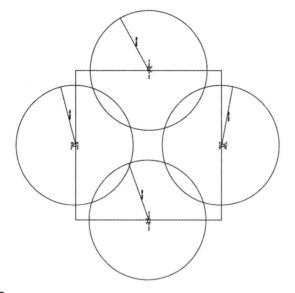

FIGURE 10.7
Elpas RFID deployment topology. *(Image courtesy of Sophie Pike, Roger Pike Associates, Ltd.)*

If an individual arrives on a new floor, and he or she receives that floor's LF beacon signal, they will be relocated to the new floor. If a tag is out of range of any of the RF receivers, they will be characterized as "lost" in the system.

The counterterrorism/security-type RFID system is a complex technology mainly because of the requirement to spatially locate an individual within a floor as well as to detect transitions in moving from zone-to-zone. This results in more complex electronic circuitry in both the card and back-end systems.

With an E-ZPass system, the location of the vehicle (and therefore the tag) is precisely known in advance. In addition, there is much more on-board real estate available in the E-ZPass tag, which is reflected in lower manufacturing costs. These devices solve very different operational problems than systems used for spatial-temporal location despite the fact that they are variants of similar technology.

Active RFID system cards use a battery to power both the signal modulation electronics and the on-board receiver/transmitter. This increases the range up to 1000-fold, but Mother Nature exacts her pound of flesh in both passive and active systems: in the former it is distance and in the latter it is battery life. It is clear from Table 10.1 that there are operational limitations of passive RFID tags.

Table 10.1 Active Versus Passive RFID Tag Attributes

Active RFID Tag Attributes:	Passive RFID Tag Attributes:
Internal Power Source	Transfers energy using RF from reader
Uses battery	No battery
Continuous power availability	Power available only in field of reader
Very low required signal strength	Very high signal strength required
Up to 100m range	Often less than 3-5 meters
Thousands of tags recognized at up to 100mph	Few hundred tags recognized within 3 meters of reader
Up to 128Kb of data storage; sophisticated search/access	128 bytes of data storage

(Information from http://rfid-info.info/.)

10.10 THE SECURITY OF CONTACTLESS SMART CARDS VERSUS MAGNETIC STRIPE TECHNOLOGIES

Physical access ID cards often use magnetic stripes to encode cardholder information. Therefore, it is useful to compare and contrast the security of magnetic stripe and contactless smart card technologies. Differences in ID card technologies have significant implications to a security strategy since they directly affect the vulnerability to threats with a risk factor of unauthorized physical access.

The focus in this section will be on evaluating card technologies that are used as part of the ID credential in the Blackboard CampusWide access control system. Recall the system infrastructure was analyzed in Chapter 9. Key details inherent to the ID/credential are evaluated here to provide a more fulsome view of risk. However, this particular system and its use of ID cards are illustrative of other access control systems, and similar analyses would apply although the details would likely vary.

In the case of CampusWide Blackboard, the maker of the contactless smart card chip is Sony, who has developed proprietary technology known as "FeliCa." FeliCa belongs to Type C of the ISO 1443 standard and includes security features such as encryption. There are other ID technologies that offer comparable security, e.g., MIFARE DESFire, HID iCLASS Elite,[a] and these are discussed later in this chapter. For the moment, the discussion will be confined to the FeliCa technology.

---

[a]Successful attacks against secure ID card technologies have been documented including I-Class Elite (e.g., Garcia, F.D., et al. "Dismantling iClass and iClass Elite." *http://www.cs.ru.nl/~rverdult/Dismantling_iClass_and_iClass_Elite-ESORICS_2012.pdf*) and MIFARE Classic (e.g., Garcia, F.D., et al. "Dismantling MIFARE Classic." *http://www.cs.ru.nl/~flaviog/publications/Dismantling.Mifare.pdf*). More detailed discussions of some secure card technologies and documented vulnerabilities are provided later in this chapter.

As is the case with other passive ID cards, the contactless smart card used in conjunction with the Blackboard CampusWide system requires no on-board power supply/battery since the antenna embedded in the card is energized by the reader interrogating signal.

The reader also detects the signal emanating from the card that is modulated by the encoded cardholder information. This process should sound quite familiar after reading the previous section. The modulated return signal contains specific information used to authorize or deny physical access to the cardholder.

The security of the information encoded on cards is a key operational issue. The information stored on the FeliCa chip is encrypted with an algorithm that has been validated by a reputable government entity.[b]

Although there have been successful cryptographic attacks against technologies like MIFARE DESFire, and iCLASS Elite, the difficulty of these attacks points to these technologies as the choice for secure applications.

Some magnetic stripe cards do encrypt the encoded data. The majority of these use the Data Encryption Algorithm (DEA), usually called DES or Data Encryption Standard. In DES, a clear text value is passed to the DES algorithm, which can be implemented either as software routines or in dedicated hardware. DES then encrypts the clear value using a key (a secret 64-bit value) and outputs an encrypted value. The MIFARE DESFire contactless smart card uses triple DES (i.e., three keys) to provide secure data storage on the credential.

The details for magnetic stripe encoding are captured in the ISO standards found in Table 10.2.

Table 10.2 ISO Standards for Magnetic Stripe Technology	
ISO 7810	Physical characteristics of credit card size document
ISO 7811-1	Embossing
ISO 7811-2	Magnetic stripe—low coercivity
ISO 7811-3	Location of embossed characters
ISO 7811-4	Location of tracks 1 and 2
ISO 7811-5	Location of track 3
ISO 7811-6	Magnetic stripe—high coercivity
ISO 7813	Financial transaction cards

[b]UK IT Security Evaluation and Certification Scheme; Certification Report No. P165, Sony FeliCa Contactless Smart Card RC-S860 ("Sony CXD9559,ROM Version 6, OS Version 3.1), and has been evaluated under the terms of the aforementioned scheme and complies with the requirements for EAL4 Common Criteria (ISO 15408) Assurance Level. *http://www.commoncriteriaportal.org/files/epfiles/CRP165.pdf.*

There are three tracks on the magnetic stripe. Each track is about one-tenth of an inch wide. For example, the ISO/IEC standard 7811, which is used by banks, specifies the following for each track:

- Track one is 210 bpi (bits per inch) and holds 79 6-bit plus parity bit read-only characters.
- Track two is 75 bpi and holds 40 4-bit plus parity bit characters.
- Track three is 210 bpi and holds 107 4-bit plus parity bit characters.

The CampusWide system uses track two (per ISO 7811) for encoding on the magnetic stripe and is designated as "read-only."

Although certain features can make magnetic stripe technology more secure from cloning, this technology is in general more vulnerable to compromise than a contactless smart card with government-validated (e.g., U.S. or UK) encryption. This is due to the strong authentication capabilities of the smart card technology as noted previously and because the contactless smart card chip is inherently resistant to cloning. The relative strengths of the magnetic stripe and smart card encryption algorithms is not entirely clear. However, successful attacks against both DES and smart card algorithms would likely require a sophisticated adversary.

How do magnetic stripes physically encode information and why is this important? The answer to the second part of the question is that understanding the encoding process provides insight into the vulnerability of the ID card to compromise.

With respect to the first part of the question, the magnetic stripe consists of an iron-based material (e.g., barium ferrite) that is capable of storing data by changing the magnetic field intensity. Each particle acts like a current loop, although these currents are in fact due to the orbital motion of electrons in the material. One of the fundamental principles of electromagnetism is that all currents create magnetic fields that can be represented by magnetic lines of flux.

The stripe can be viewed as a magnetic circuit with a magnetomotive force measured in ampere-turns. The magnetomotive force is related to the magnetic flux caused by the circulatory motion of the electrons, and the flux is "conducted" by the stripe consisting of iron-like particles.

This magnetomotive force may be distributed over a magnetic circuit of considerable length or it may be concentrated in a circuit of shorter length. In the latter case, the magnetic effect is more intense than the former. The difference is described by the magnetic field intensity, which is the magnetomotive force-per-unit-length of material and is usually denoted by the letter H.

The Oersted (Oe) is a unit of magnetic field intensity in centimeter-gram-second (cgs) units. Low coercivity materials are those of approximately 300 Oe and high-coercivity material ranges from about 2000 to 4000 Oe.

High coercivity magnetic material is often preferred in magnetic media because of its resistance to erasure. High coercivity materials offer incremental security benefits relative to low coercivity materials because more sophisticated commercial equipment is required to copy the data encoded on the stripe.

In practice, the magnetic stripe is characterized by a distribution of coercivity values. In other words, the quoted coercivity figure represents a statistical average of many magnetic field intensities and therefore should only be considered a nominal value. The shape of that Gaussian distribution of coercivity values for the magnetic domains will affect the vulnerability to erasure.

There have been a number of documented successes in exploiting the vulnerability of magnetic stripe-type cards, sometimes by copying the stripe using commercially available technology.[2] However, there are methods to reduce the risk of copying. They generally work by adding noise or a unique signature to each card, thereby linking a specific card to the encoded data. For example, a magnetic stripe could be encoded with a multidigit ISO number in identifying a particular organization. This could then be concatenated with a multidigit, unique, and randomly generated number to associate a cardholder with a specific card. The use of an unpredictable number as a unique identifier reduces the vulnerability to creating a card out of whole cloth (i.e., without possessing a physical card), but this is not an antidote to copying a card if it is lost or stolen.

Access control systems can include a feature that displays the cardholder photo on a security monitor following a swipe. This is a good security feature, but it is not likely to be sufficient to manage the risk of unauthorized physical access due to a compromised or stolen ID card, especially during times when there is a high volume of pedestrian traffic entering a facility.

Publicized card compromises such as the one cited in the reference have exploited the fact that the ID cards were encoded with an easily guessed numbering scheme. This facilitates the creation of bogus cards by eliminating the need to steal a legitimate card. It should be readily apparent that using unpredictable ID numbers is a positive security feature.

But as noted above, this will not prevent a card that has been stolen or lost from being copied unless there is some specific anticopying feature inherent to the encoding itself. For this reason, all access control ID cardholders should be regularly reminded to report a lost or stolen card immediately.

Proximity cards arguably represent a small step up from magnetic stripe cards in terms of security. However, proximity cards are also susceptible to compromise because the cards can definitely be cloned. Security professionals typically turn to technologies like MIFARE DESFire and HID iCLASS Elite for environments requiring enhanced security.

The MIkron FARE Collection System (MIFARE) includes seven variations of contactless smart cards as follows[3]:

MIFARE Classic—Employs a proprietary protocol that is compliant with elements of ISO/IEC 14443-3 Type A and uses an NXP-proprietary security protocol for authentication and encryption.
MIFARE Ultralight—Uses low-cost integrated circuits that employ the same protocol as MIFARE Classic but without the security elements and uses slightly different commands.
MIFARE Ultralight C—Uses the first low-cost integrated circuits for limited-use applications and offers triple Data Encryption Standard (DES) cryptography.
MIFARE DESFire—These are smart cards that comply with ISO/IEC 14443-4 Type A with a mask-read only memory (ROM) operating system from the manufacturer, NXP (*http://www.nxp.com/*).
MIFARE DESFire EV1—Similar to DESFire but includes advanced encryption standard (AES) encryption.
MIFARE Plus—A drop-in replacement for MIFARE Classic with a certified security level (i.e., 128-bit AES encryption).
MIFARE SAM AV2—A secure access module that provides for the secure storage of cryptographic keys and functions.

MIFARE Classic is probably the most popular contactless smart card technology in use today, with hundreds of millions of users. A number of high-profile customers make use of contactless smart cards for access control. For example, they are used for payment in various public transport systems like the Octopus card in Hong Kong, the Oyster card in London, and the OV-Chipkaart in The Netherlands.[4]

There are a number of well-documented attacks against MIFARE Classic technology. These include three papers by the same research group in the Netherlands. [4–6] In the "Dismantling MIFARE Classic" paper, the authors studied the architecture of the card and the communication protocol between the card and the reader. They were able to recover secret information from the memory of the card. Due to a weakness in the pseudorandom generator, they recovered the key stream generated by the CRYPTO1 stream cipher (i.e., the encryption algorithm).

They exploited the malleability of the stream cipher to read-all memory blocks of the first sector of the card. Moreover, they were able to read any sector of the card memory provided that one memory block within this sector was known.

Finally, they were also able to modify memory blocks if one memory block within a sector was known. There have also been successful attacks on MIFARE Classic cards that do not require a valid reader device.[7,8]

By contrast, the MIFARE DESFire card is based on triple Digital Encryption Standard (DES) encryption technology and is therefore considered by experts to be more secure than the MIFARE Classic and likely comparable in security to the iCLASS Elite (see below). However, a successful "side-channel" attack against the card using equipment that can be built for less than $3000 has been documented.[9]

Another popular technology used for enhanced security applications is the HID iClass technology. This is an ISO/IEC 15693-compatible contactless smart card manufactured by HID Global. It was introduced in the market in 2002 as a secure replacement for the HID Proximity card since these cards did not use encryption.

Migration to technology such as MIFARE DESFire or the HID iCLASS Elite would reduce the risk of ID card compromise by remote interception of the modulated access control radio frequency signal. That said, unauthorized access to the keys used to encrypt the card data is a risk factor for replay attacks (discussed below) against any physical access control system. The use of dynamically generated keys used to encrypt card data would be one possible means of preventing such an attack. iCLASS uses a proprietary encryption algorithm to provide data integrity and mutual authentication between the card and the reader. The cipher uses a 64-bit diversified key that is derived from a 56-bit master key plus the serial number of the card. This key diversification algorithm is built into all iClass readers.

The card technology is covered by U.S. Patent 6058481 and EP 0890157. The manufacturer keeps the exact descriptions of both the cipher and the key diversification algorithms secret. An important security issue is that all iCLASS-standard cards worldwide share the same master key for the iCLASS application.[10] This master key is stored in the electrically erasable programmable read-only memory (EEPROM) of every iCLASS reader. It is possible to let HID generate and manage a custom key for an individual system, but this costs more. The iClass Elite uses an additional key diversification algorithm and a custom master key-per-system that provides "the highest level of security" according to HID.

However, despite the acknowledged security enhancement inherent to iCLASS Elite, it does not eliminate the risk of card compromise. Successful attacks are documented in the open literature as noted previously.[10]

Encryption is a critical feature to prevent card compromise. However and as alluded to previously, no method of encryption would counter an attacker who successfully captures the reradiated signal emanating from an RFID or contactless smart card when presented to a turnstile if the native signal was available. This is because covertly capturing and recording this signal would enable a would-be terrorist to play back this same signal and thereby facilitate unauthorized physical access.

The attacker would not care that the data encoded on the card is encrypted. Fortunately, card manufacturers are aware of this attack vector, and even the less secure MIFARE Classic uses a unique variable, previously noted in this chapter and referred to as a nonce, to thwart replay attacks.

The credential/ID card would certainly be a logical point of attack in attempting to gain unauthorized physical access to restricted space. It is easily concealable and is a relatively easy target for theft. It is often the weak link in the access control technology chain.

But it is certainly not the only vulnerability that could be exploited for this purpose. So it is important to analyze physical security issues at both the component and system levels as discussed in Chapter 9. Such an analysis reinforces the need to understand physical and electronic system interdependencies.

10.11 MULTIFACTOR AUTHENTICATION OF IDENTITY

There is an important distinction between security controls that are used to authenticate identity versus those that merely confirm authorization for physical access. The operational requirements associated with each of these controls should be central to a well-formulated counterterrorism strategy. For example, if an individual presents a valid ID at a card reader linked to a turnstile, the machine has no way of determining if the card belongs to the cardholder. This is an issue that is frequently highlighted in this book. That individual could be intent on accessing internal areas of the building and could have either stolen or fortuitously located a legitimate ID. The machine cannot be blamed for affording access to the impostor since it is programmed to merely accept or reject a valid or invalid card, respectively.

So the machine can successfully determine that the cardholder has authorized entry, but it cannot confirm that the card belongs to the rightful owner. Fortunately there is a relatively simple method to significantly reduce this risk. This method is referred to as dual-factor authentication, but the more general term is multifactor authentication. Note that this method is used in both electronic and physical security environments.

Dual-factor authentication is often implemented through "something you possess" in conjunction with "something you know." The "something you possess" is the physical card. The "something you know" is a password or personal identification number (PIN). The familiar RSA token that generates a varying random number that represents the "something you know" is commonly used to implement dual-factor authentication, especially for remote access to internal IT resources.

Returning to the stolen ID card scenario, the card would be relatively useless unless the thief also knows the password or PIN if two-factor authentication is being used. The use of an RSA token adds an extra element of precaution by using a randomly generated number whose value changes every minute and functions as "something you know" plus "something you possess." A separate password (e.g., Windows account password) should be used with the RSA token.

So one needs to be in physical possession of the token as well as know the separate password to compromise this scheme. The RSA token counters the vulnerability of a static PIN, which is a constant form of "something you know." The RSA token forces an attacker to physically have access to the "something you know" since that something is always changing in an unpredictable way. Therefore, systems that use an RSA token for authentication all but eliminate the problem of shared passwords.

RSA "soft tokens" are also available on Blackberries and iPhones as an alternative to a physical token. Multiple levels of authentication should be required to access the soft token. This is definitely the case with respect to my company-issued Blackberry. As an aside, the 10-try limit on password attempts, the ability to enforce password complexity, and end-to-end encryption are important security features of Blackberries.

Dual/multifactor authentication is a control that reduces the risk of unauthorized physical or electronic access. In general, implementation of an enhanced authentication method such as this is strongly recommended for higher-risk scenarios.

10.12   BIOMETRIC AUTHENTICATION OF IDENTITY

The use of biometrics is another popular method of enhanced authentication. The theory behind these devices is that specific biological features are unique to individual humans, and such features can be used to confirm the identity of an individual with statistical certainty.

The technology associated with biometric security devices has improved considerably over the last 10 years. Specifically, enhancements in their ease of use and a diminution in the rate of false rejections and false acceptances has occurred. Iris recognition systems have particularly low false acceptance/rejection rates and have become easier to implement.

10.12.1   Biometric Error Statistics

A brief technical digression about false acceptances and false rejections is required since these concepts are crucial to evaluating biometric technologies and security sensors in general (see Chapter 12).

Biometric readers essentially provide a "yes" or "no" response to the presentation of card-borne biometric data. However, these devices are not perfect. On occasion, they will falsely accept or falsely reject individuals. These error rates will vary according to the specific biometric technology in question and will therefore yield a statistical distribution of outcomes. The areas under the distribution curve correspond to the possible outcomes, and these are linked to how tightly thresholds are set on the device. These thresholds represent the criteria that trigger the "yes" or "no" outcome.

The statistics of acceptance and rejection rates are important to biometrics and apply equally to other security sensors. The importance derives from the tolerance for risk, and more specifically, to the tolerance for unauthorized physical access relative to mistaken rejections of those with legitimate access privileges.

Sensor acceptance and rejection statistics are predicated on confirming or denying the so-called null hypothesis. This states simply that there is no relationship between two measured phenomena, i.e., that a certain condition either exists or does not exist and that both conditions cannot exist simultaneously.

A type I error, or error of the first kind, is the incorrect rejection of a true null hypothesis. A type II error, or error of the second kind, is the failure to reject a false null hypothesis. A type I error is equivalent to a false positive or false acceptance. Usually a type I error leads one to conclude that a thing or relationship exists when really it does not. For example, a patient has a disease for which he or she is being tested but the patient does not have the disease, or a medical treatment cures a disease when in reality it does not cure it, or a biometric reading specifies that it is associated with a specific individual on record when it is not.

A type II error is a false negative. Examples of type II errors would be a blood test failing to detect the disease it was designed to detect in a patient who actually does have the disease, a clinical trial of a medical treatment failing to show that the treatment works when it actually does work, or more relevantly, a biometric reader indicating that a record does not belong to a specific individual on record when it in fact it does.

When comparing two means (i.e., averages) of statistical distributions, concluding the means were different when in reality they were not different would be a type I error. Concluding the means were not different when in reality they were different would constitute a type II error.

From a security perspective, a false acceptance could have disastrous consequences since an unauthorized person would be afforded physical access to a restricted space. In contrast, a false rejection usually results in a temporary if potentially embarrassing inconvenience.

As noted above, the null hypothesis states that there is no relationship between two measured phenomena. In this case, a null hypothesis would be that the biometric reading is either true or false. The four possible outcomes are as one would expect:

- TN = true negative.
- TP = true positive.
- FN = false negative.
- FP = false positive.

For any biometric system, the main performance indicator is the receiver operating characteristic (ROC) curve, which is a plot of true acceptance rate (TAR) (note: TAR = TP = 1-FRR = the false rejection rate) against the false acceptance rate (FAR) = FP.

Figure 10.8 shows an ROC curve in action along with a table showing the outcomes of the null hypothesis. The two Gaussian curves represent the distribution

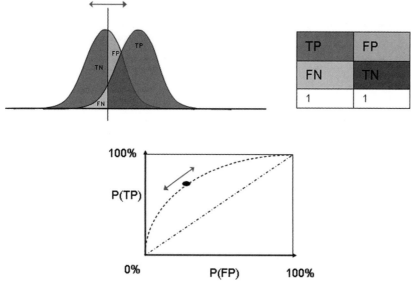

FIGURE 10.8
The ROC curve and statistical representations of the null hypothesis. *(Source: Wikipedia. "Receiver Operating Characteristic."* http://en.wikipedia.org/wiki/Receiver_operating_characteristic.)

of outcomes for the possible null hypothesis outcomes. The optimal position on the ROC curve is at the top left corner. This corresponds to a 100 percent probability of a TP and 0 percent likelihood of an FP.

In theory, one can adjust the threshold (i.e., the black vertical line between the two Gaussian curves) that determines acceptance and rejection rates. For example, in comparing fingerprints, one might require fewer characteristics to declare a match. Decreasing the threshold in this way would result in more false positives.

Conversely, increasing the threshold would result in fewer false positives (and more false negatives), corresponding to a leftward movement along the curve. The actual shape of the ROC curve is determined by how much overlap there is between the two distributions.

Each type of biometric technology (e.g., hand geometry, fingerprints, and iris recognition) has specified false acceptance and false rejection rates based on industry test results, and these are important parameters in selecting an appropriate security technology.

10.12.2 Comparative Biometric Performance

Considerations other than acceptance and rejection rates can be important in deploying biometrics. At Goldman Sachs we considered using thumbprint or hand geometry readers in offices in Asia to enhance authentication at specific locations. There was significant resistance to this idea based on health considerations. People in Asia were wary of touching surfaces for fear of physical contact with influenza-type contagions.

Table 10.3 compares the performance of various biometric technologies with respect to the following parameters:

- Universality describes how commonly a biometric is found in each individual.
- Uniqueness is how well the biometric distinguishes one individual from another.
- Permanence measures how well a biometric resists aging.
- Collectability explains how easy it is to acquire a biometric for measurement.
- Performance indicates the accuracy, speed, and robustness of the system capturing the biometric.
- Acceptability indicates the degree of approval of a technology by the public in everyday life.
- Circumvention is how easy it is to fool the authentication system.

Table 10.3 Performance Characteristics of Biometric Methods

Biometrics	Universality	Uniqueness	Permanence	Collectability	Performance	Acceptability	Circumvention
Face	H	L	M	H	L	H	L
Fingerprint	M	H	H	M	H	M	H
Hand Geometry	M	M	M	H	M	M	M
Keystroke Dynamics	L	L	L	M	L	M	M
Hand Vein	M	M	M	M	M	M	H
Iris	H	H	H	M	H	L	H
Retina	H	H	M	L	H	L	H
Signature	L	L	L	H	L	H	L
Voice	M	L	L	M	L	H	L
Facial Thermogram	H	H	L	H	M	H	H
DNA	H	H	H	L	H	L	L

H = High, M = Medium, L = Low
(Used with permission from Yun, Y.W. 2003. "Biometrics." The '123' of Biometric Technology: Chapter 13.)

10.12.3 Biometric Deployment Considerations

In a scenario that arose in my role as a security consultant, we contemplated the use of biometrics to authenticate workers entering a construction site. Construction sites are notoriously dirty, so the use of a fingerprint reader was dismissed as a potential solution.

Furthermore, the turnstile throughput rate is an important consideration. A long queue at the site entrance might cause delays in construction. Based on these constraints, a hand geometry reader emerged as the leading biometric candidate. These are currently being used at construction sites in Britain as a means of confirming hours worked.

As noted previously in this chapter, smart cards can be used to store information to include biometric data associated with the cardholder. Comparing a person's biometric characteristics with the biometric data stored on his or her ID card offers several advantages over comparing an individual's biometric reading with data stored in a database.

First is the fact that this comparison is a strong form of two-factor authentication. Not only is the data itself unique to the individual requesting access (i.e., the cardholder), but the cardholder is also presenting something one "knows" (biological data) and something one possesses (the card).

On a practical level, this mode of authentication and authorization represents a one-to-one search, whereas a search of a database of biometric files represents a one-to-many search. For example, hand geometry readers make 90 measurements to evaluate 30,000 data points. However, this corresponds to only 9 bytes of data that must be stored on a card. Hand geometry is recognized as a particularly economical biometric method in terms of data storage.

Performing this analysis and making a record-by-record comparison for a large number of records could be a lengthy process. Anecdotal input from at least one vendor and other sources suggest that this mode of querying might introduce system latency for large organizations.

The laws of probability come in handy in understanding how likely there is to be a "collision" of biometric templates stored in a database. The reference cited in Table 10.3 was the source for the following problem: if there are N possible biometric templates, and n individuals, how large must n be so that there is a 0.5 probability that two people have the same template?

This is a variation of the so-called birthday paradox, where the probability of an individual having the same birthday as others in a room is calculated relative to *any* two people in the room having the same birthday. It turns out the probability of the former is much less than the latter. Note that this problem is not at all equivalent to the probability that any two people in the world have identical patterns for a given biometric technology.

The probability of no duplicate for n individuals is given by

$$(N-1)/N \times (N-2)/Nx...x(N-n+1)/N$$
$$= (1-(1/N)) \times (1-(2/N))x...x(1-(n-1)/N)$$

But $1-\gamma < e^{-\gamma}$ where $e^{-\gamma} \sim 1-\gamma$.

$$1-(1/N) \times (1-(2/N)x...x(1-(n-1)/N)) < e^{-1/N} xe^{-2/N} x...xe^{-(n-1)/N}$$
$$= e^{-n(n-1)/2N}$$

Setting $e^{-n(n-1)/2N} = 0.5$, approximating $n(n-1)$ as n^2, and solving for n yields $n = \sqrt{(N \ln 2)}$.

If there is a pool of 1 billion biometric templates N, and the values taken by individuals are uniformly distributed throughout the population, n must equal 693,147,100 to yield a 0.5 probability of a template match with a specific individual. But n must only = 26,327 for *any* two people out of the billion to possess the same template.

Finally, the hierarchy of typical authentication and authorization controls for restricting physical access to restricted space is depicted in Figure 10.9.

FIGURE 10.9

Hierarchy of physical access controls. *(Source: U.S. Department of Transportation. "Entry-Point Screening."* http://transit-safety.fta.dot.gov/security/SecurityInitiatives/DesignConsiderations/CD/sec5.htm.*)*

SUMMARY

Authentication, authorization, and affiliation are fundamental physical security and counterterrorism controls. They represent the core of any physical security risk-mitigation strategy. Implementation of these controls is the key to effectively managing identified security risks.

Ensuring that the criteria required for affiliation with an organization are satisfied should be confirmed via background investigations. This is based on the supposition that past actions are a prologue to future behaviors. Organizations must determine the strictness of these criteria based on their culture and tolerance for risk.

Biometric devices are used to confirm authentication of identity and authorization for physical access to restricted space. There are a number of biometric device types, each with specific technical and operational features that may be more or less relevant to a given scenario of interest. The rate of biometric device errors will vary by device type, and like any sensor, error rates are statistical that are affected by performance thresholds.

Physical access control systems combine a method of confirming authorization to physically access restricted areas with a means to restrict such access. It is the ability to remotely and automatically confirm authorization to access restricted space that makes physical access control systems useful.

Biometrics and/or systems requiring multifactors for authentication of identity are often applied to higher-risk scenarios. All sensors have varying rates of false acceptance and false rejection rates. Adjusting the sensitivity of these devices will affect the relative rates of error types.

The most common technique to verify authorization to enter restricted space is via the use of an ID or credential linked to a card reader. There are many forms of IDs in use that vary according to the technology used to encode and store cardholder information. These include ID cards with magnetic stripes, proximity cards using discrete electronic components (e.g., L-C circuit and antenna), and contactless smart cards that contain an embedded electronic chip connected to an antenna.

ID cards or credentials are central to confirming authorization to physically access a restricted space. However, ID cards arguably represent the most vulnerable elements of a physical access control system due to their portability and broad distribution among the user population.

For this reason, encrypting the on-board information is important in managing the risk of card misuse in the event the card is lost or stolen and this incident goes unreported. The greater the resilience of the encoded card information with respect to unauthorized disclosure, the more secure is the access control system relative to unauthorized physical access.

Radiofrequency ID (RFID) tags can also be used to confirm authorization of physical access and to track the whereabouts of inventory. These are generally divided into passive and active systems, which are distinguished primarily by their respective range of operation. Passive systems are further divided into near- and far-field versions. Operational requirements will dictate the efficacy of various RFID options.

REFERENCES

[1]   Congressional Documents. An assessment of the Aldrich H. Ames Espionage case and its implications for U.S. Intelligence. http://www.fas.org/irp/congress/1994_rpt/ssci_ames.htm.

[2]   Ramsbrock D, Moskovchenko S, Conroy C. Magnetic swipe card system security. http://www.cs.umd.edu/jkatz/THESES/ramsbrock.pdf.

[3]   Wikipedia. MIFARE. http://en.wikipedia.org/wiki/MIFARE.

[4]   de Koning Gans G, Hoepman J-H, Garcia FD. A practical attack on the MIFARE classic. http://www.cs.ru.nl/flaviog/publications/Attack.MIFARE.pdf.

[5]   Garcia FS, de Koning Gans G, et al. Dismantling MIFARE classic. http://www.cs.ru.nl/flaviog/publications/Dismantling.Mifare.pdf.

[6]   Garcia FS, van Rossum P, Verdult R, Schreur RW. Wirelessly pickpocketing a MIFARE classic card. http://www.cs.ru.nl/flaviog/publications/Pickpocketing.Mifare.pdf.

[7]   Courtois NT. Conditional multiple differential attack on MIFARE classic. April 28, 2009 Cologne, Germany: Eurocrypt Conference.

[8]   Courtois NT. The dark side of security by obscurity and cloning MiFare classic rail and building passes anywhere, anytime. SECRYPT 2009—International Conference on Security and Cryptography. Italy: Milan; July 7, 2007.

[9]   Oswald D, Paar C. Breaking mifare DESFire MF3ICD40: power analysis and templates in the real world. September 30, 2011. http://www.chesworkshop.org/ches2011/presentations/Session%205/CHES2011_Session5_1.pdf.

[10] Garcia FD, de Koning Gans G, Verdult R, Meriac M. Dismantling iClass and iClass elite, http://www.cs.ru.nl/flaviog/publications/dismantling.iClass.pdf.

Problems

1. You are the global head of security technology for a major U.S. corporation. You intend to install a biometric device at the turnstiles in the lobby of your headquarters facility. Your strategy and financial justification is to reduce security officer costs by providing automated authentication of individuals. Completely made-up statistics on performance for the various options are given directly below. Note that a false acceptance rate (FAR) is the rate the system incorrectly permitted physical access and a false rejection rate (FRR) is the rate the system incorrectly refused an individual physical access:

	FAR	FRR
Iris Recognition	0.0001	0.00001
Hand Geometry	0.001	0.0001
Fingerprint Scan	0.001	0.001
Voice Recognition	0.01	0.001
Face Recognition	0.1	0.01

Explain the risk implications associated with both the FAR/FRR values for each method. Are these rates of false acceptance and rejection acceptable in terms of reducing the vulnerability component of risk? Why or why not?

2. Specify high-level differences in the vulnerability of proximity cards, magnetic stripes, contactless smart cards, and RFID technologies to compromise.

3. Explain in precise terms why the hierarchy depicted in Figure 10.9 is progressively more secure.

4. You are the Director of Physical Security at your firm. You are advocating the use of an RFID system to track contractors on campus. The price and complexity of the system under consideration is causing senior management to question your selection, and they are perplexed by their awareness of similar systems that seem far less involved (e.g., E-ZPass). Explain the operational differences between an E-ZPass system that interrogates cars at a tollbooth versus an RFID system that must track people and how relevant operational requirements are affected by various technical features of each system.

5. Explain the concept of coercivity in simple terms as it applies to magnetic stripe technology and how differences in coercivity might affect card vulnerability to compromise.

6. You are the Director of Physical Security at your company and you are concerned about the increase in thefts occurring after-hours in office scenarios. You want to install an RFID system to track individuals' whereabouts while in the office. Explain the high-level technical differences in a passive versus an active RFID system and the operational implications of each. How would you address concerns over privacy?

7. You are the Director of Security for a large construction company. The payroll system associated with a major project will be linked to the physical access control system in order to determine hours worked. Explain how the use of a biometric reader at the turnstile might improve the accuracy of payroll data. What concerns might you have in requiring additional authentication to access the site? Would you require workers to swipe-in and swipe-out? If so, provide a risk-based justification.

8. Figure 10.3 depicts the effect of separation distance on signal intensity for a passive RFID system operating in the far-field. Specifically, it shows the $1/r^4$ decrease in signal intensity, where r is the distance between the RFID tag and the reader. If the initial intensity is i as measured at separation distance d, what is the signal intensity at a distance of $2d$? $3d$? $4d$? Plot your results.

9. What would you expect the effect of separation distance to be with respect to an active RFID system and why? Based on your answer, plot the intensity in units of I versus r_o/r for an active system, where I is signal intensity and r_o/r is the ratio of the initial distance to the increased separation distance.

10. You are the Director of Security at a company that manufacturers technology that is highly profitable and unique to your company. Lately foreign competitors have begun manufacturing devices that are remarkably similar to your company's products. You suspect an insider may have divulged proprietary information. Your CEO is extremely concerned and has asked you to investigate.
    a. What controls/physical security would you consider implementing in attempting to identify a potential insider?
    b. Would you coordinate with the Director of IT? Why or why not? What IT controls might be useful in this context?
    c. Would you consider discussing this problem with any other individuals at your company? If so, with whom would you discuss this issue?

11. Which of the following criteria do you consider to be important for verification during a background investigation and why? Are there any others?
    a. Employment history.
    b. Criminal record checks.
    c. Credit/financial checks.
    d. Education confirmations.
    e. Internet profile.

12. Specify relevant operational conditions that affect the use of a passive versus active RFID system. In other words, discuss various on-site issues that might impact system deployment and a decision to use one or other technology.

13. Your company is considering revamping its access control system. It is in the throes of considering various ID card technology options, and the choice is between a standard proximity card and a contactless smart card. Of course, cost is an issue given the thousands of cards that will be created. The company is losing money, and it is looking for savings in all areas. Provide a risk-based argument for choosing proximity cards or contactless smart cards.

14. Describe specific scenarios where you might consider deploying biometric technology for authentication. Compare the risk and relevant operational features of a biometric plus ID card versus the use of a PIN code and ID card.

15. Big shots at your company are insisting on a remote access solution that affords them office-equivalent privileges at home. These privileges include printing, downloading, and storing company information. The proposed solution includes a firewall located in the relevant executives' homes. The firewall provides an unauthenticated connection to your company's internal network resources.
    a. Specify a security vulnerability of this set-up.
    b. What security measure(s) might be imposed to minimize the risk associated with the vulnerability noted in a above? (Hint: Authentication).

CHAPTER 11

Closed Circuit Television

11.1 INTRODUCTION

Closed circuit television (CCTV) is one of the most important physical security controls to address terrorism and other security threats. CCTV has incomparable value as a forensic tool as well as in deterring all types of physical and electronic threats. It has been used to great effect ex post facto in counterterrorism investigations. For example, in the 2005 London Tube and bus bombings, CCTV was instrumental in identifying the bombers soon after the incidents occurred. CCTV would not likely deter most suicide bombers, but that does not detract from its general value as a security countermeasure.

Although CCTV is used to monitor specific situations in real time, especially during crises or as incidents evolve, it is unrealistic to expect that multiple CCTV cameras will be effectively monitored for extended periods. In theory, one could leverage CCTV analytic technology to selectively highlight high-risk scenarios (e.g., "the package left behind"), with the goal of reducing human involvement. Unfortunately, intelligent CCTV systems require controlled environments to be effective.

A CCTV system consists of basic components that do not vary much from system-to-system. At a high level, these include a camera (with a lens), cabling, a digital video recorder (DVR) or network video recorder (NVR), and a video monitor. Unlike many other security systems that either detect or facilitate an event, CCTV detects and processes a series of events, and its performance is tied to the perception of the user. A CCTV system is relatively useless unless the imagery produced by the system is satisfactory to the viewer. Such satisfaction depends on electronic and optical specifications at the component and system levels.

At a deeper level, the laws of physics govern CCTV system performance and, in particular, the optical characteristics that affect key features such as image resolution and the field-of-view. Moreover, the overall system performance of CCTV depends on the ambient conditions. This is a distinguishing feature of CCTV relative to many other security systems.

359

Finally, the technical revolution occurring in CCTV systems as a result of Internet protocol (IP)-based technology has yielded enhancements to certain aspects of system performance. The potential for future enhancements and the integration with other security systems bodes well for the future of this technology.

However, a central theme of this book is that although networked security solutions enhance performance, they also introduce risk. It is no longer appropriate to view a CCTV camera as an isolated device. Connectivity to the network carries risk that can affect both the electronic and physical security risk profiles.

11.2   ANALOG AND IP CCTV CAMERAS

There are two basic food groups of CCTV camera types: analog and IP. The deployment trend is clearly toward the latter technology. The UK and Europe have been moving in this direction for many years. The key distinctions are touched on here because these have security implications.

The terms "analog" and "IP" refer to the signals transmitted by the CCTV system. In truth, the term "analog" is a misnomer, since analog CCTV system signals are digitized and compressed before being converted back to analog for viewing. Indeed, all CCTV images begin their journey as an analog signal since any camera detects reflected light in its native form from illuminated objects. Mother Nature operates in analog mode.

The principal difference between IP and pure analog systems is that the former encode the digital signal as packets in the camera and utilize the standard transmission control protocol (TCP)/IP signal protocol for Internet traffic, Ethernet, etc. However, the difference has profound implications to system performance as well as network security, as discussed in Chapter 9.

Table 11.1 shows high-level hardware requirements for variations of analog CCTV systems versus an IP CCTV system.

IP-based CCTV systems can suffer from the same security vulnerabilities as any device on the network. Attack vectors facilitated by physical and electronic access can exist at a number of points along the signal path.

Although CCTV cameras themselves do not use operating systems like Windows and Linux, and are therefore less vulnerable to attack, they communicate with devices that do, most notably digital video recorders (DVR) and network video recorders (NVR). Therefore, unauthorized electronic access to the network via an unsecured network port on a CCTV camera represents a potential conduit to broader network vulnerabilities.

Table 11.1 Requirements for Analog and IP-based CCTV

	Camera	Power	Transmission	Encoding	Recording
Pure IP	IP	POE	Cat5/6 Ethernet cable	IP encoding at camera	NVR
Hybrid analog/IP	Analog	Panel and power cable to camera	Cat5/6 Ethernet cable to network switch; Cat5/6 to NVR	Analog-to-IP encoder	NVR
Pure analog	Analog	Coaxial cable and power panel	Coaxial cable	N/A	DVR
Analog over Cat5 cable	Analog camera with UTP connection	Video power to balun hub	Video power over UTP (Cat5/6)	N/A	BNC patch cable to DVR

POE = Power over Ethernet; BNC = Bayonet Neill-Concelman.
(Data from Aventura Technologies. www.aventuracctv.com.)

It is useful to take a more detailed look at the analog-to-IP conversion process and, in particular, where that conversion occurs. In pure IP systems, the analog-to-digital conversion plus IP encoding occurs in the camera itself. The camera has an IP address and communicates with a switch or router just like many other IT network devices.

Hybrid analog-IP devices encode the digital signal as an IP-compatible signal in IP encoders (previously referred to as IP converters in Chapter 9) before being sent to the recording device. Both cameras and IP encoders must be physically and electronically secured, a point emphasized in Chapter 9.

As noted above, the principal difference between analog and IP CCTV systems is the fact that analog signals are not IP-encoded, or if they are, the encoding does not occur in the camera itself. An IP-encoded signal is sent directly to an NVR for recording. In contrast, analog cameras interface with a DVR, where the image processing, compression, Web interfacing, and encoding occurs. In an IP camera, these functions are handled by the digital signal processing chip that is part of the camera.

Both hybrid analog and pure IP systems utilize NVRs for image recording and processing. Pure analog systems use a DVR, although a modern DVR should include a CAT5 network port so the device can be given an IP address and is addressable via an Ethernet network.

The system-level implications of where this encoding and compression take place can be profound. First and foremost, NVRs can be located anywhere there is a network port. This can have huge benefits to system capacity since the NVR can be placed on a local area network (LAN) or near (from a network perspective, not necessarily from a physical perspective) a cluster of cameras.

Second, NVRs can handle many more signal inputs and process much more data than a DVR. This is important if you require many cameras to operate simultaneously and especially where each has megapixel resolution. Detailed information specifying the relative advantages of using NVRs versus DVRs can be found at *http://www.softsite32.com/DVR_VS_NVR.htm*.

In general, an IP camera is connected to an addressable router or a switch. The router and camera are accessible through other computers on the Internet with electronic access privileges. This has its own set of security implications, as discussed in Chapters 8 and 9.

11.3   CCTV CAMERAS AND OPTICS

A fundamental component of all CCTV systems is, of course, the camera. Since cameras use visible and/or infrared light to form electronic images, the laws of optics affect system performance. The good news is that one need not know a lot about optics to make competent choices regarding CCTV. But it helps to be familiar with the fundamental concepts in order to have an appreciation for the implications of system performance specifications to the security risk profile. In other words, it is helpful to know how changes in key system parameters affect CCTV performance and thereby impact the operational requirements.

We will first discuss the basic workings of a CCTV camera at a high level.

The camera lens focuses the incoming light reflecting off an object in the field-of-view, an important concept discussed in detail later in this chapter. The light emerging from the lens is focused onto a charge-coupled device (CCD) sensor. Such sensors are made up of photo-reactive pixels. The light causes a charge to build up on each pixel that is proportional to the light intensity.

A control circuit sends the accumulated charge to a charge amplifier, and the charge amplifier converts the charge to a sequential analog signal. The CCD detector sends the analog signal to metal-oxide semiconductor (CMOS) transistors. The signal is read at the output of one of the transistors. Other transistors buffer and reset the photo detector.

Figure 11.1 shows the guts of a CCTV camera and the photon-to-electron conversion process that produces the images that appear on a monitor.

Key optical and electronic parameters that affect CCTV system performance are listed below. As noted above, the discussion on each focuses on their effect on security operational requirements and, ultimately, their effect on risk:

- Lighting.
- Focal length and f-number.

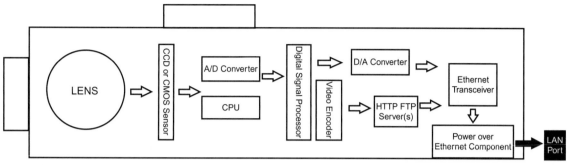

FIGURE 11.1

The CCTV camera. *(Information from Adair, G. "Understanding Megapixel Camera Technology for Network Video Surveillance Systems." BICSI.* https://www.bicsi.org/pdf/presentations/northeast10/Understanding%20Megapixel%20Camera%20Technology.pdf.)

- Angle-of-view and field-of-view.
- Depth of field.
- Sensitivity.
- Signal-to-noise ratio.
- Image resolution.
- Image recording.

11.4 LIGHTING

The proper light level is critical to any CCTV system. Without light, or more precisely, absent reflecting electromagnetic energy, CCTV systems are useless. As discussed in Chapter 4, the signal intensity or power density is the physical parameter often detected by sensors such as the human eye, human ear, or a CCTV camera charge-coupled device. The unit of intensity commonly used for optical sensors is the lux (lx) or lumen (lm)/m². One lux = 0.09 foot candles (fc).

Unfocused light emanating from a small fixture can be considered a point source since the distance from the source to the object is typically much greater than the dimensions of the source. Table 11.2 specifies the light intensity as a function of distance from the source, and these numbers follow directly from the inverse square law first mentioned in Chapter 4.

Table 11.2 Light Intensity and Distance

Lux	64	16	4	1
Meters	1	2	4	8

To gain some appreciation for the relative magnitude of ambient light intensities in units of lux, the following approximations might be helpful:

- Full summer sunlight ~ 50,000 lx
- Dull daylight ~ 10,000 lx
- Shop/office environment ~ 500 lx
- Dawn/dusk ~ 1–10 lx
- Main street lighting ~ 30 lx
- Side street lighting ~ 0.5 to 3 lx

Of course, a camera must operate at the location in which it is installed and at the times required. Light intensities will vary by location and time of day, so this must be accounted for in designing a CCTV system that is fit for purpose. A camera will usually have a specification for the minimum light level required to function. This specification relates to the concept of sensitivity, which is also discussed later in this section.

Of course, one can artificially enhance the ambient light intensity to meet CCTV system illumination requirements. How much enhancement is necessary? There is an informal "Golden Rule" that generalizes the requirement for illumination: utilize a light level corresponding to 10× the brightness required to provide minimum scene illumination. This is not meant to be gospel, but it should be viewed as a rule of thumb.

Megapixel cameras require more light to achieve high-quality images at night than lower-resolution cameras. There is one simple rule to remember: as the resolution of a camera increases, its sensitivity to light decreases. This is due to the size of the individual pixels on a sensor, which decreases with higher pixel densities.

It is helpful to think of the pixel ("picture element") formed on the charge-coupled device (CCD) sensor as a small bucket to collect light. The larger pixels are capable of collecting more light and are therefore able to deliver better performance in lower-light conditions. Therefore, more light intensity is needed for megapixel cameras than submegapixel cameras, all other conditions being equal.

11.5   FOCAL LENGTH AND f-NUMBER

All CCTV cameras contain lenses. Although lenses and radiofrequency antennae function differently, a lens is to optics what an antenna is to radio waves. It produces optical "gain" just like the antenna on your FM radio. Gain means that signal energy is not evenly distributed in space. Certain regions of space will have greater signal intensity than others as a result of lens design features that produce a specific pattern. The goal of the antenna designer is to produce antenna gain in areas most likely to require signal reception.

The diopter is an optical unit that specifies the focusing "power" of lenses. A diopter is equal to 1/focal length, where the focal length is specified in meters. The term may be familiar to the over-40 crowd who are purchasing cheap reading glasses in ever-increasing units of diopters as they advance in years.

How does a lens work? First, you may be shocked to learn that the speed of light is not constant. The speed actually varies with the medium in which it travels. It is a good thing, too, or the glasses you might be using to read this page would be useless.

FIGURE 11.2
The effect of diffraction. *(Source: Mission:Science. NASA. "Reflection." http:// missionscience.nasa.gov/ ems/03_behaviors.html.)*

Light traveling through materials such as glass slows down relative to the speed of light traveling through air. Since the thickness of the lens is made to vary this causes the light rays to converge to a spot by virtue of the relative differences in the speed of light in the two media.

So the thicker the area of the lens, the greater the path length traveled at a slower speed by the light relative to thinner portions of the lens. Lens designers shape the lens according to the distance required for convergence. The distance from the lens to this area of convergence is defined as the focal length.

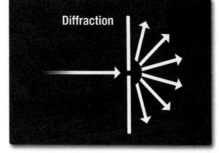

The diameter of the area of convergence is determined by the ratio of the light wavelength to the diameter of the lens. For circular lenses the angular divergence is 1.22 (λ/d) radians, where λ is wavelength and d is the lens diameter.

This minimum area of convergence is referred to as the diffraction limit since it is dictated by diffraction, as the name implies. Diffraction is a wave phenomenon and occurs whenever a wave (any wave, not just light) encounters an obstacle. When light, which can be described as a wave or a particle, impinges on an obstacle, the light bends and spreads out because of diffraction. This effect is especially pronounced when the obstacle size is on the order of a wavelength of the impinging wave. Figure 11.2 illustrates the concept of diffraction, where a collinear beam of light is impinging on a slit and emerges in many directions.

FIGURE 11.3
Focal length.

The focal length of a camera lens greatly affects the camera field-of-view and other optical features, as we will see in the next section. The focal length can also be defined as the distance where initially collimated light rays are brought to a focus. Figure 11.3 graphically illustrates the concept of focal length.

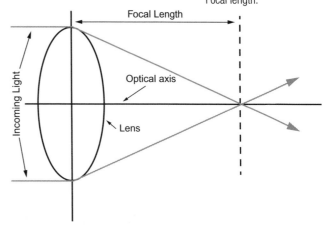

Lenses are sometimes characterized by their f-number, which is defined as the lens focal length divided by their diameter. Therefore, a small f-number means the lens has either a big aperture or a small focal length.

11.6 ANGLE-OF-VIEW AND FIELD-OF-VIEW

A CCTV camera is not of much use if it is unable to image the required area as dictated by the operational requirements. If full-area coverage of a lobby is required, a camera or series of cameras must be able to image the entire scene. The lens of the camera, the dimensions of the optical sensor (CCD), and the distance of the lens from the object determine the field-of-view. The CCD is to a CCTV camera what the retina is to the human eye.

The angle-of-view of a camera lens determines the angle of acceptance of the imaged scene along the relevant dimension of the CCD sensor (i.e., horizontal or vertical). It is also important in determining the camera resolution because it relates to the density of pixels.

The angle-of-view is typically expressed in radians. There are 2π radians in a complete circle, which can also be characterized in terms of degrees. As the reader is probably aware, there are 360 degrees in a circle. To convert radians into degrees, multiply the number of radians (rad) by $180/\pi$. For example an angle of 1 rad is roughly equal to $180/3.14 \sim 57$ degrees.

It can be shown by geometric arguments that an approximate expression for the angle-of-view equals the CCD sensor dimension (CCD_w), divided by the lens focal length (f), or CCD_w/f. In other words, the angle-of-view is a function of the relevant dimension of the sensor (i.e., horizontal or vertical) divided by the lens focal length. CCD_w is often fixed, so the variable in determining the angle-of-view defaults to the lens focal length.

For example, a standard dimension for a CCTV camera CCD is 1/3 in. A 1/3-in CCD has a horizontal dimension of 4.4 mm. We will later observe that the number of pixels-per-foot across the horizontal angle-of-view is a key specification for camera resolution. If the lens focal length is 3.5 mm and the camera uses a 1/3-in CCD, then the horizontal angle-of-view of the lens is given by 4.4 mm/3.5 mm = 1.25 rad or 72 degrees.

Similarly, if the focal length is 10 mm, the horizontal angle-of-view is 0.44 rad (i.e., 4.4 mm/10 mm) or 25 degrees. *Increasing the focal length decreases the angle-of-view and decreasing the focal length does the opposite.* This is a very important relationship in understanding CCTV system performance relative to satisfying security operational requirements. Figure 11.4 depicts the angle-of-view as seen by a CCTV camera lens.

Figure 11.5 illustrates this important relationship between focal length and the angle-of-view. Understanding this inverse relationship is critical when designing a security system to monitor a doorway as opposed to a parking lot.

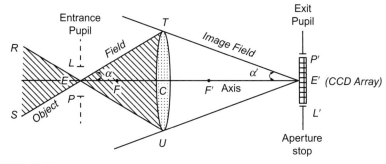

FIGURE 11.4

CCTV angle-of-view. *(Source: Federal Highway Administration. "Sensor-Installation Techniques." Traffic Detector Handbook. Third Edition—Volume II.* http://www.fhwa.dot.gov/publications/research/operations/its/06139/chapt5d.cfm.*)*

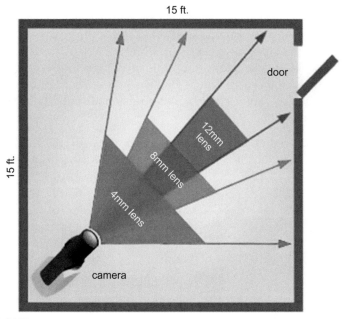

FIGURE 11.5

Field-of-view and focal length. *(Used with permission from A. S. Security & Surveillance.* http://www.assecurity.ca/.*)*

As noted above, the dimensions of the CCD sensor and the focal length determine the angle-of-view. Table 11.3 specifies the difference in the angle-of-view in the horizontal direction as a function of focal length and CCD sensor size. The data confirms that the angle-of-view decreases with increasing focal length and decreasing chip size.

Table 11.3 Camera CCD Chip Size and Approximate Angles-of-View (degrees)

Focal Length (mm)	2/3 in	1/2 in	1/3 in	1/4 in
2.0	-	-	-	82
2.8	-	-	86	57
4.0	-	77	67	47
4.8	83	67	57	40
6.0	70	56	48	32
8.0	56	44	36	25
12	39	30	25	17
16	30	23	17	13
25	18	15	12	8
50	10	7	6	4

(Data from http://www.ezcctv.com/.)

A closely related concept is the field-of-view. This is the actual width (if using the horizontal dimension of the sensor) of the scene subtended by the angle-of-view. The field-of-view equals the angle-of-view times the distance of the camera lens from the object. Figure 11.6 shows a series of photographs that gives an appreciation for the effect of both focal length and distance from lens-to-object on the total field-of-view.

Fortunately one need not memorize camera focal lengths to select the appropriate CCTV camera, but it is helpful to understand that it is a combination

3.6mm @ 5 meters

3.6 mm @ 10 meters

3.6 mm @ 15 meters

12 mm @ 5 meters

12mm @ 10 meters

12 mm @ 15 meters

FIGURE 11.6

The effect of focal length and distance. *(Reproduced with permission from EZCCTV.com.)*

of the lens focal length, the distance from the lens to the object, and the CCD sensor size that determines the field-of-view, a crucial CCTV feature with significant security implications.

The operational implications of the field-of-view are obvious. If the field-of-view is too narrow, there is a risk of missing a risk-relevant event. If the field-of-view is too wide, the resolution may be insufficient to meet a scenario-specific operational requirement (e.g., facial recognition).

Online calculators exist to help with CCTV system design (e.g., *http://www.jvsg.com/online/#*), and these can take some of the pain out of the process. However, it is instructive to at least be aware of the theory behind these calculations so that one appreciates that changing certain parameters can greatly affect system performance for a given scenario. The ability to do back-of-the-envelope calculations is especially handy if an online calculator is inaccessible.

11.7 DEPTH-OF-FIELD

A camera's depth-of-field specifies the distance between the nearest and farthest point from the lens for which the image appears in focus. The precise point-of-focus for a given lens can occur at only one distance at a given wavelength, but the transition between an in-focus and out-of-focus condition can be quite gradual. This can be an issue for infrared cameras since the lens area of focus is different at infrared and visible wavelengths.

Strictly speaking, at any distance from the lens other than the focal point, the light converges to a circle. The diameter of that circle increases for increasing distances from the lens focal point.

Importantly, increasing the f-number (i.e., decreasing the aperture or increasing the focal length) increases the depth-of-field. However, it also decreases the light intensity and increases the effects of diffraction, since the diffraction limit is proportional to the wavelength divided by the lens diameter. Diffraction sets a practical limit on increasing the depth-of-field by reducing the lens diameter as well as resolution in general.

11.8 SENSITIVITY

Sensitivity is the minimum amount of signal required to register detection by a sensor. It is related to the signal-to-noise ratio discussed below. In the case of CCTV, sensitivity is determined by the response of the CCD sensor to the light intensity from the lens. The greater the sensitivity of the camera, the less ambient light is required for detection. As noted previously, higher megapixel cameras are generally less sensitive than their less pixilated counterparts.

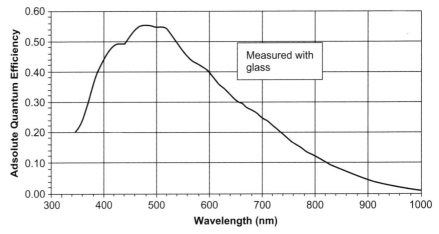

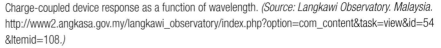

FIGURE 11.7

Charge-coupled device response as a function of wavelength. *(Source: Langkawi Observatory. Malaysia. http://www2.angkasa.gov.my/langkawi_observatory/index.php?option=com_content&task=view&id=54 &Itemid=108.)*

The response of the CCD sensor is a function of the wavelength of light. Figure 11.7 shows the normalized response of a CCD sensor in both the visible and infrared regions of the spectrum. This figure demonstrates why a standard CCTV system only works well over the visible portion of the spectrum (i.e., 400 to 700 nm). Note the sharp falloff in the CCD response as the wavelength increases from the visible to the infrared.

11.9   SIGNAL-TO-NOISE (S/N) RATIO

As its name implies, the signal-to-noise ratio specifies the relative magnitudes of the signal power to the existing noise power. The character of the noise will depend on the specific process responsible for generating that noise. Moreover, the required S/N for acceptable system performance will vary by technology. Various sources of noise are more prominent in specific frequency bands, although some noise sources can be quite broadband.

S/N is often specified in units of decibels (dBs) that are based on powers of 10 (i.e., logarithms). See Appendix D for a more detailed discussion of decibels, an extremely common unit of relative magnitude used in many areas of engineering and science. Table 11.4 specifies S/N in units of decibels and the corresponding linear representation, as well as the effect of S/N on CCTV picture quality.

Table 11.4 Signal-to-Noise Ratio and CCTV Picture Quality

S/N (dB)	S/N (linear)	Picture Quality
60	1000	Excellent; very low noise
50	316	Good; a small amount of noise but good picture quality
40	100	Reasonable; fine grain snow in the picture, fine detail lost
30	32	Poor picture quality with substantial noise
20	10	Unusable picture

11.10   CCTV IMAGE CREATION

It is useful to know something about CCTV image creation since it affects both camera resolution and system bandwidth requirements, a growing concern with the increasing use of megapixel cameras. Bandwidth and storage requirements for CCTV will be discussed in Section 11.12.

Cameras can vary by the type of scanning they use to create an image, which also affects image resolution. IP cameras use so-called progressive or noninterlaced scanning. In this type of scanning, the lines of each frame are drawn in sequence. Figure 11.8 illustrates the concept of progressive scanning.

In contrast, analog cameras use interlacing to create an image. Here the odd lines of each frame are drawn first, which are followed by the even lines.

Specifically, the CCD is scanned across and down exactly 312.5× and is reproduced on the monitor. A second scan of 312.5 lines is reproduced exactly ½ line down and interlaced with the first scan to form a picture of 625 lines. This is referred to as a 2:1 interlaced picture. The combined 625 lines constitute a frame of video (without compression), and the frame therefore consists of these two interlaced fields. Note that some loss of resolution (~ 25 percent) is often experienced due to digital filtering. Figure 11.9 illustrates the concept of an interlaced scan.

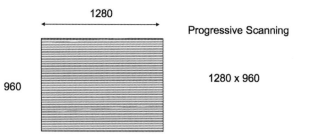

FIGURE 11.8

Progressively scanned CCTV image. *(Source: Adair, G. "Understanding Megapixel Camera Technology for Network Video Surveillance Systems." Bicsi.* https://www.bicsi.org/pdf/presentations/northeast10/Understanding%20Megapixel%20Camera%20Technology.pdf.*)*

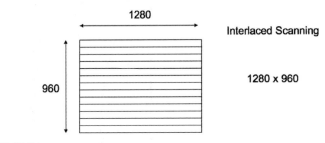

FIGURE 11.9

Interlaced scanned CCTV image. *(Source: Adair, G. "Understanding Megapixel Camera Technology for Network Video Surveillance Systems." Bicsi.* https://www.bicsi.org/pdf/presentations/northeast10/ Understanding%20Megapixel%20Camera%20Technology.pdf.*)*

The advantages of progressive scanning include the following:

1. Higher vertical resolution than interlaced video with the same frame rate.
2. Absence of visual artifacts (e.g., interline twitter) that may accompany interlaced video of the same line rate.
3. Intentional blurring is not required. This is sometimes referred to as anti-aliasing, where aliasing results from under sampling of the analog signal to create a digital signal intended to reduce interline twitter and eyestrain.[a]
4. Better results when scaling to higher resolutions than equivalent interlaced video. Scaling works well with full frames, so interlaced video must be deinterlaced before it is scaled. Deinterlacing can result in comb-like artifacts.
5. Frames have no interlaced artifacts and can be used as still photographs.

A disadvantage of progressive scanning is that it requires higher bandwidths than interlaced video with the same frame size and vertical refresh rate.

11.11   CCTV IMAGE RECORDING

The recording capability of the CCTV system is a key operational feature. Unless you happen to catch a terrorist in the act, a review of recorded imagery ex post facto will be the likely mode of operation. Because of network bandwidth limitations, and the preponderance of data derived from multicamera systems, CCTV cameras are often configured to record on motion as prescribed in the section entitled "CCTV Operational Requirements and Performance Specifications."

Analog cameras interface with DVRs for recording, and IP cameras can interface with either DVRs or NVRs. An NVR is really a server, and a simple personal

---

[a]The Nyquist theorem states that a faithful digital representation of an analog signal requires a sampling rate of twice the highest frequency component contained in the signal. Sampling at a lower rate will cause signal distortion known as aliasing.

Table 11.5 DVR and NVR Technical Specifications

Feature	DVR		NVR	
	Low Performance	**High Performance**	**Low Performance**	**High Performance**
Camera counts	16	64	50	1000
Max Frames-Per-Second (FPS) total	64	480	300	2000
Max FPS per camera	4	30	10	60+
Resolution per image	320×240	640×480	320×240	2500×1600

(Source: Softsite32.com. "DVR vs NVR Comparison." http://www.softsite32.com/DVR_VS_NVR.htm.)

computer (PC) can be configured to function as an NVR. Table 11.5 summarizes indicative technical specifications of DVRs and NVRs.

The number of required NVRs to support the camera population will be determined by a number of factors. These include the following[1]:

1. **Video resolution**—The higher the recorded resolution, the lower the total number of cameras the NVR can support. This is because a higher resolution translates to a higher number of bits being processed. This factor has become increasingly relevant with the widespread deployment of megapixel cameras.
2. **Frame rate**—The higher the recorded frames-per-second (fps), the lower the total number of cameras the NVR will support. The reasoning is the same as in item number 1 above.
3. **Target hard drive**—An NVR writing to a redundant array of independent disks (RAID) storage unit (internal or external) will support more cameras than one writing to a direct internal drive.
4. **Video compression**—The ability to reduce signal bandwidth is extraordinarily important. According to a Bosch white paper on video compression (*http://www.pinders.com/Video%20Compression%20for%20 CCTV.pdf*), because a digitized video signal has a very high data transfer rate of 216 Mbit/s (according to CCIR 601), suitable data compression methods must be used for processing and transmission. An entire DVD, capable of storing about 8 GB of data, would store less than 5 min of a movie without compression. Various compression schemes have been developed with different varying technical features and performance specifications. For example, cameras that use M-JPEG-based compression utilize much higher bandwidth (i.e., bits per second) signals than if using MPEG or H.264-based compression. As noted above regarding video resolution, this places greater demands on the NVR especially if there are multiple megapixel CCTV camera inputs. A more detailed discussion on video compression is provided below.

Table 11.6 Bandwidth Setting for NVRs

	5 FPS	**10 FPS**	**12/15 FPS**	**25/30 FPS**
CIF	128 Kbps	256 Kbps	384 Kbps	750 Kbps
4CIF/D1	384 Kbps	500 Kbps	750 Kbps	1500 Kbps
800×600	750 Kbps	1500 Kbps	2000 Kbps	3000 Kbps
1280×720	1000 Kbps	1250 Kbps	1750 Kbps	3500 Kbps
1280×1024	1000 Kbps	1500 Kbps	2000 Kbps	3800 Kbps
1920×1080	1250 Kbps	1500 Kbps	2500 Kbps	4000 Kbps
1600×1200	1250 Kbps	1500 Kbps	2500 Kbps	4000 Kbps

(Source: Arazi, G. 2005. Camera-to-NVR Ratio for Recording. White paper, Vicon. viconsecurity.com.)

5. **Scene activity**—The motion being recorded in the field-of-view will impact the overall bandwidth and picture sizes and will therefore affect the NVR recording.

In addition, greater resolution requirements and record rates will affect the required bandwidth for recording. Table 11.6 shows indicative bandwidth settings for an NVR as a function of frame rate and resolution setting.

Table 11.7 shows the number of cameras supported by a single NVR for various camera resolutions, frame rates, and storage drives for one NVR manufacturer (Vicon). Note that the source of the information listed in Table 11.5 indicates that high-performance NVRs can actually support 1000 cameras.

Table 11.7 Number of Cameras Supported by a Single NVR

	Resolution	**Max Cameras Internal Drive**	**Max Cameras RAID Drive**
	320×240	38	50
	640×480	35	50
	702×480	35	50
	800×600	32	47
	1280×720	30	45
Recording at 25/30 fps	1280×1024	29	42
	1920×1080	24	35
	1600×1200	24	35
	2048×1536	22	32
	2288×1712	19	28
	2600×1950	17	25

Table 11.7 Number of Cameras Supported by a Single NVR—Cont'd

	Resolution	Max Cameras Internal Drive	Max Cameras RAID Drive
	320×240	42	70
	640×480	40	55
	702×480	40	55
	800×600	37	52
	1280×720	35	49
Recording at 12/15 fps	1280×1024	31	45
	1920×1080	28	38
	1600×1200	28	38
	2048×1536	24	35
	2288×1712	21	31
	2600×1950	19	27
	320×240	60	80
	640×480	50	70
	702×480	50	70
	800×600	45	57
	1280×720	40	54
Recording at 7 fps	1280×1024	32	49
	1920×1080	31	42
	1600×1200	31	42
	2048×1536	27	38
	2288×1712	23	34
	2600×1950	21	29

(Data from Arazi, G. 2005. Camera-to-NVR Ratio for Recording. White paper, Vicon. viconsecurity.com.)

11.12   CCTV SIGNAL BANDWIDTH AND STORAGE REQUIREMENTS

Calculation of the video bandwidth and storage requirements imposed by a CCTV system must take into consideration the total number of networked cameras as well as the network on which those cameras reside. Typical transmission rates for various network types are as follows (*http://www.jvsg.com/bandwidth-storage-space-calculation/*):

■   1 Gb Ethernet: 500 Mb/s
■   100 Mb fast Ethernet: 55 to 60 Mb/s

- 10 Mb Ethernet: 6 to 7 Mb/s
- WiFi 802.11 g 54 Mb: 12 to 25 Mb/s

CCTV image storage is typically measured in bytes (B), kilobytes (kB), megabytes (MB), gigabytes (GB), or terabytes (TB). Bandwidth, a measure of a frequency limit or range, is typically measured in bits per second (bps or baud), kilobits (kb) per second (kbps), megabits per second (Mbps), and gigabits per second (Gbps).

The formulas for bandwidth and storage requirements are as follows, and are available at *http://www.jvsg.com/bandwidth-storage-space-calculation/*. Note that the type of compression will influence the frame size.

- Bandwidth (Mbps) = (frame size (kb) × 1024 × 8 × frames-per-second × number of cameras)/1,000,000
- Storage requirements (GB) = (frame size (MB) × 1024 × frames-per-second × number of cameras × number of days × 24 hr/day × 60 min/hr × 60 s/min × fraction of a day of recorded activity)/1,000,000,000

Some worked examples are shown immediately below as derived from the following source: *http://www.pinders.com/Video%20Compression%20for%20CCTV.pdf*.

If a camera produces 10 images/s where each image is 15 kB, how many cameras can be shared across a 100-Mbps Ethernet connection, and how long would a 200-GB hard disk drive last before it fills up and begins to record over itself?

The amount of data transmitted per second =
10 images/camera-sec × 15 kB/image = 150 kBps/camera

So, 150 kBps/camera × 8 b/B = 1200 kbps/camera
1200 kbps/camera/1024 = 1.17 Mbps/camera
100 Mbps connection can support 100 Mbps/1.17Mbps/camera = 85 cameras

Therefore, 85 cameras can be supported by a 100-Mbps Ethernet connection. However, a network should not be run at 100 percent utilization, so a more realistic bandwidth target should be selected in real life (or choose a bigger pipe!). With respect to the storage time available before rewrite, the following calculation applies:

A 200-GB hard drive = 200 GB × 1024 = 204,800 MB
204,800 MB × 8 bits per byte = 1,638,400 Mb

The drive is being filled at the rate of 1.17 Mbps as calculated previously.
So 1,638,400 Mb/1.17 Mbps = 1,400,340 s

Table 11.8 Indicative Recording Rates for Various Operational Scenarios

Operational Scenario	Typical Recording Rates (fps)
Car parking and external people movement	0.5 to 2
Office or shop	2
Money counting	3.5 to 7.5
Traffic monitoring	5 to 25
Maximum (i.e., full frame rate)	30 (rarely required)

Now $(1,400,430\,s)/(3600\,s/hr)/(24\,hr/day) = 16.2$ days

Therefore, the 200-GB drive would provide just over 16 days of recording time. The above calculation was performed in terms of bit rate.

An equivalent calculation can be performed in terms of bytes:

A 200-GB hard drive = $200\,GB \times 1024 = 204,800\,MB$
$204,800\,MB \times 1,024 = 209,715,200\,kB$

The drive is being filled at the rate of 150 kBps so
$209,715,200\,kB/150\,kBps = 1,398,101\,s$
$1,398,101\,s/3600\,s/hr/24\,hr/day = 16.2$ days.

Table 11.8 suggests recording rates for various operational scenarios. My colleagues at Goldman Sachs conducted an informal experiment and determined that a recording rate of 5 frames-per-second (fps) appeared adequate for relevant operational scenarios, but 7.5 fps is often the generally accepted minimum.

11.13   CCTV IMAGE RESOLUTION

CCTV components must be selected such that the specified operational requirements are satisfied. Anticipated risk scenarios should dictate these operational requirements, and technical specifications of components will affect the overall system performance. This section will build on the previous discussion of the field-of-view to explain optical resolution in terms of operationally relevant features. Some of the details in this section are derived from information provided by Axis, a well-known manufacturer of high-quality CCTV equipment.[2]

Let's explore image creation at the pixel level. When light reflects off an object in the CCTV camera field-of-view, the light impinges on the camera lens. The

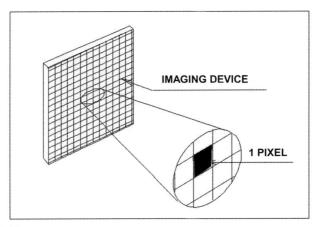

FIGURE 11.10

The pixel. *(Source: Security Camera World. "Cameras and Lenses Made Simple."* http://www. securitycameraworld.com/TECHNICAL-ARTICLES/CAMERA-AND-LENSES-MADE-SIMPLE.ASP.)

lens focuses the optical energy on the CCD sensor. As noted earlier in this chapter, the CCD is the device that converts an analog image to a series of pixels or small dots that correspond to black-to-white transitions. Figure 11.10 illustrates the concept of a pixel.

One can appreciate why the focal length of the lens is so important to camera performance. The image must be in focus at the CCD plane for a given distance between the lens and the object.

The number of pixels is a critical parameter in determining the resolution of a CCTV image (the other is the method of scanning). Furthermore, there is a direct relationship between the CCD sensor size and the number of pixels that are packed onto its surface area. The dimensions of the CCD sensor, and hence the number of pixels, are inexorably linked to image resolution.

Larger-area CCD sensors can provide greater pixel densities and therefore offer greater resolution. A recommended pixel density, defined in terms of pixels-per-foot, will be suggested later in this chapter. Table 11.9 lists the resolution levels for common CCTV formats.

IP cameras can have megapixel resolution, which means each frame has millions of bits of data. We learned in Section 11.11 that network video recorders are capable of handling the massive quantities of digital data that stream across a network when multiple high-resolution cameras are in operation.

The horizontal resolution is a particularly useful specification because it directly relates to the width of a scene and the level of observable detail across the field-of-view corresponding to that scene. Horizontal resolution is often

Table 11.9 Common CCTV Resolution Levels

Format Standard	Video Resolution (horizontal×vertical)
CIF (Common Interchange Format) based on the PAL standard in UK/Europe	352×240
SQCIF	128×96
QCIF	176×144
SIF (Standard Interchange Format) based on the NTSC standard in North America	352×240
WCIF (Wide CIF)	512×288
4CIF	704×576
4SIF	704×480
16CIF	1408×1152
DCIF	528×384
D1	704×480 NTSC
D1	704×576 PAL

PAL=phase alternating line; SQCIF=sub-quarter common intermediate format; QCIF=quarter common intermediate format; WCIF=wide common intermediate format; SIF=standard interchange format; NTSC=national television system committee.

a key operational requirement, although some scenarios might call for vertical resolution (See Problem 9 at the end of the chapter). For example, do you need to be able to see general activity across a scene or do you need to be able to recognize a particular individual within that scene?

We now know that it is the type of scanning (i.e., progressive or interlaced) and the pixel density that determine the resolution of the image. When analog video is digitized, the maximum number of pixels that can be created is based on the number of TV lines available to be digitized. Prior to the introduction of megapixel resolution cameras, the most commonly used resolution was 4CIF/SIF.

When displayed on a computer monitor, digitized analog video may demonstrate interlacing effects such as tearing. In addition, shapes may be slightly distorted since the pixels may not conform to the square pixels common to computer screens. Interlacing effects can be reduced using deinterlacing techniques, while aspect ratio correction can be applied to video before it is displayed to ensure (for example) that a circle in an analog video remains a circle when it is shown on a computer screen.

With digital network cameras, standardized resolution levels derived from the computer industry can be provided. This allows for better flexibility, and the limitations imposed by the NTSC and PAL standards become irrelevant.

VGA (video graphics array) is a graphics display system for PCs originally developed by IBM. The resolution is defined as 640×480 pixels, which is a

Table 11.10 VGA Formats and Pixels

Display Format	Pixels
QVGA (SIF)	320×240
VGA	640×480
SVGA	800×600
XVGA	1024×768
4× VGA	1280×960

QUVG = quarter video graphics array; VGA = video graphics array; SVGA = super video graphics array; XVGA = extended video graphics array.

common format used by nonmegapixel network cameras. The VGA resolution is normally better suited for network cameras since VGA-based video produces square pixels that dovetail with those on computer monitors. Computer monitors can handle resolutions in VGA or multiples of VGA. Table 11.10 shows VGA display formats and the corresponding numbers of pixels.

A network camera with megapixel resolution uses a megapixel CCD sensor to provide an image that contains 1 million or more pixels (hence the prefix "mega"). As noted above, cameras with a larger number of pixels have a greater potential for capturing finer detail and therefore in general produce a higher-quality image.

However, the discussion on scanning revealed that the number of pixels is not the whole story on image resolution. In addition, and this will be discussed in detail later in the chapter, it is the pixel *density* rather than the absolute number of pixels that determines resolution. In general cameras with greater numbers of pixels provide higher pixel densities if other parameters are the same. In particular, megapixel network cameras in conjunction with megapixel lenses allow users to see more image detail and/or to view a larger area of a scene than lower-resolution cameras. Table 11.11 shows the number of megapixels as a function of display format.

Table 11.11 Megapixel Resolution

Number of Megapixels	Horizontal × Vertical Pixels
1.3	1280×1024
1.4	1400×1050
1.9	1600×1200
2.3	1920×1200
3.1	2048×1536
4.1	2560×1600
5.2	2560×2048

Megapixel resolution also provides greater flexibility in providing images with different aspect ratios. The aspect ratio is defined as the ratio of the width of an image to its height. A conventional TV monitor displays an image with an aspect ratio of 4:3.

Megapixel network cameras can offer the same ratio, in addition to others, such as 16:9. The advantage of a 16:9 aspect ratio is that unimportant details, usually located in the upper and lower part of a conventional-sized image, are missing and therefore can be removed by filtering so that bandwidth and storage requirements can be reduced.

Finally, let's summarize the high-level analog-to-digital conversion process during image capture. The object being viewed by the camera lens is located some distance from the lens, and the scene to be viewed has a certain width. The lens viewing the scene focuses the reflected light rays from the field-of-view onto the CCD sensor. The CCD sensor consists of a fixed number of pixels in the horizontal and vertical dimensions. Therefore, the analog field-of-view is transformed into a digital representation of the scene by the CCD sensor.

11.14 RESOLUTION REQUIREMENTS FOR SUBMEGAPIXEL CCTV SYSTEMS

What if you do not own megapixel CCTV cameras? A specific pixel-per-foot metric might be difficult to achieve at significant distances. That does not mean adequate resolution cannot be achieved with lower-resolution cameras. However, it might mean more cameras will be required to cover the same area or the camera must be located closer to the object.

A special CCTV system will be described at the end of this chapter that can help to address scenarios where the coverage of large areas is required and the network bandwidth and/or storage capability is limited.

To provide for realistic operational conditions when using submegapixel CCTV systems, a specification other than a fixed pixel density is required. The following standard provides such specifications and is publicly available through the Centre for Protection of National Infrastructure, a British government organization (*http://www.cpni.gov.uk/*), as communicated by Roger Pike of RPA Ltd, UK.

The choice of a CCTV camera, and the field-of-view in particular, will depend on the nature of the activity to be observed. Five general observation categories have been defined that are based on the relative size of an individual as he or she appears on a monitor. A CCTV system rated to 4CIF (i.e., 720×480 pixels) should meet the stated visual monitoring requirement *for both live and recorded images*.

1. **Monitor and control**—A human figure occupies *at least 5 percent* of the screen height and the scene portrayed is not unduly cluttered. From this level of detail an observer should be capable of monitoring the number, direction, and speed of movement of individuals across a wide area, provided their presence is known (i.e., searching is not required).

2. **Detection**—The figure occupies *at least 10 percent* of the available screen height. Following an alert, an observer would be able to search the display screens and ascertain the presence of an individual with a high degree of certainty.

3. **Observation**—The figure occupies *between 25 and 30 percent* of the screen height. At this scale, some characteristic details of the individual, such as distinctive clothing, can be seen, and the view remains sufficiently wide to allow monitoring of some activity surrounding an incident.

4. **Recognition**—The figure occupies *at least 50 percent* of the screen height. A viewer can say with a high degree of certainty that an individual is the same as one that had been seen previously.

5. **Identification**—The figure occupies *100 percent* of the screen height. The picture quality and detail should be sufficient to enable the identity of an individual to be established beyond a reasonable doubt.

The purpose of the aforementioned categories is to suggest representative image sizes when specifying a system in order to meet a particular operational requirement rather than define a minimum standard. It does not follow that it will be impossible to recognize or identify an individual if the image size is smaller than the percentages suggested. Equally, there is no guarantee that individuals will be identifiable because they occupy 100 percent of the screen. Other factors such as lighting and angle-of-view will also play a role.

It should also be noted that when these guidelines were first developed, all CCTV systems were based on a common standard (e.g., NTSC in the United States and PAL in Europe/UK) for video capture and display. Therefore general observation categories could be developed that were valid for all CCTV equipment.

Since the introduction of IP systems there is now variability in the capture, recording, and display resolution. So a "Recognition" requirement cannot be directly equated to 50 percent of the screen height. Moreover, with the introduction of megapixel cameras and higher-resolution displays, it is now possible to provide the same image resolution using a fraction of the screen area that was previously required with older digital formats. This issue will be addressed in detail in the next section. Table 11.12 shows the equivalent screen height percentages needed to maintain 4CIF resolution.

Table 11.12 Equivalent Percentage Screen Height for Varying Digital Resolutions

Category	4CIF/SIF	080p	720p	WSVGA	SVGA	VGA	CIF	CIF	QCIF
Identify	100	38	56	67	67	84	*139*	*139*	*278*
Recognize	50	19	28	34	34	42	70	70	*139*
Observe	25	10	14	17	47	21	35	35	70
Detect	10	4	6	7	7	9	14	14	28
Monitor	5	2	3	3	3	5	7	7	14

The figures in standard font indicate achievable percentages. Figures in italics might be impossible to achieve.

Note that the following caveats apply:

1. The resolution reflects the lowest resolution in the system chain and not necessarily the monitor display resolution.
2. There is no significant image compression being applied to the image.
3. The person imaged is of average height (5 ft 4 in to 5 ft 8 in or equivalently 1.64 to 1.76 m).

The situation can be more complicated for recorded imagery. This is because the recording process is likely to utilize image compression technology (e.g., H.264) that can cause a reduction in picture quality. So a figure that occupies 50 percent of the screen height and can be recognized in real time may not be recognizable from the recorded image because the compression process has introduced loss in picture detail. For this reason, stated requirements must relate to both the recorded image and the live image for all CCTV cameras.

11.15 RESOLUTION REQUIREMENTS FOR MEGAPIXEL CCTV SYSTEMS

The resolution specification for a CCTV *system* (i.e., all components to include lens, camera, cabling, and monitor) must satisfy the stated operational requirements. As we now understand from previous chapters, the operational requirements are driven by the assessed risk.

As discussed in the previous section, resolution requirements for submegapixel CCTV cameras are characterized by the fraction of the screen occupied by the object being imaged. Therefore, the "Identification" level operational requirement associated with 4CIF requires the image to occupy 100 percent of the screen height, etc.

However, and as also noted previously, this metric is not applicable to megapixel cameras since an object can be fully represented using a small fraction of the screen area, even when significant distances separate the lens and the object. Therefore, a different metric is required to specify resolution requirements for megapixel CCTV systems.

For thin convergent lenses, it can be shown by geometric arguments that the width of the field-of-view, W, can be approximated by the distance from the lens to the object, D, times the horizontal dimension of the CCD sensor, CCD_w, divided by the focal length of the lens, f:

$$\mathbf{W \sim D \times (CCD_w / f)}$$

If there is one formula relating to CCTV worth memorizing, this is the one (hence the enlarged font). Why? Estimating a specific camera type or the number of such cameras required to cover a particular scenario is a common exercise in developing a counterterrorism/security strategy. This expression provides the physical basis for such estimates. It also offers insight into the trade-offs that are involved in ensuring adequate CCTV coverage (e.g., focal length versus distance to the object, field-of-view relative to focal length, etc.).

As noted previously, the CCD sensor converts the light reflecting off an object and focused by the lens into pixels. The sensor comes in various sizes, and the number of pixels along a horizontal or vertical dimension will vary and will scale according to those dimensions.

The ratio of the width of the CCD sensor to the lens focal length, CCD_w/f, is an important expression in its own right. This is the lens angle-of-view that was discussed in Section 11.6. CCD_w/f is an approximation to a more precise expression. It is worth showing how the simplified expression is derived.

Figure 11.11 illustrates the relevant physical parameters in determining the lens angle-of-view: the distance from the object being viewed to the lens (S_1), the distance from the lens to the image plane (S_2), the length of the image (d), and the angle between the central axis of the lens and one end of the image, α. By simple trigonometry it is easy to show that for the half-angle $\alpha/2$, $\tan(\alpha/2) = (d/2)/S_2 = d/2S_2$.

For small angles, $\tan(\alpha/2) \sim \alpha/2 = (d/2S_2)$, so the angle-of-view, $\alpha = d/S_2$. In order to create a sharp image, S_2 must equal the focal length of the lens. This condition is attained when the lens is focused at infinity, i.e., when the rays incident on the lens are parallel.

α is given in radians, so we can multiply the angle-of-view by the distance from the object to the lens in order to determine the camera field-of-view. Importantly, this is the width of the scene that can be imaged by the lens and is given by the expression for the field-of-view, W, above.

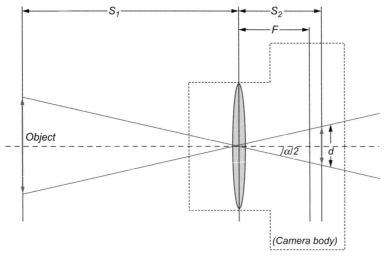

FIGURE 11.11

Angle-of-view revisited. *(Source: Wikipedia. "File:Lens Angle of View.svg."* http://en.wikipedia.org/wiki/
File:Lens_angle_of_view.svg.*)*

The expression for W allows one to easily determine the required camera lens
focal length if the CCD dimensions (and associated number of pixels) and the
distance from the lens to the object are known. Notice that W scales linearly
with both the distance from the scene, D, and the angle-of-view. This scaling is
important to keep in mind when thinking about configuring a CCTV system to
adequately cover a scene. Figure 11.12 tells the story.

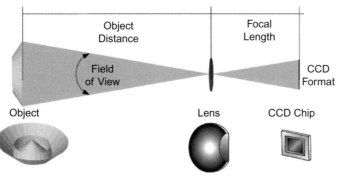

FIGURE 11.12

Key optical parameters and CCTV resolution. *(Permission granted courtesy of Photogrammetry Software.*
http://www.photogrammetry-software.com/2011/11/what-is-photogrammetric-cameras-field.html.*)*

The key to maintaining the required resolution for a given scenario is to ensure the pixel density remains above a specific threshold for any distance between the object and lens. The image resolution can be specified in terms of a convenient and intuitive metric: the ratio of the number of pixels to the width of the horizontal field-of-view or "pixels-per-foot."

This ratio maps the CCD dimension per number of pixels to the size of the object being imaged. The greater the number of pixels-per-foot across the field-of-view, the greater the amount of detail will be discernible on the monitor, assuming the monitor itself has sufficient resolution.

According to the expression for the field-of-view, W, in order to maintain a constant pixel density, an increase in the number of horizontal pixels is required whenever any of the following scenario changes occur:

- The distance increases between the object and the lens.
- The lens focal length decreases.
- The CCD sensor width increases (Note that increasing the CCD sensor width is automatically accompanied by an increase in the number of pixels in that dimension).

The previous discussion implies that when the number of pixels is increased, wider fields-of-view are achievable at greater distances assuming a constant focal length and pixels-per-foot specification. This implies that higher-resolution cameras can cover areas that would require multiple lower-resolution cameras or shorter distances between the camera and object to achieve the same resolution.

Table 11.13 specifies experimentally determined results on camera resolution relative to other parameters and confirms the theory presented herein. The horizontal field-of-view (HFOV) scales linearly with the distance from an object to the camera lens, assuming a constant focal length.

Table 11.13 Number of Pixels and Horizontal Field-Of-View

Camera Resolution	Focal Length	HFOV (feet)	Pixel-per-Foot	Distance from Object to Camera Lens
640×480 (analog)	4.8	14	40	14
1.3 MP	4.8	33	40	35
2 MP	4.8	40	40	42

MP=megapixel. (From Toshiba. "Designing an IP Camera Project." http://www.toshibasecurity.com/support/docs/Toshiba_Design_an_IPSystem_WhitePaper.pdf.)

The implication is that using expensive megapixel cameras might actually be cheaper than opting for a lower-resolution variety depending on the scenario since less cameras would be required to cover the same scene.

But the key question yet to be resolved is, "How many pixels-per-foot are adequate to satisfy a specified operational requirement?" According to the reference that is the source of the information listed in Table 11.13, 40 pixels-per-foot is the minimum pixel density required for facial recognition, license plate reading, or any scenario where detail must be resolved. In other words, this is the threshold figure that separates a general surveillance requirement from a forensics specification or other scenarios requiring greater detail.

However, there is not universal agreement on this specification. The FBI specification for facial recognition-level performance is listed as 80 pixels/ft.[3] It is important to keep in mind that this metric is subjective, and it will likely vary according to scenario-specific operational requirements.

It is also important to appreciate that a given pixels-per-foot specification is inversely related to the distance between the object and camera. What do we mean by this?

Let's assume the distance between the object and the camera is x and the horizontal resolution specification is 40 pixels/ft. In order to satisfy a resolution requirement of 80 pixels/ft without changing other camera features, this mandates that the distance between the camera lens and the object be $x/2$. Many operational scenarios might preclude moving CCTV cameras significantly closer to the object.

One can easily determine the maximum horizontal field-of-view (HFOV) that can be viewed by the camera assuming a 40 pixels/ft pixel density is the required camera resolution. If we assume a 5 MP camera (i.e., 2560 horizontal pixels. See Table 11.11), the maximum horizontal field-of-view for a single camera is 2560 pixels/40 pixels/ft = 64 ft.

This yields a simple means of determining the minimum number of cameras required to cover the width of a given area. For example, if one needs to monitor a perimeter fence line circumscribing a building using 5 MP CCTV cameras, the minimum number of cameras required for a 1000-ft perimeter is the width of the area to be monitored divided by the maximum horizontal field-of-view for a single camera. In other words:

$$(1000\,\text{ft})/(64\,\text{ft}/\text{camera}) \sim 16\,\text{cameras}$$

Clearly an increased number of lower-resolution cameras will be required to cover the same perimeter.

Conversely, if we know the field-of-view required for viewing and the pixel-per-foot requirement, we can specify the minimum camera resolution as follows:

$$\text{field-of-view (feet)} \times \text{(pixels-per-foot)/camera} = \text{number of required pixels/camera}$$

Note that some scenarios may require a calculation using the vertical field-of-view. Imagine the cameras were positioned on the fence line focused downward rather than facing the fence, and the requirement was to capture activity along the fence line. In that case, the vertical dimension of the CCD camera is relevant, and the calculation would use the number of CCD pixels along its vertical dimension for that particular camera.

11.16 CCTV VIDEO COMPRESSION

Video compression is used to reduce transmission bandwidth and video storage requirements. It was noted previously that video compression is a practical necessity these days due to the inherently high-signal bandwidths that are common to modern CCTV systems.

Various compression algorithms have been developed for use in CCTV since the high bandwidth of video imagery can severely affect network performance. This and the attendant costs of data storage mandate lower signal transmission and recording rates.

Most current DVRs offer the H.264 codec algorithm to compress video imagery. A codec is a device capable of encoding or decoding a digital data stream. Historically, the two video compression formats for DVRs before H.264 were Motion JPEG, or M-JPEG (Joint Photographic Experts Group), and MPEG-4 (Moving Picture Experts Group). These three compression options can all display and record up to 30 frames/s (fps). However, there are areas in which they differ, and these are worth noting (*http://www.2mcctv.com/blog/2012_05_09-h-264-compression-dvr-mjpeg-mpeg4/*). Only cursory treatments of some of the more prominent compression algorithms are included here in order to provide basic information on key features that are likely to affect operational requirements.

11.16.1 M-JPEG

M-JPEG results from the sequencing of separately compressed JPEG images. When such images are combined in this way, a M-JPEG video image is created. M-JPEG offers lower frame rates, but offers increased image resolution.

M-JPEG images require significant storage due to their high resolution. However, the image size and therefore the total number of pixels-per-image can be restricted.

11.16.2   MPEG-4

MPEG-4 uses techniques similar to M-JPEG. It works by comparing two compressed images and saves the difference from each sequential image. This involves a technique known as difference coding, which compares a frame with a reference frame, and only pixels that have changed from the reference frame are coded. The objective is to save memory and processing power.

A higher compression rate is one of the advantages of MPEG-4. Therefore, it is useful in applications where low-bandwidth signals are required. However, MPEG-4 provides a lower picture quality than M-JPEG and also supports less megapixel cameras than M-JPEG.

11.16.3   H.264

H.264 is another name given to MPEG-4 Part 10 and is also known as advanced video coding (AVC). Like JPEG, MPEG-4, and MPEG-2, H.264 is a discrete cosine transform (DCT)-based codec. It uses interframe predictive coding to reduce video data between a series of frames. It also utilizes difference coding and is quickly becoming the industry standard for CCTV video compression.

The DCT expresses data points in terms of cosine functions at different frequencies. Compression algorithms that use this method discard low-amplitude, high-frequency components to facilitate signal compression, and thereby reduce bandwidth. Therefore, the number of transmitted pixels is reduced. H.264 codec is capable of producing compressed video streams with 80 Mb/s bandwidth, limited to 8-bit resolution.

H.264 codec is designed to be at least 50 percent more efficient than MPEG-2 and MPEG-4 Part 2 while maintaining the same video quality. It is also designed to fit many applications and accommodate high and low resolutions, high and low bandwidths, and can be used with multiple media types.

H.264 is more demanding that MPEG-4 Part 2, which means decreases in the frame rate can occur. H.264 offers higher compression rates and requires less storage space than MPEG-4 and M-JPEG. It supports audio-to-video (AV) synchronization (also known as lip syncing), and it is designed for use in viewing video imagery in real time.

A negative feature of H.264 is its somewhat reduced robustness. For example, if a frame drops because of bandwidth issues, the video could be adversely affected.

11.16.4   JPEG 2000

JPEG 2000 is a wavelet-based image compression standard and coding system.[4] It is known for its superior visual quality in contrast to H.264 and MPEG-2. JPEG 2000 can operate over a complete frame, while other compression schemes require the image to be broken up into smaller blocks, causing quality to diminish unevenly and vary within the frame. This creates the digital artifact known as blocking. Quality loss occurs evenly across the entire frame with JPEG 2000 and has visually beneficial effects relative to blocking.

Figure 11.13 shows the difference in bit rate for various compression algorithms. The x-axis indicates the bit rate after compression. The y-axis specifies image quality. Higher numbers indicate lower quality. The graph shows that JPEG 2000 outperforms MPEG-2 Intra throughout the bit-rate range and can scale to higher rates than H.264. At the low end of the bit-rate spectrum, H.264 outperforms JPEG 2000.

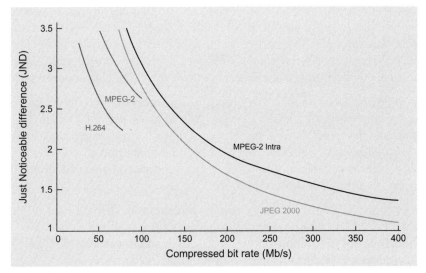

FIGURE 11.13

Bit rate and compression technology *(Used with permission from Koh, C. Broadcast Engineering. "Video Compression."* http://broadcastengineering.com/storage-amp-networking/video-compression.*)*

11.17   CCTV AND SECURITY SYSTEMS INTEGRATION

Chapter 9, Section 9.6 discussed the benefits of integrating physical security systems with Windows Active Directory. In addition, IP-based security systems provide opportunities to enhance controls based on physical and electronic security systems integration. Specifically, designating the physical access control system devices as objects within Windows Active Directory can facilitate highly customized and sophisticated security monitoring. For example and as noted previously, it would be possible to prevent an individual from logging onto a workstation unless that person has physically swiped his or her ID at a designated card reader. Imagine the surprise to piggybackers!

Other opportunities for enhanced monitoring exist by linking the physical access control and CCTV systems. A CCTV system with analytic software could be used to deny access at specific portals if the CCTV camera detected a high-risk individual who was known to be wearing a red sweater, blue blazer, etc.

One company, 3VR, advertises an analytics product that could be deployed in this way as part of its Advanced Object Tracking/Video Intelligence Platform. [5] It works by detecting physical features such as a specific color of clothing, object shape, etc., and storing these features in a database that can be queried. This obviates the need to search through the video imagery, which can be extremely laborious and time consuming.

Significant enhancement of monitoring might be achieved if a CCTV system with this capability is integrated with the physical access control system. Searching a structured database for a specific word that corresponds to a video image is much easier than searching the video imagery itself.

The resulting possibilities for enhanced security-risk monitoring and intelligent restriction are notable. For example, a CCTV camera could zoom and record activity at workstations where multiple passwords were attempted or if one attempted to plug into a network port with an unauthorized device.

If the security setup included a "swipe out" function (i.e., swipe an ID card at a card reader to exit a space), an integrated security solution could prevent logging on to a machine if he or she was physically located elsewhere (i.e., the person did not badge out from the original location).

In addition, the CCTV system could be used to locate a specific individual and restrict access and/or immediately identify his or her physical access history.

In general, physical access privileges and historical data from physical access control systems plus CCTV records can be tied to an organization's Windows Active Directory to ensure current access privileges are enforced. It also ensures that physical and electronic risk management efforts are aligned.

11.18 CCTV CABLING

Attention thus far has been paid to the optical and processing-related features of CCTV systems. Optics and image processing are clearly important, but CCTV performance also depends on the type of cable used to connect system components (assuming a wireless system is not in use), and is especially important when transmitting signals over significant distances.

Cabling can also represent a big driver of cost in a large security project and should be factored into the system-level analysis. In the next sections we will review the most common forms of cable used to interconnect CCTV components.

11.18.1　Coaxial Cable (Coax)

Coax has been the industry standard for CCTV for many years and was first introduced in 1929. A coax consists of a copper conductor surrounded by a polyethylene dielectric. Coaxial cable is called "coaxial" because it includes one physical channel (the copper core) that carries the signal surrounded by a concentric physical channel (a metallic foil or braid) and an outer cover or sheath, all running along the same axis. Hence the "co" prefix in the term, "coaxial."

The outer channel serves as a shield (or ground). The metal foil or braid reduces the effects of electromagnetic interference. In addition to promoting signal integrity, electromagnetic shielding helps deter adversaries from intercepting signals without authorization, although this is not necessarily its intended function. Figure 11.14 illustrates the anatomy of a coax cable. Various types of coax exist for use in CCTV. Table 11.14 specifies coax types and associated cable run distances.

An important feature of all electronic devices that connect to each other is their respective electrical impedance. The source or internal impedance refers to the opposition to alternating electrical current exhibited by the output terminals of a device due to a combination of resistance, inductance, and capacitance.

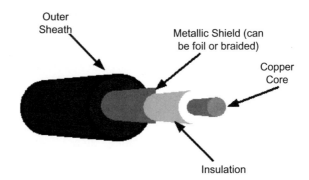

FIGURE 11.14

Coaxial cable. *(Source: Federal Highway Administration. "Fundamentals of Telecommunications."*
Telecommunications Handbook for Transportation Professionals: The Basics of Telecommunications.
http://ops.fhwa.dot.gov/publications/telecomm_handbook/chapter2_01.htm.)

Table 11.14 Coaxial Cable Types and Distance Specifications for CCTV Application

RG59/U	<225 m
RG6/U	Superior performance from 0-225 m
	OK performance from 225 to 545 m
RG11/U	>545 m

(Data from Access Communications Pty Ltd. "Coaxial Cables." http://www.accesscomms.com.au/reference/coax.htm.)

The source impedance of an electronic component will vary with frequency where electrical resistance is constant with frequency. As noted above, and this is worth repeating for emphasis, impedance is a key electrical parameter when interfacing electronic components. Moreover, interfacing electronic components is the whole point of using a cable.

If the output/internal impedance of a device does not match the impedance of a device that is connected to it at the frequency of operation, an impedance mismatch exists. Such mismatches result in an inefficient or ineffective transfer of power and can cause equipment to underperform or fail.

The vast majority of coaxial cables are either 50 or 75 ohm (Ω) characteristic impedance. The characteristic impedance of coax is determined by the ratio of the diameters of the shield and core wire plus the dielectric constant of the insulating material between the core wire and the shield. The CCTV industry selected 75-Ω as the characteristic impedance standard for coaxial cable.

A coaxial cable must be terminated at both ends of the cable with resistances that are equal to the cable characteristic impedance. That is, to prevent spurious reflections from impairing the picture, CCTV cameras that are intended to connect to 75-Ω coax must have an internal source impedance of 75-Ω, and likewise, monitors must be provided with a 75-Ω termination.

CCTV cameras should be configured for 75-Ω source impedances when delivered out of the box. But instances where this has not been the case have occurred and might explain problems experienced with a new unit. Some cameras have exhibited almost zero output impedance notwithstanding the fact that the specification sheets indicated 75-Ω.[6]

When CCTV impedance mismatches occur, signal "ghosts" and ringing effects become more evident as the length of the coaxial cable increases. The ringing effect (i.e., when a white-to-black or black-to-white transition in the picture is repeated many times in close succession) can occur with impedance mismatches even with short cable runs of 50 to 200 ft. Readily apparent ghosts are likely to appear when the cable approaches 500 to 1000 ft in length.

Another problem caused by a camera with zero source impedance when interfaced to a 75-Ω coax is that signals placed on the coax to control pan and tilt of the camera will be shorted out by the 0-Ω output of the camera and may cause affected systems to operate intermittently or fail.

The same intermittent or failed condition may be induced in other equipment that uses the same coaxial cable to transmit special control signals. The point is that such conditions can be caused by a CCTV camera with zero-output impedance and not by a failure in, say, the pan and tilt functions themselves.

Almost all CCTV cameras and monitors include coax connections. Requirements for additional impedance measurements should be a relative rarity, but it is useful to know how to recognize this condition. How can one be sure that a particular camera actually has 75-Ω output impedance and thereby confirm the listed specification?

The optimum solution is to test the output impedance before installation. This measurement cannot be made directly with a simple resistance measurement. This is due to the fact that the output impedance of a CCTV camera is not a static direct current (DC) resistance reading; it is a dynamic alternating current (AC) reactance measurement. The following is a prescription for measuring the output impedance of a CCTV camera[6]:

1. Connect the CCTV camera through a short, 75-Ω coaxial cable to an oscilloscope or waveform monitor.
2. Place a precision termination (i.e., 75 Ω±1 percent) at the oscilloscope or meter.
3. Measure the amplitude of the sync pulse with the termination in place. The sync pulse should read about 40 IRE[b] or 0.286 V peak-to-peak.
4. Remove the 75-Ω termination. The sync level will double (i.e., 80 IRE or 0.572 V peak-to-peak) if the camera has the correct source impedance. A defective camera will typically read the same amplitude with or without the termination in place.

The following formula can be used to calculate the precise source impedance:

$$S = \left(\frac{U - T}{T}\right) \times 75$$

---

[b]A brief explanation of units is required here. IRE is a unit used in the measurement of composite video signals. Its name is derived from the initials of the Institute of Radio Engineers. A value of 100 IRE is defined to be the range from black-to-white in a video signal. A value of 0 IRE corresponds to the zero voltage value during the blanking period. The CCTV sync pulse is normally 40 IRE below the zero value, so an all-white signal should equal 140 IRE peak-to-peak. http://en.wikipedia.org/wiki/IRE_(unit).

U = Unterminated reading of sync IRE or voltage.
T = Terminated reading of sync IRE or voltage.
S = Internal source termination in ohms.

The low attenuation and resistance to electromagnetic interference (EMI) of coax make it a popular choice for transmission distances up to 1500 ft. Longer distances are possible if repeaters are used in the transmission path. Both inbound video and outbound pan-tilt-zoom (PTZ) commands can travel over the same cable.

11.18.2   Unshielded Twisted Pair (UTP) Cable

Unshielded twisted pair (UTP) cable is relatively new in the CCTV industry, although the concept has been around for a long time. It is now the standard for data networks (e.g., Ethernet). In fact, the patent on twisted pair cabling is held by Alexander Graham Bell. Figure 11.15 illustrates twisted pair technology as presented in that patent.

UTP cable consists of a pair of insulated copper wires that are twisted together to improve transmission performance. The twisting reduces crosstalk and offers some protection against EMI, although it is not as effective as coax in this regard.

There are two types of UTP cables used for CCTV: Cat5 and Cat6. There are physical differences between the two, but the most important difference is that Cat5 is rated for signal bandwidths of 100 Mbps, Cat5e is rated for 350 Mbps, and Cat6 is rated at 1000 Mbps. Table 11.15 specifies various UTP cable categories, data rates, and applications.

UTP requires impedance matching to modify 75-Ω video signals for transport over 100-Ω UTP cable. This is done using a so-called balance-to-unbalanced element or "balun." Baluns are electronic devices that ensure the same impedance exists at the source and load. This in turn means that any electromagnetic interference will induce the same noise voltage on each of the two wires connecting circuit elements. Differential amplifiers work by amplifying voltage *differences*. Therefore a differential amplifier can eliminate this noise voltage since the difference in the noise across the terminals is zero.

One issue to consider when deploying UTP cable is that not all baluns permit pan-tilt-zoom (PTZ) commands to travel to the camera. UTP cable offers reasonable performance up to 1000 ft and longer if the baluns are powered (i.e., active).

UTP cable is increasingly becoming the cable of choice for integrated security systems where video, alarm monitoring, access control, and asset tracking are all carried over a single network. The small diameter, low weight, low cost, and broad usage in data transmission applications all contribute to the popularity of UTP cable relative to coax.

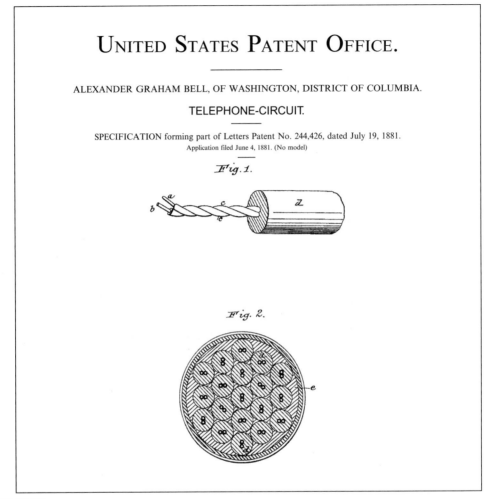

FIGURE 11.15

Alexander Graham Bell telephone circuit. *(Source: Patent number: 244426, Issue date: Jul 19, 1881. http://www.google.com/patents?id= DEBJAAAAEBAJ&printsec=abstract&zoom=4#v=onepage&q&f=false.)*

What about system performance over distance for various cable types? At 500 ft, coax delivers better signal quality to the monitor and the DVR than UTP cable. At 1000 ft, coax still offers better performance than UTP cable. However, at 3000 ft, coax performance drops off sharply. At 4000 ft, a CCTV system is unusable with either coax or UTP cable. Coax performance could be improved by using amplifiers along the cable route. However, another type of cable, fiber optics, offers the best performance at this distance. Fiber optic cable is discussed below.

As noted above, coax does not require impedance-matching electronics since the output impedance of CCTV cameras is matched to the characteristic impedance

Table 11.15 Unshielded Twisted Pair (UTP) Cable Types and Applications

Category	Maximum Data Rate	Typical Application
CAT1	Less than 1 Mbps	Analog Voice (POTS), basic rate ISDN, doorbell wiring
CAT2	4 Mbps	Primarily used for token ring networks
CAT3	16 Mbps	Voice and data, 10 Base-T Ethernet, basic telephone service
CAT4	20 Mbps	Used for 16 Mbps token ring
CAT5	100 Mbps up to 1 Gbps	10 Base-T, 100 Base-T (fast Ethernet), GigE, FDDI, 155 Mbps ATM
CAT5E	100 Mbps	FDDI, ATM, CCTV
CAT6	Greater than 100 Mbps	Broadband applications (e.g., CCTV)
CAT7	Emerging standard	GigE plus

POTS = plain old telephone service; ISDN = integrated services for digital network; FDDI = fiber distributed data interface; ATM = asynchronous transfer mode.
(Source: Federal Highway Administration. Telecommunications Handbook for Transportation Professionals: The Basics of Telecommunications. "Fundamentals of Telecommunications." http://ops.fhwa.dot.gov/publications/telecomm_handbook/chapter2_01.htm.)

of the cable. Therefore, coax has fewer connection points that could lead to signal loss or breakdown. It is also well-shielded against EMI. Coax also tends to introduce fewer digital artifacts than UTP.

UTP disadvantages are that impedance-matching electronics are required, and UTP offers reduced protection against EMI relative to coax or fiber. Higher category UTP (e.g., Cat6) offers somewhat better EMI protection than medium-to-lower category UTP (e.g., Cat3).

Legacy CCTV systems often utilize coax for connecting system components. Therefore, rewiring with UTP cable can represent a cost-prohibitive barrier to upgrading to IP-based technology. Note that technology is now available that allows IP-based systems to be used with coaxial cable (e.g., *http://www.nitek.net/solutions/ip-cameras-over-coax.html*).

Finally, if it were not for the cost of electro-optical impedance-matching electronics, fiber optic cable would be the overwhelming choice for CCTV applications, especially when long distance transmission is required given the low rate of attenuation.

11.18.3 Fiber Optic Cable

Fiber optic cable uses light as the communication signal. The cable itself consists of an inner glass core that is surrounded by a sheath known as a cladding. The cladding has a lower index of refraction than the glass core. The light remains confined to the core as a result of a phenomenon known as total internal reflection. Total internal reflection occurs because of differences in the core and cladding indexes of refraction, n_1 and n_2, respectively and is based on a principle known as Snell's Law.

If the ratio of refractive indices n_2/n_1 is less than unity (i.e., n_2 is less than n_1), where n_2 is the index of refraction of the cladding and n_1 is the index of refraction of glass, there will be a "critical" angle of incidence above which the angle of refraction is always greater than 90 degrees. When this is true, none of the incident light is transmitted through the glass and all of it is reflected. When this condition holds, total internal reflection occurs. The condition for the critical angle, θ_c, is

$$\theta_c = \sin^{-1}(n_2/n_1)$$

Figure 11.16 depicts the anatomy of a fiber optic cable.

Various modes of propagation in the core can be supported as a result of the fiber geometry although single mode fibers do exist. Figure 11.17 depicts light

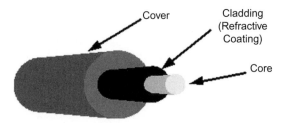

FIGURE 11.16
Fiber optic cable. *(Source: Federal Highway Administration. Telecommunications Handbook for Transportation Professionals: The Basics of Telecommunications. "Fundamentals of Communications." http://ops.fhwa.dot.gov/publications/telecomm_handbook/chapter2_01.htm.)*

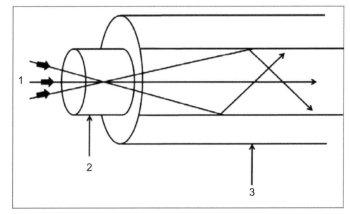

FIGURE 11.17
Total internal reflection of light in a fiber optic cable. *(Source: Shah, R.Y. and Y.K. Agrawal. Open I. National Institutes of Health. "Introduction to Fiber Optics: Sensors for Biomedical Applications." http://openi.nlm .nih.gov/detailedresult.php?img=3224405_IJPhS-73-17-g001&req=4.)*

launched at one end of a fiber and then propagating within the core as a result of total internal reflection.

Fiber optic cable maintains signal integrity over significant distances. Attenuation of a signal within coax at 5 MHz can be 20 dB/km where fiber optic cable varies between 0.3 and 3 dB/km.[7] As a result, links over 60 km can be achieved with fiber over multiple frequencies. This allows for long distance transmission of multiple signals.

We now know that fiber optic cables are made of glass and transmit visible or infrared light. They do not rely on currents resulting from an applied voltage. Hence, they are immune to electromagnetic interference as well as ground loops, where the latter are caused by differences in the potential between terminal equipment ground connections.

Since the electromagnetic signal (i.e., light) in fiber optic cables is confined to the glass fiber core, they do not radiate electromagnetic energy. So they are inherently more secure than cables that support the propagation of electric currents with fluxing magnetic fields. The magnitude of the magnetic flux density is directly proportional to the current, but varies inversely and non-linearly with the distance from the cable.

We know from Chapter 7 that all electric currents generate magnetic fields. These fields do not remain completely confined within coax or UTP cables (Note: coax typically provides better shielding). Although fiber could potentially be compromised if physical access to the cable is achieved, remote signal collection by an adversary is not possible if the fiber optic cable is functioning properly.

Fiber optic cable is considerably smaller than coax. The bare glass fiber itself is 0.125 mm in diameter. The diameter of a single fiber core patch lead is 3 mm, and an 8-fiber bundle is 3 mm. Contrast this with the 6.5-mm diameter of a 75-Ω coax copper cable. Therefore, optical fiber is well-suited to scenarios where space is limited and weight is a concern. Table 11.16 specifies various fiber optic parameters of interest. Table 11.17 summarizes key performance characteristics of coax, UTP, and fiber optic cable for CCTV applications.

Table 11.16 Fiber Optic Parameters

Core Diameter (Microns)	Numerical Aperture	Attenuation at 850 nm (dB/km)	Attenuation at 1300 nm	Attenuation at 1550 nm	Bandwidth at 850 nm (MHz/km)	Bandwidth at 1300 nm	Bandwidth at 1550 nm
8	0.11	N/A	0.5	0.3	-	-	-
50	0.20	3.0	1.2	N/A	400	600	N/A
62.5	0.275	3.5	1.5	N/A	160	500	N/A
(Data from Impath Networks. http://iMPathnetworks.com/site/media/IMPath/GuidetoCCTV.pdf.)							

Table 11.17 Comparison of Performance Characteristics for CCTV Cable Types

	Cable Diameter (inches)	Cable Weight (lb/1000 inches)	Attenuation @ 5 MHz (dB/100 inches)	Shielding (dB)	Rated Distance (feet)
Mini coax	0.146	16	1.3	80	350
RG 59 coax	0.242	35	0.58	80	750
RG 6 coax	0.272	42	0.47	80	1500
Cat 5e UTP (passive)	0.2	20.9	1.22	40	1000
Cat 5e UTP (active)	0.2	20.9	1.22	40	3000
Fiber (multimode)	0.13 × 0.23	13.5	< 0.5	N/A	6500

(Data from Wessels, R. Uniprise Solutions. "Choosing the Correct Cable for Security CCTV." http://www.gocsc.com/uploads/white_papers/e0690f07348745f68d22dba7ccb798ab.pdf.)

11.19   CCTV SIGNAL SECURITY

Since UTP cables are often the transmission medium for CCTV in networked environments such as Ethernet, it is instructive to estimate their vulnerability to interception. Consider an insider who has been coopted by a terrorist organization that is interested in viewing or disrupting what appears on a facility's CCTV monitors, but the insider cannot physically access the monitors directly.

What specific aspect of a CCTV signal might be a target for interception? In other words, what would give an adversary cause for optimism with respect to successful signal interception and demodulation? Consider the flat-panel display used by most CCTV systems. They work by storing interlaced and non-interlaced video lines in digital memory. They require video information not only as binary-encoded shades of color but also as a sequence of discrete pixel values.

Flat-panel displays digitally buffer only a few pixel rows. The entire image is stored in the frame buffer of the video controller. Therefore, flat-panel video interfaces have to continuously refresh the entire image between 60 and 85 times per second. This continuous refreshment of the image ensures that the signals on the video interface are periodic, at least between changes in the displayed information. Periodic signal features represent the Holy Grail to those looking to conduct covert signal collection.

A periodic signal has a frequency spectrum that consists of narrow lines spaced by the repetition frequency (i.e., if the signal peaks are separated in the time domain by t seconds, they will be separated by $1/t$ in the frequency domain). A covert receiver could attempt to suppress all other spectral content by periodic averaging with that precise repetition frequency, thereby lifting the signal emanating from cables and/or connectors out of the background noise.[8] Noise is the bane of overt and covert signal processors.

Let's assume an unshielded twisted pair (UTP) cable, which in fact does provide some shielding as noted in Table 11.15, is used to route CCTV signals via Ethernet. The signal frequency is 5 MHz, and the cable voltage is at 2.5 V with an impedance of 100 Ω. Therefore, according to Ohm's law the current in the cable is 0.025 A (amperes). From Ampere's law, a current-carrying wire produces a magnetic flux density, B in units of webers per meter squared (Wb/m²).

Specifically, at a distance of a meters and I amperes, this flux density equals $(2 \times 10^{-7})I/a$.[c] So the magnetic flux density at a distance of 1 m from a wire carrying 0.025 A of current equals 5×10^{-9} Wb/m². The terrorist uses a simple pickup device similar to the one shown in Figure 11.18, but he will likely need to do some signal averaging to suppress noise as noted above.

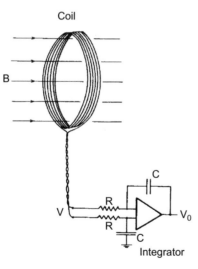

Magnetic field measurements

FIGURE 11.18
Simple magnetic field pick-up coil. *(Source: Wurden, G.A., C.W. Barnes, and K.F. Schoenberg. "Steady-State Position Control for the Tokamak Physics Experiment (TPX). http://wsx.lanl.gov/tpx/steady.html.)*

---

[c] The magnetic field will actually decrease $\sim 1/a^6$ because at a distance of 1 m the loop is well within the near-field or $c/2\pi f = 10$ m. However, we will assume optimum conditions for the terrorist so that the falloff decreases by only $1/a$.

Since the voltage $\sim -d\emptyset/dt$ as sensed by the coil, the changing magnetic flux could be integrated with respect to time to determine the magnetic field corresponding to the CCTV signal.

To make life modestly easier we will assume a favorable geometry. To that end, let's assume the terrorist's antenna is circular in shape with a modestly covert radius of 0.1 m (about 4 in) and is positioned so that the magnetic flux through the loop is a maximum (i.e., the plane of the loop is facing the wire). Since the dimensions of the loop are much smaller than a wavelength of the magnetic flux, we can safely assume the field does not vary over the loop diameter.

The change in magnetic flux passing through the loop induces a voltage. This is the principle of electromagnetic induction. The magnetic flux density, B, at 5 MHz is given by the following expression:

$$B = 5 \times 10^{-9} \sin(2\pi \times 5 \times 10^6 \, t) = 5 \times 10^{-9} \sin(31.4 \times 10^6 \, t) \, \text{Wb/m}^2$$

The area of the loop is $\pi r^2 = 0.03 \, \text{m}^2$.

$$\text{Therefore, the flux, } \emptyset \text{ through the loop} = 0.03 \times 5 \times 10^{-9} \sin(31.4 \times 10^6 \, t) \, \text{Wb}$$
$$= 0.15 \times 10^{-9} \sin(31.4 \times 10^6 \, t) \, \text{Wb}$$

The electromotive force (emf) induced in the single coil is given by

$$-(10^{-8})d\emptyset/dt = \text{the time rate of change of flux through the coil}$$
$$= -(10^{-8}) \times 0.15 \times 10^{-9} \times 31.4 \times 10^6 \cos(31.4 \times 10^6 \, t) \, \text{volts}$$
$$= -4.7 \times 10^{-11} \, \text{volts (at the maximum point in the cycle)}$$

This is indeed a small number, but our terrorist is no dummy. He understands that to improve the performance of his covert detection device one can construct a solenoid consisting of high permeability material, μ, surrounded by N turns of wire. This has the effect of concentrating the lines of magnetic flux and thereby inducing a greater voltage.

Let's assume the following parameters for the terrorist's coil antenna. The material used to concentrate magnetic flux has a magnetic permeability relative to air of 25,000 (e.g., a material consisting of 50 to 80 percent iron and nickel), 5 MHz signal frequency corresponding to the CCTV Ethernet signal, the same induced voltage as calculated above for a single loop of wire, and $N = 1000$ turns of wire.

These parameters are actually optimistic from the terrorist's point of view since the demagnetization factor of the magnetic material would likely decrease the permeability. My colleague Dave Chang has pointed out that the effective permeability depends on both the relative area and length dimensions of the core and on the 1/3 power of the ratio of the winding length to core length. In addition, the permeability is greatly affected by the ratio of the length-to-diameter of the magnetic field concentrator.

Figure 11.19 plots the permeability of a ferrite rod versus the effective permeability for a range of length-to-diameter ratios (from 1 to 100). The plot shows

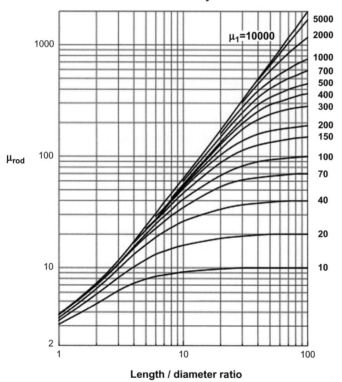

FIGURE 11.19

The permeability of a ferrite rod versus the effective permeability for a range of length-to-diameter ratios (from 1 to 100). *(Source: National Magnetics Group, Inc. "Effective Permeability of Ferrite Rods." http://magneticsgroup.com/pdf/erods.pdf.)*

that for small length-to-diameter ratio, the effective permeability is much much smaller than the intrinsic permeability of the ferrite rod.

However, we assume the worst case from the defender's perspective, so the induced voltage is given by

$$-10^{-8}N\mu\, d\varnothing/dt = -4.7\times1000\times25{,}000\times10^{-11}$$
$$= -117.75\times10^{6}\times10^{-11}$$
$$\sim -10^{-3}V = 1\,mV$$

One millivolt is a decent signal that could be demodulated by even the most pedestrian receiver.

But life is not so easy for the terrorist in spite of his cleverness. Terrorists must contend with the presence of noise just like the rest us. Such noise derives from a variety of sources, and it is a corrupting influence on all electromagnetic signals. The terrestrial and cosmic noise density at 5 MHz is roughly 30 dB/kHz relative to 1 μV/m.[9][d]

Therefore, we calculate the electric field strength due to the ambient noise to be 0.16 V/m. If the circumference of the circular loop is 0.63 m, the interfering noise voltage is about 0.10 V. Therefore, the magnitude of the noise power would dominate the signal power at this frequency.

The terrorist could invoke signal processing such as the coherent detection scheme mentioned at the beginning of the section in an attempt to dig out the signal from the noise. The signal-to-noise ratio is $10^{-2}=-40\,dB$. Therefore, + 50 dB of processing gain would be required to achieve 10 dB of signal margin, the minimum for successful detection.

Fortunately, life gets even worse for the terrorist. Referencing Table 11.15, we observe that an unshielded twisted pair does provide some shielding. According to the chart there is 40 dB of electromagnetic signal attenuation. (Note: the quoted figure of 40 dB attenuation actually specifies the level of immunity of the cable signal from *external* interference, but the existing shielding also acts to reduce signal leakage.)

So the radiated magnetic flux density due to the current in the unshielded twisted pair CCTV cable at 1 m is actually reduced by a factor of 100 in voltage since 40 dB = 20 log(V_1/V_2). Therefore, log(V_1/V_2) = 2 so V_1 = 100 V_2.

---

[d]Since signal power is what the terrorist's receiver measures, and power scales as voltage squared, then dB = 10 log [(V_1/V_2)²] = 20 log(V_1/V_2).

The presence of UTP shielding would attenuate the terrorist's 1-mV signal to roughly 10^{-5} volts or $10\,\mu V$, which translates to a S/N of 10^{-4} at the frequency of interest. Based on this rough estimate, the radiated signal from the unshielded twisted pair cable is at a relatively low risk of remote compromise at a distance of 1 m from the cable.

11.20   CCTV OPERATIONAL SUMMARY

It is critical that the required resolution and other performance specifications align with stated operational requirements. Rules of thumb and back-of-the-envelope calculations as specified in this chapter can help determine ballpark estimates of system performance which are driven by drive operational requirements. As noted above, online calculators can take some of the pain out of these calculations, but it is important to appreciate the basic science and key technical features.

There are certain fundamental features that apply to CCTV technology in general. The following are high-level principles and factoids associated with CCTV technology that are relevant to CCTV systems:

1. If a digital video recorder (DVR) is used, the analog-to-digital converted image is stored on a disk.
2. If a network video recorder (NVR) is used, the digital-to-IP converted image is stored on a network storage device (e.g., RAID hard drive) or server.
3. The higher the resolution (i.e., more pixels-per-frame), the more storage space is required.
4. The higher the frame rate, the more storage is required for an equivalent number of pixels-per-image.
5. Motion detection/activation should be invoked to conserve storage.
6. Video compression, using the H.264 or M-JPEG compression algorithms, for example, should be invoked to conserve storage, although there are differences in the resulting bandwidth among each of these options.
7. CCD sensor size and lens focal length are key camera specifications.
8. A variable focus 3.8- to 9.5-mm focal length lens is ideal for monitoring hallways, doorways, and average size rooms.
9. 5- to 50-mm focal length lenses are appropriate for monitoring hallways and doorways, but these can be adjusted to monitor long passageways or areas several hundred feet from the camera.
10. The field-of-view is inversely related to focal length, i.e., the longer the focal length, the narrower the field-of-view.
11. Wide lens apertures imply narrow depths of field and conversely.

12. Illuminate to 10× the minimum brightness required to observe an image.
13. Resolution is a function of the density of pixels across the field-of-view in addition to the mode of scanning. A minimum suggested pixel density for higher-resolution requirements and megapixel cameras is 40 pixels-per-foot across the horizontal field-of-view.
14. For submegapixel cameras, 4 CIF (UK/Europe) and 4 SIF (North America) should be the minimum image resolution.
15. 7.5 fps is frequently quoted as the minimum required recording rate for CCTV.
16. Be aware of the impact of frame rate and resolution on system bandwidth and image storage requirements.
17. Plan for day and nighttime operation; ensure adequate lighting (e.g., minimum 20 lx intensity) or infrared illumination at night.

11.21 SPECIAL CCTV SYSTEM REQUIREMENTS

11.21.1 Wide Area Coverage

Operational requirements dictate the specifications for CCTV systems and for any security technology, for that matter. We observed that CCTV coverage of a wide scene could drive a requirement to install numerous cameras or perhaps a lesser number of high-resolution units. Each of these approaches has cost implications associated with hardware, installation, bandwidth, and storage.

There is no fooling Mother Nature, as the expression goes. The laws of physics dictate how camera lenses function, and the number of pixels per unit length across the field-of-view significantly affect resolution. This resolution requirement may limit options for CCTV deployment since it directly affects the number of required cameras for a given scenario.

However, a clever system has been developed in the UK that takes a different operational approach and has produced a less resource-intensive system. Specifically, the company is called Viseum (*www.viseum.co*). The system they have developed is for wide-area coverage, but it does not continuously record activity across the entire area to be monitored.

In practice, the Viseum system can be used to identify and record a particular event at a specific location at an instant in time. Specifically, the recording camera (i.e., the PTZ) captures discrete images among the continuous motion in the panorama. It does not continuously capture all activity unless an object happens to be the only entity moving within the 360-degree field-of-view. How does it do this?

The Viseum system consists of five or six high-resolution and stationary cameras that are arranged in a circle to provide a 360-degree field-of-view (i.e., ~ 60 degrees per camera) in a horizontal plane. These cameras are programmed to detect motion, and their function is to direct a PTZ camera that sits above the circular array of cameras. The PTZ camera continuously moves in response to the detected motion. So envision the PTZ constantly moving in three dimensions to capture movement detected in the 360-degree field-of-view of the fixed array.

The streaming video output of the PTZ is the only camera being recorded by the NVR, thereby limiting bandwidth and storage requirements. In crowded scenarios with significant motion, the Viseum system is only capturing events that occur at a moment in time and then moving on to the next detected motion. However, this ephemeral glimpse of activity is enough to confirm where and when an incident occurred and, depending on the optical parameters, who is in the area at the time of an incident.

Table 11.18 compares the coverage of a Viseum system with very high-resolution cameras that record continuously.

According to the referenced source, the data in Table 11.15 implies that as many as ten megapixel cameras are required to achieve the same coverage as one Viseum unit. Of course, it is important to reiterate that the Viseum is not recording all motion at all times in the field-of-view since the recorded output only derives from the pan-tilt-zoom camera. With respect to bandwidth and storage, Table 11.19 illustrates the significant savings offered by Viseum.

Table 11.18 Performance of Traditional Megapixel Cameras Versus Viseum

Coverage (degrees)	Visual Identification Distance (m)	Visual Identification Distance (m)
	Megapixel Camera	*Viseum System*
360	14	61
180	28	61

(Data from Monitor. http://www.viseum.co.uk/wp-pdf/The-Viseum-IMC-compared-with-megapixel-cameras.pdf)

Table 11.19 Comparison of Bandwidth and Storage Requirements for Viseum and Megapixel Cameras with 180-Degree Coverage

	Coverage (degrees)	Bandwidth (Mbps)	Storage for 30 Days (TB)
Megapixel cameras	180	76	12
Viseum	180	6.4	1.0

(Data from Monitor. http://www.viseum.co.uk/wp-pdf/The-Viseum-IMC-compared-with-megapixel-cameras.pdf)

11.21.2 Nighttime Monitoring

Nighttime operation of CCTV systems presents its own challenges to visual monitoring and requires specific technology. Since camera lenses and optics require visible light to function under normal operating conditions, the absence of light renders a traditional camera useless.

Traditional CCTV lenses and associated electronics are designed for use at visible wavelengths. Artificial lighting is typically provided to ensure appropriate illumination of a scene of interest, and a minimum of 20 lx of intensity is specified in the visible portion of the spectrum (see Section 11.22, "CCTV System Performance Specifications").

Fortunately, lenses and electronics that function at infrared wavelengths exist. Infrared radiation is discussed in Chapter 12 in connection with passive infrared detectors. Figure 7.18 shows where infrared energy resides in the electromagnetic spectrum.

Infrared CCTV should not be confused with thermal imaging. The latter exploits the fact that humans radiate energy at a wavelength of about 10 μm. In that case, the object being viewed is the source of optical energy, and it is that energy that is detected by an infrared sensor. In contrast, infrared CCTV uses illuminators that actively radiate infrared light that reflects off objects in the field-of-view.

The distance between the illuminator and the object under illumination is an important operational issue. In fact, the inverse square law that was first introduced in Chapter 4 applies once again since the illuminator can be considered a point source of light. Therefore, if the distance between source and illuminated object is x and the light intensity is I, at a distance of $2x$ the illuminating infrared light intensity is $I/4$. At a distance of $3x$ the intensity will be $I/9$, etc.

However, the illuminating intensity or "illuminance" is also impacted by the angle of illumination. Specifically, the intensity of reflected light resulting from the illumination of a diffuse target will be proportional to the cosine of the incident angle and the reflectance of the target. So, at an angle of 0 degrees (i.e., the illuminator directly faces the object), the cosine is unity, so the reflected intensity is only a function of the distance from the source according to the inverse square law (i.e., $1/r^2$).

However, at an angle of 90 degrees, the intensity of the reflected light will be 0 since no light will impinge on the object. For all illumination angles between 0 and 90 degrees, the intensity will decrease according to the inverse square law multiplied by the cosine of the angle between illuminator and object.

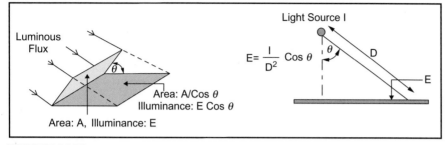

FIGURE 11.20

Cosine Law of illumination. *(Source: Security Camera World. "Infrared Illumination, How Far Does Your Light Shine?* http://www.securitycameraworld.com/Technical-Articles/infrared-illumination.asp.)

Note that this is only true for a diffuse reflector. If a very highly reflective surface is encountered, virtually no energy will be reflected back along the incident light path to the camera. This is why a mirror may appear black when viewed at an angle. Figure 11.20 illustrates the geometry of illumination and the Cosine Law.

The camera spectral response (i.e., response as a function of wavelength) relative to the illuminating source is another important operational feature. A high-power infrared illuminator generally consists of a tungsten halogen bulb, which as a result of its operating temperature emits a high proportion of light in both the infrared and visible portions of the spectrum. See Chapter 12 regarding the relation between an object's temperature and the wavelength of radiated energy. Some longer-life infrared illuminators use quartz halogen bulbs.

In front of the light source is a filter that blocks visible wavelengths, which are below the infrared portion of the spectrum. Recall that infrared wavelengths are longer than their visible neighbors in the electromagnetic spectrum. Infrared filters have different wavelength cutoffs. The most common varieties allow wavelengths greater than 715 nm (nanometers) (i.e., $10^{-9}\,\text{m} = 1\,\text{nm}$) to pass.

If optimum camera performance is to be achieved, it is necessary to match the camera spectral response to that of the filtered light source. The important area of the spectrum in terms of camera effectiveness is where the camera response overlaps with the infrared-filtered lamp response.

The camera sensor effectively integrates all the wavelengths of light falling on it within the response curve. Therefore, the camera sensitivity to reflected infrared radiation relates to the area where the respective camera sensor and infrared filter spectral response curves overlap, and not the camera response at a filter threshold.

This is why one must know the shape of both the camera and infrared filter spectral response curves in order to predict infrared CCTV performance. To reiterate, it is not the height or amplitude of the response curve at the filter cutoff that determines performance, but rather the area enclosed by the overlap of the camera and illuminator response curves.

Figure 11.21 shows the spectral response for two cameras relative to an infrared (IR) illuminator with an 830-nm filter cutoff. Camera A responds only in the visible portion of the spectrum, but Camera B's spectral response extends further into the infrared and overlaps with the spectrum of the IR-filtered illumination lamp.

Finally, the wavelengths of the illuminating light source will determine its relative covertness as noted below:

- 715 to 730 nm: overt infrared—produces a soft red glow.
- 815 to 850 nm: semicovert infrared—produces a faint red glow faintly visible to the human eye.
- 940 to 950 nm: covert infrared—invisible to the human eye.

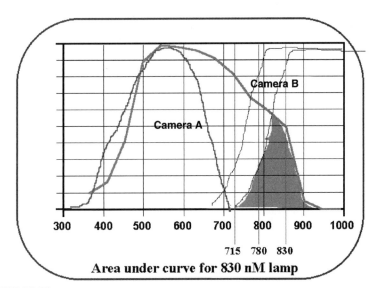

FIGURE 11.21

Infrared CCTV camera and illuminator spectral response. *(Used with permission from Security Camera World. "Infrared Illumination, How Far Does Your Light Shine?* http://www.securitycameraworld.com/Technical-Articles/infrared-illumination.asp.)*

11.22   CCTV SYSTEM PERFORMANCE SPECIFICATIONS

11.22.1   Optical Features

1. Implement full area coverage for the space being monitored.
2. Capture additional detail for areas with limited fields-of-view (e.g., doors or portals) according to stated operational requirements.
3. Optical resolution requirement: minimum of 40 pixels-per-foot of the relevant dimension of the field-of-view.
4. Display color images.

11.22.2   CCTV System Architecture[e]

1. Implement IP- and NVR-based systems in conjunction with IP cameras.
2. If analog cameras must be maintained from a legacy system or where IP devices are contraindicated based on security considerations, card reader outputs should interface with an IP encoder that is mounted within a secure area that connects to an NVR.
3. Video storage should be scalable to support significantly more than the minimum number of cameras. Note this figure will depend on the size and number of facilities.
4. If utilizing the IT network to route CCTV signals, segregate these devices using a firewall or router to create a VLAN. If this is not viable due to system limitations, a dedicated, TCP/IP-based network should be installed with the capacity to handle all networked physical security devices. Additional electronic controls should be implemented according to security best practices and the assessed risk.

11.22.3   Security Incident Triggering and Interfacing

1. Contact trigger inputs (one per camera) to provide for activation by external devices.
2. Instant replay on alarms associated with a security event should include pre- and postevent-triggered recordings for up to 1 hr.
3. In the event of a trigger-activated input, a replay loop sequence will be initiated consisting of a sequence of pre- and post-event images replayed continuously in a loop.

---

[e]Much of this material was provided courtesy of Roger Pike, RPA Ltd., UK.

4. A live image from the camera will also be displayed, thereby allowing the user to view the current security situation.
5. The pre- and post-event time will be user-definable on a per-camera basis.
6. In the event of an alarm, an image sequence will be displayed on the screen within 1 s of the alarm being received in the security control room or monitoring point.
7. Utilize alarm stacking so new alarms will be held in a stack for sequential review.
8. Provide for an audio alarm that is generated in the control room or monitoring point based on the triggering of an alarm input.
9. Include video-loss detection with continuous confirmation of the integrity of video inputs. An alarm should be generated with associated screen text that should appear at the monitoring point when a "healthy" video input signal is lost.
10. Implement record-on-motion capability with sensitivity suited to specified operational requirements.

11.22.4 CCTV Image Recording

1. Provide for separate recorded video streams in high definition television (HDTV) (minimum 1280×720) resolution at 15 fps that is activated on motion, and 1 fps at a minimum of 4 CIF (704×480) otherwise, using H.264 or Motion JPEG compression over a TCP/IP protocol-based network.
2. The aforementioned frame rate and resolution specifications apply *on a per-camera basis.*
3. Provide quality imagery under anticipated ambient lighting conditions to achieve the stated operational requirement and provide supplementary lighting to establish a minimum 20 lx intensity level.
4. Provide for audio detection, transmission, and recording based on risk and operational requirements.

11.22.5 CCTV System Security, Resilience, and Additional Features

1. Imagery should be stored for a minimum of 31 days with overwriting on a first-in/first-overwrite basis.
2. Provide secure data backup for 31 days.
3. Support color and black/white in the event of low-light conditions.

4. Adjust capture rate and resolution on a per-camera basis, but the system should not exceed the total rate allotted across all cameras on the network.
5. Provide for separately selectable recording intervals for each camera.
6. Ensure the system is compatible with an organization's IT-network infrastructure and operating system.
7. Include date and time search, alarm list search, bookmarked search, and motion search. Consider enhanced video analytic software to facilitate searching (e.g., 3VR; see Section 11.17).
8. Utilize continuous (time lapse) recording, event/alarm recording, and pre- and postevent recording.
9. Include dual-mode recording (i.e., a camera records at one rate/resolution (typically lower) and then increases to a higher rate based on detection of activity).
10. Use dome fixtures for indoor use and sufficiently robust units for outdoor deployments.
11. Images should be exportable via the network or removable storage media (e.g., USB storage drive, DVD) to include an audit trail with time, date, camera name, and number indicated within the data. Note that this capability carries profound information security risks and should be permitted only if implemented in a manner consistent with an organization's information security policy and standards.
12. IP-based devices should not be installed in publicly accessible spaces. Use analog devices that link to appropriately secured IP encoders. If an IP-based device must be installed in a public space, MAC address restrictions, antitampering, and network end-point protection should be implemented.
13. Provide for an appropriately secure encryption standard (e.g., AES 256) in support of signal transmission and storage.
14. Utilize physical tamperproofing for devices and cabling. Restrict electronic access to CCTV ports via MAC address filtering and other end point controls.
15. Secure NVRs and DVRs with appropriate physical security controls and auditing of physical access. See the "Data Center Security Standard" in Section 9.4.

11.22.6   CCTV System Security Risk Metrics

1. Mean time between equipment failures.
2. Number of devices that do not meet the stated performance specifications based on a security risk assessment.
3. A recorded history of security incidents to include time of incident, date of incident, incident type, incident location, and incident disposition.

SUMMARY

CCTV is a key control in almost any modern counterterrorism strategy. It has significant value as a forensic tool as well as for remotely viewing the details of an incident or suspected incident in real time.

There are two main types of CCTV systems: analog and Internet Protocol (IP). Analog systems are actually digital devices since the image plane contains a charge-coupled device (CCD) that converts the analog signal to tiny dots or pixels. The CCD sensor is analogous to the retina in the human eye. Both analog and IP cameras use CCDs, and the number of pixels across their horizontal and vertical dimensions is an important factor in determining image resolution.

CCTV cameras use lenses to create an image, and lenses obey the laws of optics. Concepts like signal-to-noise ratio, sensitivity, depth-of-field, focal length, angle-of-view, and width of the field-of-view are central to understanding CCTV system performance.

In particular, the expression for the horizontal field-of-view is important in developing an analytic if intuitive appreciation for CCTV performance relative to stated operational requirements. The expression for the horizontal field-of-view, W, is given by the following approximate expression:

$$W \sim D \times CCD_w / f$$

D = distance from the object to the lens.
CCD_w = width of the CCD sensor. (Note: if the vertical field-of-view is of interest, then CCD_w in the expression is replaced by the vertical dimension of the CCD sensor, CCD_v)
f = lens focal length.

Megapixel cameras are so named because the images produced by these devices consist of millions of pixels. The number of pixels in the image in conjunction with the method of scanning (i.e., interlaced or progressive), determines the resolution. Because of their high-resolution capability, a useful metric for megapixel cameras is the number of pixels-per-foot in the horizontal or vertical dimensions depending on the viewing requirement. Forty pixels-per-foot is suggested as the threshold for higher-resolution requirements.

If a pixel-per-foot resolution metric is established, and the number of pixels in the CCD sensor is known, it is easy to determine the maximum width of the field-of-view for a given camera. This is given by the following expression:

$$\text{Horizontal Field-of-view} = (\# \text{Horizontal CCD Pixels})/(\text{Pixel Density})$$

This expression allows one to determine the minimum number of megapixel cameras required to cover a given scene at the specified camera resolution. An analogous expression exists for the vertical field-of-view.

There are a number of operational features and performance specifications associated with CCTV systems. Required features will vary according to the operational requirements. In addition, specialized cameras exist that are capable of providing higher-resolution imagery and extensive areal coverage using a combination of multiple fixed cameras in conjunction with a pan-tilt-zoom (PTZ) device. Active illumination of a scene with infrared light and special infrared detection equipment will sometimes be required for nighttime CCTV operation.

REFERENCES

[1] Arazi G. Camera-to-NVR ratio for recording. White paper, Vicon; 2005. viconsecurity.com.

[2] Axis Communications. Resolutions. http://www.axis.com/products/video/about_networkvideo/resolution.htm.

[3] CCTV Chat. IP cameras and megapixel cameras for facial identification. http://www.cctvchat.com/archive/index.php/t-464.html?s=f950854892b164f1148110683ba36f60.

[4] Koh C, Broadcast Engineering. Video compression. http://broadcastengineering.com/storage-amp-networking/video-compression.

[5] 3VR. Advanced object tracking. http://www.3vr.com/products/videoanalytics/advancedobjecttracking.

[6] McClatchie FF, FM Sytems, Inc. Why and how to measure CCTV camera output impedance. http://www.fmsystems-inc.com/manuals/CCTVTERMart.pdf.

[7] Impath Networks. http://iMPathnetworks.com/site/media/IMPath/GuidetoCCTV.pdf.

[8] Kuhn M. Electromagnetic eavesdropping risks of flat-panel displays. In: Workshop on Privacy Enhancing Technologies, 26–28 May, Toronto, Canada; 2004.

[9] Bianchi C, Meloni A. Natural and man-made terrestrial electromagnetic noise: an outlook. Ann Geophys June 2007;50(3). http://www.earth-prints.org/bitstream/2122/3674/1/11bianchi.pdf.

Problems

1. As the newly appointed security director of a large urban facility you are shocked to learn that your predecessor had not established any performance specifications for physical security infrastructure. Therefore, your first task is to develop such specifications for the CCTV system. To that end, indicate the appropriate optical characteristics to provide identification-level resolution for the following scenarios. Be as quantitative and specific as possible. You have carte blanche to specify the ambient conditions and CCTV system characteristics (e.g., pixel-per-foot for the horizontal field-of-view, distance from camera to object, ambient light level, etc.) and any other scenario-specific parameters, but you must justify the chosen system specifications based on operational requirements.
   a. Door entrance.
   b. Long corridor.
   c. Parking lot.
   d. Office space.
   e. Lobby area.

2. You are the head of physical security technology for a major investment bank. The new corporate headquarters requires significant visual monitoring, and your security strategy includes the installation of hundreds of IP cameras. You anticipate significant pushback on many levels, but most assuredly this will cause angst among the IT network team that must provide adequate bandwidth and electronic storage to accommodate the data so generated. Specify how various system parameters and/or features might be adjusted to limit the bandwidth/storage requirements of the system. Indicate what effect, if any, such adjustments could have on the risk profile and what you might do in terms of compensating controls.

3. The physical access control system in your facility indicates an alarm when there is a "forced door" or "door held open" condition detected. As expected, heavily trafficked areas are subject to numerous false alarms. The vast majority of these are false positives. Indicate a strategy to deal with this issue and specify how CCTV could play a role (or not). Explicitly discuss the cost versus benefit to your organization with respect to any proposed strategy.

4. You are the Security Director of a large company contemplating the construction of a new facility. You have been asked to provide a security strategy to the building designers. To that end, you have designated the lobby of your building as a "high risk" area in the security strategy. Create a rough sketch of an indicative building lobby. Indicate camera types based on their position (e.g., camera type "a" covering a key area, camera type "b" covering another key area, etc.) and specify the role each camera type plays with respect to the lobby security strategy. Indicate performance specifications for each camera type based on defined operational requirements.

5. You are the Director of Security for a large metropolitan hospital located in a high-crime area. The security strategy includes the installation of external CCTV cameras around the perimeter of the building.
   a. Indicate the operational requirements for a CCTV system.
   b. Calculate the minimum number of cameras for total perimeter coverage. Assume the perimeter is 10,000 ft in circumference, 5-MP (megapixel) cameras, 40 pixel-per-foot minimum camera resolution, and the distance from each camera to the fence line is 100 ft.

6. You have an operational requirement of identification-level resolution for a 1-megapixel CCTV camera focused on a doorway. What is the maximum horizontal field-of-view for this camera? What is the maximum horizontal field-of-view for a 3-MP camera with the same operational requirement? Repeat the calculation for a 5-MP camera. (Hint: see the text.)

7. You are moonlighting by performing technical security consulting. The CEO of the company where you work as the Security Director is requesting a system design for perimeter surveillance cameras at his posh residence. You are due for a raise at work, and therefore decide to accept the job. After conducting a risk assessment of the property, you determine that an area of enhanced vulnerability to unauthorized physical access is the back of the house. The horizontal field-of-view is 50 ft

and the camera will be installed 25 ft from the façade. You also decide to use a 5-MP camera. What focal length lens do you need to cover the entire horizontal field-of-view?

8. Explain the effect of each of the following on the horizontal field-of-view:
   a. Increasing the distance from the object to the camera lens.
   b. Decreasing the lens focal length.

9. A section of fence that is 200 ft in length requires complete CCTV coverage. As the Director of Security, you are asked to determine how many cameras are required to cover that portion of the fence line. The physical security standard mandates a minimum resolution of 40 pixels-per-foot in the relevant dimension and also calls for 5-MP cameras.
   a. How many cameras are required to cover the entire section of fence if the cameras are facing the fence line?
   b. How many cameras are required to cover the entire section of fence if the cameras are positioned along the fence line? (Hint: consider the vertical field-of-view.)

10. You are the newly appointed Security Director for a large manufacturing company. The previous security director was fired because of massive incompetence. Your first assignment is to conduct a physical security risk assessment at a manufacturing facility in a country where the potential for various terrorism attack vectors is assessed to be high. The physical security standard for the organization calls for a minimum of 40 pixels-per-foot resolution across the horizontal field-of-view. In one particular venue and using the technical specifications of the cameras already purchased by your predecessor, you calculate that you will only achieve 20 pixels-per-foot horizontal resolution. This will not satisfy the identification-level operational requirement.
    a. Assuming you could position the cameras anywhere you deem appropriate, what would you do to satisfy the 40-pixel-per-foot requirement? Justify your answer.
    b. If you could replace the cameras, what technical specification would be enhanced to achieve 40 pixels-per-foot and by how much?

11. If a camera produces 7.5 images per second and each image is 10 kB, how many cameras can be shared across the following network types?
    a. 1-Gbit Ethernet: 500 Mbit/s.
    b. 100-Mbit fast Ethernet: 60 Mbit/s.
    c. 10-Mbit Ethernet: 7 Mbit/s.
    d. WIFI 802.11 g 54 Mbit: 25 Mbit/s.

12. For each of the network types specified in Problem 11, calculate the length of time a 1-TB hard disk drive would be available for recording before it fills up and begins to record over itself.

13. You are a terrorist that is interested in compromising an organization's CCTV system. Unfortunately (for you) the organization wisely decided to invest in fiber optic technology for signal routing. You have managed to gain physical access to

the organization's headquarters and, even better, to the fiber optic cable that leads to the network video recorder (NVR). How would you attempt to access the signal inside the cable?

14. Use Table 11.15 to calculate the signal attenuation for the following cable types after a 1000-ft cable run. Express your answer in linear terms. (Hint: calculate the loss in dBs and convert from dBs to its equivalent linear representation):

   a. Fiber.

   b. RG-59.

   c. Cat5E.

15. You are concerned that the unshielded twisted pair cable carrying your CCTV signals is leaky and therefore subject to compromise. Indicate some options you might consider to reduce the vulnerability component of risk. Specify the operational and/or technical pros and cons of each option.

16. Explain the concept of video compression at a high level, and indicate why it is important.

CHAPTER 12

Physical Access Restriction, Incident Detection, and Scenario Monitoring

12.1 INTRODUCTION

Restricting physical access to higher-risk areas is essential to any counterterrorism strategy. Like many other security-related controls, restricting physical access is intended to address the risk factor of unauthorized physical access. Physical arguments presented in Chapters 4 to 7 reinforce intuition that physical proximity to a facility and/or its occupants enhances the vulnerability to various terrorism attack vectors. Moreover, physical models first presented in Chapter 4 make it possible to quantitatively estimate the vulnerability component of risk for some of these attack vectors.

Since a "No Trespassing" sign might only deter the most diffident terrorist, more stringent countermeasures are typically required. Security controls that restrict physical access are often programmed according to defined access privileges. Practical physical access control systems combine methods of automated authorization and/or authentication with physical restriction. This integration is what makes these devices useful.

With respect to physical access restrictions, a barrier such as a turnstile or a door with a magnetic locking mechanism is released in response to the presentation of a token or credential such as a picture ID. The ID validates an individual's affiliation with an organization. This affiliation is confirmed by querying a back-end database that associates an individual with their respective access privileges. It all sounds fantastically simple, but recall the discussion in Chapter 5 on the statistical likelihood of unauthorized physical access arising from random errors in access privilege assignments, especially in large organizations.

Once authorization to enter a restricted space has occurred, thereby confirming an individual's affiliation and good standing within the organization, physical entry is granted by the system. In purely technical terms, the confirmation of physical access privilege initiates a signal that triggers a relay and releases a locking mechanism.

Sometimes these systems also incorporate a means of authenticating the identity of the ID holder. I repeat for emphasis that *merely presenting an ID card at a turnstile does not authenticate the identity of the cardholder.* Rigorous authentication of identity is the essence of multi-factor authentication that was discussed in Chapter 10.

The use of a credential that incorporates a biometric or personal identification number (PIN) code is intended to confirm organizational affiliation as well as validate the identity of the cardholder. In the case of the PIN, the process is based on the presumption that the legitimate cardholder is the only individual who knows the PIN code *and* is the unique individual who possesses that particular physical card. Hence the importance of not revealing a bank card PIN to any other human on earth.

With respect to biometrics, the inherent uniqueness of biological features inexorably links the rightful cardholder to a specific card or credential. The presumption is that the biological features captured on the card are unique to the cardholder.

Of course, no matter how strict the authentication and authorization methods, an access control system must be enforceable. In other words, physical access can only be achieved once proper authorization has been validated. Therefore, there must be some mechanism that facilitates physical access to authorized individuals and restricts physical access otherwise. This is the principal motivation for deploying commandable locking mechanisms on doors and portals.

12.2 ELECTRIC STRIKES AND MAGNETIC LOCKS

Although the use of credentials discussed in Chapter 10 are central to implementing authentication and authorization controls, they would not be much use unless there was a means of restricting physical access to spaces that are off-limits to nonauthorized individuals.

The method of limiting physical access according to defined access privileges is often accomplished through the use of a card reader that is linked to an electric strike or magnetic lock. The mechanics of each are straightforward.

When an individual presents a valid ID card to the reader, a confirming signal from the local access control panel causes a current to flow to the electric strike or magnetic lock. A magnetic field is generated by the current which releases or retracts the holding mechanism. For those individuals inside the space, a mechanical release via a card reader or button on the inside/secure side of the room allows individuals to exit the space by overriding the locking mechanism.

Unless fire safety rules dictate otherwise, best practices dictate that door locks function as fail-secure devices. That means that if power is not applied to the device it remains in a locked state. A decision to operate in a fail-secure or fail-insecure mode has operational implications since a fail-secure configuration mandates the use of a battery backup in the event building power is interrupted.

It is important to clarify one point that could be a source of confusion because of terminology. An electric strike is an active mechanism (i.e., it has moving parts) that consists of a bolt that is retracted when current is applied to a solenoid. The bolt is the mechanism that prevents the door from opening. Figure 12.1 illustrates the concept of an electric strike.

In contrast, a so-called "magnetic lock" is a passive device, so there are no moving parts. How does that device work? It is a fact of life that all electric currents generate a magnetic field. Recall we encountered the concept of magnetic flux and flux density in Chapter 11 when calculating signal emanations from a twisted pair cable (e.g., Cat5) carrying an Ethernet CCTV signal.

The magnetic flux generated by an electrical current creates the force that holds the door in a closed position. Cessation of the current turns off the flux and thereby allows the door to be opened. Figure 12.2 shows a magnetic door lock in operation.

Despite the difference in their names, electric strikes and magnetic locks both function as a result of magnetic fields generated by electric currents. Again, it is the magnetic field generated by an electric current flowing through the

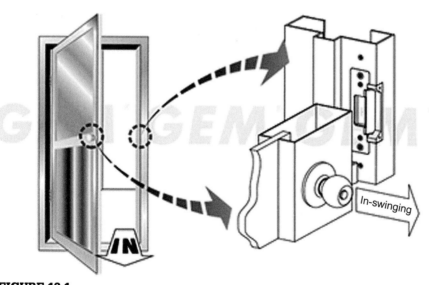

FIGURE 12.1
Electric strike. *(Image used with permission from PanicExitPro.com.* http://www.panicexitpro.com/product_detail_10840.aspx.)

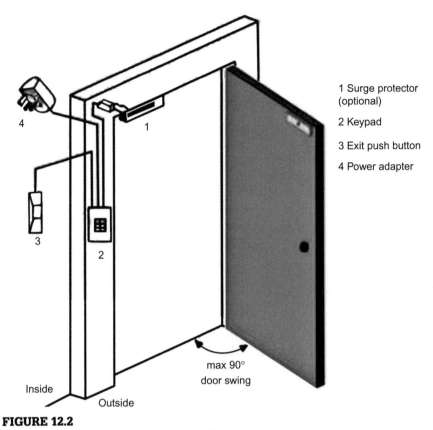

1 Surge protector
(optional)

2 Keypad

3 Exit push button

4 Power adapter

max 90°
door swing

Inside

Outside

FIGURE 12.2

Magnetic lock. *(Adapted from* http://www.eslisurveillance.com/security_door_lock_
kits.htm.*)*

windings of a solenoid that generates the force that retracts the security bolt
in an electric strike. So the term "electric strike" is not technically a misnomer,
but it could be confusing when considering the term "magnetic lock" in the
same context.

12.3   DOORS AND PORTALS

To state the obvious, doors and portals exist to prevent physical access to
restricted space by those who do not have access privileges. Doors and portals are required to facilitate access to individuals with legitimate access rights.
Electric strikes and magnetic locks are the devices that facilitate authorized
door openings by authenticated individuals.

However, the use of magnetic locks and electric strikes alone is often insufficient to address the unauthorized physical access risk factor. No matter how robust, a lock can do nothing to prevent the door from being held open for unauthorized individuals by those with legitimate physical access privileges.

The phenomenon where an individual follows another into a restricted space without confirming authorization to enter is known as "piggybacking." Not surprisingly, various technologies have been created to address piggybacking. Two of these that are typically used for this purpose include turnstiles and mantraps.

Turnstiles are designed to allow only one person at a time to pass through a doorway or portal. A rotatable tripod fixture is commonly used for this purpose, although many variations on this theme exist. Tripod turnstiles are ubiquitous in the New York Subway system, and swinging panels are common on the Tube in London.

In exact analogy with locks applied to doors, the user presents a card or registered body part to a reader. Upon successful authorization and possibly authentication, a signal is sent from the access control panel to a magnetic relay that releases the locking mechanism on the turnstile. When released, the tripod sprocket can be rotated in one direction so that it facilitates physical access to the requesting individual.

This type of turnstile is not foolproof since some individuals are quite adept at jumping over, crawling under, or squeezing past such devices. For that reason, turnstiles of varying heights are available, where the height of the turnstile is presumably related to the assessed risk of someone jumping over it. In addition, the tripod barrels can be manufactured in varying lengths to reduce the vulnerability associated with a particularly lean individual.

Full-height turnstiles are also available to reduce the risk of jumpers, limbo rockers, and squeezers. These are also used throughout the New York Subway system, especially when there is no attendant present at the station.

A mantrap, or more correctly in today's world, a "person trap," is a more extreme contraption that requires the person seeking entry to authenticate himself or herself after entering an antechamber. Once his or her identity has been authenticated, and authorization to enter has been confirmed, a second door opens and allows physical entry into the space.

A mantrap can be quite effective in preventing piggybacking, but it will do nothing to address the risk of unauthorized physical access by someone who has recovered a lost or stolen access token/ID. Only enhanced authentication via multifactor and/or biometric methods can address the risk factors for this threat vector.

The decision regarding the appropriate level of technology for restricting physical access boils down to cost versus benefit. Mantraps are relatively expensive, and costs can increase significantly when structural modifications to a facility are required to accommodate such a device as a retrofit.

As noted previously in other contexts, this type of decision is quite common in security. Issues associated with cost in terms of money or convenience and juxtaposed against the assessed risk drive a security strategy. There is no right or wrong answer, but such decisions should be justifiable based on the results of the risk assessment and the availability of resources.

12.4 THE TEN PLUS ONE COMMANDMENTS OF PHYSICAL ACCESS

12.4.1 Restriction

It is useful to define a set of fundamental principles for physical access restriction pursuant to developing a generally applicable security strategy. Ideally, such principles would constitute the first section of a physical security policy, and this would link to a standard that specifies the performance of identified controls. For those readers with a religious bent, the following are the *Ten Plus One Commandments of Physical Access Restriction*:

1. Physical access privileges should be granted on a strictly "need-to-know" and/or "need-to-access" basis. Such privileges should be periodically reviewed as well as the access control lists that are linked to those privileges.
2. A proper security risk assessment should be used to identify areas of enhanced risk relative to identified threats, and the relative magnitude of their respective components of risk.
3. All areas in a facility that require physical access restriction must confirm an individual's access privilege prior to entry.
4. Access privilege should be confirmed via a card reader and/or biometric or a multi-factor authentication scheme that is linked to an appropriate door locking mechanism.
5. Areas deemed to be of higher risk relative to identified threats should require authentication of identity prior to entry.
6. Multifactor and/or positive authentication (e.g., a biometric) should be used to authenticate individual identity prior to entering higher-risk areas.
7. Higher-risk areas should either be alarmed or guarded after business hours, and qualified security personnel should monitor such alarms.
8. An incident response protocol should be developed, communicated, and practiced in the event of alarm activation and/or other security incidents.

9. Any space storing confidential or sensitive physical media (e.g., documents and portable memory devices) should be designated as a higher-risk area.
10. Any space housing IT infrastructure and/or telephone equipment should be designated as a higher-risk area.
11. A facility security risk assessment should be conducted periodically with the periodicity determined by the tolerance for risk and/or any significant changes in the security risk profile.

12.5 THE IMPORTANCE OF PHYSICAL ACCESS CONTROL SYSTEM SPECIFICATIONS

To review elements of Chapter 1, a physical security policy represents the operational core of the enterprise security strategy. The policy evolves from fundamental principles such as those specified in Section 12.4 and forms the basis for the creation of security standards.

Security standards specify the requirements for security controls and methods of implementation such as technology. These technologies must perform at a certain level in order to satisfy articulated operational requirements for a given physical area or electronic application or device.

The level of performance of identified controls is dictated by system specifications that are determined by the operational requirements. This is why such specifications are important. If the system specifications are missing or inaccurate, the system may not perform at a level necessary to satisfy the operational requirements that are relevant to addressing identified risk factors.

Finally, the operational requirements are determined by intuition and judgment informed by experience. In contrast, the technology specifications are determined by analyses using established scientific and engineering principles.

12.6 PHYSICAL ACCESS CONTROL SYSTEM ARCHITECTURE AND SIGNALING

Chapter 9 detailed physical and electronic vulnerabilities associated with the physical access control infrastructure. This section explores physical access control system functionality more generally, and its relevance to the security risk profile.

Figure 12.3 depicts a generic physical access control system architecture at a high level. Note that specific system components such as the access control panels that store local card access information and the access control server that sends and receives instructions to and from the panels should be physically protected from unauthorized physical access.

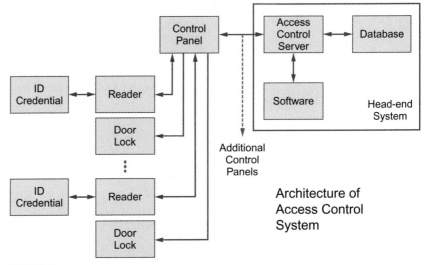

FIGURE 12.3

Physical access control system architecture. *(Reprinted with permission from Raviraj Technologies.* http://www.ravirajtech.com/architecture-of-access-control-system.html.*)*

As noted in Chapters 9 and 11, if IP-based technology is used in publicly accessible space, appropriate electronic and/or physical controls should be applied to prevent the compromise of electronic and physical assets.

As is evident from Figure 12.3, the system architecture is relatively simple, and this was discussed previously in Chapter 9. An ID credential is presented to a card reader that is linked to a door locking mechanism. The information on the ID is read by the reader and transmitted to the local panel that controls that particular reader-door combination. The panel receives updated access privilege information from the access control server on a periodic basis. The central server communicates with all system panels in this way. Local access privilege data is stored on each panel.

The public facing or "sharp end" of a physical access control system is the card reader. The ID credential is arguably the most vulnerable component in a physical access control system. It is highly portable, and unless special provisions for user authentication are invoked, anyone on the planet could pick it up and use it to gain physical access to restricted space. Chapter 10 discussed specific physical access card technologies and associated vulnerabilities in detail.

Although two-factor authentication mechanisms in the form of a PIN or biometric in conjunction with the card are advisable to reduce risk of unauthorized physical access in higher-risk venues, a lower-tech option is available, namely visually comparing the cardholder with the photograph on his or her card. However, at least one human resource will be required to implement this control at all times.

A photograph on an ID card linked to an updated access database is also a form of two-factor authentication; the card is something you possess and the photograph is something you are. The bigger the better is the rule in terms of the size of the photograph in order to facilitate effective inspections.

It is always a good security practice to include a photograph of the legitimate cardholder on an ID card but not the name or logo of the organization. If the card is lost or stolen, the name of the organization on the card makes it more susceptible to unauthorized use.

If two-factor authentication is implemented, the system can be configured to operate in conjunction with another authentication mechanism such as a biometric reader (e.g., fingerprint, hand geometry, etc.). Two types of comparisons can be implemented as noted in Chapter 10: (1) the biometric reader data is compared against user data that is stored in a database or (2) the biometric reader data is compared to the cardholder's biometric data that is stored on the card.

The latter mode is preferred for several reasons. The first is that it represents a one-to-one comparison and therefore is typically faster than option number two for significant user populations.

The second reason is that there can be privacy concerns if an individual's biometric information is stored in a database belonging to a company or organization. The one-to-one comparison eliminates that issue, since the cardholder data is stored on the card that is in the possession of the cardholder.

However, invoking the one-to-one comparison option places constraints on possible card technologies. Specifically, smart card technology is required since these possess sufficient on-board memory to accommodate biometric data. Use of smart cards is a good idea in general because of their enhanced security relative to proximity cards.

Recalling the dissection of a physical access control system in Chapter 9, enterprise physical access control systems often piggyback on the existing IT network for signal routing. We also observed that non-IP-based access control readers and panels would require the use of an IP converter or encoder to leverage typical local area and wide area networks. Such devices convert digital card reader or panel signals into packets so that such signals are compatible with the TCP/IP protocol.

Referring to Figure 12.3, after an ID card is presented to a reader, the information encoded on the card is relayed to a local access panel. The standard signaling format for physical access control devices is known as Wiegand, named after the Wiegand magnetic effect that formed the basis for access card technology.

In the standard 26-bit Wiegand format, bit 1 is an even parity bit. Bits 2 to 9 are a facility code. Bits 10 to 25 are the card number. Bit 26 is an odd parity bit. Other formats have a similar structure of leading with the facility code followed by card number and include parity bits for error checking.

The Wiegand interface uses three wires, one of which is a common ground and two of which are data transmission wires usually called DATA0 and DATA1, alternately labeled "D0" and "D1" or "Data Low" and "Data High."

When no data signals are sent, both DATA0 and DATA1 are pulled to the "high" voltage level, i.e., +5 VDC. When a 0 is sent, the DATA0 wire is pulled to a low voltage while the DATA1 wire remains at a high voltage. When a 1 is sent, the DATA1 wire is pulled to a low voltage while DATA0 remains at a high voltage.

Numerous access control system manufacturers adopted Wiegand technology but were not satisfied with the limitations of only 8 bits for site codes (i.e., 0 to 255 values) and 16 bits for card numbers (i.e., 0 to 65,535 values). They subsequently designed their own formats with varying complexities of field numbers, lengths, and parity checking.

Each access control panel is electronically linked to a reader or set of readers that control a prescribed set of doors. The panel stores relevant access data that facilitates physical access for those cardholders authorized to enter space controlled by those specific doors. In some IP-based configurations, a local control panel is linked directly to a set of doors and communicates to a master control panel that in turn communicates via RS-485 to an Ethernet hub or switch. The Ethernet cabling is typically Category 5 (Cat5) or Cat6, i.e., unshielded twisted pair cable as discussed in Chapter 11 in connection with CCTV.

Facilitating physical access literally means that the reader sends cardholder information via an electrical signal to the panel. Upon comparing the received signal with the card data and the stored data, the panel responds by sending a signal to the magnetic lock or electric strike to open a relay. This stops electric current from flowing to the lock. Without current to create the requisite magnetic field, the bolt on the strike is no longer held in place or the two poles of a magnetic lock are not energized, and the door or turnstile is then free to rotate.

The astute reader might ask, "In a dynamic user population, how do specific panels know who has legitimate access at any point in time?" This is a good question and raises an important security risk issue.

In a distributed physical access control system, the panels connect to the access control server that is updated periodically with a file that contains the most current physical access privilege information. This information is pushed out to the local panels. But the panels are dependent on the "brain," i.e., the server, to supply the local panels with ground truth regarding current physical access privilege information. Ground truth must be updated at some reasonable time interval since the environment is changing with the addition, subtraction, and transfer of access privileges for the user population.

We have learned that the local panel makes physical access "decisions" following the presentation of a card to a reader. Another good question might be the following: "What happens if the server cannot communicate with the panel?" This situation might occur in a power failure, assuming the panel has a battery backup or the building is under UPS power, but the server is down.

The panel will facilitate access to the readers/doors under its control, but only with the most recently updated information. So let's say "Carl Young" has been fired from the company or changes to a role that has different access privileges, a decidedly cheerier notion. Suppose further that the access control system server goes down before the change in Carl Young's status can be communicated to the panel. In that case the panel will allow "Carl Young" to enter space to which he may no longer have access privileges.

The good news is that if the panels do have backup power, physical access control of doors and portals can at least be maintained during a power outage, recognizing the incremental risk of unauthorized access just described.

Signal routing is a relative cinch if a local Intranet is used, since one can leverage the IT infrastructure wherever there is network connectivity. It also facilitates enhanced monitoring through security system integration as discussed in Sections 9.6 and 11.16. However, these same components are vulnerable to electronic attack if electronic or physical security vulnerabilities exist on this network.

For example, a publicly accessible IP card reader or IP encoder provides a physical network connection that is potentially vulnerable to scanning for open ports and other internal network vulnerabilities. Therefore, and as noted many times previously, IP-based physical access control devices must be electronically and/or physically secured. Appropriate controls include filtering by media access control (MAC) address and end point protection as well as securing the device from physical tampering. The ideal situation is to avoid installing IP-based devices in public spaces.

The bottom line is that the access control server, database, and panels require the kinds of physical and electronic controls discussed throughout this book. In fact, because of its central role in the system, compromising the physical access system server could lead to unauthorized physical access to restricted space across the enterprise.

Now that the functionality of a physical access control system is understood, some useful access control system features and functions for an indicative system are presented below.

12.7 PHYSICAL ACCESS CONTROL SYSTEM SPECIFICATIONS*

12.7.1 General Networking and Security Requirements

1. Utilize an IP-based system to facilitate communication, control, and security systems integration.
2. Provide IT-network connections and assign IP addresses to access control components, excluding devices in publically accessible locations unless appropriate physical and electronic security controls are in place.
3. Integrate a physical access control system with CCTV and other physical security sensors or systems (e.g., intercom, intruder alarm, visitor management system) in order to manage identified physical security threats.
4. Utilize the corporate IT network, but segregate access control infrastructure via a secure subnet configuration (e.g., virtual local area network (VLAN)) with appropriate interzone traffic monitoring as noted in Chapter 8. If this is not viable, a dedicated IP network should be installed with the capacity to accommodate all networked security devices.
5. Use system controllers/panels that support hardware protocols from multiple manufacturers.
6. Utilize power over Ethernet (POE) for components wherever possible and practical. (Note: for reference, the "Enforcer" electromagnetic lock with 1200 lb of retention force draws 500 mA at 12 VDC or 250 mA at 24 VDC. Therefore, 6 W of peak power are required).
7. Provide for multiple card reader connections to local controllers/panels.
8. If alarms are required in a given space, utilize passive infrared (PIR) proximity alarm sensors positioned for 100 percent internal area coverage and mounted out of physical reach. Monitor all alarm outputs in a proper control room if possible.

12.7.2 Physical Access Control System Authorization and Authentication Requirements

1. Utilize HID i-CLASS Elite or MIFARE DESFire ID credentials with enlarged photographs and no corporate designation.
2. Provide for enhanced authentication (e.g., biometrics or two-factor authentication) for higher-risk environments (e.g., data centers).
3. Control visitor access with designated visitor IDs that limit physical access privileges and utilize configurable expiration dates/times.

---

*With acknowledgement to Roger Pike, RPA Ltd, UK as an important source of information.

4. Integrate the physical access control and CCTV systems with Windows Active Directory to establish a nexus between physical and electronic access systems for enhanced security monitoring as required.
5. Ensure physical and electronic access privileges are current.
6. Include an "antipass back" feature at all physical access control points.
7. Utilize antipiggybacking methods in high-risk or highly trafficked areas (e.g., building lobby turnstiles) wherever possible.
8. Consider ¾-height turnstile/gates to discourage "jumpers" in areas where this is warranted and based on the assessed risk.

12.7.3   Physical Access Control System Security Conditions, Locking, and Signaling

1. Provide appropriate door/portal locking mechanism using magnetic locking components rated to a minimum of 1200 lb on internal doors leading to common/public space (see Section 12.7.1 #6 for more technical details).
2. Provide a suitable doorframe to accommodate magnetic locking mechanisms noted in number 1 immediately above.
3. Provide electronic contacts to monitor door status.
4. Establish a unique physical access code for each segregated area and program the ID cards based on defined physical access privileges.
5. Provide physical alerts/alarms based on "door held open" and "door forced" risk conditions with configurable settings for additional alarm/event parameters.
6. Provide visible confirmation of authorized physical access at a card reader (e.g., green and red light-emitting diodes).
7. Consider increasing the time interval triggering "door held open" alarms for areas with historically high false-positive alarm rates as well as eliminating the alarm during highly trafficked and low-risk times. Consider the cost-effectiveness of CCTV coverage as a compensating control to resolve potential false-positive alarms.

12.7.4   Physical Access Control System Information Storage and Transmission

1. Provide secure storage, analysis, and routing of historical physical access information.
2. Coordinate the installation and management of physical access servers and any other network devices with the organization's IT department.
3. Provide secure storage of physical access histories for up to 5 years or as dictated by local, state, and federal regulations.
4. Regularly review physical access logs for anomalies and correlate with results of analyses of electronic risk.

12.7.5 Physical Access Control System Event Logging and Reporting

1. Provide for a customized, easily configurable, and secure reporting capability.
2. Provide an auditable record of all physical access events (e.g., access history of transactions to and from restricted areas) and signal conditions.

12.7.6 Physical Access Control System Security and Resilience

1. Incorporate system security and redundancy using multiple and physically separated physical access control servers linked to local panels/door controllers.
2. Ensure all physical access control equipment including servers, controllers, and edge devices are secure with respect to physical tampering.
3. Encrypt physical access historical data and signal transmissions. Ensure the resilience and reliability of the decryption capability.
4. Utilize on-board memory for signal controllers, thereby providing additional system resilience. Consider encryption of access control data stored therein.
5. Provide a battery backup for critical system components such as access control panels.
6. Install IP devices only in physically secure spaces unless compensating electronic controls are implemented (e.g., antitampering, MAC address filtering, and end point restrictions). Restrict electronic and physical access to IT network ports. For insecure spaces, utilize analog equipment linked to IP encoders installed in secure spaces.

12.7.7 Physical Access Control System Security Risk Metrics

1. Mean time between equipment failures.
2. System false acceptances and false rejection rates.
3. An historical record of security incidents to include incident type, incident time, incident date, incident location, and disposition.

12.8 SECURITY INCIDENT MONITORING AND DETECTION

Detecting and monitoring risk-relevant security activity is a key physical security control to counter the threat of terrorism. Security sensors operate by sensing a change in a physical parameter that relates to some change in a risk factor.

Note that these sensors are not sensing terrorism per se. Typically they alert on a disturbance of the environment, and this disturbance may signify unauthorized physical access, for example, a risk factor for terrorism and other threats.

12.8.1   Security Sensors

There are many potential options for sensors applied to security scenarios. Scientists and engineers have developed numerous technologies based on various physical phenomena that have found their way into the security world. There are pros and cons to each of these sensors with varying applicability based on scenario-specific constraints.

However, the use of sensors to monitor the environment for risk-relevant security issues often amounts to a "signal-to-noise" problem. That is, identifying a real alert amid a preponderance of false positives can negate the effectiveness of the most sensitive sensor. In fact, you might be tempted to believe that an ultrasensitive sensor is preferable in security applications because of the ability to detect smaller disturbances to the environment. This might be the case in some scenarios, but the problem is that greater sensitivity is potentially more likely to generate greater numbers of false positives. An analogous problem was discussed in Chapter 10 regarding false acceptance and rejection rates for biometric devices.

Determining the appropriate sensor sensitivity is a balancing act. That is, the risks of false positives due to high sensitivity must be weighed against the risks of false negatives arising from attenuated detection capabilities. Maximum sensor sensitivity is limited by the signal-to-noise ratio of the device. In general, the process of determining the appropriate sensor sensitivity requires a working knowledge of the device and, importantly, the specific deployment conditions.

A good example of this balance is the use of metal detectors for weapons inspections. If the sensitivity of the device is set too high (i.e., the machine senses very small quantities of metal), everyone with a nail clipper or belt buckle will be subject to further search and the queue could be overwhelming. Over time this has a negative impact on both the inspectors and those being inspected.

On the other hand, if one sets the sensitivity too low, the armed terrorist might go undetected. Testing and statistical analyses of both test data and data *in situ* plus a detailed appreciation of operational conditions are essential to getting this right. A more rigorous explanation of sensor sensitivity and other important concepts will be provided in the next section.

One must therefore be judicious in identifying incidents that pose an actual threat or that can provoke a meaningful response by security officials when establishing sensor sensitivity. System "noise" characterized by false positives jeopardizes the proper response to a legitimate security incident. There are many real and anecdotal stories of security officers ignoring alarms after becoming inured to repeated false activations.

This is a scenario that should be avoided at all costs. However, it would be a mistake to level criticism exclusively at the security officer, if at all. This situation reveals an underlying issue with the risk management strategy. The remedy is to rigorously evaluate security risk at each affected location, adjust security technology to match operational conditions in proportion to risk, and develop practical response protocols.

12.8.2   Security Sensor Performance and Statistics

Although security sensors are designed to sense anomalies, it is helpful to understand sensor fundamentals to appreciate their functional limits relative to such anomalies. Although it may appear that a sensor magically begins working perfectly upon installation, the reality is more nuanced. In fact, much work has transpired behind the scenes to ensure that the sensor works as advertised. The notion of "working" in this context entails calibration along with a firm understanding of relevant environmental factors.

The first sensor concept to explore is sensitivity. Sensitivity is the minimum sensor input required to produce a detectable output. Recall this concept was first introduced in Chapter 11 in connection with CCTV. For example, thermometer sensitivity would be the minimum temperature increase/decrease that would cause the thermometer to register a different reading. If one plotted the temperature reading versus the actual temperature on the y- and x-axes of a graph, respectively, the slope of the resulting line is the sensitivity. Ideally the slope of that line is straight (i.e., linear) so that the sensor behaves reasonably within a defined range of operation.

The range of sensor operation is the so-called dynamic range. It represents the difference between the minimum possible sensor value and its maximum value. The dynamic range does not dictate the sensor operating range per se but rather the absolute value or difference between the maximum and minimum values of its total operating range.

But what if you recorded 100 readings from a sensor where the measurement conditions didn't vary, but the sensor readings were wildly different from one another? This should cause you to question the viability of the instrument since a functional sensor should yield similar results under congruent conditions.

The concept of precision refers to the repeatability, or equally, the reproducibility of measurements. It is instructive to be more quantitative since precision is essential to making accurate measurements of risk or anything else for that matter.

Suppose you had sufficient ambition to calculate the mean and standard deviation of 100 sensor readings. The unusually astute reader might ask, "Well, what if the mean measured from 100 sensor readings differs from the true mean? How can one determine whether the sensor is working according to Hoyle?" The same highly intelligent individual might ask a follow-up question, "What if the readings are in fact different from one another, but the instrument is unable to detect those differences?"

Answering the first question quantitatively requires an elementary statistical analysis of sensor performance. Let's assume a doctor takes a patient's temperature, but she wants to know if her thermometer is appropriately calibrated. Calibration implies that the device consistently performs within specified limits. The tolerance for those limits is determined by the context.

First, she might assume the sensor temperature reading is a normally distributed random variable, and the patient's true mean temperature is supposed to be $37.00°$ C with a standard deviation of, say, $4°$ C.

Suppose she records a sample of 100 temperature readings. The standard error is defined as the population standard deviation, σ, divided by the square root of the sample size, N, or $\sigma/\sqrt{N}$. In this case $N = 100$ so $\sqrt{100} = 10$. Therefore, the standard error equals $4°$ $C/10 = 0.4°$ C.

Suppose the physician now measures the mean of the sampled temperature readings to be $37.10°$ C, recalling that the true mean is $37.00°$ C. What can the doctor conclude about the performance of her thermometer based on the sample mean and the standard error? Is the thermometer appropriately calibrated?

To be specific, the physician wants to know the range of thermometer readings such that 95 percent of the time a mean $\underline{X}$, calculated from a sample of measurements, should fall within a specific range of values determined by the statistics of a normally distributed random variable.

It turns out that the so-called 95 percent confidence interval can be constructed in terms of the standard error and yields the desired result. This range of values of the sampled mean about the true mean is given by the following expression:

$$\underline{X} - 1.96(\sigma/\sqrt{N}) < \mu < \underline{X} + 1.96(\sigma/\sqrt{N})$$

$\underline{X}$ is the sampled mean, σ is the true standard deviation, μ is the true mean, and N is the sample size.

Plugging the appropriate values into this expression shows that the lower and upper bounds on the 95 percent confidence interval for the mean of sampled temperatures is

$$\underline{X} - 1.96(\sigma/\sqrt{N}) = 37.10 - 1.96(4/10) = 37.10 - 0.78 \sim 36.3°C$$
$$\underline{X} + 1.96(\sigma/\sqrt{N}) = 37.10 + 1.96(4/10) = 37.10 + 0.78 \sim 37.9°C$$

The 95 percent confidence interval for the sampled mean is approximately between 36.3 and 37.9° C. Since the true mean of the sensor is 37.0° C., and the sampled mean falls within the 95 percent confidence interval of the true mean, we can conclude that the temperature sensor is appropriately calibrated.

For interested readers, the 99 percent confidence interval for a sampled mean is given by $\underline{X} \pm 2.58(\sigma/\sqrt{N})$ and the 99.9 percent confidence interval equals $\underline{X} \pm 3.29(\sigma/\sqrt{N})$. The bigger the interval, the more likely it is that the sampled mean will be a number within the defined interval.

But recall the intelligent reader posed two questions. The second question relates to the situation where the temperature sensor readings fluctuate, but the values are too coarse to actually observe the fluctuation. This question naturally leads to the concept of sensor resolution.

Resolution is the smallest detectable incremental change of an input parameter that can be detected in the output signal. Resolution can be measured as a percentage of the full sensor scale or in absolute terms. In the case of a doctor evaluating a patient, the resolution of the thermometer must comport with her "operational requirements."

That is, the thermometer values might be seen to be fluctuating wildly if the device is capable of discriminating temperatures to within 0.000001° C. However, for diagnostic purposes this level of resolution matters little to the doctor because the human body is presumably agnostic to fluctuations at this level. On the other hand, degree-level changes are important in determining a patient's health. Therefore, a thermometer that could resolve temperature to only 10° C would be useless.

Accuracy is the maximum difference between the actual value being measured and the value indicated by the sensor. Like resolution, accuracy can be measured as a percentage of the full sensor scale or in absolute terms.

But accuracy is not the same as precision. Imagine you and a friend are at the local pub competing in a friendly game of darts. The objective is to hit the bull's-eye at the center of the target. The loser pays for a round of beer for everyone at the bar. Let's say a cluster of darts thrown by your friend hits the target in the outer circle of the target, but these darts all fall within a 1-cm radius of each other. This is indeed a show of extreme precision. However, it is also a highly inaccurate performance given the disparity between where the darts landed and where they should have landed, i.e., the bull's-eye. Figure 12.4 graphically illustrates the difference.

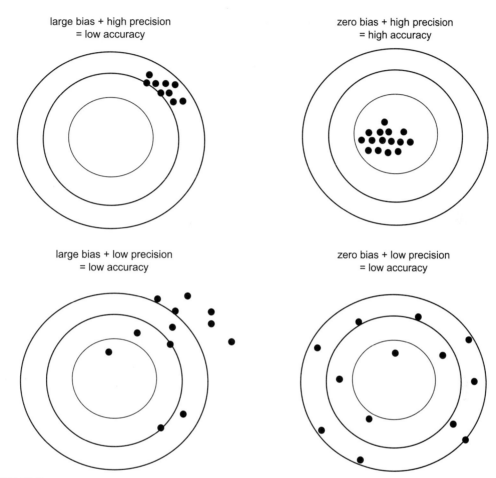

FIGURE 12.4

Accuracy versus precision. *(Source: U.S. Food and Drug Administration. "Equipment and Calibration."* http://www.fda.gov/ MedicalDevices/DeviceRegulationandGuidance/PostmarketRequirements/QualitySystemsRegulations/MedicalDeviceQualitySystemsManual/ ucm122460.htm.*)*

Offset is another common sensor parameter. Offset is defined as the reading of the sensor when it should be zero or no input. Many people have experienced offset error when they weigh themselves on a bathroom scale. If the scale reads 3 lb when no one is on the scale, this offset will be added to the weight of the individual when he or she actually steps on the scale.

The linearity of a sensor or transducer (i.e., a device that converts one type of energy into another—an audio speaker is a transducer since it converts electrical signal energy into mechanical energy) indicates the magnitude of the departure of the measured curve of a sensor from its ideal curve. In the linear portion of a sensor's operating curve, increases in an input should produce proportionate changes in the sensor output. Linearity is a terrifically important concept in all areas of science and engineering, and this includes security. Appendix A discusses the general concept of linearity.

Finally, the notion of hysteresis is relevant to sensors. This is most commonly associated with magnetization curves (i.e., the change in magnetic flux density, B, resulting from a change in magnetic intensity, H). In general, hysteresis is a measure of a sensor's sensitivity to the direction of the change of an input parameter. A sensor should in theory be "direction agnostic" and therefore respond identically regardless of whether a change occurs from a positive or negative direction. But this is not always the case.

As noted previously, it is not necessary to understand the aforementioned concepts in detail when using security sensors. Security sensors typically respond or do not respond based on the magnitude of a change in the monitored parameter (e.g., capacitance, spatial variations in the infrared energy background, Doppler shift associated with moving objects, etc.).

However, sensor performance is a function of factors such as sensitivity, accuracy, precision, resolution, etc. Therefore, understanding sensor fundamentals can help ensure security operational requirements are satisfied.

12.8.3 Security Sensor Operational Requirements

Assuming one has rigorously evaluated the risk factors associated with the threats affecting a particular area or space within a facility and then identified controls, the next step is to identify methods to implement those controls. This typically requires the implementation of a sensor. Even physical access control and CCTV systems, the two most popular access control technologies, utilize sensors that affect system functionality.

Ideally, any candidate sensor technology would be characterized by the following performance criteria:

- Low rate of false positives and false negatives.
- Appropriate performance under scenario-specific conditions.
- Sufficient areal or volumetric coverage.

Recall the concepts of false acceptance and false rejection were discussed in Chapter 10 in connection with biometric devices. The same statistical principles apply to sensors more generally since biometric readers are just another type of sensor. In this case, the sensor is measuring a deviation from expected ambient conditions rather than the acceptance or rejection of a credential.

False acceptance and false rejection for biometrics are now replaced by false positive and false negative, respectively, for sensors. A false positive is a condition where a sensor erroneously detects an environmental anomaly. A false negative is a condition where the sensor does not detect an environmental anomaly and should have done so. Both conditions are not good from a security perspective. A false negative implies that a legitimate security issue exists but is not detected. This can represent a serious security condition.

A false positive is an erroneous detection of a scenario anomaly. Repeated false positives lead to desensitization of risk conditions and potentially ignoring a condition signifying an actual increase in security risk. Sensor sensitivity plays a major role in the statistics of false positives and false negatives as it sets the threshold on detection.

Ambient conditions must also be factored into the requirements for sensor performance. Issues like weather/temperature, lighting, etc. will drive sensor selection and the overall strategy. For example, if detection is required in external space, and this is not possible based on a sensor's performance specifications, compensating controls must be instituted. Again, such reasoning represents the essence of an effective security strategy.

Tables 12.1 and 12.2 specify various security sensor technologies, as well as key operational requirements for interior and exterior deployments. These are not meant to be exhaustive, but should provide some perspective

Table 12.1 Interior Security Sensors			
INTERIOR SENSORS	**Passive/Active**	**Covert/Visible**	**Volumetric/Line**
Boundary or Penetration Sensors			
Electromechanical	p	c/v	L
Infrared	p/a	v	L
Vibration	p	c	L
Capacitance	p	c	L
Fiber Optic Cable	p	c/v	L
Interior Motion Sensors			
Microwave	a	v	V
Ultrasonic	a	v	V
Sonic	a	v	V
Passive IR	p	v	L
Proximity Sensors			
Capacitance	a	c	L
Pressure	p	c	L
(From Garcia. M. 2008. The Design and Evaluation of Physical Protection Systems, Second Ed. Waltham, MA: Butterworth Heinemann.)			

Table 12.2 Exterior Security Sensors

EXTERIOR SENSORS	Passive or Active	Convert or Visible	Line-of-Sight (LOS) or Terrain-Following (TF)	Volumetric (VOL) or Line Detection (LD)
Buried Line Sensors				
Seismic Pressure	P	C	TF	LD
Magnetic Field	P	C	TF	VOL
Ported Coaxial Cable	A	C	TF	VOL
Fiber Optic Cable	P	C	TF	LD
Fence-Associated Sensors				
Fence Disturbance	P	V	TF	LD
Sensor Fence	P	V	TF	LD
Electric Field	A	V	TF	VOL
Freestanding Sensors				
Active Infrared	A	V	LOS	LD
Passive Infrared	P	V	LOS	VOL
Bi-static Microwave	A	V	LOS	VOL
Dual Technology	A/P	V	LOS	VOL
Video Motion Detection	P	C	LOS	VOL

(From Garcia. M. 2008. The Design and Evaluation of Physical Protection Systems, Second Ed. Waltham, MA: Butterworth Heinemann.)

on the types of commercial security sensors that are available. In addition, the sensors have been organized according to interior or exterior deployment. This makes the information contained therein particularly handy for reference.

Entire books could be devoted to some of the sensors listed in these tables. A security requirement might inspire the reader to identify a potential candidate sensor and then do more in-depth reading on a particular technology. The cited source lines would be a good place to begin that research.

Clearly there are performance limitations for each sensor, and specific security scenarios lend themselves to various deployment options. As always, the risk factors associated with the specific threat attack vectors of concern coupled with on-site operational requirements should drive the selection. As the security technology guru Roger Pike likes to remind his clients (patiently), "First, tell me what you're trying to achieve."

Rather than superficially describing technical features for a list of sensors, the next several sections provide a more in-depth treatment of three sensor technologies that are important to counterterrorism and security: passive infrared sensors (PIR), ultrasonic sensors, and metal detectors. Understanding the fundamentals of these three sensor technologies will highlight issues that apply to sensors more generally, and should help drive decisions related to specific deployment opportunities.

PIRs and ultrasonic sensors are so-called proximity sensors. The name derives from the detection of objects *in proximity*, i.e., without actually touching them. Proximity sensors are a general type of sensor. At a high level, proximity sensors utilize some form of detector that registers a change in a physical parameter such as the infrared energy background or a Doppler shift caused by relative motion between the object and the detector.

PIR sensors linked to alarm systems are used in many security scenarios these days. They are relatively simple devices, yet if deployed correctly they can be extremely effective as a means of detecting unauthorized physical access. If they are deployed haphazardly, they are surprisingly easy to defeat. Therefore, deployment configurations are an important consideration and will be discussed here.

Ultrasonic sensors are used in scenarios that are similar to PIR sensors. Although less popular these days, they are still applicable to certain security scenarios. Ultrasonic and PIRs have some complementary operational features, and a combination of the two technologies could be a formidable detection methodology.

Metal detectors are ubiquitous these days. Anyone who has traveled by air in the United States during the last 30 years has stepped through a detector archway or has been worked over by a wand searching for metal objects. A number of commercial buildings deploy them in lobbies as well. They are a natural complement to X-ray inspection devices intended to detect bombs and/or weapons.

Moreover, conventional weapons such as handguns and other firearms do not receive sufficient attention as terrorist weapons. Maybe this is because they are so common in the United States. Nevertheless, and in part as a result of their accessibility, it is important to understand the principal technology used to detect firearms.

12.8.4   Passive Infrared Sensors

PIR sensors are a common form of proximity sensor. The use of PIR sensors can be effective in triggering alarms signifying attempts at unauthorized physical access. Proper installation of these devices is critical in order to not increase their vulnerability to disarming or introduce high rates of false positives.

A little science can help to take the mystery out of PIRs and also highlight their utility and limitations. We have already discovered that infrared energy is a type of electromagnetic radiation with wavelengths between 700 nm to 300 µm. These wavelengths are longer than visible light and hence are not detectable by the unaided eye.

Electromagnetic energy is radiated at infrared wavelengths by human beings and other living creatures as a result of their body temperature. The theory of black body radiation explains the association between temperature and the wavelength of the emitted radiation. Recall Figure 7.18 illustrates where infrared energy exists in the electromagnetic spectrum.

Objects that radiate light or, equivalently, thermal energy do so according to the laws of thermodynamics. The radiated power and wavelength of the emitted radiation depends on the object's temperature. Figure 12.5 illustrates the relationship between radiated thermal power (kilowatts) and the temperature of an object at a given wavelength.

It turns out that the wavelength of thermal radiation and thermal power can both be described by simple expressions (Note: wavelength corresponds to color if the radiation is visible). With respect to wavelength, the Wien Displacement Law applies and is written as follows:

$$\lambda \, (cm) = 3000/T$$

λ = wavelength.
T = absolute temperature (degrees Kelvin).

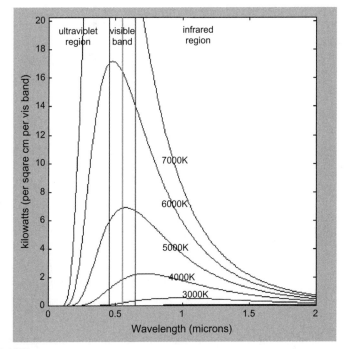

FIGURE 12.5

Radiated thermal power and temperature. *(Source: Muller, R.A. 2001. "Invisible Light."* http://muller.lbl.gov/teaching/physics10/old%20physics%2010/chapters%20(old)/12-InvisibleLight.html.*)*

Therefore, if the temperature of a human at the surface (i.e., the skin) is roughly 300 K, the wavelength of radiated thermal power as seen by a detector is 10 μm. A thermal sensor programmed to detect the presence of humans should be designed for optimum sensitivity at this wavelength.

The total radiated thermal power (P) emitted by humans, or any object for that matter, is given by the following expression:

$$P = A\sigma T^4$$

Here A is the area of the object, σ is the Stephan-Boltzmann constant $= 5.68 \times 10^{-8}\,W/m^2 K^4$, and T is the absolute temperature. The important point is that the total radiated power is proportional to the temperature to the fourth power.

As we know from numerous discussions on scaling, this implies that small changes in the temperature of an object will have a big impact on its radiated thermal power. If object A is twice as hot as object B, the total radiated power of object A is 16 times that of object B (i.e., the temperature of $A = 2\,B$ so the power emitted by $A \sim 2^4\,B = 16\,B$). The total thermal power radiated by humans has been calculated to be about 150 W, which makes them relatively easy to detect against a typically cooler background.

In a PIR sensor, the sensing element is a pyroelectric device that generates a temporary electric potential when there is a change in detected infrared radiation. The potential disappears following the dielectric relaxation time, allowing for continuous detection. The device is referred to as "passive" because it is detecting the presence of ambient infrared energy, and it is not actively illuminating an object. Recall the discussion on infrared CCTV in Chapter 11, which uses illumination to detect reflected infrared energy. Although both devices leverage infrared energy, they function in completely different ways.

A Fresnel lens, possibly familiar to readers who have inspected photocopier platens, is then placed over the pyroelectric device to prevent false triggers, supply uniform sensitivity, and extend the field-of-view, which has been quoted as 60 degrees for one model.[1] The Fresnel lens effectively creates spatial zones across the field-of-view. Figure 12.6 illustrates the concept.

The intensity of thermal energy radiated per solid angle subtended by the lens is what the Fresnel lens "sees." A solid angle is defined as the two-dimensional angle in three-dimensional space that an object subtends at a point. Qualitatively it is a measure of how large the object appears to an observer looking from that point. In the International System of Units (SI), a solid angle is a dimensionless unit of measurement called a steradian (sr).

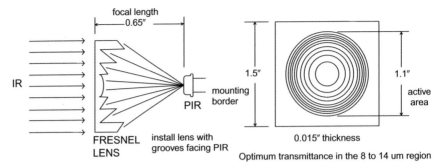

FIGURE 12.6

A Fresnel lens and PIRs. *(Source: www.nyu.edu.)*

Technically, the solid angle is the angle determined by the surface area of a sphere, *S*, divided by the radius squared, r^2. Therefore, if the surface of interest is an entire sphere, the solid angle is given by $4\pi r^2/r^2 = 4\pi$ sr. Figure 12.7 illustrates the geometry of thermal radiation detection in terms of a solid angle.

But this is not the complete story with respect to infrared detection and PIRs. PIRs work by examining spatial changes in infrared energy within the field-of-view and across the zones created by the Fresnel lens. It is these spatial differences between the source of infrared energy and its surroundings that are used to detect the presence of a potential intruder.

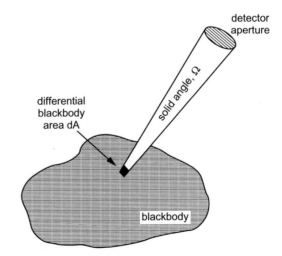

FIGURE 12.7

Thermal detection geometry. *(Soure: NASA. GOES Science Project. "Blackbody Radiation." http://goes. gsfc.nasa.gov/text/MITRE-GOES_MP93W62/a-a/a-a.html.)*

Specifically, the PIR is configured to provide an electric signal in response to spatial changes in the infrared background across the solid angle zones within the field-of-view. Figure 12.8 depicts the physical situation and the electronic signal output.

Specifically, the Fresnel lens views the area of coverage as a series of fan-shaped zones, with small gaps in between. Movement between these zones is interpreted as human activity. It is most sensitive to motion that occurs between each zone, lateral to the sensor. The farther the distance from the sensor, the wider the spaces between these zones become. This increases the potential for gaps in coverage.

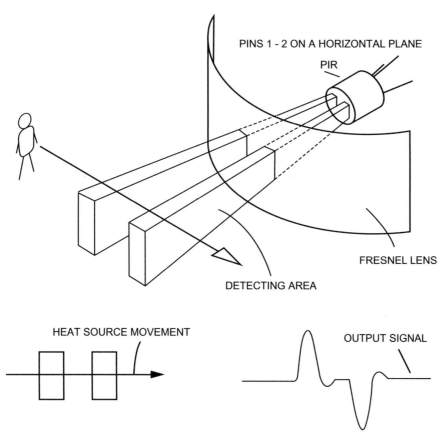

FIGURE 12.8

PIR sensor detection and signal output. *(Source: Sensor Workshop at ITP. "Reports/Passive Infrared Sensor." http://itp.nyu.edu/physcomp/sensors/Reports/PassiveInfraRedSensor.)*

The PIR sensitivity decreases linearly with distance. Most PIR sensors are sensitive to full-body movement up to around 40 ft but are only sensitive to hand movement, which is more discrete (and discreet!), up to about 15 ft.

Passive infrared sensors are difficult to defeat *unless* physical access to the lens is possible. This could happen if there is a physical route to the lens that is outside the lens field-of-view. This is possible if the device is mounted low on the wall near the entrance to a room, and where the field-of-view does not include the doorway. In addition, placing PIRs near air vents or open windows increases the risk of false positives because of temperature gradients.

Since the device focuses infrared energy radiating from a source, if the lens is opaque to the radiated energy the device will not work. So someone wishing to defeat the device might slip a cover over the lens or spray the lens with infrared-absorbing material.

The countermeasure to this potential compromise of the device is to mount the lens in a physically inaccessible place. Therefore, the objective is to detect the intruder before he or she can physically approach the device. PIRs are often mounted in the upper corners of rooms, in part for this reason, and also because this optimizes detection since it captures individuals walking across the field-of-view. This motion will cause a maximum angular rate of signal change with respect to the infrared background as seen by the sensor.

12.8.5   Ultrasonic Sensors

Ultrasonic sensors work in ways that are similar to radar and sonar by exploiting the Doppler principle. Many readers are qualitatively familiar with this effect after hearing the sound of an approaching or retreating siren. This sound is characterized by increasing pitch (i.e., frequency) as the vehicle approaches the observer and a decreasing pitch as the vehicle moves away from the observer.

This frequency change or Doppler shift results from relative motion between the stationary sensor (e.g., the human ear or an ultrasonic transducer) and a moving object. It is a natural phenomenon that occurs whenever energy emanates from a moving object relative to a stationary observer or vice versa. It is this relative movement that is exploited by ultrasonic sensors and is used to detect motion.

It is difficult to envision a scenario where an individual gaining unauthorized physical access to a space does not move within that space. But an object that is in fact stationary relative to the sensor will not produce a Doppler shift (i.e., $v_s = 0$ in the expression for Δf below) and therefore will not be detected by this type of sensor. This is not the case with PIRs, although they have their own operational limitations as noted previously.

An ultrasonic sensor consists of a piezoelectric transducer that converts electrical energy into an ultrasonic acoustic wave, typically between 40 and 50 kHz. This high-frequency sound, which is beyond the capability of human hearing,[a] impacts an object and is reflected back toward another transducer that converts the acoustic energy into electrical energy. The distance of an object from the sensor can be evaluated once this echo is received using the following simple expression:

$$d = 2(c \times \underline{t})$$

d = distance
c = speed of sound
t = elapsed time of the signal

The coefficient of 2 arises from the fact that the ultrasonic signal travels out toward the object and is reflected back to the sensor along the same path.

When the medium of propagation is air, the speed of sound, c, is equal to 340 m/s under standard conditions. The control circuitry on the ultrasonic sensor can distinguish between stationary objects and objects in motion by interpreting changes in frequency as motion according to the Doppler effect.

For interested readers, the precise change in frequency that results from the motion between a stationary source and an object moving toward the source can be calculated from the following formula:

$$\text{Change in frequency, } \Delta f = \frac{(c + v)f}{c}$$

f = sound frequency
c = velocity of sound
v = velocity of the object

Figure 12.9 depicts the relativistic effect on the source frequency of sound emanating from a moving vehicle due to the Doppler effect. Note that although this is an instance of the Doppler principle, it is not the same as the ultrasonic sensor. In the ultrasonic sensor case, the "observer" (i.e., intruder) is moving toward the stationary source of ultrasonic energy. In the case of the vehicle, the source of sound energy (e.g., a siren) is moving toward a stationary observer.

---

[a]The maximum audible frequency for humans is about 20 kHz. Note that this is not beyond the frequency range of dogs!

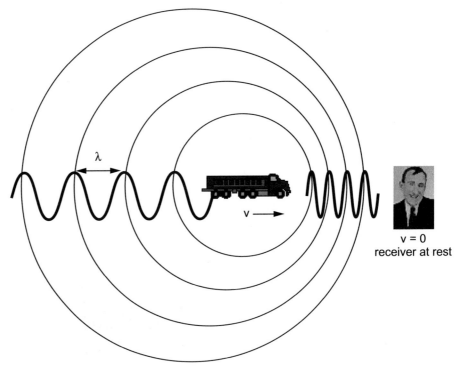

FIGURE 12.9
The Doppler effect. *(Source: Goddard Space Flight Center. NASA. "Doppler Shift."* http://imagine.gsfc.
nasa.gov/YBA/M31-velocity/Doppler-shift-2.html.*)*

Ultrasonic sensors can detect hand motion up to about 20 ft, arm and torso movement to about 30 ft, and full-body motion to roughly 40 ft. Ultrasonic sensors do not have gaps in the zone of coverage such as those exhibited by PIR sensors and can be sensitive to slight motions at nearly twice the distance. However, the overall detection range of an ultrasonic sensor is comparable to that of a PIR sensor. The ultrasonic sensor can also detect motion behind partial obstructions. One of the advantages of the ultrasonic sensor is the ability to calculate distance to the object in motion.

However, very slow motion relative to the fixed sensor could represent an operational issue, which is not the case for PIRs. Data specifying ultrasonic sensor sensitivity to the rate of motion was unfortunately not available.

It might also be interesting to understand the difference in response as a function of the relative direction between a sensor and an object, and this is analyzed below.

As noted previously, the Doppler shift, Δf, for the signal reflected off an object moving directly toward a stationary source of sound is given by $[(v+c)/c]f$, where c is the velocity of sound, v is the velocity of the moving object, and f is the frequency of the ultrasonic transmitter. Therefore, the transmitted frequency will be increasing since $(v+c)/c$ will always be greater than unity (so $\Delta f > f$).

What is the Doppler shift for objects moving at right angles to the ultrasonic sensor? The so-called transverse Doppler shift is given by $\Delta f = [\sqrt{(1-(v/c)^2}]f$. We see from this expression that the frequency of the transmitted frequency will be decreasing since $1-(v/c)^2$ will always be less than unity (so $\Delta f < f$).

In the limit where $v \sim c$ we see that $\Delta f = 2f$ for motion directly toward the sensor, and $\Delta f = 0$ for motion at right angles to the sensor. In the limit where $v << c$, $\Delta f = f$ for motion directly toward the sensor as well as at right angles to the sensor.

Therefore, the shift in frequency for objects moving at right angles to the source will in general be smaller (i.e., less sensor sensitivity) than when objects move directly toward the source except in the limit of extremely slow motion when the Doppler shifts are similar in magnitude. Slow motion should be the rule in this case since people generally do not move at or even near the speed of sound. So there should be no appreciable difference in system performance for motion at right angles to the sensor versus motion directly at the sensor.

Differences in the performance of PIRs and ultrasonic sensors suggest potential benefits derived from dual technology devices. In fact, dual technology sensors are manufactured, and several URLs advertising such devices are listed directly below:

1. *http://www.smarthome.com/36528/Leviton-OSSMT-MDW-Multi-Tech-PIR-Ultrasonic-Occupancy-Sensor-Decora-Wall-Switch-White/p.aspx.* (Note: this particular device is used for automatic light switches, but the operational principle is identical to a device used in a security scenario.)
2. *http://updates.clipsal.com/clipsalonline/Files/Brochures/W0001310.pdf.*

12.8.6 Metal Detectors

Metal detectors might be the most common technical security device in use today. Every commercial airport in the United States deploys at least one of these devices to screen passengers for weapons in conjunction with X-ray technology that is used to screen baggage.

Metal detectors, as distinguished from magnetometers, are active devices. They generate a magnetic field that interacts with metallic objects to produce a specific effect. Namely, a changing magnetic field produces an electric field that induces currents to flow in the metal. All electrical currents produce a magnetic field. The metal detector detects the magnetic field that is generated by the so-called eddy

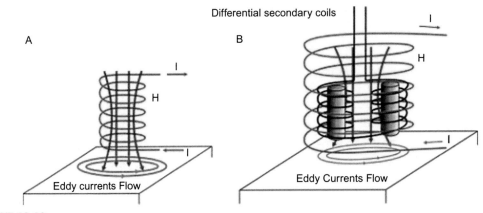

FIGURE 12.10

Eddy currents. *(Source: Garcia-Martin, J., J. Gomez-Gil, E. Vazquez-Sanchez, "Non-Destructive Techniques Based on Eddy Current Testing." Open I Beta.* http://openi.nlm.nih.gov/detailedresult.php?img=3231639_sensors-11-02525f20&req=4.)*

currents in the metal. Figure 12.10 illustrates eddy current generation using single coil and opposing coil configurations.

How do metal detectors such as those deployed in airports exploit eddy currents to detect metal objects such as weapons?[2] Almost all of these devices use a technique known as pulse induction (PI). Recall the archway you pass through during a typical screening in advance of catching a flight at the airport.

Typical PI systems use a coil of wire (or more likely multiple coils) on one side of the arch as the transmitter and receiver. This coil sends powerful, short pulses of current through the coil of wire. Each pulse generates a brief magnetic field as a result of this current. When the pulse stops, the magnetic field reverses polarity and collapses very suddenly, resulting in a sharp electrical spike. This spike lasts a few microseconds and causes another current to flow through the coil. This subsequent current is called the reflected pulse and lasts only about $30\,\mu s$.

The transmitting coil then sends another pulse and the process repeats. A typical PI-based metal detector sends about 100 pulses/s, but the number can vary greatly based on the manufacturer and model, ranging from about 25 pulses/s to over 1000 pulses/s.

If a metal object passes through the metal detector, the pulse creates a magnetic field in the object as a result of the changing electric fields (according to Maxwell's equations). Recall that when the pulse's magnetic field collapses, the changing magnetic field causes a reflected pulse. The magnetic field generated in the metal object as a result of the induced eddy current causes the reflected pulse to take longer to completely disappear.

A sampling circuit in the metal detector monitors the duration of the reflected pulse. By comparing the actual result to the expected duration, the circuit can determine if another magnetic field has caused an increase in the reflected pulse decay time. If the decay time of the reflected pulse takes a few microseconds longer than expected, the presumption is that the presence of a metal object is what is causing the interference (i.e., the metal detector has been calibrated to respond accordingly). The pulsing circuit is set to operate continuously to reduce the risk of someone slipping a weapon through the portal while an inspector is not looking.

The sensitivity of a metal detector is a key security issue that has significant operational implications. As noted previously in this chapter, sensor sensitivity settings represent a balancing act of risk management and should be based on the tolerance for risk. Setting the sensitivity of the device too high will result in an abundance of false positives. However, a sensitivity setting that is too low would represent a significant security issue since a legitimate weapon could go undetected, i.e., a false negative occurs.

Perhaps contrary to intuition, the mass of a metal object is less significant in metal detection than other physical features.[3] The size, shape, electrical conductivity, and magnetic properties are more important in eliciting a detector response.

For example, when a long thin wire is passed through a portal-type metal detector, and the wire is configured such that no two points on the wire are touching, it is less likely to be detected. However, if the same wire is in the shape of a closed loop, the metal detector will more likely respond, even though the mass of the wire has not changed.

The orientation of an object is also a factor in how a metal detector responds to the presence of metal. Suppose one passes the same closed-loop wire described above through a metal detector. Lay this loop on its side so that it is parallel to the ground. In this configuration the portal-type metal detector is less likely to detect the presence of metal. However, if the wire loop is held upright such that the face is parallel to the detector side panels, the metal detector will be more likely to respond as a result of this orientation. Let's examine why this is so.

The maximum-induced electric field in the receive coil occurs when the rate of change of magnetic flux is a maximum. Therefore, the maximum signal occurs when the planes of the transmitter and receiver coils face each other. The so-called "right hand rule" shows why this is the case.

If the current, *I*, is flowing in a particular direction through the transmit coil, then the magnetic field associated with that coil circulates around the coil. The direction of the fluxing field around the current-carrying wire can be determined by the right hand rule: grasp the wire in your right hand with the thumb pointing in the direction of the current. The orientation of your curled fingers corresponds to the direction of the magnetic flux. Figure 12.11 shows the right hand rule in action where *B* is the fluxing field and *I* is the current.

Therefore, it is easy to see that a receive coil intended to maximize the flux through the boundary would be oriented such that its face was parallel to the transmit coil. Recall a similar geometry was discussed in Chapter 11 when we examined the scenario of a covert receive coil that was used to detect emanations from a Cat5 Ethernet cable carrying CCTV signals. Figure 12.12 illustrates the direction of a fluxing magnetic field as a result of current flow in a wire.

Finally, electromagnetic interference (EMI) is an issue with metal detectors as well as any sensor that functions due to induction. Various models of metal detectors are better shielded than others. Common metal objects in close proximity such as stools, trash cans, chain-link fence, vibrating pipes, and expanding air ducts have reportedly interfered with metal detector performance.

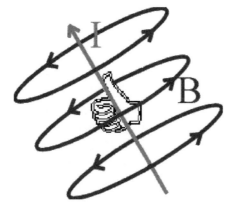

FIGURE 12-11

The right hand rule. *(Source: NASA. Stargazers. "Electromagnetism."* http://stargazers.gsfc.nasa. gov/resources/electromagnetism.htm.*)*

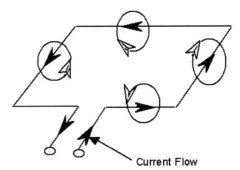

Current Flow

FIGURE 12.12

Magnetic flux generated by current flow. *(Source: Federal Highway Administration. "Sensor Technology." Traffic Detector Handbook. Third Edition—Vol. I.* http://www.fhwa.dot.gov/ publications/research/operations/its/06108/02.cfm.*)*

SUMMARY

Physical access restriction is a key control to address the terrorism risk factor of unauthorized physical access. Standard security infrastructure used to implement this control includes electric strikes and magnetic locks. However, the real security challenge involves facilitating physical access to restricted areas for authorized individuals and preventing physical access otherwise.

Electric strikes and magnetic locks are useful because they can be controlled by devices that authorize physical access and/or authenticate identity. These include ID card readers and biometric readers. The biometric device actually confirms authorization as well as authenticates identity.

Security sensors that work in conjunction with alarms complement controls dedicated to restricting physical access. They respond to changes in the environment that signify an increased vulnerability to unauthorized physical access as well as other risk factors, depending on the threat and sensor type.

However, no sensor is perfect, and statistical analyses of performance provide important insights into their effectiveness. Moreover, adjustment of sensor sensitivity will affect the rate of false positives and false negatives. The organizational tolerance for risk will in part determine the required level of sensor sensitivity.

Three sensors are analyzed in this chapter: PIRs, ultrasonic motion detectors, and metal detectors. Issues associated with each are illustrative of the type of analysis required for any sensor prior to deployment. However, each of these has very specific operational features and performance capabilities. All sensors require an understanding of the specific deployment conditions relative to stated operational requirements in order to be most effective in scenarios of interest.

REFERENCES

[1] Hodges L, Michigan State University. Ultrasonic and passive infrared sensor integration for duel technology user detection sensors. http://www.egr.msu.edu/classes/ece480/capstone/fall09/group05/docs/ece480_dt5_application_note_lhodges.pdf.

[2] Tyson J, About.com. How metal detectors work. http://tattoo.about.com/gi/o.htm?zi=1/XJ&zTi=1&sdn=tattoo&cdn=style&tm=7&f=00&su=p284.13.342.ip_p504.6.342.ip_&tt=2&bt=4&bts=4&zu=http%3A//home.howstuffworks.com//metal-detector.htm.

[3] National Criminal Justice Reference Service. Metal detection. https://www.ncjrs.gov/school/178265_8.pdf.

Problems

1. You are the Security Director of a major international company, and you are doing a preliminary assessment of security requirements for your new headquarters facility. This facility will be located in midtown Manhattan. Your facility will also be located in close proximity to "iconic" facilities in the vicinity, and the general crime rate is considered low.

   a. Specify at least one significant threat of concern for the following areas in and around this facility and identify the relevant components of risk associated with each threat:
      i. Building perimeter.
      ii. Building lobby.
      iii. Entrance to internal office areas.

   b. Note at least one risk factor for the threats noted above. Recall a risk factor is a characteristic/feature that enhances one or more components of risk.

   c. Choose one building area and indicate how the following controls would address the risk factor associated with the threat you identified for that building area: (a) visual monitoring; (b) authentication; (c) authorization; and (d) physical restrictions.

   d. Specify at least one *technical* method to implement one of the relevant controls for that area and describe the operational requirements for your choice of method.

   e. Provide one technical specification for the method noted above. Indicate how it satisfies the stated operational requirement.

2. You are planning to install a suite of security equipment in an internal room that requires special access. The room has one window and one door. This security equipment includes a visual monitoring control method (CCTV) and a card reader controlling a magnetic lock on the door as a method to implement physical access restriction.

   a. If the distance from the camera to the door is 20 ft, the camera is 1 megapixel, and the operational requirement is facial recognition thereby dictating a minimum of 40 pixels/ft resolution in the horizontal field of view, indicate a reasonable value for the lens focal length required to cover the doorway. Use an online calculator or the formula specified in Chapter 11.

   b. Research various models on the Web and specify the force of the electromagnet required when the lock is engaged. Justify your answer based on risk and cost.

   c. Specify a response protocol in the event a "door forced" or "door held open" alarm is registered. Would this response include the triggering of any other sensors/equipment?

   d. What other security controls would you use if any?

3. You are a terrorist attempting to gain unauthorized access to a data center. In doing a reconnaissance of a target facility, you notice the passive infrared sensors

inside the facility are within reach of the entrance. Indicate how you might defeat these sensors. Specify procedures or compensating controls to correct the problem or manage the risk.

4. Explain why unauthorized physical access to the physical access control system panels should not be allowed. What security controls to include sensors would you invoke to protect the panels? Would you provide the same controls for the readers? Why or why not?

5. A physical access control system similar to the one illustrated in Figure 12.3 is installed in your building. Building air conditioning (AC) power has been lost, but fortunately the panels are backed up by an uninterruptable power supply (UPS). However, the central server that communicates to the panel is not so fortunate. Explain the potential effect on unauthorized physical access to restricted space while the server is down. Be as specific as possible with respect to the scenarios of concern.

6. Explain why a PIR should be installed so that it detects motion perpendicular to the face of the sensor. Would you expect motion detection to be more sensitive if an individual is closer or farther away from the PIR? Why?

7. Would an ultrasonic sensor detect a human standing perfectly still in its field of detection? Why or why not? What about a PIR?

8. Would you expect a PIR to work if the temperature inside a building was 37° C? What if the human was wrapped in tinfoil?

9. Explain in your own words the statement that a sampled mean is within a 95% confidence interval of the true mean for a sensor. If one stated the sampled mean is within a 70% confidence interval of the true mean, would you expect the interval to be wider or narrower than a 95% confidence interval? Why?

10. Explain the difference in functionality between a magnetic lock and an electric strike.

11. Explain the risks associated with the following scenarios:
    a. Building AC power is lost and a magnetic lock on a door fails unsecure, i.e., the lock is not energized.
    b. Building AC power is lost and the electric strike on a door fails secure because of a battery backup.
    c. The fire alarm is activated and the magnetic lock on a door is released.
    d. The fire alarm is activated and the electric strike on a door remains active. (Note: this likely violates the fire code in most jurisdictions.)

12. Explain the difference between "accuracy" and "resolution" in the context of sensor measurements. Give an example of a measurement with high resolution and poor accuracy.

13. You are a frequent flier and, of course, are subject to the preflight security at airports. You have done informal experiments to test TSA screening procedures and noticed that the metal detectors at some airports detect your pocketknife and at other airports they do not. Provide a qualitative explanation of the risk

associated with this phenomenon. What would you do to correct this issue if you deem it necessary to correct it, and what vulnerabilities if any does your correction introduce?

14. You are the Security Director of an iconic building in Manhattan with a number of high-profile tenants. After a series of publicized shootings, you evaluate the components of risk and decide to install a metal detector in the lobby for visitors. What experiments would you conduct to determine the appropriate sensitivity setting on the machine for your organization? Recall that the problem is to reduce the number of false positive activations but not to the extent that a legitimate weapon would go undetected. What false positive rate would be acceptable and why? (Note: there is no right or wrong answer here.)

15. Extra Credit! Design a high-level technical security strategy for a data center, incorporating appropriate security sensor technology in various areas as part of the regimen. Specify which security sensors should be mounted within these areas and how they mitigate the risk of identified threats.

Epilogue

Attempting to capture the essential elements of terrorism risk and risk mitigation in one book can be tricky. Most notably, it is a field populated by individuals with wildly dissimilar backgrounds. For example, many of its practitioners in the United States are from law enforcement and the Intelligence Community. Although such individuals may possess years of operational experience, and may have developed a strong intuition about risk, they often have little or no technical or quantitative skills. At the other end of the personnel spectrum are engineers who lack operational experience but possess solid technical backgrounds, and apply their skills to the complex problems that arise in modern terrorism scenarios.

This mixture of backgrounds coupled with the sheer breadth of the field makes counterterrorism challenging from an educational perspective. Specifically, there is no agreed set of fundamental principles, methods, and/or materials that forms the basis for problem solving. Consider the field of medicine where students learn anatomy, physiology, biochemistry, and so on as part of a core curriculum. Similar core curricula exist in other disciplines, but not in counterterrorism.

It would be quite presumptuous to claim that this book provides *the* exclusive corpus of material required to address the many varieties of terrorism risk problems. But it does present one framework that facilitates rigorous thinking about security risk, and therefore might be included in a candidate security curriculum. This framework entails analyzing the magnitude of each component of risk (qualitatively or quantitatively) and addressing the risk factors that enhance each component. Assessing electronic risk can appear more challenging because the very existence of a network, which is essential to modern electronic communication, is itself a risk factor for the threats of concern. But the basis for assessing security risk as specified in this framework is actually the same across all threat types.

Of course, the Holy Grail of security is to actually *measure* risk. This often proves elusive in a field with low numbers of incidents and/or rapidly evolving risk profiles. But the absence of security incidents does not imply an absence of risk. The workaround is that one can measure incidents that relate to a risk factor for a threat rather than instances of the threat itself.

Moreover, certain simple physical models can be applied to a variety of terrorism scenarios, and thereby yield estimates of the vulnerability component of risk. In addition, there is a strong statistical component to analyzing terrorism risk, and probabilistic methods can be used to estimate the likelihood that risk mitigation will be effective.

Some risk factors related to electronic terrorism lend themselves to quantitative analyses (e.g., dropped packets, attempts at establishing TCP/IP connections). But in general, looking for and responding to risk factor events in inter-zone network traffic is required to effectively manage electronic terrorism risk, and constitutes a form of measurement in this context.

Unfortunately, in counterterrorism there can be a tendency to quantify inherently qualitative issues and handwave on topics where quantifiable results are actually achievable. It is essential to understand when quantitative methods apply, and when they don't, and thereby provide truly useful recommendations on security risk management.

Even when quantitative methods are applicable, estimates rather than exact solutions yield results that are often good enough. The ultimate goal is to develop enough insight to make an informed decision on risk in light of competing security priorities and restricted budgets. Such insights can often be achieved with merely order-of-magnitude precision.

Of course, determining the set of required security controls is essential to managing terrorism risk. The final three chapters of this book focus on key counterterrorism controls. These provide the underlying theory and functional details to assess their applicability and effectiveness across a spectrum of terrorism scenarios.

Finally, the modern security professional faces many challenges. In addition to the actual terrorists, he or she must deal with pampered executives, shrinking budgets, and competing priorities. All these drive an increasing need for risk-based decision making. The hope is that this book provides a useful balance of theoretical and practical material that can help enable, prioritize, and ultimately justify such decisions.

Linearity, Nonlinearity, and Parametric Scaling

Risk can sometimes be evaluated more precisely because of a relationship to physical quantities that obey natural laws. These physical quantities are themselves a function of parameters like distance and time. One can then examine the effect of these quantities on risk using a range of parameter values dictated by scenario-specific conditions.

For example, if one hopes to evaluate the vulnerability of a facility to vehicle-borne explosives, one must do so for various payloads and standoff distances in order to develop an effective mitigation strategy. It is unlikely an adversary will advertise the plan of attack, and therefore a distribution of possible attack scenarios is required.

Because an estimate of the vulnerability to explosive damage is related to physical quantities such as impulse, overpressure, etc., it is necessary to accurately determine their dependence on parameters such as the distance from the source to the target and the explosive payload. This process of identifying key physical quantities and their dependent physical parameters is a mainstay of assessing the vulnerability component of security risk. Moreover, understanding the resultant *change* in risk as these scenario-dependent parameters vary is essential in developing a risk-mitigation strategy. We speak of the effect of such changes in parameter values as "parametric scaling."

Several key scaling concepts are the notions of linearity and nonlinearity. As one might guess, the term linearity is rooted in the word "line." If two variables are linearly related it means a change in one variable causes a proportionate change in the other. Suppose, for example, age and body weight are linearly related for humans. Let's write down a made-up expression that depicts a hypothesized relationship between chronological age and body weight:

$$\text{BODY WEIGHT} = (4 \times \text{AGE}) + 25$$

Based on this simple equation, we can calculate body weight by simply substituting representative values for age:

Age (Years)	Body Weight (Pounds)
10	65
20	105
30	145
40	185
50	225

In this case age and body weight are linearly related because an increase in age causes a *proportionate* increase in body weight for all values of age. Specifically, an increase in age from 10 to 20 years, yields a weight difference of $105 - 65 = 40$ lb. If one doubles the age difference from 20 to 40 years, this yields a weight difference of $185 - 105 = 40 \times 2 = 80$ lb. In other words, doubling the age results in a doubling of weight.

This fixed relationship between related variables is the essence of linearity. The fact that such changes are always proportionate throughout the range of the function is the key element here. A graph of the expression Weight $= (4 \times \text{Age}) + 25$ is depicted in Figure A.1, and it is worth noting the very straight and hence *linear* appearance. Linearity is an important characteristic of physical quantities that affect risk.

However, the physical world is replete with examples of processes or quantities that display *nonlinear* behavior. A nonlinear relationship between variables or parameters is one where successive changes in one variable cause *disproportionate* changes in a related variable. An example of a nonlinear relationship

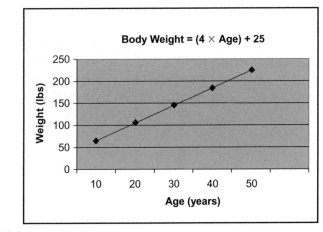

FIGURE A.1

Linearity.

is that of the velocity of an object and its kinetic energy. The kinetic energy of an object is proportional to the square of its velocity. The exact expression is Kinetic Energy $(KE) = 1/2mv^2$, where m is mass. Let's plot some representative values of kinetic energy in terms of velocity without specifying any particular units (we assume the mass is one or unity):

Velocity	Energy
10	50
20	200
30	450
40	800
50	1250

If we double the velocity from 10 to 20, this results in a difference of $200 - 50 = 150$ units in energy. However, doubling the velocity once more from 20 to 40 units yields a change in value of $800 - 200 = 600$ energy units. We see that a doubling of the velocity results in a quadrupling of the kinetic energy.

This disproportionate relationship between the related quantities, in this case energy and velocity, is the defining characteristic of a nonlinear functions. As the difference in the values of velocity increase, the difference in the kinetic energy becomes disproportionately larger. A graph of the expression for $KE = 1/2mv^2$ using the above values is shown in Figure A.2, and note its non-straight-looking appearance.

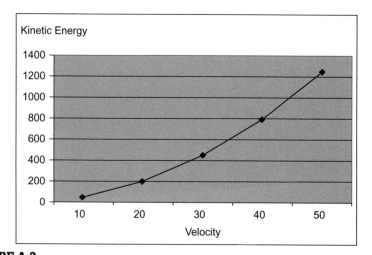

FIGURE A.2
Nonlinear function: $KE = 1/2mv^2$.

This is a good time to point out an important feature of the expression for kinetic energy. The exponent of the velocity variable indicates the number of times that variable is multiplied by itself. In other words, for any variable x, $x^2 = x \times x$, $x^3 = x \times x \times x$, etc. In particular, an exponent of 2 is referred to as the square of a variable, so $x^2 = x$ "squared." In the same vein, a variable with an exponent of three as in x^3 is referred to as x "cubed". x^4 is referred to as "x to the fourth power," x^5 is "x to the fifth," and it continues from there ad infinitum.

Linear and nonlinear functions tell an important story about how physical quantities and scenario-dependent parameters are changing with respect to one another. In understanding risk it is sometimes more important to know how relevant physical quantities such as intensity, signal/noise, etc. change with angle, distance, time, etc. than it is to know the magnitude of that quantity at a specific point in space or time.

The range of possible threat scenarios can vary considerably. So it is important to use all relevant information to estimate the limits of vulnerability associated with scenarios of interest and plan accordingly.

In fact, security strategies often call for an explicit relationship between a physical quantity affecting risk and some dependent parameter. Examples might include the intensity of a signal as a function of distance from the signal source or the volumetric density of a chemical agent as a function of time. Once this relationship is understood, a graphical representation of the dependence can be useful in developing a physically realistic mitigation strategy.

For example, it might be important to know how the sound intensity changes from one side of a wall to the other as a function of the thickness of the wall material. This information might be of particular value when designing a conference room intended for meetings with clients. Or maybe the intensity of radioactivity from a radioisotope source as a function of distance from that source is of interest in order to determine the characteristics of a proposed radiation shield.

When armed with such physical insights, effective mitigation strategies are more likely to emerge. The shape of the curve depicting the intensity versus distance from a source emitting some form of nasty energy yields important information regarding security risk that in turn facilitates effective and proportionate mitigation. In fact it is difficult to imagine a complete picture of risk for many physical security threats without such a model.

But a function of the form $y = x^2$ such as in the equation characterizing kinetic energy is not the only nonlinear expression around. However, it is important because it is quite common in security risk and elsewhere in describing the physical world.

An exponent can in fact assume any value. As discussed in the text, an important physical quantity that influences the response of building structural elements to explosive blasts is the so-called impulse. The impulse characterizes how long the pressure wave interacts with a structure and is measured in units of pressure multiplied by time (e.g., pounds-per-square-inch-millisecond or "psi-ms").

For those more familiar with physics principles, the impulse represents the time integral of the momentum imparted to the structure by the explosive force.

According to one source, the explosive impulse varies inversely with distance from the source (i.e., as $1/r = r^{-1}$). Compare how the explosive impulse and sound intensity scale with distance from their respective sources. If one doubles the distance from a point source of acoustic energy the sound intensity decreases by one quarter.

However, a doubling of the distance from an explosive source would result in a decrease by 1/2 in the magnitude of the impulse. Therefore, the effect of distance on the explosive impulse is considerably less than its effect on sound intensity. I have neglected the effect of explosive overpressure, which, as we know from Chapter 6, scales as $1/r^3$ according to some references.

Understanding the dependence of a physical quantity on a parameter such as distance is often a central theme in understanding the vulnerability component of risk.

Representations of sound intensity and explosive impulse as a function of distance from their respective sources are examples of decreasing nonlinear functions. Several "generic" decreasing nonlinear functions are shown if Figure A.3, where the function $f(r)$ is plotted relative to the variable r. We see

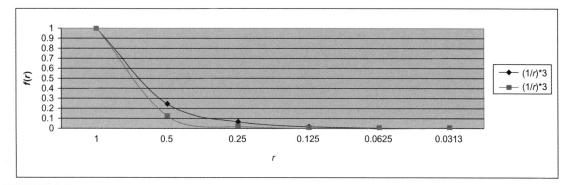

FIGURE A.3
Decreasing nonlinear functions.

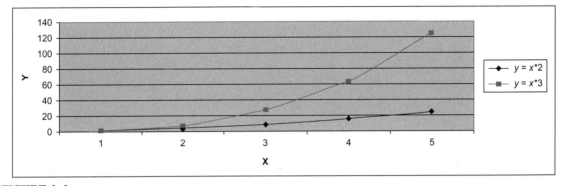

FIGURE A.4
Increasing nonlinear functions.

that $f(r)$ approaches 0 as r becomes larger in value but never actually equals 0. Mathematicians refer to functions like $f(r)$ as *asymptotically* approaching a limiting value.

We could just as easily encounter nonlinear functions that *increase* with distance, time, etc. Two examples, $y=x^2$ and $y=x^3$, are plotted in Figure A.4.

Exponents, Logarithms, and Sensitivity to Change

Linear and nonlinear expressions that describe the behavior of physical quantities affecting security risk can provide insight into the sensitivity to change of scenario-dependent parameters. Let's write a few examples of such expressions using the shorthand called exponents and observe this sensitivity firsthand.

We now know that $r^3 = r \times r \times r$, $r^6 = r \times r \times r \times r \times r \times r$, $r^9 = r \times r \times r \times r \times r \times r \times r \times r \times r$, and so on. According to the definition of exponents, the number of "r"s on the right-hand side of the equation corresponds exactly to the superscript above the r on the left side of the equation. If we substitute the number 10 for r, the value of these functions is a thousand, a million, and a billion, respectively (i.e., $10 \times 10 \times 10 = 10^3$, etc.). Clearly small differences in the exponent can make a big difference in the magnitude of the function.

A personal story may serve to drive this point home. I once deposited a check for \$10,000 in my bank account resulting from the sale of my home. When I checked my balance, the bank had credited my account for only \$1000. The \$9000 discrepancy was reflected in the omission of a single 0. This was equivalent to reducing the exponent of 10^4 (i.e., 10,000) by one to 10^3 (i.e., 1000). I was ultimately reimbursed in full after producing my deposit slip. So the moral of this story is to keep all deposit slips and to pay close attention to the exponents in any transaction.

Speaking of money, exponents play an important role in the financial world. Each of us with an interest-bearing bank account is affected by the time period over which interest on the principal is calculated. The general formula is Future Value = (Present Value) $\times (1 + I/n)^n$, where I is interest rate and n is the number of times interest is applied to the principal.

Consider the difference in the value of your bank account after 1 year if the interest rate was applied once-per-day versus once-per-year using the same interest rate! That translates to the exponent n equaling 365 in the former and 1 in the latter case. As I write this I am lamenting the pathetic rate of return I am experiencing in my conventional savings account.

Exponents are often small numbers, but they have a powerful effect on the range of values of a function. Furthermore, they tell an important story about the processes they characterize. It is the exponent that determines the degree of nonlinearity and hence how rapidly a quantity is changing as a function of a specific parameter.

In the expression $I = r^n$, the exponent is $n = 2$ and it determines the sensitivity of the intensity to changes in the variable, r. For example, doubling r results in a quadrupling of I. Tripling the value of r causes I to increase by a factor of nine, and so forth.

The logarithm is the inverse of exponentiation. In other words, it "undoes" the effect of the exponent. For example, the logarithm of 1000 in base 10 is the value of n in the expression $10^n = 1000$. So in this case $n = 3$. Similarly, the logarithm (often abbreviated as "log") of 100 equals 2, and the log of 1,000,000 equals 6, etc. A list of exponents in base 10 and their integer equivalent expressions is as follows:

$$10^0 = 1$$
$$10^1 = 10$$
$$10^2 = 100$$
$$10^3 = 1000$$
$$10^4 = 10,000$$
$$10^5 = 100,000$$
$$10^6 = 1,000,000$$
$$10^7 = 10,000,000$$
$$10^8 = 100,000,000$$
$$10^9 = 1,000,000,000$$
$$10^{10} = 10,000,000,000$$

By the way, the previously esoteric mathematical term "googol" that is now familiar to nearly everyone in the world, albeit with a different spelling, is defined as 10^{100}.

The logarithm is important in presenting information about risk for several reasons. First, it represents a compact way of displaying the full range of values when plotting a broad range of numbers. Consider a graph of $y = x^3$ for $x = 1$ through $x = 100$. The corresponding values of y range from 1 through 1,000,000. If we plot the logarithm of y instead of the absolute value of y, the y-axis only extends from 0 to 6.

Figure B.1 shows a plot of $y = x^3$ for $x = 1$ to 100 using a semilogarithmic (i.e., only one axis is logarithmic) scale. Contrast this with the form of the y-axis if we plotted the absolute value of y instead, i.e., from 1 to 1,000,000.

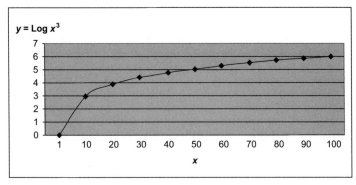

FIGURE B.1
Semilogarithmic plot.

Furthermore, sometimes functions describing physical processes vary as the logarithm of a parameter rather than the value of the parameter itself. Examples of this abound in the physical world. Processes or quantities that vary as log (x) have a more gradual dependence on x than those that scale linearly with x.

The Exponential Functions e^x and e^{-x}

For some reason certain numbers and expressions occur more frequently than others in natural phenomena. One of these is the number "e" and is defined by the following expression (written to only four decimal places; e is a so-called irrational number and therefore does not have a finite decimal representation), $e = (1 + 1/n)^n = 2.7183 \ldots$ as n approaches infinity.

The exponential function is defined as $f(x) = e^x$, where x is some arbitrary exponent. This function appears in many contexts in the natural world and is the solution to a number of equations related to physical processes that characterize risk. The exponential function is also the solution to simple first order differential equations that express the rate of change of some quantity Q, with time, t (or with respect to any other parameter), and where r is a proportionality constant: $dQ/dt = -rQ$ for processes where the quantity Q is decreasing and $dQ/dt = rQ$ for processes where Q is increasing.

The logarithm in base "e" has a special designation and is referred to as the "natural logarithm." This does not imply that the logarithm for other bases is in some way unnatural. The natural logarithm is abbreviated as "ln." We now know from the previous discussion on logarithms that $\ln (e^x) = x$. This is because the natural logarithm undoes exponentiation for functions where "e" is the base in exactly the same way that regular logarithms do for expressions in base 10 or any other base for that matter.

Figure C.1 shows a plot of $y = e^x$ where the exponent varies from $x = 1$ to $x = 5$. It is immediately obvious from the graph that this is a nonlinear function. Hence, increasing the exponent x has disproportionately greater effects on the value of y.

The exponential function is a solution to a common and relatively simple differential equation that governs a number of processes relevant to physical security. This statement applies equally to the *decreasing* exponential function $y = e^{-x}$ depicted in Figure C.2. Understanding the general behavior of the exponential function can lead to important insights into the vulnerability component of risk.

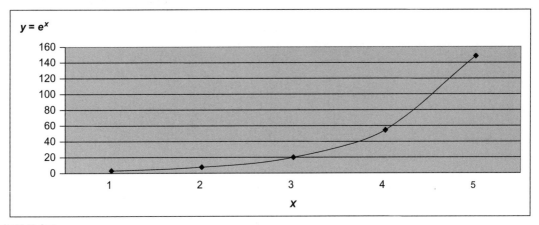

FIGURE C.1
Increasing exponential function.

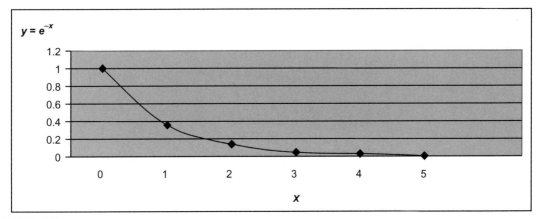

FIGURE C.2
Decreasing exponential function.

The Decibel (dB)

The decibel is very useful in depicting relative changes in quantities related to security. Decibels can be intimidating, especially if logarithms are themselves scary since the logarithm is an inherent part of the definition of the decibel. Simply put, a decibel is merely one means of expressing a ratio between two quantities. The decibel indicates the magnitude of one quantity relative to another expressed in logarithmic units.

It makes no sense to say a signal is 30 dB, 40 dB, 100 dB, etc., although such statements are made all the time. A response to this statement must be, "30 dB compared to what?" You may have in fact seen sound pressure levels seemingly expressed without such a comparative reference.

For example, conversation-level speech is sometimes expressed as 60 dB. In this case dB are actually referenced to the minimum threshold of human hearing (10^{-12} W/m²), and this figure forms the basis for the sound pressure level (SPL) scale. So, the full expression is 60 dB SPL and is consistent with the definition of the decibel as a unit expressing *relative* magnitudes.

The strict definition of a decibel when used to compare quantities like power or intensity is $10 \log(x/y)$. We could just as easily be comparing the value of Joe versus Tom's bank account or any comparison for that matter.

For example, if I happen to mention that the magnitude of my affinity for vanilla ice cream is twice that of chocolate, and we let $x =$ the magnitude of my taste for vanilla ice cream and $y =$ the magnitude of my taste for chocolate ice cream, then the ratio of magnitudes = (magnitude of x)/(magnitude of y) = 2.

Plugging that into the definition of a decibel we get $10 \log(2) = 3$, since the logarithm of 2 in base 10 is 0.3. Therefore, an equivalent statement for my liking vanilla ice cream twice as much as chocolate is that my fondness for vanilla is 3 dB more than chocolate. If the taste for vanilla ice cream actually exceeded that of chocolate ice cream by a factor of 1000, then $10 \log(1000) = 30$. In this case my lust for vanilla exceeds that of chocolate by 30 dB, etc. It is really that simple, and once you become accustomed to thinking in terms of decibels it becomes second nature.

If we want to convert 30 dB back to its equivalent linear expression we must first divide 30 by 10. This "undoes" the multiplicative factor of 10. This act of undoing yields the number 3. Now we must deal with the logarithm portion of the expression. Exponentiation undoes the logarithm function, so if we operate in reverse and raise 10 to the third power (i.e., 10^3) we restore the original linear value of 1000.

Decibels are sometimes expressed in terms of a predefined physical quantity for reference. Examples include dBm (decibels relative to a milliwatt), dBV (decibels relative to a volt), etc. 0 dBm is defined as 1 mW (i.e., one thousandth of a watt) and a 30-dBm signal is therefore equal to 30 dB above 1 mW or 1 W.

Also, I noted above that a decibel often compares quantities like power and intensity and is given by $10 \log(x/y)$. When comparing amplitudes it is convenient to compare the square of the respective quantities. So dB = 10 log (A^2_1/A^2_2) = 20 log (A_1/A_2) based on the properties of logarithms.

If all this seems somewhat confusing, then it may be helpful to merely memorize some common decibel values. You have already seen that 3 dB is a factor of 2. Continuing, 10 dB is roughly a factor of 10, 20 dB is a factor of 100, 30 dB a factor of 1000, and 60 dB represents a factor of 1,000,000. Do you detect a pattern here?

Each increase of 10 dB represents a factor of 10 increase in the equivalent linear expression. One of the really nice things about decibels is that they can be added together, thereby obviating the need to multiply large numbers. This convenient feature derives from the decibel being defined in terms of a logarithm.

For example, if we know that each acoustic barrier offers 30 dB = 10 log 1000 or a factor of 1000 of sound attenuation from one side of the barrier to the other, and there are three identical barriers between the source and listener, it is easy to determine the total attenuation.

This is accomplished by simply adding 30 dB + 30 db + 30 dB = 90 dB = 10 log (10^9) or a total attenuation factor of 1,000,000,000. The alternative method would require multiplying each factor, i.e., $1000 \times 1000 \times 1000 = 1,000,000,000 = 10^9$, which can be more cumbersome.

Parameters for Anti-Explosive and Bullet-Resistant Window Treatments[a]

Typical Design Guidelines for Blasts

From the *Architectural Record* at *http://archrecord.construction.com/print.asp*, we find:

> **Common blast level:** 4 psi overpressure at an impulse of 28 psi × milliseconds
>
> **Enhanced blast level:** 10 psi overpressure at an impulse of 89 psi × milliseconds
>
> **Certain government agencies' requirement:** 40 + psi overpressure and a blast duration of several hundred milliseconds

Note that $1 \text{ psi} = 6.9 \times 10^4$ dynes/cm^2. In centimeter-gram-second (cgs) units the above translates to:

Window Glass Properties		
	Overpressure (dynes/cm^2)	**Duration (sec)**
Common	2.8×10^5	7×10^{-3}
Enhanced	6.9×10^5	8.9×10^{-3}

Table 1-91 of the *CRC Handbook of Tables for Applied Engineering Science*, 2nd Ed., Table 1-91. Ed. Ray E. Bolz and George L. Tuve, Boca Raton, FL: CRC Press, Inc., 1986, gives:

Window Glass Specifications Satisfying Federal Specification Standard DD-G-451c	
Density	2.5 g/cc
Young's modulus	6.9×1011 dyn/cm^2
Poisson ratio	0.23
Tensile strength	4.1 to 4.5×108 dyn/cm^2

---

[a]From Chang, D.B. and C.S. Young. (2012) "Probabilistic Estimates of Vulnerability to Explosive Overpressures and Impulses." *Journal of Physical Security.* 6(1), 45 – 57.

Properties of 3M Scotchshield™ Ultra Safety and Security Window Films

The 3M website, *http://www.3m.com/*, gives the following parameters:

Recommendations of Applied Products for Explosion Protection			
	SCLARL150	**Ultra 400 Series**	**Ultra 600**
Film thickness	0.051 mm	0.1 mm	0.152 mm
Young's modulus	$> 3.45 \times 1010 \, dyn/cm^2$	$>3.45 \times 1010 \, dyn/cm^2$	$>3.45 \times 1010 \, dyn/cm^2$
Tensile strength	$2.08 \times 109 \, dyn/cm^2$	$2.08 \times 109 \, dyn/cm^2$	$2.08 \times 109 \, dyn/cm^2$

The website *http://www.cpni.gov.uk/advice/physical-security/ebp/in-depth-anti-shatter-film/* gives the following recommendations for antishatter film:

- Polyester film at least $175 \, \mu m$ (0.175 mm) should be used: 300-μm (0.3-mm) film should be considered for panes over $10 \, m^2$ or for ground floor windows over $3 \, m^2$.
- The specification can be lowered to at least $100 \, \mu m$ (0.1 mm) if bomb blast net curtains are also to be used.

Recommendations of the British Security Service (MI5)

The film specifications that Applied Products gives are those cited in the MI5 recommendations for antishatter film in its document "Protection Against Flying Glass," *https://www.mi5.gov.uk/home.html*.

In addition MI5 recommends the use of blast-resistant glass (i.e., laminated glass) with the following specifications:

- Minimum thickness: 7.5 mm.
- Inclusion of polyvinyl butryal interlayer of minimum thickness: 1.5 mm.
- Frame mounting able to withstand $7 \times 104 \, dyn/cm^2$.

These specifications apply to a windowpane with area $< 2 \, m^2$. A 1-m^2 window has an increased blast resistance, so the numbers should be increased by 50 percent to match the increased resistance.

For larger windows, the recommendation is that the $7 \times 10^4 \, dyn/cm^2$ should not be decreased when designing the accompanying frames.

Tempered Glass Properties

In the production of regular glass, a molten silica-based mix is cooled slowly under carefully controlled conditions. The slow cooling (annealing) relieves undesirable stresses from the glass. Increased strength can be obtained by heating the annealed glass to a temperature near its softening point and then cooling it rapidly. The resulting heat-treated glass is classified either as "fully tempered" or "heat-strengthened."

From *http://www.alumaxbath.com/tech/tgp.htm* we find that the typical breaking stresses and typical impact velocities for fracture are as follows:

Bullet-Resistant Glass		
	Annealed glass	**Tempered glass**
Breaking stress (60 s load)	4.14×10^8 dyn/cm^2	16.6×10^8 dyn/cm^2
Impact velocity (1/4 inch 5 g missile)	914 cm/s	1829 cm/s

The website *http://science.howstuffworks.com/question476htm* states that bullet-resistant glass typically consists of a layer of polycarbonate between pieces of ordinary glass. The polycarbonate is a tough transparent plastic that is marketed under the brand names Lexan, Tuffak, or Cyrolon. Bullet-resistant glass typically has thickness between 7 and 75 mm.

For the properties of polycarbonate we refer to the website *http://en.wikipedia.org/wiki/Polycarbonate*, which provides the following specifications:

Polycarbonate	
Young's modulus	$2-2.4 \times 10^{10}$ dyn/cm^2
Density	1.2 g/cc
Poisson's ratio	0.37
Tensile strength	5.5 to 7.5×10^8 dyn/ cm^2

Half-Life

The half-life is defined as the time it takes for a quantity to be reduced by one half its initial value.

An important process is one where the rate of change of the amount of a quantity is proportional to the amount that exists. The interest accrued from a bank account, no matter how paltry, is an example of such a process. Consider the rate of accumulation from interest for an account with \$100 versus \$1 million.

This phenomenon can be characterized by a simple differential equation as follows:

$$dC/dt = \lambda t$$

The proportionality constant is specified in terms of a process-related rate constant denoted by the Greek letter lambda (λ).

The solution to this equation is a simple exponential. Staying with our bank balance example, in that case C_o is the initial amount of cash, C is the amount of cash, λ is the interest rate, and t is time:

$$C = C_o e^{\lambda t}$$

Radioactive intensity obeys the same relation, and the intensity *decays* with time according to

$$I(t) = I_o e^{-\lambda t}$$

In other words, the number of radioactive counts per unit time is proportional to the amount of the radioactive substance.

Let's solve for t when the ratio of the intensity relative to the initial intensity I_o is ½. In other words, we seek the time t, such that the intensity of the radioactivity from the radioisotope has been halved in value, i.e., the radioactive half-life.

Taking the natural logarithm of both sides we get $\ln(I/I_o) = \ln(\frac{1}{2}) = -\lambda t$. In this case, λ would likely have units of decays per second.

The natural logarithm of $\frac{1}{2}$ is 0.693 (a good number to remember), so solving for t we get

$$t = 0.693/\lambda \; ***$$

To reiterate, t is the time in seconds required for the intensity of radiation to decay to half its original value.

Note this simple expression for half-life holds for any exponential process, and one merely needs to know the process rate, λ, to immediately yield the desired result.

Therefore, you can impress your friends at parties by using *** to immediately determine the half-life of exponentially decaying processes simply by knowing the process rate.

Near Fields from Radiated Radio-Frequency Identification (RFID) Power Data

We assume the radiation is from a printed circuit antenna on an RFID-like transponder that has the shape of a planar coil, and represent this source as a magnetic dipole **M** oscillating at an angular frequency $\omega = 2\pi\ 10^9/s$. (*Note*: we do not take into account any differences in the magnitude of the current at different portions of the antenna.)

The magnetic and electric fields from this dipole are given by the following expressions. Note that the bolded letters are vectors, a bolded x represents the vector (i.e., cross) product of two vectors, and a bolded dot represents the scalar (i.e., dot) product of two vectors:

$$\mathbf{B} = (\mu_o/4\pi)\,[k^2\,(\mathbf{I}\times\mathbf{M})\times\mathbf{i}\,\{\exp(ikr)/r\} + \{3i(\mathbf{I}\cdot\mathbf{M})-\mathbf{M}\}\,\{(1/r^3)-(ik/r^2)\}\exp(ikr)] \qquad [1]$$

$$\mathbf{E} = -(1/4\pi)(\mu_o/\varepsilon_o)^{1/2}k^2\,(\mathbf{I}\times\mathbf{M})\,\{\exp(ikr)/r\}\{1-(1/ikr)\} \qquad [2]$$

In these expressions:

$\mu_o = 4\pi10^{-7}\,H/m$ is the magnetic permeability of free space (H = henry).
$\varepsilon_o = 1/(36\pi10^9)$ F/m is the dielectric permittivity of free space (F = farad).
r (in meters) is the distance of the observation point from the magnetic dipole.
i is the unit vector pointing from the magnetic dipole **M** to the observation point.
$k = \omega/c$ is the wave number of the radiation (where $c = 3 \times 10^8\,m/s$).

The magnetic flux density B has units of webers per meter^2 (Tesla) and the electric field strength E has units of volts per meter.

The associated Poynting power flux vector is

$$\mathbf{P} = (\mu_o\omega^4/16\pi^2c^3)\,M^2\sin^2\theta\,\mathbf{i}/r^2\,W/m^2 \qquad [3]$$

And the total power radiated is

$$P_{total} = (\mu_o \omega^4 / 12\pi c^3) M^2 \, watts \qquad [4]$$

When $kr \ll 1$, i.e., in the near field, the magnetic flux density becomes:

$$\mathbf{B} = (\mu_o / 4\pi)\{3\mathbf{i}(\mathbf{i}.\mathbf{M}) - \mathbf{M}\}(1/r^3) \, Wb/m^2 \qquad [5]$$

DEDUCTION OF M FROM THE RADIATED POWER

Equation [4] can be solved for M in terms of the total power radiated:

$$M^2 = (P_{total} 12\pi c^3) / (\mu_o \omega^4) \qquad [6]$$

If we assume $10\,\mu W$ of radiated power from the RFID transponder, this gives

$$M = 2.2797 \times 10^{-6} \, A/m^2 \qquad [7]$$

MAGNETIC FIELD MAGNITUDE IN THE NEAR FIELD

Equation [5] yields a rough magnitude of the magnetic field close to the magnetic dipole:

$$B = \mu_o M / 4\pi r^3 \qquad [8]$$

As an example, consider

$$r = 1\,cm = 0.01\,m \qquad [9]$$

Then, with the magnetic moment of Equation [7], we find

$$B = 2.2797 \times 10^{-7} \, W/m^2 \qquad [10]$$

This corresponds to a field intensity of

$$H = B/\mu_o = 0.18 \, A \, turns/m = 0.0125664 \times 0.18 = 0.00226 \, Oe \, (Oersted) \qquad [11]$$

Index

Note: Page numbers followed by *f* indicate figures, *t* indicate tables and *np* indicate footnote.

481